MORGAN COMMUNITY
COLLEGE LIBRARY

D0480015

MP3
The Definitive Guide

WITHDRAWN BY
MORGAN COMMUNITY
COLLEGE LIBRARY

MORGAN COMMUNITY
COLLEGE LIBRARY

MP3
The Definitive Guide

Scot Hacker

O'REILLY®

Beijing · Cambridge · Farnham · Köln · Paris · Sebastopol · Taipei · Tokyo

MP3: The Definitive Guide
by Scot Hacker

Copyright © 2000 O'Reilly & Associates, Inc. All rights reserved.
Printed in the United States of America.

Published by O'Reilly & Associates, Inc., 101 Morris Street, Sebastopol, CA 95472.

Editor: Simon Hayes

Production Editor: Maureen Dempsey

Cover Designer: Hanna Dyer

Printing History:

March 2000:	First Edition.

Nutshell Handbook, the Nutshell Handbook logo, and the O'Reilly logo are registered trademarks. Many of the designations used by manufacturers and sellers to distinguish their products are claimed as trademarks. Where those designations appear in this book, and O'Reilly & Associates, Inc. was aware of a trademark claim, the designations have been printed in caps or initial caps. The association between the image of a hermit crab and MP3 is a trademark of O'Reilly & Associates, Inc.

While every precaution has been taken in the preparation of this book, the publisher assumes no responsibility for errors or omissions, or for damages resulting from the use of the information contained herein.

Library of Congress Cataloging-in-Publication Data

Hacker, Scot
   MP3: the definitive guide/Scot Hacker.—1st ed. p. cm.
   ISBN 1-56592-661-7 (alk. paper)
      1. MP3. 2.MP3 players. 3. Music—Computer programs. 4. Internet (Computer network)—
      Computer programs. I. Title.

ML74.4.M6 H33 2000
780'.285'65—dc21   00-025403

ISBN: 1-56592-661-7   [6/00]
[M]

Table of Contents

Preface

This book has a simple premise: People want to build MP3 collections of the music they like and respect. To do justice to that music requires that the MP3 files constituting a personal music collection be of a high audio quality. But MP3 is generally considered to be a convenience format, not an audiophile format—its main advantages are its flexibility and its portability.

While the press generally refers to MP3 audio as being "near CD quality," audiophiles often point to anomalies in the fidelity of the typical MP3 download. But there's a big difference between the average MP3 file downloaded from the Internet and a file you encode yourself, at a decent bitrate, from your own source material, using the encoder you feel yields the highest quality. MP3 is very much capable of achieving CD quality—you just have to pay a little attention to the variables. As I began to research the MP3 scene in earnest, I found that only a small fraction of available resources were paying close attention to MP3 quality issues. As a hobbyist audiophile, I found this dissatisfying, and felt that it was important to provide readers with a "no-compromise" approach to MP3—you *can* have your convenience factors and a quality audio experience at the same time.

While this book provides plenty of introductory material that will coach any reader through the basic mechanics of MPEG audio, it puts quite a bit of emphasis on fidelity issues, in addition to some of the peripheral topics not covered in depth in other books and online resources. Beyond the basics, for example, we'll be taking a close look at the many legal issues surrounding the MP3 scene, the challenges of building your own MP3 playback hardware, the technical details involved in setting up your own MP3 streaming server, and more.

It was also important to me that this book not be overly Windows-centric. Microsoft Windows may be king in terms of both the number of users and the number of MP3 applications available, but I'm not convinced it's the best possible

MP3 playback and creation platform, for reasons we'll go into elsewhere in the book. The number of MacOS users is increasing once again, Linux use is rising at an incredible clip, and BeOS is highly optimized for media content creation and consumption, with lots of built-in MP3-specific goodies. Accordingly, I've tried to balance coverage of non-Windows operating systems evenly throughout this book. Even if you use only one operating system, I hope you'll find reading about some of the alternative approaches illuminating.

It practically goes without saying that the amount and variety of available MP3 playback and creation software is growing at an incredible rate, as are the number of MP3 hardware options available. I don't pretend to have covered everything available in this book, and plenty of new applications and gear not covered here will undoubtedly be available by the time you read this. I've tried to structure the coverage of available products with an eye toward concepts, rather than specifics, so that the provided coverage will (hopefully) be applicable even to products that have yet to be invented. Please regard the coverage in this book, even where application-specific, as a guide to MP3 creation and playback principles in general.

MP3 is a truly amazing codec and a great feat of engineering. In conjunction with the huge array of "peripheral" technologies and tools available, MP3 has single-handedly ushered in a new era of file-based digital music distribution. It is my hope that this book will help you get the most out of the codec and its surrounding technology, so you can get back down to what this is all supposed to be about: enjoying the music you love.

Conventions in This Book

The following typographical conventions are used in this book:

`Constant width`
> Indicates command-line elements, computer output, and code examples.

Italic
> Introduces new terms and URLs, commands, file extensions, filenames, directory or folder names, and UNC pathnames.

 Indicates a tip, suggestion, or general note. For example, we'll tell you how to increase performance or save space, or we'll list links to useful web sites.

Indicates a warning or caution. For example, we'll warn you about easy-to-overwrite traps, crucial plug-ins you should not delete, or where it is important to re-encode your material.

How to Contact Us

We have tested and verified the information in this book to the best of our ability, but you may find that features have changed (or even that we have made mistakes!). Please let us know about any errors you find, as well as your suggestions for future editions, by writing to:

O'Reilly & Associates, Inc.
101 Morris Street
Sebastopol, CA 95472
(800) 998-9938 (in the U.S. or Canada)
(707) 829-0515 (international/local)
(707) 829-0104 (FAX)

You can also send us messages electronically. To be put on the mailing list or request a catalog, send email to:

info@oreilly.com

To ask technical questions or comment on the book, send email to:

bookquestions@oreilly.com

We have a web site for the book, where we'll list examples, errata, and any plans for future editions. You can access this page at:

http://www.oreilly.com/catalog/mp3/

For more information about this book and others, see the O'Reilly web site:

http://www.oreilly.com

Acknowledgments

As with any book of this scope, I did not work alone. I am much indebted to my editor, Simon Hayes, for helping to get this project off the ground and for his guidance in structuring and shaping this book in the "big picture." I am also most grateful for the many contributions made by our pool of technical editors:

- mp3tech.org's Gabriel Bouvigne, who possesses a nearly encyclopedic knowledge of MPEG's technical arcana and who helped to flesh out the details of this book in numerous ways.

- Lifelong audiophile Mike Knapp, who can build high-end amplifiers in his sleep and who contributed immeasurably to Hi-Fi issues throughout the book.

- Bruno Prior, who literally built a house around an extensive room-to-room home MP3 network, and who seems to have used every MP3 tool on the planet extensively. Prior also contributed much on the topic of encoding from analog sources.

- MP3.com's "High Geek" Sander van Zoest, who offered much behind the scenes information, especially on the broadcasting and streaming side of things, and who turned me on to MP3 products and technologies before they happened.

In addition, I'd like to thank the members of the WinAmp, mp3stereo, SHOUTcast, and icecast mailing lists, as well as the community inhabiting various MP3 USENET groups. The following individuals have also offered assistance: John Hedtke, Malcolm Humes, Michael James, Henry Kingman, Bruce Lash, Marco Nelissen, Peter Urbanec, Rob Voisey, and Franc Zijderveld.

This book is dedicated to my wife, Amy Kubes, who cheerfully put up with the endless stream of music (both good and bad) flowing from my office over the past year, and for her unwavering support during the course of this project.

1

The Nuts and Bolts of MP3

In April of 1999, the term "MP3" surpassed "sex" as the most-searched-on term at some of the Internet's top search engines—a phenomenal achievement for a complicated digital music encoding algorithm devised over the course of a decade by a few scientists and audiophiles in an obscure German laboratory.

What is it about MP3 that inspires such unprecedented levels of enthusiasm? For some, it's the prospect of being able to store vast quantities of music on a computer's hard drive, and to shuffle and rearrange tracks from that collection around at a moment's notice. For others, it's the promise of an entirely new model for the music universe—one that allows creative artists to publish their own work without the assistance of the established industry. But for millions of users, the thrill of MP3 is more simple than that: it's the possibility of getting their hands on piles of high-quality music, free of charge.

In this chapter, we'll get a bird's-eye view of the format and the MP3 phenomenon: what it is, how it works, how to download and create MP3 files, and how to listen to them. Then we'll take a look at some of the many issues surrounding MP3, including piracy, politics, digital rights, and the recording industry's stance on the matter. Finally, we'll examine the correlation between the MP3 and open source software movements, and find out why file-based digital music distribution is here to stay.

MP3 Basics

If you're new to the MP3 game, you'll want to know exactly what MP3 files are, where to get them, how they work, and how to make the most of a growing MP3 collection. As you read through this brief overview, keep in mind that these topics are covered in much greater detail elsewhere in this book.

What Is MP3?

Simply put, MP3 is an audio compression technique. Raw audio files—such as those extracted from an audio CD—are very large, consuming around 10 MB of storage space per minute. But MP3 files representing the same audio material may consume only 1 MB of space per minute while still retaining an acceptable level of quality. By drastically reducing the size of digital audio files, it has become feasible for music lovers to transfer songs over the Internet, for users to build enormous digital music collections on their hard drives, to play them back in any order at any time, and to move them around between different types of playback hardware. These possibilities have far-reaching ramifications not just for music lovers, but for artists and the recording industry as well. We'll explore the politics and philosophical issues raised by MP3 in the second part of this chapter.

Why the term "MP3?"

"MP3" is the quick way of referring to an encoding algorithm called "MPEG-1, Layer III," developed primarily by a German technology group called Fraunhofer and Thomson and now officially codified by the International Standards Organization, or ISO. The name, of course, corresponds to the extension found on MP3 files: *After_the_Goldrush.mp3*, for example. More on Fraunhofer and Co. can be found in the section "About the Codec," later in this chapter.

Small is beautiful: How MP3 works

Raw audio does not compress well via traditional techniques: if you try to zip up a WAV file, for instance, you'll find that the resulting archive is only marginally smaller than the uncompressed original.

MP3 takes a different tack on the compression problem. Rather than just seeking out redundancies like zip does, MP3 provides a means of analyzing patterns in an audio stream and comparing them to models of human hearing and perception. Also unlike zip compression, MP3 actually discards huge amounts of information, preserving only the data absolutely necessary to reproduce an intelligible signal. The amount of data preserved is configurable by the person doing the compressing, so an optimal balance between file size and quality can be achieved. The tool or software used to achieve the compression is called an "encoder," while the playback software is called a "decoder" or, more simply, an "MP3 player."

By running uncompressed audio files through an MP3 encoder, files can shrink to around one-tenth of their original size, while still retaining most of their quality. By compressing a little less (to around one-eighth of the original size), MP3 quality can be virtually indistinguishable from that of the original source material. As a result, a three-minute song can be transformed into a 3 MB file, which is something most people can find room for on their hard drives, and that most web surfers can download in a reasonable time frame. In other words, a 640 MB compact disc stuffed full of MP3 files rather than uncompressed audio can store around 10–11 hours worth of music. And since DVDs store around eight times as much as compact discs, a recordable DVD could hold nearly five days worth of continuous music on a single 5″ platter.

The mechanics of the MP3 codec and perceptual encoding principles can be found in Chapter 2, *How MP3 Works: Inside the Codec.*

Working with MP3 Files

If you know how to download files from the Internet, have a grasp of basic file management concepts, and aren't afraid to experiment with new applications, you can probably get started on your own MP3 collection without much coaching. However, there are a lot of options and considerations to take into account, including the quality and efficiency of MP3 encoders and players, advanced features and functions, techniques used for organizing and customizing large MP3 collections, and so on. We've dedicated all of Chapter 3, *Getting and Playing MP3 Files*, and Chapter 4, *Playlists, Tags, and Skins: MP3 Options*, to these topics. For now, here's a brief tour of the basics.

Downloading MP3s

In order to start playing MP3 files, you'll need to get your hands on some, of course. There are two ways to do this: You can either download MP3s that other people have created, or you can create them from the music you already own.

 Before you start downloading MP3s, you should know that the vast majority of files available out there are distributed illegally. Many people encode music they legally own, and then make it available on the Internet to people who do not own that music, which is illegal (see Chapter 7, *The Not-So-Fine-Print: Legal Bits and Pieces*, for more information). Whether you choose to download pirated music is a moral choice that only you can make. The wide availability of pirated music, however, should not stop you from seeking out legal MP3s. While there are far fewer of these available, you'll be surprised by the quality of the gems you'll find hiding out in the haystacks. A great place to find legal MP3s is *MP3.com*, though that site is certainly not the only source of legitimate files. If you use a commercial MP3 tool like RealJukebox (Chapter 3), you'll probably find a button or link in the interface that will take you directly to an MP3 download site.

Finding MP3 files

While most users start out by simply typing "MP3" into their favorite search engine, that probably isn't the most efficient way of going about things. You might want to start instead at a major site dedicated to indexing or distributing MP3 files, such as *mp3.lycos.com, www.listen.com, www.scour.net,* or *www.rioport.com.* Search engines can, however, be very useful for finding smaller sites run by individuals—but be prepared to encounter lots of broken links and unresponsive sites. Because many user-run sites are quickly shut down by Internet Service Providers (ISPs) under pressure from record labels, search engines often index links to sites that no longer exist.

The Web isn't the only way to find MP3 files—you'll also find plenty of files on FTP servers, in binary Usenet groups, and in IRC channels. Details on using these venues for MP3 downloading can be found in Chapters 3 and 4.

Users looking to swap MP3 files easily with music fans all over the world may want to check out Napster (*www.napster.com*), which is a sort of combined IRC, FTP, and search client with a twist. Rather than searching the Web, you'll be searching the hard drives of other Napster users for songs you like. Since you'll only see files on the systems of people currently using the service, you won't have to worry about broken links and downed servers. Log in to the Napster server, register your collection with a specific genre, and you'll be able to search for files on other people's systems by song name or artist. Find a song or songs you like and transfer them to your hard drive, while other people do the same with your music collection. Meanwhile, you can chat with other music lovers in the background as your transfer proceeds. Great idea, but the potential for copyright abuse inherent in this product is extreme, and none of the music we found during testing was legitimate. Nevertheless, Napster has single-handedly ushered in a whole new era of user-to-user file sharing, and has the music industry more worried than ever.

Creating your own MP3 files

Creating your own MP3s is only slightly more difficult than downloading them, but the payoff is worth it. You know for a fact that the music in your collection is the music you like, you can personally control the quality of the encodings, and you don't have to worry about whether any of your tracks are illegal.

Encoding tracks from your CD collection is a two-step process. First, bits from an audio CD must be transferred to your system as uncompressed audio, typically as a WAV file. This extraction process is known as *ripping*. The uncompressed audio is then run through an MP3 encoder to create an MP3 file. However, there are dozens of tools available that take care of all the hard work behind the scenes, ripping and encoding transparently in a single step. You'll meet a handful of ripper/encoder combination tools in Chapter 5, *Ripping and Encoding: Creating MP3 Files.*

Playback basics

Think of an MP3 file like any other document you might store on your computer and open in an application. You can open a document by using an application's File → Open menu, by double-clicking a document icon, or by dragging a document onto the application's icon. MP3 files are no different, and can typically be played in any of these ways. There are hundreds of MP3 players available for virtually all operating systems, and all of them are capable of playing all MP3 files. As a user, you have tons of options when it comes to picking your tools. In Chapter 3, you'll meet some of the most popular MP3 players available for Windows, MacOS, Linux, and BeOS, and be introduced to the fundamental principles of MP3 playback.

Playlists

One of the most liberating aspects of working with file-based music (as opposed to music stored on media such as CDs, tapes, or LPs) is the fact that you suddenly gain the ability to organize, randomize, and mix the tunes in your music collection in an infinitude of ways. If you've ever created custom mixed-music cassette tapes, you know how fun—and how time consuming—this can be. MP3 playlists let you enjoy the fun part while skipping the time-consuming part.

The vast majority of MP3 players include a "playlist" window or editor, into which you can drag any random collection of tracks. Any playlist can be saved for posterity, to be played again at a later date. A playlist can be as short as a single song or as long as your entire collection (some people have playlists referencing months of nonrepeating music). A playlist can reference all the music in a folder or an entire directory structure, or can be composed by querying your system for all songs matching a certain criteria. For example, you can create playlists of all country music written prior to 1965, or all of your acid jazz tracks, or all of your schmaltzy disco. Playlist creation and manipulation is covered in detail in Chapter 4.

Playlists are simple text files listing references to the actual locations of MP3 files on your system or on a network. As such, they consume almost no disk space. Because playlists reference songs on your system, it is usually not useful to trade them with other users. There are, however, playlists comprised only of URLs to MP3 files on the Internet, and these will, of course, work on anyone's system.

ID3 tags

MP3 files are capable of storing a certain amount of "meta-data"—extra information about each file—inside the file itself. Data on track title, artist, album, year, genre, and your personal comments on the track can all be stored in an MP3 file's *ID3 tags*. These tags will be inserted automatically by most tools as you rip and encode, or can be added or edited later on, often directly through your MP3 player's interface. ID3 tags become more important as your collection grows, especially when you start using database-oriented MP3 organizers, as described in Chapter 4.

Internet radio

Some people have neither the time nor the inclination to create and manage a huge MP3 collection. Fortunately, they don't have to. Thanks to the rise of outfits like SHOUTcast (*www.shoutcast.com*) and icecast (*www.icecast.org*), thousands of users are *streaming* MP3 audio from their computers to the Internet at large, running live broadcasts much like a radio station. There are several key differences between MP3 downloads and MP3 streaming:

- MP3 broadcasts aren't saved to the listener's hard disk, unlike MP3 downloads. When you tune in to a broadcast, the only thing that's saved to disk is a tiny text file containing some meta-data about the broadcast in question, including the server's address and a playlist. This file is passed to the MP3 player, which in turn receives and handles (buffers) the ongoing broadcast.

- Broadcasts are synchronous, while downloads are asynchronous. In other words, when you tune in to a broadcast, you hear exactly what's being played from a given server at that moment in time, just like the radio. When you download a file, you get to listen to it any time you want.

- Because of bandwidth constraints on most listeners, broadcasts are typically of a lower fidelity than MP3 downloads. MP3 broadcast servers usually send out MP3s that have either been down-sampled to a lower frequency, encoded at a lower-than-normal bitrate, or sent as a mono rather than stereo stream.

Full details on tuning in to MP3 broadcasts can be found in Chapter 4. The process of running your own Internet radio station is described in Chapter 8, *Webcasting and Servers: Internet Distribution*.

Beyond the computer

While you'll almost certainly create all of your MP3 files on your computer, and will most likely begin your MP3 explorations by playing them back through your computer as well, part of the magic of file-based digital audio is the flexibility. There's no reason an MP3 file can't be transferred to any device that includes a storage and playback mechanism. And sure enough, a whole new class of devices has arisen to meet this need: portable units similar to the classic Sony Walkman but geared for MP3 playback, rather than tape or CD, are becoming hugely popular. Meanwhile, we're beginning to see the emergence of a whole new range of home stereo MP3 components, capable of storing gigabytes of digital audio and being operated just like any other home stereo component. Of course, the technology is being applied to car stereos as well. Even hand-held computers such as the Handspring Visor are gaining MP3 playback capabilities.

Users with some technical know-how and a soldering iron are hacking out techniques for building MP3 playback hardware of their own, free from SDMI and other security mechanisms (see Chapter 7 for more about MP3 security and legal issues) that ultimately limit the functionality of commercial MP3 hardware. Chapter 6, *Hardware, Portables, Home Stereos, and Kits*, includes comparative analysis of MP3 portables, an early look at a few MP3 home stereo components, and introduces the concepts of building your own MP3 hardware from scratch.

About the Codec

So, what exactly is MPEG audio compression, and MP3 specifically? Technically, that's a bit of a long story, so we'll go into great detail on that in Chapter 2. You don't need to know how MP3 works in order to start playing with it, but to shed a little light on the subject now, MPEG audio compression is a "psychoacoustic" technique that exploits various limitations in both the human ear and the mind's ability to process certain kinds of sounds at very high resolutions. MPEG encoders store "maps" of human auditory perception in a table, and compare an incoming bitstream to those maps. The person doing the encoding gets to specify how many bits per second will be allocated to storing the final product. Taking note of that restriction, the encoder does its best to strip away as much data as possible (within the specified data storage limitation, or "bitrate") while still retaining the maximum possible audio quality. The more bits per second the user allows, the better described the final output will be, and the larger the resulting file. With fewer bits per second, the user will get a smaller file (better compression), and a corresponding decrease in audio quality. Again, we'll go into the process in greater detail in Chapter 2.

The MPEG family

MPEG is not a single standard, but rather a "family" of standards defined by the Moving Picture Experts Group, which was formed in 1998 to arrive at a single compression format for digital audio and avoid a standards war between various competing technologies. All of the MPEG standards are used for the coding of audio-visual data into compressed formats.

Coding in this sense of the word refers to the process of running a stream of bits through an algorithm, or set of rules. *Encoding* is the process of taking an uncompressed bitstream and running it through the algorithm to generate a compressed bitstream or file. *Decoding* is, naturally, the opposite—taking a compressed bitstream and turning it into an uncompressed file or an audible signal. The term *codec* is short for compressor/decompressor,* and refers to any algorithm capable of performing this bidirectional function.

The MPEG family is broken down into major classes (MPEG-1, MPEG-2, MPEG-4), which are further broken down into sub-classifications called *layers*. Each major class and layer is optimized for specific real-world applications, such as compressed movie soundtracks, broadcast, or file-based musical coding. Each successive layer is more complex than the preceding layer. For example, a layer III decoder will be 2.5 times more complex than a layer I decoder. The MPEG "layers" are described in sub-documents of each class, with audio coding schemes described in a document labeled "ISO/IEC11172-3." The MPEG coding technique that interests us in this book is MPEG-1/MPEG-2 Layer III, referred to throughout this book simply as "MP3."

Technically, MPEG-1 Layer III and MPEG-2 Layer III are both referred to as MP3, as are the rather obscure MPEG 2.5 extensions. MPEG-1 Layer III is used for 32, 44.1, and 48kHz sampling rates, while MPEG-2 Layer III is for 16, 22.05, and 24kHz sampling rates. The MPEG 2.5 extensions allow for 8 and 11kHz. MP3 players can play any of these, and the specs are very similar.† The vast majority of files you'll encounter in the wild are simple MPEG-1 Layer III.

Do not confuse MPEG-1 Layer III (MP3) with MPEG-3—there is no such animal. There was once an MPEG-3 classification in development, which was intended to address high-quality video. However, MPEG-2 was shown to deliver sufficiently high quality, so MPEG-3 was conjoined with the existing MPEG-2 specification. The spec now skips from MPEG-2 to MPEG-4.

---

* In some circles, the term stands for enCOder/DECoder, though this interpretation has lost favor to compressor/decompressor.

† MPEG-2 also allows for multichannel extensions of up to five channels, though few people have ever actually seen this in action. Multichannel efforts are concentrated on MPEG-4, covered in Chapter 9, *Competing Codecs and Other File Formats*.

The MP3 patent

The fact that the MP3 spec is maintained by the MPEG Working Group doesn't mean they invented the technology. The working group merely codifies standards to guarantee interoperability between various applications, operating systems, and implementations. One of the very first tasks of the working group was to circumscribe the conditions of the ownership of intellectual property under the umbrella of international standards. Their conclusion was that patented technologies are allowed to be codified as standards, but that those patents must be fairly and equitably licensable to all comers, so that no single company could gain a monopoly on a specific audio/video compression technology.

The MP3 codec itself was devised by the Fraunhofer Institute of Germany and Thomson Multimedia SA of France (referred to throughout this book simply as "Fraunhofer"), who originally published the standard in 1993.* Fraunhofer and Co. own the intellectual copyright on any technology capable of creating "an MP3-compliant bitstream." While Fraunhofer publishes low-grade sample code that can be used as a basis for more sophisticated MP3 coding tools, Fraunhofer still requires developers of MP3 encoders to pay hefty licensing fees (full details on that can be found in Chapter 5).

To learn more about the MPEG working group and MPEG specifications in general, there is no better starting point than *www.mpeg.org*. To learn more about Fraunhofer and MP3 licensing issues, see *www.iis.fhg.de*. The official web site of the MPEG Consortium is *drogo.cselt.stet.it/mpeg/*.

Rights, Piracy, and Politics

The flexibility and portability of MP3 has left the recording industry wondering where to turn, unsigned musicians newly empowered, signed artists with mixed reactions, and fans making out like bandits. The debate centers on a quest for the right balance between exploiting the promotional power of this new medium and protecting the intellectual copyright of artists and labels.

MP3's Impact on the Recording Industry

In July of 1999, the International Federation of Phonographic Industries (IFPI) estimated that around three million tracks were downloaded from the Internet every day, most of them without the permission of their copyright holders. The Recording Industry Association of America (RIAA) claims to have lost as much as $10 billion through music piracy in 1998. It's not just record company executives and

---

* Fraunhofer did not work alone; other companies and organizations (notably AT&T) contributed to the development of the encoder as well.

artists who stand to lose; the digital music revolution has implications for everyone in the channel: record store owners, CD pressing plants, and even truck drivers. Of course, most signed artists resent having their intellectual property illegally distributed as well. Well-known artists ask the RIAA every day to clamp down on pirate sites hosting their music (although it's also the case that many signed artists are much more supportive of MP3 than are their labels). In the rest of this chapter, we'll take a look at some of the many difficult issues currently being faced by the industry and music lovers alike, and take a look at some of the techniques the industry is proposing to deal with the situation. The legal nitty-gritty of MP3 is discussed in more detail in Chapter 7.

File-based digital audio changes the game

For nearly a century, the record industry has held the distribution of musical content in a hammerlock. If you wanted to own music, you had to do it on their terms, purchasing music distributed on the media they had officially blessed, and only through their approved channels. While the industry's stranglehold on music distribution slipped for the first time in the 1950s with the advent of reel-to-reel tape decks, and even more in the '70s with the popularization of the cassette tape, tape technologies had a major Achilles' heel: analog copies always lose a little quality as successive copies are made—a third-generation copy of a well-recorded LP doesn't sound so well-recorded anymore. In addition, the person making the copy is burdened with having to create a new physical instance for each person to whom she wants to distribute her tunes.

I don't have to tell you that MP3 has changed all of that. Digital copies (of anything) are virtually bit-perfect, so no quality is lost in successive generations—a 74th-generation copy sounds every bit as good as the original. And then there's the Internet. Because digital music can be file-based rather than media-based, a single file representing any kind of content can be placed on a web or FTP server and made available to the entire world at once. The burden of making physical copies, which naturally limited the rampancy of tape-based copies to a large extent, has vanished.

But until recently, there's been another "gating factor" that has limited the spread of file-based audio distribution: size. While it's always been possible to rip an audio track from a compact disc and make it available on the Internet, doing so was impractical because uncompressed audio consumes around 10 MB per minute of storage space. Few people had the available bandwidth or storage space to be whipping 30 MB pop songs around.

If all of us had Internet connections with unlimited bandwidth and hard drives large enough to store terabytes or petabytes of data, MP3 would be unnecessary. Limited bandwidth and small hard drives are the only reason MP3 even exists (or, at least, the only reasons it's become popular). Ironically, the MP3 phenomenon hit at a time when both of these issues were being addressed at a rapid clip. More and more, people are having DSL or cable modem connections installed in their homes, and 36 GB hard disks are available for a few hundred bucks at this writing. If the trend continues, and there's no reason to think that it won't, one can almost imagine audio compression in general becoming obsolete due to a lack of demand. But for the foreseeable future, limited bandwidth and modest hard drives are a reality, so digital audio compression is a necessity.

If you can't beat 'em, join 'em

Will the recording industry be able to put an end to MP3? If not, how will it cope with the phenomenon? There are several factors at work here. While people commonly claim that the cassette revolution had little impact on the industry, the truth is that, for whatever reason, sales today aren't as great as they were in the '70s. Of course, there are several reasons for this, such as the fact that CDs cost twice what LPs used to cost, and the fact that we no longer seem to have anything like the giant mega-stars of the '70s. Pink Floyd's "Dark Side of the Moon" stayed in Billboard's Top 100 for the better part of a *decade*. While we still have stars, the days of the Beatles and the Stones are, most likely, gone for good. Of course, the industry feels that illegal MP3 downloads are making these problems worse.

But a 1999 report from industry analyst Jupiter Communications concluded that only three percent of consumers would be purchasing downloaded music by the year 2003. While the industry has good reason to be concerned, some see that last factoid as a wake-up call to the industry—either adapt to a world in which downloadable copyrighted music is a reality, or be left out altogether. If this projection turns out to be true, the industry will either have to find a way to crush unprotected MP3 distribution (unlikely), or accept the fact that MP3s and other digital audio files will continue to be distributed without hope of a significant revenue return.

In the short term, the RIAA launched a campaign to start shutting down pirate sites. For the most part, this has consisted of cease-and-desist letters being sent to Internet service providers, warning them to remove illegal files from users' sites or face prosecution (see Chapters 7 and 8). ISPs are generally quick to oblige (and are bound by law to do so). But even with the best lawyers in the land at their disposal, the industry has found that trying to crush pirate sites in the midst of a phenomenon this large is like playing a vast and endless game of Whack-a-Mole—eliminate one site and six others spring up in its place. Even with the cooperation of ISPs, the task is futile and the industry knows it, though they are still obliged to continue trying.

Beat 'em: The Secure Digital Music Initiative (SDMI). In the face of this apparent futility, the industry has decided to approach the problem from another angle: Chop it off at the knees. Since the sprawling and largely ungovernable Internet cannot be easily controlled, the industry has decided to work with its partners and make it harder to create copy-able digital music files to begin with. By colluding with the makers of compact discs, sound cards, and software vendors, and by embedding special codes into newly created CDs, the industry hopes to get as many people using copy protection-enabled equipment and source material as possible.* According to a quote made by SDMI Executive Chairman Dr. Leonardo Chiariglione in *Billboard* magazine:

> You will be able to play your MP3 files on the portable devices of today, but at a certain point in time, which may happen quite soon, the record companies will start embedding some signals into their future content so that it can become playable only on SDMI devices.

As you'll see throughout this book, it is logically and practically impossible to create a 100% secure system, since savvy users can always trap music as it's heading out of the computer and toward the sound card. The industry's goal, then, is to create a fence high enough that the vast majority of users will lack the technical know-how or wherewithal to try and jump over it. This plan, known as the Strategic Digital Music Initiative (SDMI), is already much-delayed in its implementation at this writing, and is, many feel, doomed for failure. Only time will tell. More on SDMI can be found in Chapters 6 and 7.

Join 'em: MP3 and electronic commerce. If illegal MP3 distribution cannot be stopped or even significantly curtailed, then the industry may learn to embrace the new paradigm and accept the fact that its role is changing in the digital world. Major labels will most likely come to appreciate the "buzz" effect that can be created by posting tracks on their own web sites. Releasing a few good tracks from an upcoming album by a big-name star is likely to result in more sales and more word-of-mouth. Already, we're beginning to see the first glimmerings of this phenomenon, as major stars such as Tom Petty, Billy Idol, The Grateful Dead, and Alanis Morissette embrace the format.

---

* Embedded codes in music, known as *watermarks*, are created such that their presence persists even when transformed from one format to another, even when "jacked" out of an audio port.

The industry faces a major obstacle in persuading hardware vendors to collude with them in making computers secure against music piracy: Consumers *want* the ability to copy music freely. If one hardware vendor adopts SDMI and another does not, many consumers are simply going to buy equipment from the one who does not. That's quite a disincentive to vendors considering implementing SDMI in hardware, and without global and enforced legislation (unlikely), the industry faces an uphill battle. Nevertheless, Sony has already developed a pair of technologies, called MagicGate (for use in devices) and OpenMG (for use in PCs), that guarantee that a signal can be moved from one place to another, but not copied. Of course, Sony is also a record label, so their desire to move on this front is understandable. But unless they can get other vendors to adopt the same or similar technology, savvy consumers will simply avoid these products.

But the industry doesn't have to *give* away MP3 files. What's wrong with selling them? One can imagine a future in which fans can log into a label's site and download tracks for a buck a pop, selecting only the songs worth purchasing and (happily) ignoring the duds. Whether this is managed via micropayments or ongoing accounts with labels, there's a big problem here: Once a fan has purchased a file, what's to stop him from hacking it into an unprotected version, placing that file on his own site, and making it available for download—enabling infinite copying of the unprotected version to the rest of the world? SDMI and audio formats with built-in security (see Chapter 9) will help here, but again, it only takes one user to break or somehow get around the security mechanism, and the file is once again in the clear and released into the wild. Right or wrong, most people are going to download the free, unprotected version rather than the 99¢ version when given a choice. One begins to appreciate the industry's dilemma.

So, if the industry decides to go for it and start selling music online in a big way, how will they do it? First of all, due to its lack of security, MP3 is very badly suited for the job. Online sales of digital music are likely to come in some other file format, and more likely in several of them. No big deal—the flexibility of software makes it easy for users to store lots of formats on their hard drives, and probably even to play them all back through the same player. Regardless, you can practically rest assured that whatever formats are used will be SDMI-compliant. Taking that as a given, here are the models:

Micropayments

Because credit card charges always incur a transaction fee, low-cost items (such as individual songs) are more awkward to sell online than are sweaters or beer. The notion of micropayments is that users maintain an account with an independent organization. Users may load up the account with money in advance, as with a phone card, and charge small purchases against it. Record labels may also run their own micropayment schemes.

CD distribution

Because the production of compact discs is relatively inexpensive, users may be able to order up a bunch of songs at once and have them pressed to an audio CD, which will then be mailed to the user. Because the cost will be higher, standard credit card transactions will be feasible. This model, in fact, has already been used by companies such as Liquid Audio (*www.liquidaudio. com*), though they have not managed to reach a significant cross-section of the population. Such a model run by a major label would likely have more success.

Subscription

In this model, users would pay a flat monthly or yearly fee and be entitled to download the latest hits from a variety of artists selected by the user or the label, in whichever format the label chooses to work.

Temptation

Perhaps the simplest model, and the one most akin to the shareware model computer users are familiar with, is to simply give away a track or two from upcoming albums, with the hope that users will like the tracks enough to purchase the entire CD, either online or from a local record store.

Advertising

Controversial for good reason, the MP3 advertising model is an extension of the banner ads on web pages with which we're all familiar. Each downloaded MP3 file comes with a brief advertisement embedded into the first few seconds, which is the first thing the user hears. While this is essentially similar to what we get on the radio every day, most users dislike the notion of having their personal MP3 collections riddled with ads. Nevertheless, this model is already in use by Amp3.com, who has managed to sign a number of big-name artists on to the program.

"Guilt sites"

This rather odd idea, which has been tossed around by many people in many forums, has yet to see a working model. The concept is that many users want to enjoy the free trade and exchange of MP3 files, but still want to pay a royalty back to the labels and artists who made the music possible. "Guilt sites" would allow people to check in anonymously and say, "I've decided to actually keep and listen to 24 of the 113 files I downloaded this month. Here's a list of the songs. Please accept my $24 in payment." A fascinating idea, but one which the recording industry is unlikely to bless.

Is MP3 Legal?

One of the questions most frequently asked by people concerned about MP3 piracy is, "Why not just make MP3 illegal?" By making MP3 illegal, they reason, it would be easy to arrest music pirates and deter others from taking part in the ongoing plundering of the traditional music business. There are several problems with this line of thinking:

- MP3 has lots of legitimate uses, and is intended for legitimate use. The mere fact that it can also be used for illegitimate purposes does not in and of itself provide sufficient reason to outlaw it.

- MP3 is a codec. Nothing more, nothing less. Nothing about MP3 is inherently dangerous. You can use a crowbar to break into a drug store, chicken manure to make bombs, or a laptop computer to crack security systems, but that doesn't mean any of those things should be illegal. You can kill yourself or others by drinking too much alcohol, swinging a machete in the wrong vector, or by eating too much bacon, but that doesn't mean those things should be illegal.

- If we were to make MP3 illegal, we would also have to outlaw all other computer file formats, from *.DOC* to *.JPEG*, since all of them can be used to store and distribute intellectual property illegally as well.

Short answer: Yes, MP3 is legal—it's just an innocent codec. Issues surrounding the protection of intellectual and creative copyright are completely separate from the mechanism of distribution. However, MP3 differs from other audio compression techniques; it provides no built-in means to prevent unrestricted copying. This is an issue the industry is struggling to solve, but MP3 itself is but one player in a larger problem, not the problem itself.

The Artist's Turn

Great talent does not automatically end up at the top of the music business. All over the world, millions of talented, creative artists are playing music for their friends, or in small clubs, or even on tour, trying to make a name for themselves. You think that a talented artist will automatically end up with a recording contract? Think again. The record business isn't necessarily looking for talent... but that's another story.

Unless you're scouring the local newspaper and heading off to local clubs night after night looking for something fresh, you may never hear thousands of great musicians and songwriters. Unless an artist is being spotlighted by the recording industry, mass exposure is almost impossible for an artist to get.

The next wave of self-publishing

The MP3 revolution addresses this concern head-on. Because any musician with a computer can encode their own songs to MP3, they can potentially expose themselves to the world at large without ever having to sign a recording contract. They can go directly to the people, bypassing the industry as we know it. This possibility is analogous to the great desktop publishing revolution of the '80s and the web publishing revolution of the 1990s—suddenly, everyone has the ability to publish their own music (no matter how bad or how good) without help from "the man."

Unsurprisingly, this—perhaps the single most liberating and legitimate aspect of the MP3 revolution—is seldom if ever mentioned by record industry executives when talking about piracy problems. An artist signed to a label generally does not have the right to post his own songs to the Internet, because the label owns the copyright to those songs. But an independent, unsigned artist can do whatever she likes with her own tunes. And while that represents a lesser threat to the industry, it represents a threat nonetheless; the prospect of a burgeoning "industry" that runs itself, outside of the RIAA's purvey, is at hand. And unlike piracy issues, there isn't a thing the RIAA can do about the rise of self-publishing musicians. Sites like MP3.com represent this concept in its full glory. Rather than requiring users to surf the Web for scattered, legitimate downloads by unsigned artists, users can search through archives of thousands of unsigned artists all in one place.

 While MP3.com is focused on and dedicated to the promotion of unsigned artists, the site does indeed enjoy an arrangement with The American Society of Composers, Authors, and Publishers (ASCAP), which allows MP3.com to stream (not offer for download) the works of musicians signed to labels. MP3.com's relationship with ASCAP is outlined at *www.mp3.com/ascap/*.

Do the math: A good deal for artists

There's more than just exposure in it for the artist. Let's do the math. According to one artist who's been struggling to make it in the business for years, a band who sells 150,000 CDs through a medium-size label will still not be generating profit for themselves—yes, there's that much overhead in being associated with a label.* Furthermore, only around 5% of signed artists end up turning a profit—signing with a label is not necessarily a "ticket to ride." But if an artist presses his or her own CDs, and sells them for $10 each over the Internet, they can make a profit by

---

* It is for reasons such as this that the relatively successful group TLC was forced to file for bankruptcy in 1999.

selling only 15,000 copies. This artist would make $5 per CD in profit, netting $75,000 in sales. And, in fact, this is exactly what MP3.com allows artists to do, using their D.A.M. CD service (see Chapter 8 for details).

Presumption of Guilt

There's another, possibly more frightening aspect to the rise of self-publishing: Anti-piracy measures instituted by the industry—such as SDMI—may have a negative impact on the rise of this new distribution mechanism. As you'll see in more detail in Chapter 7, SDMI and similar mechanisms operate on a presumption of guilt. Because so much music in MP3 format is pirated, security mechanisms tend to make the assumption that anything in MP3 format is probably pirated. This is nothing but a slap in the face to the unsigned, unrepresented artist using the MP3 codec for legitimate purposes, to willfully and legally publish his own music. If security formats, technologies, and hardware are pushed on users by the industry, unsigned artists will be left right where they were before MP3 promised them an alternative.

Legitimate uses of MP3 are not constrained to music. One doesn't have to look too far to find other creative, legal, and legitimate uses of the technology. *The New York Times* makes spoken-word versions of its news available for download from its site. MP3LiT.com features hundreds of published and unpublished authors reading excerpts from their books, going on political rants, reading or improvising poetry, and offering self-help material, all in MP3 format. These and other legitimate uses of MP3 will be adversely affected by any attempt by the record industry to squash unprotected MP3 files in general.

Why MP3 Is Here to Stay

As you've probably heard, MP3 isn't the only digital audio compression format out there. As you'll see in Chapter 9, there are numerous alternatives to the format available to the public. In fact, many of them achieve even better compression ratios and/or better sound quality than MP3.

Not the best, but good enough

So why hasn't the public moved toward competing formats in a wild rush? Even MP3's most staunch supporters readily admit that MP3 is a less-than-ideal solution from an audiophile perspective. But like Betamax or the Macintosh, history proves that the best technology doesn't always win. The VQF and AAC formats are great examples of this in action: both offer superior quality, and often, smaller file sizes than MP3 as well.* Nevertheless, MP3 is entrenched—you might say that MP3 is to

---

* Many MP3 players also handle VQF and other audio formats; you can switch between them seamlessly.

the Internet audio industry as Windows is to the operating system market—functional and workable, but not the ideal solution, even though the depth of its penetration practically guarantees that it isn't going anywhere anytime soon.

More often than not, standards are set by the technology that establishes a strong user base first. And establishing that user base has as much to do with marketing, wide availability, and ease-of-use as it has to do with quality. And history also shows that a superior technology doesn't just have to be a little better in order to turn heads—it has to be way, way better. While some of MP3's competing formats are better than MP3, the fact of the matter is that MP3 is good enough. At decent bitrates, it sounds great, and the compression ratios are perfectly acceptable to most people. While some people make the point that the public will migrate to another technology as soon as something better comes along, this is not proving to be the case. Excellent alternatives do exist, but they're not taking hold (at least, they're not as of early 2000). For another format to surpass the momentum of MP3, it would have to have all of the following attributes:

- Smaller file sizes
- Superior audio quality
- Be free and unprotected

Ironically, it's that third point that makes all the difference. The first and second points are already satisfied by other file formats and codecs. But the public wants what the public wants, and they have spoken very clearly: they want lots of choice, available source code, and freedom from copying restrictions. The fact that this also means a huge headache when it comes to protecting intellectual property is another matter.

The source, Luke, use the source

Another important key to MP3's popularity is the fact that it's highly available. Rather than hanging from the awnings of a single company, literally hundreds of MP3 encoders and players are available for virtually every operating system under the sun. And, of course, there are millions of MP3 files out there. Most people don't have the time or the inclination to evaluate all the competing formats—they go with what works.

But perhaps most importantly, Fraunhofer and Thomson have made sample code available to the world. As you'll see in Chapter 7, that doesn't mean the MPEG codec is open source exactly (technically, developers still owe licensing fees to the codecs copyright holders), but it does mean that it's been possible for competition to take root and for a multiplicity of approaches to flourish. From the most complex and exacting command-line applications to dirt-simple, all-in-one GUI applications, a quick search of any MP3-related site will uncover as many approaches to MP3 encoding and playback as there are types of computer users. That kind of diversity has a way of generating a deep, grassroots kind of spirit around a technology—one need look no further than the amazing success of Linux to witness the kind of results that can arise in an open, "biologically diverse" environment.

 Among the contenders to MP3 is Microsoft's own digital audio compression format, Windows Media. To be sure, Windows Media does deliver good sound at much smaller file sizes than MP3 (at the lower bitrates).* Windows Media offers security features for artists and labels who want to take advantage of it. It's built-in streaming features make it competitive with MP3 and RealAudio simultaneously. But the real kicker, of course, is the fact that Windows Media is built into later versions of Windows, giving it a level of direct access with which no one can hope to compete. But at this writing, Windows Media was not gaining any kind of serious buy-in from users (though that doesn't mean it never will). Think about that: if not even Microsoft can break into a market it desperately wants to occupy, then it's a pretty safe bet MP3 will be sticking around for a good long time. MP3 is in a position relative to digital audio compression that Microsoft itself is in relative to operating systems—it got in on the game early and established a strong user base, making it the standard. And standards have a way of remaining standards (imagine what would happen if you purchased a new toaster and it came with an electrical plug that didn't fit your wall sockets). Windows Media and other competitive codecs are covered in Chapter 9.

"Open source" music

To be sure, there are a handful of bands who have adopted the "open source" approach to music. The Grateful Dead is probably the most famous example of this force in motion. For decades, attendees at Dead shows were not patted down for hidden microphones; rather, taping of live shows was actively encouraged by the band and its management. The Grateful Dead realized that when you encourage a meme to spread and make your fans feel like they're an integral part of the process, the fans become loyal to the family; the Dead always sold out their concert venues. While industry execs still fear that giving things away means cannibalizing their own business, the important lesson is that if what you give away is good, then people want more of it, not less.

---

* Though the consensus is that the format creates noticeable artifacts, especially with certain types of sounds—see Chapter 9 for more information.

Today, with the Dead a thing of the past, this spirit lives on at sites like *www. deadabase.com*, where users can trade MP3 versions of all those live shows. The only restriction placed on people downloading tracks is that they aren't allowed to profit from them, even by selling ad space on their sites. In subsequent years, bands such as Phish, Metallica, the Black Crowes, and the Dave Matthews Band have all jumped on the "open source music" bandwagon, although this always applies to tapes of live shows rather than of albums.

Comparison between the MP3 movement and the open source software movement doesn't stop there. Some argue that the entire history of music is open-source-like, noting that Homer's *Iliad* and *Odyssey* were composed collectively over the years by "skilled Greek emcees," and that the modern practice of resampling, remixing, and audio collage forms a perfect audio analog to the open source movement.[*]

Give the people what they want

Finally, there's the fact that MP3 is unprotected. Ironically, it is this fact that labels and signed artists fear the most—any MP3 file can be duplicated a bazillion times, traveling from one user to the next like an unrestrained virus. Right or wrong, millions of MP3 users are interested in the technology simply because it's so easy to get "free" music. While the record industry struggles to introduce protected formats that will allow us only to copy our own music, for our own use, the public apparently wants just the opposite—a simple format that works the way they expect the rest of our computer documents to work, not one that imposes restrictions and limitations on who can get at the contents of a particular file, and on what machine.

Protected audio compression formats are going to make some headway, because the industry is going to make sure that they do. But there are too many people who appreciate MP3 precisely for its openness for it ever to go away. While some songs may eventually become available only in protected formats, people will continue to use available MP3 tools.

Biting the hand that feeds

The question is, does the freedom afforded by MP3 ultimately threaten the very industry it so enjoys? The industry certainly made this argument at the dawn of cassette tapes, and again at the dawn of video tapes, only to be proven wrong for the most part. But as mentioned earlier, infinite digital copying really is a horse of a different color, and this time around, the industry has a right to be afraid. But is that really such a bad thing? MP3 may force the industry to change the way it does

---

[*] Julian Dibbell, "You Say You Want a Revolution?," *www.mp3.com/news/258.html.*

business. Labels may ultimately *have* to give a few tunes away in order to sell an album. They may at some point *have* to start selling songs one tune at a time rather than as complete albums—the whole concept of what constitutes an "album," which is currently an artifact of the amount of recording time that can be fit onto a vinyl LP or CD, may be permanently affected. They may even be forced to lower the unjustifiably high prices they currently charge for compact discs.

In short, MP3 and related formats may force the record industry to downsize its approach to the whole game, and to come to grips with the fact that they can't fight this phenomenon forever. For its part in the debate, the watchdog organization Electronic Freedom Foundation (*www.eff.org*), has stated that:

> ...architecture is policy. Given the choice, consumers would choose to purchase music in open formats. We believe that artists who allowed their works to be distributed in open formats would gain competitive advantages over artists who locked up their work.

The EFF's fear is that if the Big 5 record companies (Sony Music Entertainment, EMI Recorded Music, Universal Music Group, BMG Entertainment, and Warner Music Group) are allowed to monopolize the trade in online music, independent artists will be stymied just as their big opportunity appears on the horizon.

Can't we all just get along?

The record industry is not going to simply go away. They'll still be around to promote artists, to manage tours, to print and sell t-shirts and bumper stickers, and to run the web sites of their artists. As one representative put it, "Without the help of the industry, the independent artist's experience may be closer to that of a street performer, rather than a stage performer." It is, after all, possible that a marketing machine more powerful than MTV itself may rise like a Phoenix from the chaos of the Internet.

The industry has yet to feel the full impact of MP3, but they will—it's inevitable. The genie is already out of the bottle.

2

In this chapter:
* *A "Perceptual" Codec*
* *The Anatomy of an MP3 File*

How MP3 Works: Inside the Codec

So what's the trick? How does the MP3 format accomplish its radical feats of compression and decompression, while still managing to maintain an acceptable level of fidelity to the original source material? The process may seem like magic, but it isn't. The entire MP3 phenomenon is made possible by the confluence of several distinct but interrelated elements: A few simple insights into the nature of human psychoacoustics, a whole lot of number crunching, and conformance to a tightly specified format for encoding and decoding audio into compact bitstreams. In this chapter, we'll take a look at these elements in detail in order to understand exactly what's going on behind the scenes of MP3 encoding and decoding software, as well as some of the chicanery that takes place between your ears.

Note that this chapter goes fairly deeply behind the scenes of MP3, and is somewhat technical in nature. You can skip this chapter if you're not interested in learning how MP3 works. If you just want to get started creating and playing MP3 audio, you can skip ahead to Chapters 3, 4, and 5.

A "Perceptual" Codec

Well-encoded MP3 files can sound pretty darn good, considering how small they are. As mentioned in Chapter 1, *The Nuts and Bolts of MP3*, your typical MP3 file is around one-tenth the size of the corresponding uncompressed audio source. How is this accomplished? That's a somewhat complex topic, so we've devoted this entire chapter to explaining the process.

MPEG Audio Compression in a Nutshell

Uncompressed audio, such as that found on CDs, stores more data than your brain can actually process. For example, if two notes are very similar and very close together, your brain may perceive only one of them. If two sounds are very different but one is much louder than the other, your brain may never perceive the quieter signal. And of course your ears are more sensitive to some frequencies than others. The study of these auditory phenomena is called *psychoacoustics*, and quite a lot is known about the process; so much so that it can be quite accurately described in tables and charts, and in mathematical models representing human hearing patterns.

MP3 encoding tools (see Chapter 5, *Ripping and Encoding: Creating MP3 Files*, for examples and usage details) analyze incoming source signal, break it down into mathematical patterns, and compare these patterns to psychoacoustic models stored in the encoder itself. The encoder can then discard most of the data that doesn't match the stored models, keeping that which does. The person doing the encoding can specify how many bits should be allotted to storing each second of music, which in effect sets a "tolerance" level—the lower the data storage allotment, the more data will be discarded, and the worse the resulting music will sound. The process is actually quite a bit more complex than that, and we'll go into more detail later on. This kind of compression is called *lossy*, because data is lost in the process. However, a second compression run is also made, which shrinks the remaining data even more via more traditional means (similar to the familiar "zip" compression process).

MP3 files are composed of a series of very short *frames*, one after another, much like a filmstrip. Each frame of data is preceded by a *header* that contains extra information about the data to come. In some encodings, these frames may interact with one another. For example, if one frame has leftover storage space and the next frame doesn't have enough, they may team up for optimal results.

At the beginning or end of an MP3 file, extra information about the file itself, such as the name of the artist, the track title, the name of the album from which the track came, the recording year, genre, and personal comments may be stored. This is called "ID3" data, and will become increasingly useful as your collection grows. We'll look at the structure of MP3 files and their ID3 tags in this chapter, and the process of creating and using ID3 tags in Chapter 4, *Playlists, Tags, and Skins: MP3 Options*. Let's zoom in for a closer look at the entire process.

 Always remember to set your encoder to store ID3 data during the encode process, if possible—doing so will save you a lot of work down the road.

Waveforms and Psychoacoustics

Everything is vibration. The universe is made of waves, and all waves oscillate at different lengths (a wavelength is defined as the distance between the peak of one wave and the peak of the next). Waves vibrating at different frequencies manifest themselves differently, all the way from the astronomically slow pulsations of the universe itself to the inconceivably fast vibration of matter (and beyond). Somewhere in between these extremes are wavelengths that are perceptible to human beings as light and sound. Just beyond the realms of light and sound are sub- and ultrasonic vibration, the infrared and ultraviolet light spectra, and zillions of other frequencies imperceptible to humans (such as radio and microwave). Our sense organs are tuned only to very narrow bandwidths of vibration in the overall picture. In fact, even our own musical instruments create many vibrational frequencies that are imperceptible to our ears. Frequencies are typically described in units called *Hertz* (Hz), which translates simply as "cycles per second." In general, humans cannot hear frequencies below 20Hz (20 cycles per second), nor above 20kHz (20,000 cycles per second), as shown in Figure 2-1.* While hearing capacities vary from one individual to the next, it's generally true that humans perceive midrange frequencies more strongly than high and low frequencies,† and that sensitivity to higher frequencies diminishes with age and prolonged exposure to loud volumes. In fact, by the time we're adults, most of us can't hear much of anything above 16kHz (although women tend to preserve the ability to hear higher frequencies later into life than do men). The most sensitive range of hearing for most people hovers between 2kHz to 4kHz, a level probably evolutionarily related to the normal range of the human voice, which runs roughly from 500Hz to 2kHz.

These are simple and well-established empirical observations on the human hearing mechanism. However, there's a second piece to this puzzle, which involves the mind itself. Some have postulated‡ that the sane mind functions as a sort of "reducing valve," systematically bringing important information to the fore and sublimating or ignoring superfluous or irrelevant data.§ In fact, it's been estimated that we really only process a *billionth* of the data available to our five senses at any given time. Clearly, one of the most important functions of the mind is to function as a sieve, sifting the most important information out of the incoming signal, leaving the conscious self to focus on the stuff that matters.

---

* Figure 2-1 is based on a chart and data produced by Xing Technology Corporation (*www.xingtech.com*).

† However, note that frequency-dependent sensitivity flattens out the louder the sound is. For more information, see the section on Fletcher-Munson curves in Chapter 4.

‡ Aldous Huxley, *The Doors of Perception*. First published by Chatto and Windus Ltd., 1954. Now available in numerous reprints.

§ Presumably, one of the distinguishing characteristics of insanity is a failure of the mind to perform its function as a reducing valve, allowing "irrelevant" information to take as much precedence as the relevant.

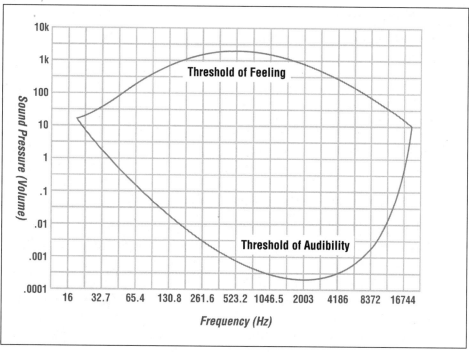

Figure 2-1. While vibratory frequencies extend both above and below, human hearing is pretty much limited to the range between 20Hz and 20kHz

The basic principle of any perceptual codec is that there's little point in storing information that can't be perceived by humans anyway. As obvious as this may sound, you may be surprised to learn that a good recording stores a tremendous amount of audio data that you never even hear, because recording equipment (microphones, guitar pickups, and so on) is sensitive to a broader range of sounds and audio resolutions than is the human ear. After getting an overview of how perceptual codecs work in general, we'll take a closer look at exactly how the MP3 codec does its thing.

The word "codec" is a foreshortening of the words "compress" and "decompress," and refers to any of a class of processes that allow for the systematic compression and decompression of data. While various codecs are fundamental to many file formats and transmission methods (for instance image and video compression formats have their own codecs, some of which are perceptual as well), it's the MP3 codec that concerns us here.

Breaking It Down

MP3 uses two compression techniques to achieve its size reduction ratios over uncompressed audio—one lossy and one lossless. First it throws away what humans can't hear anyway (or at least it makes acceptable compromises), and then it encodes the redundancies to achieve further compression. However, it's the first part of the process that does most of the grunt work, requires most of the complexity, and chiefly concerns us here.

Perceptual codecs are highly complex beasts, and all of them work a little differently. However, the general principles of perceptual coding remain the same from one codec to the next. In brief, the MP3 encoding process can be subdivided into a handful of discrete tasks (not necessarily in this order):

- Break the signal into smaller component pieces called "frames," each typically lasting a fraction of a second. You can think of frames much as you would the frames in a movie film.

- Analyze the signal to determine its "spectral energy distribution." In other words, on the entire spectrum of audible frequencies, find out how the bits will need to be distributed to best account for the audio to be encoded. Because different portions of the frequency spectrum are most efficiently encoded via slight variants of the same algorithm, this step breaks the signal into *sub-bands*, which can be processed independently for optimal results (but note that all sub-bands use the algorithm—they just allocate the number of bits differently, as determined by the encoder).

- The encoding bitrate is taken into account, and the maximum number of bits that can be allocated to each frame is calculated. For instance, if you're encoding at 128 kbps, you have an upper limit on how much data can be stored in each frame (unless you're encoding with variable bitrates, but we'll get to that later). This step determines how much of the available audio data will be stored, and how much will be left on the cutting room floor.

- The frequency spread for each frame is compared to mathematical models of human psychoacoustics, which are stored in the codec as a reference table. From this model, it can be determined which frequencies need to be rendered accurately, since they'll be perceptible to humans, and which ones can be dropped or allocated fewer bits, since we wouldn't be able to hear them anyway. Why store data that can't be heard?

- The bitstream is run through the process of "Huffman coding," which compresses redundant information throughout the sample. The Huffman coding does not work with a psychoacoustic model, but achieves additional compression via more traditional means.* Thus, you can see the entire MP3 encoding

---

* See the glossary for definition and more information.

process as a two-pass system: First you run all of the psychoacoustic models, discarding data in the process, and then you compress what's left to shrink the storage space required by any redundancies. This second step, the Huffman coding, does not discard any data—it just lets you store what's left in a smaller amount of space.

- The collection of frames is assembled into a serial bitstream, with header information preceding each data frame. The headers contain instructional "metadata" specific to that frame (see "The Anatomy of an MP3 File" in this chapter).

Along the way, many other factors enter into the equation, often as the result of options chosen prior to beginning the encoding (more on those in Chapter 5). In addition, algorithms for the encoding of an individual frame often rely on the results of an encoding for the frames that precede or follow it. The entire process usually includes some degree of simultaneity; the preceding steps are not necessarily run in order. We'll take a deeper look at much of this process in the sections that follow.

Notes on "Lossiness"

Compression formats, whether they operate on audio, video, images, or random collections of files, are either *lossless* or *lossy*. The distinction is simple: Lossless formats are identical to the original(s) after being decompressed, while lossy formats are not. A good example of a lossless compression format is the ubiquitous .zip archiving scheme. When you unpack a zip archive containing a backup of your system from last month, losing even a single byte is unacceptable. However, some types of data can withstand having information thrown away, on the grounds that either you'll never notice what's missing, or you're willing to make a compromise: Smaller files in exchange for missing but unimportant data.

A good example of a lossy compression format is JPEG, which banks on the fact that image files often store more information than necessary to display an image of acceptable quality. By throwing away some of the information, and by encoding redundant information with mathematical algorithms, excellent compression ratios can be achieved for images that don't need to be displayed at high resolutions.

While the JPEG analogy doesn't depict the MP3 compression process accurately, it does illustrate the concept of lossiness, and it's important to understand that all MP3 files, no matter how well-encoded, have discarded some of the information that was stored in the original, uncompressed signal.

Many lossy compression formats work by scanning for redundant data and reducing it to a mathematical depiction which can be "unpacked" later on. Think for a moment of a photograph depicting a clear blue sky, and below it a beach. If you were to scan and store this image on your hard drive, you could end up storing hundreds of thousands of pixels of perfect blue, all identical to one another, and therefore redundant. The secret of a photographic compression method like GIF is that this redundant information is reduced to a single description. Rather than store all the bits individually, they may be represented as the mathematical equivalent of "repeat blue pixel 273,000 times." When the part of the image depicting the sand is encountered, the sand is analyzed for redundancy and similar reductions can be achieved. This is why simple images can be stored as small files, while complex images don't compress as well—they contain less redundancy. On the other hand, JPEG compression works in accord with user-defined "tolerance thresholds"; determining how similar two adjacent pixels (or, more accurately, frequencies) have to be before they're considered redundant with one another is the key to determining the degree of lossiness. If JPEG compression is set high, light blue and medium blue pixels may be treated as being redundant with one another. If JPEG compression is set low, the codec will be more fussy about determining which pixels are redundant. The end result will be a clearer picture and a larger image file.

Masking Effects

Part of the process of mental filtering, described earlier in this chapter, which occurs unconsciously at every moment for all of us, involves a process called *masking*, and is of much interest to students of psychoacoustics: the study of the interrelation between the ear, the mind, and vibratory audio signal. Two separate masking effects come into play in MP3 encoding: auditory and temporal.

Simultaneous (auditory) masking

The simultaneous masking effect (sometimes referred to as "auditory masking") may be best described by analogy. Think of a bird flying in front of the sun. You see the bird flying in from the left, then it seems to disappear, because the sun's light is so strong in contrast. As it moves past the sun to the right, it becomes visible again. In more concrete audio terms, recall how you can sometimes hear an acoustic guitarist's fingers sliding over the ridged spirals of the guitar strings during quiet passages. Of course, you seldom if ever hear this effect during a full-on rock anthem, because the wall of sound surrounding the guitar all but completely drowns these subtle effects.

The MP3 codec, of course, is unconcerned with guitar stings; all it knows are relative frequencies and volume levels. So, to put simultaneous masking into more concrete terms, let's say you have an audio signal consisting of a perfect sine wave fluctuating at 1,000Hz. Now you introduce a second perfect sine wave, this one fluctuating at a pitch just slightly higher—let's make it 1,100Hz—but also much quieter—say, −10db.* Most humans will not be able to detect the second pitch at

---

* Decibels are a unit of sound pressure, more commonly known as "volume." The measurement of decibels is always relative, so −10db does not imply something quieter than silence, only that the second tone is quieter than the first.

all. However, the reason the second pitch is inaudible is not just because it's quieter; it's because its frequency is very close (similar) to that of the first. To illustrate this fact, we'll slowly change the frequency (pitch) of the second tone until it's fluctuating at, say, 4,000Hz. However, we'll leave its volume exactly as it was, at –10db. As the second pitch becomes more dissimilar from the first, it becomes more audible, until at a certain point, most humans will hear two distinct tones, one louder than the other, as illustrated in Figure 2-2. At Point A, Tone 2 is barely audible next to Tone 1. At Point B, Tone 2 is quite audible, even though its volume remains unchanged.

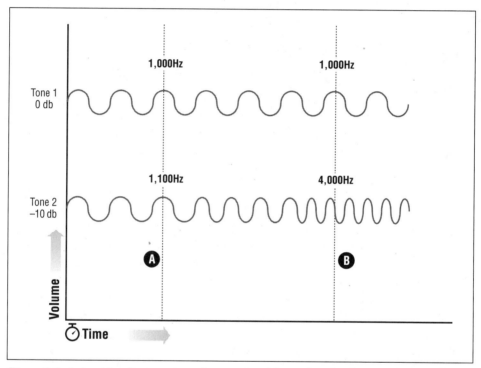

Figure 2-2. As two simultaneous tones become more dissimilar, they become recognizable as separate entities

What's going on here is a psychoacoustic phenomenon called "simultaneous masking," which demonstrates an important aspect of the mind's role in hearing: Any time frequencies are close to one another, we have difficulty perceiving them as unique, much as mountains on the distant horizon may appear to be evenly textured and similarly colored, even while the same mountains might be full of variation and rich flora if one were hiking in them. In effect, we have the aural equivalent of an optical illusion—a trick of our perceptual capacity that contributes to our brain's ability to filter out the less relevant and give focus to stronger elements.

Now consider for a moment the fact that an audio signal consisting of two sine waves—even if one is quieter—contains almost twice as much data as a signal containing a single wave. If you were to try and compress an audio signal containing two sine waves, you would want the ability to devote less disk storage space to the nearly inaudible signal, and more to the dominant signal. And, of course, this is precisely what the algorithms behind most audio compression formats do—they exploit certain aspects of human psychoacoustic phenomena to allocate storage space intelligently. Whereas a raw (waveform or PCM*) audio storage format will use just as much disk space to store a texturally constant passage in a symphonic work as it will for a dynamically textured one, an MP3 file will not. Thus, MP3 and similar audio compression formats are called "perceptual codecs" because they are, in a sense, mathematical descriptions of the limitations of human auditory perception. The MP3 codec is based on perceptual principles but also encapsulates many other factors, such as the number of bits per second allocated to storing the data and the number of channels being stored, i.e., mono, stereo, or in the case of other formats such as AAC or MP3 with MPEG-2 extensions, multi-channel audio.

Temporal masking

In addition to auditory masking, which is dependent on the relationship between frequencies and their relative volumes, there's a second sort of masking which also comes into play, based on time rather than on frequency. The idea behind temporal masking is that humans also have trouble hearing distinct sounds that are close to one another in time. For example, if a loud sound and a quiet sound are played simultaneously, you won't be able to hear the quiet sound. If, however, there is sufficient delay between the two sounds, you will hear the second, quieter sound. The key to the success of temporal masking is in determining (quantifying) the length of time between the two tones at which the second tone becomes audible, i.e., significant enough to keep it in the bitstream rather than throwing it away. This distance, or threshold, turns out to be around five milliseconds when working with pure tones, though it varies up and down in accordance with different audio passages.

Of course, this process also works in reverse—you may not hear a quiet tone if it comes directly before a louder one, so premasking and postmasking both occur, and are accounted for in the algorithm.

---

* Pulse Code Modulation is the standard designator for the digitization of uncompressed audio, such as that found on audio CDs. PCM audio is sampled 8000 times per second at 8 bits, for a total storage consumption of 64 kbps.

For more information on psychoacoustics, read any of the excellent papers on the subject at *www.cpl.umn.edu/auditory.htm.*

Enter Bitrates, Stage Left

While MP3 users cannot control the degree of lossiness specifically, as they might do with a JPEG image, they can control the number of bits per second to be devoted to data storage, which has a similar net result.

In the process of coding, the "irrelevant" portions of the signal are mapped against two factors: a mathematical model of human psychoacoustics (i.e., the masking requirements), and the bitrate, which is established at the time of encoding (see Chapter 5). The bitrate simply refers to the number of bits per second that should be devoted to storing the final product—the higher the bitrate, the greater the audio resolution of the final product, as shown in Figure 2-3. An easy way to visualize the effect of bitrate on audio quality is to think of an old, turn-of-the-century film. Old movies appear herky-jerky to us because fewer frames per second are being displayed,* which means less data is distributed over a given time frame.

Analog Signal   Digital Signal at 64 kbps   Digital Signal at 128 kbps

Figure 2-3. More bits per second means more audio resolution, pure and simple

For example, the current de facto standard is to encode MP3 at 128 kbps, or 128,000 bits per second. The codec takes the bitrate into consideration as it writes each frame to the bitstream. If the bitrate is low, the irrelevancy and redundancy criteria will be measured harshly, and more subtlety will be stripped out, resulting in a lower-quality product. If the bitrate is high, the codec will be applied with leniency, and the end result will sound better. Of course, the file size of the end product corresponds directly with the bitrate: If you want small files, you have to settle for less quality. If you don't mind larger files, you can go for higher bitrates.

---

* And because old movie cameras did not operate at a constant rate, nor was the frame rate accurate with the passage of time in the real world.

Bitrates refer to the total rate for all encoded channels. In other words, a 128 kbps stereo MP3 is equivalent in size and quality to two separate 64 kbps mono files. However, a 128 kbps stereo file will enjoy better quality than two separate 64 kbps mono files, since in a stereo file, bits will be allocated according to the complexity of the channels. In a given time, one channel may utilize 60% of the bits while the other uses only 40%. The cumulative size in bits will, however, remain constant.

CBR vs. VBR

Most of the information you'll read in this book and elsewhere assumes that the bitstream is being encoded at a constant bitrate (CBR). In other words, if you specify a 128 kbps encoding, then that's what you're going to get, start to finish. The drawback to CBR is that most music isn't structured with anything approaching a constant rate. Passages with many instruments or voices are succeeded by passages with few, simplicity follows complexity, and so on. The response to this situation has been the development of variable bitrate (VBR) encoders and decoders, which vary the bitrate in accordance with the dynamics of the signal flowing through each frame. VBR technology was first implemented by Xing, which is now owned by Real Networks, but is now supported by dozens, if not hundreds, of third-party products.

Rather than specifying a bitrate before encoding begins, the user specifies a threshold, or tolerance, when encoding with VBR. All notions of bits per second go right out the window, of course; instead, one selects VBR quality on a variable scale. Confusingly, this scale is represented differently in different encoders. While MusicMatch Jukebox gives you a scale of 1 to 100, the LAME command-line encoder lets you specify a quality of 0 to 9, where the scale represents a distortion ratio. Therefore, you can't just assume that higher numbers mean higher quality—see the documentation for your encoder before proceeding, or run the tests yourself. In any case, the scales are essentially arbitrary; think of them as though you were using a slider to control the overall quality versus file size ratio as you might with a JPEG editor.

While VBR files may achieve smaller file sizes than those encoded in CBR at a roughly equivalent fidelity, they present a number of drawbacks of their own. First, these files may not be playable in older-generation decoders, which had no notion of VBR concepts (although the ISO standard specifies that a player must handle VBR files if it's to be considered ISO-compliant). Second, VBR files may present timing difficulties for decoders. You may expect your MP3 player to display inaccurate timing readouts—or no timing information at all—when playing back VBR files. However, VBR techniques conveniently take some of the guess work out of trying to find an optimal bitrate for any given track—whereas you might have to encode a file several times with CBR to find the perfect balance, you can just set your encoder to use a relatively high quality level and let the computer figure out an optimal bitrate for each frame automatically.

> In general, the header data in most CBR files is same for each frame, while header data is necessarily different for each frame of a VBR file. However, VBR files don't incur more processing power, as all MP3 players read the header data for each frame regardless of whether they're playing a CBR or VBR file.

Bitrates vs. samplerates

Bitrates aren't quite the final arbiter of quality. The resolution of audio signal in general is in large part determined by the number of source samples per second stored in a given format. While bitrates are a measure of the *amount of data stored* for every second of audio, samplerates measure the *frequency with which the signal is stored*, and are measured in kiloHertz, or thousands of samples per second. The standard samplerate of CD audio is 44.1kHz, so this is the default samplerate used by most encoders, and found in most downloadable MP3 files. Audio professionals often work with 48kHz audio (and, more recently, 96kHz*). Digital audio storage of lectures and plain speech is sometimes recorded as low as 8kHz. Streamed MP3 audio is often sent out at half, or even a quarter of the CD rate in order to compensate for slow Internet connection speeds. If you need to minimize storage space, or are planning to run your own Internet radio station, and are willing to sacrifice some quality, you'll want to do some experimenting with various samplerates. More details can be found in Chapter 5.

> Note that nothing is ever actually played or heard during the encoding process—you can encode MP3 on a computer with no sound card or speakers, if you need to for some reason. In fact, this is exactly how things are done in some professional organizations, particularly those dedicated to Internet broadcasting (see Chapter 8, *Webcasting and Servers: Internet Distribution*). In such instances, one computer may be used for auditioning and selecting files, a second used for the actual encoding process, and a third dedicated to serving the files to the Internet. Of course, the beefiest machine available will always be used as the encoding machine in such a scenario.

---

* Generally, stored audio frequencies cannot be higher than half the samplerate, so a 96kHz samplerate allows for storage of frequencies well outside the human 20kHz threshold.

Freedom of Implementation

Interestingly enough, the MP3 specification (ISO 11172-3) does not specify exactly *how* the encoding is to be accomplished. Rather, it outlines techniques and specifies a level of conformance; in other words, it tells developers that their resulting MP3 files must meet certain structural criteria.* This is necessary for the same reason that any standard exists: To allow for the proliferation of MP3 encoders and players by various vendors and developers. The specification only serves to guarantee a baseline consensus in the community regarding how certain things will operate. An encoder developed according to the MP3 specification will be capable of outputting a "compliant bitstream" that can be played successfully with any MP3-compliant decoder, just as you can create a JPEG file in any image editor under any operating system and expect it to display properly in any JPEG-compliant image viewer on any operating system.

It's important to maintain the distinction between the primary developers of the codec itself, The Fraunhofer Institute, and the committee that codified the work of Fraunhofer into the MPEG-I Layer 3 specification, the International Standards Organization (ISO). Standards are often created this way: A company produces a technology, other companies apply to become a part of the standards-creation process, and together they lay down the laws of implementation so that all vendors can compete around that technology. Note, however, that just because MP3 has been standardized by ISO does not mean that Fraunhofer (and their partners Thomson Multimedia) don't still hold the patent on the technology itself. As you'll see in Chapter 7, *The Not-So-Fine-Print: Legal Bits and Pieces*, Fraunhofer's patent is being aggressively exercised, making it difficult for small-time developers to affordably implement the ISO standard.

In any case, while the standard specifies exactly how *de*coding is to be accomplished, it only provides sample implementations (one simple and one complex) for *en*coding. As a result, there's a certain degree of headroom available for developers to make up some of the rules as they go along. In general, encoder developers work toward two goals: speed and quality. While there is some difference in the quality of audio files output by various encoders (as you'll see in Chapter 5), there are vast differences in the speed at which encoders operate. Sometimes, encoding speed comes at a distinct disadvantage to the quality of the resulting bitstream, though this is not necessarily the case.

A good example of the kind of freedom left to developers is the fact that the MP3 standard does not specify exactly how to treat the upper end of the spectrum, above 16kHz. Since human auditory perception begins to diminish greatly (with

---

* Documentation on the MP3 specification can be ordered for around $150 from *www.iso.ch*.

age and exposure to loud volumes) between 16kHz and 20kHz, some developers have historically chosen to simply chop off frequencies above 16kHz, which can be beneficial at low bitrates, since it leaves more bits available for encoding more audible frequencies. Xing, for example, did this with the first versions of their very fast codec. Later, they rewrote their codec to handle frequencies up to 20kHz (probably at the behest of the audiophile MP3 community).

If you're curious about the upper and lower thresholds of your own hearing, download a sine wave generation program for your platform and run some tests. If you find a graphical program, you can simply turn the dial or drag the slider up the frequency spectrum until you can no longer hear it. If the program works from the command line, you can either generate sweep frequencies or generate a series of files at different frequencies at the upper end of the range and play them in sequence. BeOS and Linux users should check out a utility called sinus, while users of any platform can generate pure tones through any of the many simple synthesizer programs available at your favorite software library. The potential problem with running this kind of test lies in the fact that your playback hardware may itself not be capable of reproducing frequencies above, say, 17kHz. A test like this is best conducted on the highest quality equipment you can find.

Other Considerations

In addition to the general principles outlined in this chapter, the MP3 codec does a lot of additional work maintaining frequency tables, storing and allocating bits optimally, handling user options set at encode time, and the like. While we don't cover everything the encoder is responsible for exhaustively, here are a few of the more important additional chores the encoder must tackle.

Dipping into the reservoir

Because the bitrate is taken into consideration at every time frame, there will inevitably be certain frames of such complexity that they cannot be adequately coded to adhere to the limitations imposed by the chosen bitrate. In such a case, the MP3 spec allows for a "reservoir of bytes," which acts as a sort of overflow buffer when the desired amount of data cannot be stored in the given timeframe. In actual practice, this reservoir is not a separate storage space in the file, but rather the "empty space" left over in frames where the necessary information was encoded into the available space with room to spare. In other words, the byte reservoir is a portion of the algorithm designed to rob Peter and pay Paul.

While the CD and DAT audio formats typically offer 16 bits of resolution, the processing of a very complex musical passage may result in only four or six bits of resolution being encoded into the final bitstream,* since there isn't enough storage space allocated to handle the data needs of each frame. What can't be drawn from the reservoir will simply result in an audible degradation of the signal quality. Thus, the byte reservoir is only a partial solution to the loss of signal quality in complex passages. The only real solution to quality loss is to encode the signal at a higher bitrate.

The joint stereo effect

Most people have had an opportunity at some point to listen to a stereo system with a separate subwoofer attached (in fact, most better-quality computer speaker systems consist of two or four satellite speakers and a separate subwoofer). And as you may have noticed, the placement of satellite speakers is critical to high-quality audio reproduction, whereas the placement of the subwoofer is almost entirely irrelevant—people stuff subwoofers under desks, behind couches, or integrate them with other pieces of living room furniture. The reason it's possible to do this without affecting sound quality is because the human ear is largely insensitive to the location of the source of sounds at the very low and very high ends of the frequency spectrum.

The MP3 spec optionally exploits this aspect of human psychoacoustics as well. A file being encoded in stereo is by definition twice as large as a monophonic file. However, this file size doubling effect can be somewhat mitigated by combining high frequencies across the left and right tracks into a single track. This is done during the encoding phase by selecting the "joint stereo" option in the encoder's preferences, or by passing an appropriate command-line option to the encoder (there are actually several subtle differences between the various joint stereo encoding "modes"—more on that in Chapter 5). Since you might not be able to tell which speaker very high signals are emanating from anyway, there may be no point in storing that data twice.

 Some hard-core audiophile tweaks claim that bass sounds are not entirely nondirectional, only that they're less so than mid- and high-frequency sounds. Listeners with ears trained this well are probably not much interested in MP3 to begin with, but those listeners might be able to tell the difference in high-frequency spatialization when comparing MP3 to unencoded audio.

---

* This isn't necessarily a bad thing; it depends on the complexity of the passage in question.

When the joint stereo option is enabled, a certain amount of "steering information" is added to the file so that these sounds can be placed spatially with some approximation of accuracy during playback. This becomes especially important at the upper edge of the bass spectrum, where the ear becomes more sensitive to the spatial location of bass signals. Joint stereo (in "Intensity" mode) really is a low-fi solution best reserved for situations where you need to keep file size at an absolute minimum.

 The joint stereo option can *in some instances* introduce audible compression artifacts which can't be removed by increasing the bitrate. The only way to find out whether this is a problem for you is to experiment. If you don't like the results, re-encode without joint stereo enabled. Remember: Your ears don't lie.

Side Information

If joint stereo is used in M/S (middle/side) mode, the left and right channels aren't encoded separately. Instead, a "middle" channel is encoded as the sum of the left and right channels, while a "side" channel is stored as the difference between the left and the right. During the decoding process, side information is read back out of the frame and applied to the bitstream so that the original signal can be reconstructed as accurately as possible. The side information is essentially a set of instructions on how the whole puzzle should be re-assembled on the other end.

Who Defines "Imperceptible?"

Before moving away from the topic of perceptual codecs, there's an important point to be made about the category as a whole: They all make baseline *assumptions* about the limitations of human perception, and about how closely the end result will be listened to. The fact of the matter is that all that stuff being stripped out adds up to something. While no recording format, whether it be vinyl, reel-to-reel, compact disk, or wax cylinder, can capture all of the overtones and subtle nuances of a live performance, nor can any playback equipment on the face of the earth reproduce the quality of a live performance. All compression formats—especially perceptual codecs—are capable of robbing the signal of subtleties. While certain frequencies may not be distinctly perceptible, their cumulative effect contributes to the overall "presence" and ambience of recorded music. Once a signal has been encoded, some of the "magic" of the original signal has been stripped away, and cannot be retrieved no matter how hard you listen or how good your playback equipment. As a result, MP3 files are sometimes described as sounding "hollow" in comparison to their uncompressed cousins. Of course, the higher the quality of the encoding, the less magic lost. You have to strike your own compromises.

Many feel that the current digital audio standard offers less resolution than the best analog recording, which is why many audiophile purists still swear by vinyl LPs. Digital audio introduced a host of distortions never before encountered with analog, but hasn't had analog's 50+ years of research and development to eradicate them. Compressing and further modifying "CD quality" audio with a lossy perceptual codec like MP3, some might say, adds insult to injury.

But then there's reality, and the reality right now is that the vast majority of us do not listen to music with the trained ears of a true audiophile, nor do most of us possess magnificent playback equipment. Most of us use middle-ground sound cards and PC speakers, most of us have limits to the amount of data we can store conveniently, and most of us connect to the Internet with relatively low-bandwidth modems. Reality dictates that we make compromises. Fortunately, the reality of our sound cards and speakers, the quality of which lags far behind the quality of decent home audio systems, also means that most of these compromises won't be perceived most of the time.

The bottom line is that the perceptual codec represents a "good enough" opportunity for us to have our cake and eat it too. As things stand now, it all comes down to a matter of file size if we want to store and transfer audio files with anything approaching a level of convenience. In a perfect world, we would all have unlimited storage and unlimited bandwidth. In such a world, the MP3 format may never have come to exist—it would have had no reason to. If necessity is the mother of invention, the invention would never have happened. Compression techniques and the perceptual codec represent a compromise we can live with until storage and bandwidth limitations vanish for good.

The Huffman Coding

At the end of the perceptual coding process, a second compression process is run. However, this second round is not a perceptual coding, but rather a more traditional compression of all the bits in the file, taken together as a whole. To use a loose analogy, you might think of this second run, called the "Huffman coding," as being similar to zip or other standard compression mechanisms (in other words, the Huffman run is completely lossless, unlike the perceptual coding techniques). Huffman coding is extremely fast, as it utilizes a look-up table for spotting possible bit substitutions. In other words, it doesn't have to "figure anything out" in order to do its job.

The chief benefit of the Huffman compression run is that it compensates for those areas where the perceptual masking is less efficient. For example, a passage of music that contains many sounds happening at once (i.e., a "polyphonous" passage) will benefit greatly from the masking filter. However, a musical phrase consisting only of a single, sustained note will not. However, this passage can be compressed very efficiently with more traditional means, due to its high level of redundancy. On average, an additional 20% of the total file size can be saved during the Huffman coding.

Raw Power

If you've surmised from all of this that encoding and decoding MP3 must require a lot of CPU cycles, you're right. In fact, unless you're into raytracing or encryption cracking, encoding MP3 is one of the few things an average computer user can do on a regular basis that consumes *all* of the horsepower you can throw at it. Note, however, that the encoding process is far more intensive than decoding (playing). Since you're likely to be decoding much more frequently than you will be encoding, this is intentional, and is in fact one of the design precepts of the MP3 system (and even more so of next-generation formats such as AAC and VQF).

Creating an MP3 file, as previously described, is a hugely complex task, taking many disparate factors into consideration. The task is one of pure, intensive mathematics. While the computer industry is notorious for hawking more processing power to consumers than they really need, this is one area where you will definitely benefit from the fastest CPU (or CPUs) you can get your hands on, if you plan to do a lot of encoding.

It's impossible to recommend any particular processor speed, for several reasons:

- People have very different encoding needs and thresholds of what constitutes acceptable speed.

- Encoders, as you'll see in Chapter 5, vary *radically* from one to the next in terms of their overall efficiency.

- Any mention of specific processor speeds would surely be out-of-date by the time you read this.

- There's more to the equation than just the speed of the CPU. While MHz may be a good measure of CPU speed when comparing processors from the same family, it's not a good performance measurement between systems. The difference in size of the chip's on-board cache may have a big impact on encoding speeds, as do floating-point optimizations, so one must be careful to note such differences when benchmarking.

In any case, it's easy enough to set up batch jobs with most encoders, so you can always let 'er rip while you go out to lunch, or even overnight. Unless you're really stuck with an old clunker of a machine (a CPU manufactured prior to 1996, for example) and your needs aren't intensive, don't even think about running out to get a new computer just to pump up your encoding speed. You'll be better off making sure you have an adequate complement of RAM, a fast and accurate DAE-capable* CD-ROM drive, a good sound card, and that you're using the most efficient encoder available for your platform (see Chapter 5).

Notes on Decoding

As noted earlier, the great bulk of the work in the MP3 system as a whole is placed on the encoding process. Since one typically plays files more frequently than one encodes them, this makes sense. Decoders do not need to store or work with a model of human psychoacoustic principles, nor do they require a bit allocation procedure. All the MP3 player has to worry about is examining the bitstream of header and data frames for spectral components and the side information stored alongside them, and then reconstructing this information to create an audio signal. The player is nothing but an (often) fancy interface onto your collection of MP3 files and playlists and your sound card, encapsulating the relatively straightforward rules of decoding the MP3 bitstream format.

While there are measurable differences in the efficiency—and audible differences in the quality—of various MP3 decoders, the differences are largely negligible on computer hardware manufactured in the last few years. That's not to say that decoders just sit in the background consuming no resources. In fact, on some machines and some operating systems you'll notice a slight (or even pronounced) sluggishness in other operations while your player is running. This is particularly true on operating systems that don't feature a finely grained threading model, such as MacOS and most versions of Windows. Linux and, to an even greater extent, BeOS are largely exempt from MP3 skipping problems, given decent hardware. And of course, if you're listening to MP3 audio streamed over the Internet, you'll get skipping problems if you don't have enough bandwidth to handle the bitrate/ sampling frequency of the stream.

Some MP3 decoders chew up more CPU time than others, but the differences between them in terms of efficiency are not as great as the differences between their feature sets, or between the efficiency of various encoders. Choosing an MP3 player becomes a question of cost, extensibility, audio quality, and appearance.

---

* DAE stands for Digital Audio Extraction, and refers to a CD-ROM drive's ability to grab audio data as raw bits from audio CDs, so you don't have to rip tracks via the sound card. More details on DAE can be found in Chapter 5.

That's still a lot to consider, but at least you don't have to worry much about benchmarking the hundreds of players available on the market (unless you've got a really slow machine).

If you're a stickler for audio quality, you've probably got a decent to excellent sound card already. However, if you've got an older sound card (such as a SoundBlaster 16) and a slower CPU (slower than a Pentium 133), be aware that the "look ahead" buffer in the MP3 player can easily become exhausted, which will result in an audible degradation of sound quality. However, sticking a better sound card (such as a SoundBlaster 64) in the same machine may eliminate these artifacts, since better sound cards perform more of the critical math in their own hardware, rather than burdening the computer's CPU with it.

While this situation won't affect many modern geeks, there's an easy way to test your equipment to determine if its lack of speed is affecting audio quality: Just pick a favorite MP3 file and decode it to a noncompressed format such as WAV, then listen to the MP3 and the WAV side-by-side. If the WAV version sounds better, you'll know that your machine isn't up to the MP3 playback task, since the uncompressed version requires very little processing power to play.

The Anatomy of an MP3 File

Aside from being familiar with the basic options available to the MP3 encoder, the typical user doesn't need to know how MP3 files are structured internally any more than she needs to know how JPEG images or Word documents are structured behind the scenes. For the morbidly curious, however, here's an x-ray view of the MP3 file format.

Inside the Header Frame

As mentioned earlier, MP3 files are segmented into zillions of frames, each containing a fraction of a second's worth of audio data, ready to be reconstructed by the decoder. Inserted at the beginning of every data frame is a "header frame," which stores 32 bits of meta-data related to the coming data frame (Figure 2-4). As illustrated in Figure 2-5,[*] the MP3 header begins with a "sync" block, consisting of 11 bits. The sync block allows players to search for and "lock onto" the first available occurrence of a valid frame, which is useful in MP3 broadcasting, for moving around quickly from one part of a track to another, and for skipping ID3 or other data that may be living at the start of the file. However, note that it's not enough

---

[*] Figure 2-5 is based on a diagram produced by ID3.org (*www.id3.org/mp3frame.html*).

for a player to simply find the sync block in any binary file and assume that it's a valid MP3 file, since the same pattern of 11 bits could theoretically be found in any random binary file. Thus, it's also necessary for the decoder to check for the validity of other header data as well, or for multiple valid frames in a row. Table 2-1 lists the total 32 bits of header data that are spread over 13 header positions.

Table 2-1. The Thirteen Header Files' Characteristics

Position	Purpose	Length (in Bits)
A	Frame sync	11
B	MPEG audio version (MPEG-1, 2, etc.)	2
C	MPEG layer (Layer I, II, III, etc.)	2
D	Protection (if off, then checksum follows header)	1
E	Bitrate index (lookup table used to specify bitrate for this MPEG version and layer)	4
F	Sampling rate frequency (44.1kHz, etc., determined by lookup table)	2
G	Padding bit (on or off, compensates for unfilled frames)	1
H	Private bit (on or off, allows for application-specific triggers)	1
I	Channel mode (stereo, joint stereo, dual channel, single channel)	2
J	Mode extension (used only with joint stereo, to conjoin channel data)	2
K	Copyright (on or off)	1
L	Original (off if copy of original, on if original)	1
M	Emphasis (respects emphasis bit in the original recording; now largely obsolete)	2
		32 total header bits

Following the sync block comes an ID bit, which specifies whether the frame has been encoded in MPEG-1 or MPEG-2. Two layer bits follow, determining whether the frame is Layer I, II, III, or not defined. If the protection bit is not set, a 16-bit checksum will be inserted prior to the beginning of the audio data.

The bitrate field, naturally, specifies the bitrate of the current frame (e.g., 128 kbps), which is followed by a specifier for the audio frequency (from 16,000Hz to 44,100Hz, depending on whether MPEG-1 or MPEG-2 is currently in use). The padding bit is used to make sure that each frame satisfies the bitrate requirements exactly. For example, a 128 kbps Layer II bitstream at 44.1kHz may end up with some frames of 417 bytes and some of 418. The 417-byte frames will have the padding bit set to "on" (1) to compensate for the discrepancy.

Locking onto the Data Stream

One of the original design goals of MP3 was that it would be suitable for broadcasting. As a result, it becomes important that MP3 receivers be able to lock onto the signal at any point in the stream. This is one of the big reasons why a header frame is placed prior to each data frame, so that a receiver tuning in at any point in the broadcast can search for sync data and start playing almost immediately. Interestingly, this fact theoretically makes it possible to cut MPEG files into smaller pieces and play the pieces individually. However, this unfortunately is not possible with Layer III files (MP3) due to the fact that frames often depend on data contained in other frames (see "Dipping into the reservoir," earlier). Thus, you can't just open any old MP3 file in your favorite audio editor for editing or tweaking.

Figure 2-4. Data describing the structural factors of that frame; this data is called the frame's "header"

The mode field refers to the stereo/mono status of the frame, and allows for the setting of stereo, joint stereo, dual channel, and mono encoding options. If joint stereo effects have been enabled, the mode extension field tells the decoder exactly how to handle it, i.e, whether high frequencies have been combined across channels.

The copyright bit does not hold copyright information per se (obviously, since it's only one bit long), but rather mimics a similar copyright bit used on CDs and DATs. If this bit is set, it's officially illegal to copy the track (some ripping programs will report this information back to you if the copyright bit is found to be set). If the data is found on its original media, the home bit will be set. The "private" bit can be used by specific applications to trigger custom events.

The emphasis field is used as a flag, in case a corresponding emphasis bit was set in the original recording. Th emphasis bit is rarely used anymore, though some recordings do still use it.

Finally, the decoder moves on through the checksum (if it exists) and on to the actual audio data frame, and the process begins all over again, with thousands of frames per audio file.

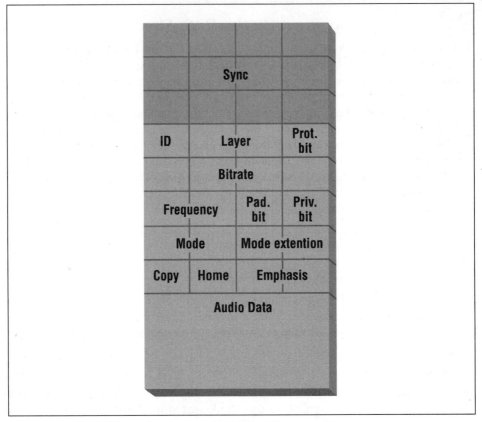

Figure 2-5. The MP3 frame header represented visually

 For more details on the structure of MP3 header frames, including the actual lookup tables necessary to derive certain details from the bit settings previously listed, see the Programmer's Corner section at *www.mp3tech.org/*. If you want to go straight to the horse's mouth, start at *www.iso.ch.*

ID3 Space

http://www.id3.org/ Tacked to the beginning or end of an MP3 file, "ID3" tag information may be stored (see Chapter 4), possibly including artist and title, copyright information, terms of use, proof of ownership, an encapsulated thumbnail image, and comments. There are actually two variants of the ID3 specification: ID3v1 and ID3v2, and while the potential differences between them are great, virtually all modern MP3 players can handle files with tags in either format (though a few older players will have problems with ID3v2 tags). Not only are ID3v2 tags capable of storing a lot more information than ID3v1 tags, but they appear at the beginning of the bitstream, rather than at the end. The reason for this is simple: When an MP3 file is being broadcast or streamed rather than simply downloaded, the player needs to be able to display all of this information throughout the duration of the track, not at the end when it's too late.

It's unfortunate that ID3 tags ever ended up being tagged onto the end of MP3 files to begin with; we'd be much better off if all MP3 files stored their ID3 data at the beginning rather than at the end of the file. As it stands, some MP3 players will simply give up if actual audio data is not encountered within the first few frames. While players developed to the actual ISO MPEG specification will know how to handle either type, the specification itself is unfortunately vague on this point. It simply states that a player should look for a "sync header," without specifying exactly where seeking should start and stop. This laxness in the spec has caused some controversy among developers of ID3-enabled applications, who naturally don't want their applications seeking blindly through 1GB image files, should the user happen to hand one to the application. Fortunately, the ID3v2 spec is more specific on the matter.

One of the more interesting portions of the ID3 specification is the numerical categorization of types of audio, as shown in the Appendix. The numerical identifiers are stored in the ID3 tag, and typically mapped to the actual names via a picklist or another widget in the MP3 player or ID3 tool.

Frames per Second

Just as the movie industry has a standard that specifies the number of frames per second in a film in order to guarantee a constant rate of playback on any projector, the MP3 spec employs a similar standard. Regardless of the bitrate of the file, a frame in an MPEG-1 file lasts for 26ms (26/1000 of a second). This works out to around 38fps. If the bitrate is higher, the frame size is simply larger, and vice versa. In addition, the number of samples stored in an MP3 frame is constant, at 1,152 samples per frame.

The total size in bytes for any given frame can be calculated with the following formula: FrameSize = 144 * BitRate / (SampleRate + Padding).

Where the bitrate is measured in bits per second (remember to add the relevant number of zeros to convert from kbps to bps), SampleRate refers to the sample-rate of the original input data, and padding refers to extra data added to the frame to fill it up completely in the event that the encoding process leaves unfilled space in the frame. For example, if you're encoding a file at 128 kbps, the original sample-rate was 44.1kHz, and no padding bit has been set, the total size of each frame will be 417.96 bytes: 144 * 128000 / (44100 + 0) = 417.96 bytes.

Keeping in mind that each frame contains the header information described above, it would be easy to think that header data accounts for a lot of redundant information being stored and read back. However, keep in mind that each frame header is only 32 bits long. At 38fps, that means you get around 1,223 bits per second of header data, total. Since a file encoded at 128 kbps contains 128,000 bits every second; the total amount of header data is miniscule in comparison to the amount of audio data in the frame itself.

3

Getting and Playing MP3 Files

At bottom, playing MP3 files is no more difficult than opening any file in any application. In fact, it's usually little more than a simple matter of drag and drop. There are, however, literally hundreds of different MP3 players out there, all of them with specific differences, features, and quirks. There are also a few considerations to keep in mind when building an MP3-optimized computer/sound system, and of course there's the question of how to get MP3 files to begin with, not to mention how to organize them once you've got them. In this chapter, we'll get an overview of the best/most popular MP3 players available for Windows, Mac OS, Linux, and BeOS, and discuss some of their more important options and features. We'll save the more advanced functions and features for Chapter 4, *Playlists, Tags, and Skins: MP3 Options.*

Of course, before you hear the first note, you'll have to get your hands on a starter MP3 file or two. You'll find a basic introduction to MP3 download concepts in Chapter 1, *The Nuts and Bolts of MP3*, and we'll treat the subject in much more detail in "Obtaining MP3 Files," later in this chapter.

Choosing and Using an MP3 Player

At this writing, there are several hundred different MP3 players out there, with new ones appearing practically on a weekly basis. While the lion's share of players exist only for the Microsoft Windows platform, there are great players for Mac OS, Unix/Linux, and BeOS as well (of course there are players for just about every audio-capable operating system in existence, but we cover just these four platforms in this book). MP3 players vary radically from one to the next. Some are more efficient than others, some have groovy psychedelic interfaces, some work only from the command line, some can be extended to do things their authors never dreamed of by way of plug-ins, and so on. You have some choices to make.

While this book gives URLs for most of the tools covered, you'll find plenty more by surfing around the "players," "encoders," or "software" sections of sites such as *www.mp3.com*, *www.emusic.com*, *www.mp3now.com*, *www.mp3tech.org*, and hundreds of other dedicated MP3 web sites.

If you're serious about MP3, there's no reason to stick with the first decoder you download. Try out a bunch of them, run some careful listening and performance tests, and think about exactly what you want to do with MP3 before making your decision. Note that most MP3 decoders play many more audio file formats than just MP3, including WAV, AIFF, AAC, VQF, RealAudio, ASF/WMA, MOD, XM, IT, S3M, and many more. Many players are also equipped to play audio CDs, and most are easy to set up as your system's default sound player if you like. Fortunately, it's not going to cost you an arm and a leg to experiment with multiple MP3 players to find the one that suits your needs, as most of them are low-cost, and some of them are even free. Even the players that aren't free generally let you test them out in some form before making any commitments.

If you're the user of a Unix-based operating system other than Linux, keep in mind throughout this book that most POSIX command-line tools will compile properly on nearly any other POSIX-compliant platform, including the BSD family, Sun's Solaris, QNX, IRIX, and many others. GUI applications may or may not be cross-platform compatible. We don't mean to leave you out here—we're just attempting to address the widest possible audience.

Basic Features

In the next section, we'll cover MP3 players for various operating systems. Note that we don't even attempt to cover all of the players for any given platform in this chapter—these are simply the best and/or most popular players available as of early 2000. While MP3 player options may increase and change over time, the basic features and functions of the players covered here will apply in some form to most players on most platforms. The decoders chosen for coverage here are represented as examples of how decoders work on their respective platforms, and don't represent endorsements of these players over and above other players that may or may not be available by the time you read this.

The Skin I'm In

As you'll see in this chapter and the next, many MP3 players live on the edge when it comes to user interface concepts. Not only do many of them employ a look and feel completely unrelated to that of the host operating system, but many also take advantage of an increasingly popular concept in UI customization. Rather than locking the user into an appearance programmed in by the developer or dictated by the operating system, more and more modern applications ship naked, like a paper doll you get to dress up yourself. Users are then free to download and apply "skins," which are collections of bitmap images custom-cut to specified dimensions.

Since skins are just collections of bitmapped images, they're completely operating-system agnostic, which means a single skin will work just fine in any operating system, and typically with any MP3 player that supports the WinAmp skin layout. Thus, you may see pictures throughout this book that *look* like WinAmp, but in fact are not—once a player is wearing a skin, it becomes impossible to tell which player it really is or which platform it's running on. Today, there are literally thousands of skins you can download and apply to the currently running player, without even having to stop and restart. Note that skins are nothing but window dressing—they don't affect the quality or capabilities of the underlying decoder in the least, and all developers seem to have found ways to tack additional functionality onto their players without mucking with the skin-imposed user interface (typically via pop-up or context menus).

It's worth noting that the WinAmp skin format isn't the only one out there. Notably, MusicMatch Jukebox, Sonique, K-Jöfol, SoundJam, and FreeAmp all have their own skin templates, which are incompatible with the WinAmp's. Smaller (but growing) collections of downloadable skins are available for these players as well. Take a closer look at creating and using skins in Chapter 4.

If you've ever used a cassette recorder or VCR, you're already familiar with the universal symbols for play, stop, pause, back, and forward, and most graphical MP3 players sport some semblance of these buttons (note, though, that back and forward buttons often skip to the previous or next track in the current playlist, rather than letting you arbitrarily fast-forward or rewind—similar to some less-full-featured home and car stereos). While MP3 decoders can vary radically from one to the next, the same basic functions are typically found in all of them. NullSoft's WinAmp is pictured in Figure 3-1, but the following basic usage instructions should apply to most players out there. Near the play controls, you'll often find what looks like an eject button. However, the "eject" function on MP3 players usually presents a file panel from which you can select a new track. A progress slider typically serves double-duty, letting you "scrub" back and forth to different points in the current file, while also showing you how much of the file has been played.

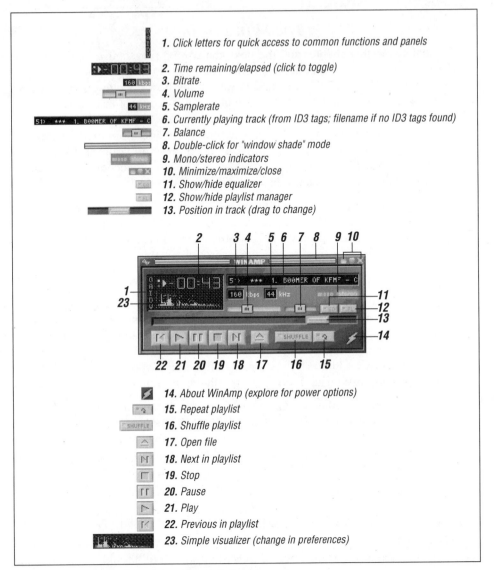

1. *Click letters for quick access to common functions and panels*

2. *Time remaining/elapsed (click to toggle)*
3. *Bitrate*
4. *Volume*
5. *Samplerate*
6. *Currently playing track (from ID3 tags; filename if no ID3 tags found)*
7. *Balance*
8. *Double-click for "window shade" mode*
9. *Mono/stereo indicators*
10. *Minimize/maximize/close*
11. *Show/hide equalizer*
12. *Show/hide playlist manager*
13. *Position in track (drag to change)*

14. *About WinAmp (explore for power options)*
15. *Repeat playlist*
16. *Shuffle playlist*
17. *Open file*
18. *Next in playlist*
19. *Stop*
20. *Pause*
21. *Play*
22. *Previous in playlist*
23. *Simple visualizer (change in preferences)*

Figure 3-1. The basic functions of an MP3 decoder

Additionally, most MP3 players will include a pair of shuffle and repeat buttons. When the shuffle function is activated, the order of any currently running playlist will be randomized, which can be a gas once you've built up playlists containing many hours of music. The repeat function is often a three-way toggle: repeat current song, repeat entire playlist, and don't repeat.

One of the most enjoyable aspects to working with MP3 players is the fact that they let you create custom "playlists," which are simply lists of audio files living anywhere on your system and grouped together under a single name. This lets you store your files in logical directory structures as described later in this chapter, but still create listening sessions based on mood, tempo, or other arbitrary criteria. For example, you could create a playlist called "Tranquilizer" that references just the slow songs from dozens of different artists. Behind the scenes, a playlist is just a plain text file naming the full paths to the selected songs. When viewed through the MP3 player's interface, playlists are often attractive and highly customizable entities that let you rearrange, sort, and skip around through vast collections with ease. Playlists for players that can handle streaming or broadcast MP3 can also store URLs to your favorite broadcast sites (actually, there are two separate types of streaming playlists; we'll cover those in Chapter 4).

Near the progress slider, you may find a pitch bender of some kind, which lets you speed up or slow down the playrate of the current file. Somewhere on the display, you'll usually find a digital readout reporting the number of elapsed seconds in the current track, the track's title or filename (depending on whether ID3 tag data is detected in the file, and often animated or scrolling), the file's rank order in the current playlist, and its encoding bitrate and sampling frequency. Many MP3 players include graphical frequency spectrum analyzers, which let you visualize the "soundscape" of the current file as it plays. Many players also offer a full graphic equalizer, which lets you control the relative emphasis of various subbands across the frequency spectrum (see Chapter 4). The equalizer may be cleverly concealed in a roll-out drawer or other hidden window; to bring it forward, look for a button labeled "EQ" somewhere in the interface. Similarly, the player's playlist function will likely be initially hidden, but can be brought forward by clicking a button marked "PL" or with an icon resembling a list.

Some of the skins available out there are *very* bizarre, and may disguise these elements behind cryptic or incomprehensible interface elements. However, note that the basic skin layout is usually fixed, so the position of elements relative to one another should remain constant for MP3 decoders that wear WinAmp skins. Thus, it's generally easy to find hidden controls once you've become familiar with the generic WinAmp layout.

Some MP3 decoder players can be resized into two or more formats, which lets you hide your player without minimizing it completely; many controls are still visible and usable. This feature, known as *window shade* mode, is generally accessed by double-clicking the player's title bar (Mac OS users will find this behavior familiar), as shown in Figure 3-2. Minimize, window shade, and close buttons will typically appear somewhere on or near the title tab as well, depending on the player. To access additional functions not obvious in the default interface, try right-clicking any unused space (Mac users: Ctrl+click or Opt+click) to access a context menu.

Figure 3-2. WinAmp running in "window shade" mode

Note that many (if not most) MP3 players aren't limited to playing MP3, but can handle a wide variety of additional audio file formats as well. Once you've settled on a player, you may want to dig through its options for a mechanism that will let you easily establish it as the default handler (favored application) for any or all audio file formats you might encounter, if your operating system permits this.

Players by Platform

With the basics out of the way, we'll take a look at some of the more idiosyncratic or less intuitive features of the most popular players available for various operating systems. The players are listed by operating system, and alphabetically within each operating system section.

Windows 95/98/NT

Needless to say, there are more applications written for Windows than for any platform on the planet, and that includes MP3 encoders and players. Search your favorite MP3 software archive and you'll find a bottomless pit of options. And because of the sheer critical mass behind Windows, its MP3 apps are also without question the most evolved and mature available.

Unfortunately, Windows users may also expect a few hitches along the way: Glitches in the sound stream, hung applications, and the dreaded blue screen of death are all part of the Windows experience that many of us have come to simultaneously respect and hate. In all fairness, these behaviors may be the exception and not the rule, and most Windows MP3 applications are very well behaved most of the time. If all you want to do is run one audio stream at a time and you have a relatively stable Windows installation, you don't have anything to worry about, and will likely enjoy trouble-free audio. However, you may also experience a perceptible impact on overall system responsiveness when working in other applications while MP3 players do their thing in the background, depending on your available horsepower and the configuration of your hardware. The primary reason for this behavior is that threading in Windows is rather coarse-grained, meaning that when multiple applications are trying to do work simultaneously, they take long turns with the processor in comparison to, say, Linux or BeOS.

You may also experience specific limitations in the architecture of Windows' audio subsystem. For example, MP3 players like WinAmp and Sonique allow you to specify "Allow multiple instances" in their preferences. Unless you have Microsoft's DirectSound installed, however, trying to open any two audio applications at once in Windows with a SoundBlaster card will result in a "Could not open audio device" message. In other words, Microsoft has added the capacity for handling multiple simultaneous audio streams to the system late in the game, and many millions of Windows users are not able to do this by default. For general-purpose MP3 playback, though, issues like this one are of little concern to the vast majority of users. Meanwhile, many Windows MP3 players are very efficient, with feature sets unmatched on any platform.

MusicMatch Jukebox

www.musicmatch.com While in most cases MP3 players and encoders are different beasts, there are a few products out there that combine CD ripping, encoding, playing, playlist management, and the rest of the kitchen sink all in a single, compact interface. MusicMatch Jukebox is a great example of a well-designed (and very fast) all-in-one package, as shown in Figure 3-3.

In addition to a standard playlist feature, MusicMatch offers a "Music Library," which optionally catalogs every supported audio file on your machine, essentially providing a database of available audio from which you can build your custom collections as playlists. As with Windows Explorer, you can sort and organize your music library by clicking the column headers, or resize columns by dragging the header separators.

Since MusicMatch includes excellent documentation of its own, there's no point in rehashing the basics here. In a nutshell, use the Music Library to database the music on your hard drive, then drag files out of the Music Library and onto the player or into the playlist window. Alternatively, drag files directly from Explorer and into the player or playlist window.

MusicMatch includes partial support for ID3v2 tagging (see Chapter 4), so you can store and display additional data related to a given title such as a bitmap image of the album cover, song lyrics, and comments from the artist. If a particular track doesn't already have this information embedded, you can add it by activating the Track Info window, then clicking the Tag microbutton. Enter or change any information related to the track from the Tag panel, then click the Tag Art button, navigate to any 100×100 *.BMP* or *.JPG* image on your system and click Done. From

Figure 3-3. MusicMatch offers all-in-one ripping, encoding, and MP3 playback environment in a handsome interface

now on, the image associated with that track will appear in place of the usual MusicMatch logo whenever you're playing that track.

If you find that you like MusicMatch's database functionality but would prefer to use WinAmp as your default MP3 player, pull down Options → Player Controls → Use WinAmp player. While you're in there, dig through the Options menu thoroughly—you'll find tons of configuration possibilities that may not be apparent at first glance.

Interestingly, MusicMatch Jukebox includes a "Line-in" encoding option, which lets you encode MP3s directly from analog sources such as LP or tape. We'll cover this functionality in depth in Chapter 5, *Ripping and Encoding: Creating MP3 Files*.

Real's Real Jukebox

www.real.com Perhaps the most consumer-friendly combination player/ripper/ encoder for Windows users is Real's Real Jukebox, which includes some nifty database-like functions to help users organize and sift through their ever-growing collections.

Installing Real Jukebox

Most Real Jukebox configuration options can be established during installation. Pay particular attention to its "security" feature, which is enabled by default. Leaving this option enabled will mark your files with ownership data, making it difficult to play them with other hardware or software MP3 players. You may want to use the Change button on the final installation setup screen to disable security checking.

 By turning security off, you are essentially taking it upon yourself to follow your own judgment and use only legal MP3s. By leaving security on, JukeBox can help prevent you from accidentally playing illegal MP3s. This is a nice option for those who choose to respect the wishes of the RIAA and steer clear of pirated music.

Playing music with Real Jukebox

Before you can play anything with Real Jukebox, you'll need to get some MP3 or other audio files into its database, called the Music Library. If you've already downloaded or encoded a collection of files using other software and just want to start playing your tracks without importing them permanently, pull down File → Open Files and Playlists. If you want to have your existing collection imported into the Music Library so you can further organize, sort and group your tracks later on, pull down File → Import Files and Playlists. The files or playlists you select will begin to play automatically, using JukeBox's built-in decoding engine. Skip to another track by double-clicking its name in the list of tracks. Pause, skip backward/forward, stop, shuffle, and repeat buttons are located in a row near the top of the JukeBox window.

Because the Music Library includes the ability to sift and sort through your collection, you'll find an Explorer-like hierarchy to one side of the main window, with expandable icons for Artist, Album, and Genre. Expand one of these trees and your Music Library will be instantly parsed according to those criteria. JukeBox also makes it very easy to create custom "playlists." Click the New Playlist button at the bottom of the screen and a blank window will appear. Now click Add Tracks and a music navigation window will let you select tracks from any hierarchy in your Music Library. Select a track (or use

Ctrl-click to select multiple tracks) and click the Add button to include that track in your new playlist. Pretty slick.

Ripping/encoding with Real Jukebox

By default, JukeBox assumes that you'll want to encode all of your files to RealAudio format, rather than MP3. Since, if you're reading this book, you probably want to build an MP3 collection, you'll also want to make this change in the preferences.

Real Jukebox is constructed as a tightly integrated system, designed to be as simple to use as possible. While it does indeed take care of some of the nasty details on your behalf, its simplicity may make it unsatisfactory for some power users, since it offers less control over sophisticated encoding parameters. Before you begin, you'll want to make sure you've set the encoding bitrate to your liking (note that the free version is limited to 96 kbps encodings; you'll need to pay to get the full range of encoding options). If you accepted the defaults during installation, pull down Options → Preferences → Encoding Options and select a quality level (allowable bitrates are listed at the right, though they're not clearly labeled as such). Real Jukebox is also configured by default to start recording audio CDs automatically upon insertion. Blech. Disable this option from the General tab of the Preferences panel.

Although frustrating for sophisticated users, Real Jukebox insists on placing all encoded tracks into a single directory, then keeping track of them with its own internal databases and playlists. Note that Real Jukebox playlists are in a completely proprietary format, and are not hand-editable like normal playlists. You'll find them stored in the *db* subdirectory of the Real Jukebox installation directory. Unlike Music-Match Jukebox, you can't tell Real Jukebox to create a new directory for every new artist, with subdirectories for each album. If you're willing to let Real Jukebox manage all of your music, this won't present a problem since its internal database does a great job of cataloging albums, artists, and genres for you. If, on the other hand, you want to keep working with a pre-existing system of carefully constructed artist/album directory structures, Real Jukebox won't let you. If you move your MP3 files around later, or manually organize them into subdirectories, Real Jukebox will complain the next time it encounters that file in one of its databases or playlists. You'll have the option to tell it where to look for the file instead, but this process quickly grows tiresome. In other words, if you want to use the Real Jukebox system, you have to use all of it—warts and all.

After inserting a CD and launching Real Jukebox, select the record/play CD icon in Real Jukebox's lefthand navigation panel. A connection will be established with the CDDB,* and the Album and Artist names will appear along with the Genre, with all track names and lengths listed in the main screen. If you want to record all tracks, just click the red Record button on the main toolbar and sit back. If you want to record only a few tracks, use the empty checkbox at the bottom of the screen to deselect all tracks, then manually select the tracks you want to record. If you'd like to start downloading a collection of MP3 files, the Real Jukebox interface includes built-in links to sites where you can find legitimate (non-pirated) MP3 files.

Sonique

www.sonique.com One of the most eagerly awaited MP3 players to be unleashed on the scene in a long time is Night 55's Sonique, one of the first new contenders to give long-reigning champ WinAmp a serious run for its money. In fact, within months of its initial release, Sonique had become the second most popular MP3 player in use under Windows, and its popularity continues to grow at this writing. So what's so great about Sonique? Well, two things: its incredibly trippy interface and its very high-quality decoder. Night 55 claims that Stardust, its MP3 decoder engine, is the best-sounding player available, and our subjective tests confirmed this claim. The audio quality of the Stardust decoder is particularly noticeable when listening to tracks encoded with lower bitrates, which sound less "swishy" than do the same tracks played through WinAmp. Night 55 attributes this quality difference to a form of audio antialiasing run built into Stardust, along with a close code similarity to the original Fraunhofer decoder.

Sonique also represents a fascinating experiment in discarding user interface conventions—Night 55 has constructed a look and feel from scratch, completely unrelated to the underlying operating system. Gone are all notions of title tabs, scrollbars, zoom boxes and the like, and in their place are organic, rounded surfaces, animated interactions, flowing menus, and unusual navigational tools, as shown in Figure 3-4. Of course, discarding all UI conventions has always been a controversial move (witness the battles that raged surrounding the initial release of Kai's Power Tools in the mid-90s). The problem with this sort of interface is that it forces the user to learn everything anew, and indeed, even experienced users will have to experiment for a while before they discover just how they're supposed to operate an application like this.

The pay-off is an aesthetic experience not often duplicated (though the MP3 world certainly does have more than its fair share of UI mad scientists). There's probably no better way to familiarize yourself with Sonique's UI than to play with it, but here's a brief guide to get you started.

---

* The Compact Disc Database, an Internet database storing track numbers, titles, and lengths for hundreds of thousands of popular compact discs. More details on the CDDB can be found in Chapter 5.

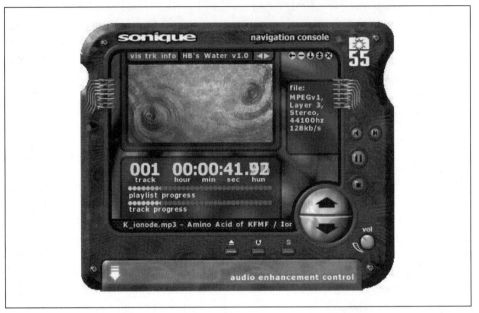

Figure 3-4. Sonique's animated interface

 Users interested in unique interface concepts may also enjoy checking out K-Jöfol, a freeware multimedia player for 95/98/NT that is among the fastest Win32 players available. See *www.kjofol.org* for more information.

Sonique sports three main window styles, or "mode states": "small-state," "mid-state," and "enlarged" or "nav-state." Each mode gives you access to basic player controls, but differ in form and in the number of additional goodies to which you have access.

There are two ways to move amongst the three modes:

- Double-click in any blank space in the application's frame.

- Use the set of four small, round icons containing arrows. The up arrow takes you to nav-state if you're in mid-state, and to mid-state if you're in small-state, while the down arrow does the opposite. Double up or double down arrows will jump you across two levels at once.

The following descriptions will allow you to choose the best mode to suit your needs:

Enlarged or nav-state

This mode lets you view the finest level of detail available on the currently playing file, including timing information down to the one-hundreth of a second and a bps (bits-per-second) readout that updates itself in real time when VBR files are being played. Perhaps most importantly, however, the enlarged mode lets you view the current visualization method at the largest possible size (a full-screen mode is also available). When in nav-state, the main screen is by default occupied by a collection of icons representing online tools, the playlist editor, size mode, setup options, info, and audio controls. Once you access any of these, a sideways arrow will appear amongst the navigational icons, which will return you to full mode's main menu. So you can think of nav-state as harboring a collection of additional horizontal options, and of the two other states as merely different aesthetic form factors. A few of the options available from nav-state bear further explanation. Since navigating amongst Sonique's many modes can be a little... odd, a wide range of navigation and playback hotkeys are provided; see Table 3-1.

The other two states are simple players, and should require no explanation. Select these if you want Sonique to consume less of your desktop real estate.

Setup Options

Perhaps the most important module available from the full mode view is the Setup Options panel, from which you can establish many aspects of Sonique's eye-candy settings such as smoke, blur, zoom, and effects levels. In addition, you'll find five "tabs" available along the right side of this mode. The general settings let you configure aspects of Sonique's windowing and playlist behavior, as well as letting you establish Sonique as your system's default audio CD player. If your machine has multiple sound cards installed, you can select which device Sonique should send its output to from the Audio tab.

The Visual tab lets you control the speed and smoothness of Sonique's window and menu animations (note that this control is separate from the control for audio visualizations, described previously). If Sonique's animations start to make you a little queasy, you can easily turn them off by dragging the Animation Speed slider to zero. This can also be useful if you have a slower machine and are finding that the sound skips or gets "crunchy" on occasion. Since the animation effects are somewhat CPU-intensive, turning them off can save you a few precious cycles (note that Sonique only runs on Pentium-class computers and higher). The File Types tab lets you specify which audio file formats are registered in Windows as being handled through Sonique by default. The Audio Controls tab brings Sonique's graphical equalizer forward, so you can fine-tune the frequency distribution across 20 sub-bands, as well as manipulating the volume (amplitude), balance, and pitch of the currently playing track. More details on equalization are in Chapter 4.

If you spend a lot of time at the command-line, note that Sonique can be launched and controlled from a DOS prompt, like so:

```
Sonique -play
```

This will cause Sonique to start playing the last current song when Sonique was last closed. Other allowable flags are:

```
appendonly <filename> (adds filename to current playlist)
clearplaylist
loop
play
stop
resume
removecursong (removes current song from playlist)
pause
seeknext
seekprev
seekto[track#] (jumps to an arbitrary numbered track in the
playlist)
shuffle
```

Of course, the path to Sonique's installation directory must be in your system path variable, or you must run these commands from within Sonique's directory itself.

Table 3-1. Sonique Hotkeys

Hotkey	Function
B	Next song
C	Pause
D	Delete current song
L	Load song
P	Playlist editor
Q	Equalizer toggle
V	Stop
X	Play/stop
Z	Previous song
Ctrl+D	Clear playlist
Ctrl+E	Enlarged mode
Ctrl+I	Announce to IRC toggle
Ctrl+M	Mid-state mode
Ctrl+N	Nav console
Ctrl+O	Online tools
Ctrl+P	Playlist
Ctrl+R	Setup options

Table 3-1. Sonique Hotkeys (continued)

Hotkey	Function
Ctrl+S	Play/stop
Ctrl+T	Always on top toggle
Ctrl+,	Small-state mode
Ctrl+Tab	Change state
1-9	Volume settings
`(~)	Mute volume
0	Full volume
Ctrl+double-click frame in enlarged mode	"Dexter" mode (try it!)

WinAmp

www.winamp.com/ Without question, NullSoft's WinAmp (Figure 3-5) is the most popular MP3 player available for the Windows platform (and thus, by definition, for any platform). While other very capable players are available, and debate continues as to whether the free WinAmp offers sound quality as good as some of its competitors, WinAmp got a big leg up in the early popularity game, and had hundreds of thousands—if not millions—of installed units before other GUI MP3 decoders even started to make headway. There's good cause for WinAmp's popularity, too—when it comes to the number of features, options, and supported goodies, nothing even comes close. Later versions of WinAmp even come with a built-in "mini-browser," which will let you search for MP3 music at Amazon.com by name or genre.

Because of its wide support for skins and plug-ins, WinAmp has spawned an entire cottage industry of innovators creating and contributing additions and extensions to the base program. Nor is WinAmp limited to playing only MP3 files— between its native capabilities and its many available plug-ins (most of which are freeware), WinAmp can play most any audio format under the sun, and can be set up as the default player for audio files, overriding Windows' built-in audio player.

Amazingly, for a program with as many possibilities as are offered by WinAmp, the program (at this writing) ships with almost no documentation whatsoever. WinAmp's interface, for the most part, is intuitive enough that most options can be figured out just by fiddling around and paying attention. In addition, the WinAmp web site hosts an array of overview information and FAQs. The Playback Basics earlier in this chapter should be all you need to get up and running with 90% of the things you'll want to do with WinAmp, so we'll just take a look at a few of the less obvious features here.

In early 1999, NullSoft was sued for $2 million by PlayMedia Systems, inventors of the original Amp engine around which the original version of WinAmp was built. Modern versions of WinAmp use the "Nitrane" decoder, which NullSoft claimed to have developed on their own. The controversy boiled down to a question of whether Nitrane contained enough intellectual property left over from the Amp days to justify an IP case on PlayMedia's behalf. The suit was later settled out of court... just before NullSoft was purchased by America Online, along with Spinner.com. Shortly after the purchase agreement, WinAmp became a 100% free player.

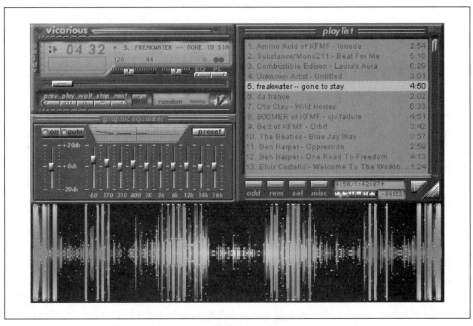

Figure 3-5. NullSoft's WinAmp wearing a third-party skin and displaying its graphic equalizer, a playlist, and a visualization plug-in

Setup

After installing WinAmp, you'll be presented with the WinAmp Setup → Settings panel, which will let you configure the way WinAmp is configured on your system. If you accept all of the default options in this panel, you'll be establishing WinAmp as the default sound player for your system, both for audio file formats and for audio CDs. If you'd like to experiment with the program before committing yourself, you may want to deselect these options. You'll also be able to specify whether a WinAmp icon should be added to the Start menu, the Desktop, and the Quick Launch bar (Win98/IE4 only). You can always access the Preferences panel again later by tapping Ctrl+P.

WinAmp options

Beyond the obvious interface elements that can be accessed by clicking buttons and dragging files onto the player or into a playlist, all additional functions and features can be accessed in one of three ways:

- Right-click any blank space in the interface itself.
- Left-click the "control" button at the top left of the WinAmp window.
- Tap Alt+F.

Any of these three actions will activate WinAmp's main context menu, from which all additional features can be accessed. In addition, WinAmp is highly keyboardable, and most features can be activated via hotkeys. To access a complete list of WinAmp hotkeys, click the lightning bolt in the lower-right corner of the interface and select the "Keyboard Info" tab.

Only non-obvious entries in the WinAmp context menu are covered here:

Play Location

WinAmp is capable of playing MP3 files being streamed or broadcast over the Internet (Chapter 8, *Webcasting and Servers: Internet Distribution*). To open an MP3 URL, just tap Ctrl+L and enter or paste in the URL (typically including a port address), and hit Enter.

View File Info

As discussed in Chapter 2, *How MP3 Works: Inside the Codec*, MP3 files may include additional "meta-data" that store information such as the track's artist, the song name, the album from which the track came, the year of publication, and more. This information may be stored in ID3v1 or ID3v2 format, though WinAmp supports ID3v1 files only at this writing (ID3v2 tags will not stop WinAmp from playing—it just won't see the tags). Access this menu item (or tap Alt+3) and a panel will appear displaying all available ID3 tags. Edit this information if you like, click OK, and your edits will be saved into the file permanently.

Options → Preferences

Accessing this item (or tapping Ctrl+P) launches a very detailed, multi-tabbed dialog from which you can establish dozens of preferred behaviors for WinAmp, or override its default settings. These options are covered in detail in Chapter 4.

Options → Skin Browser

Accessing this item (or tapping Alt+S) launches a chooser from which you can select any of your installed WinAmp skins. By default, WinAmp looks in a subdirectory of its own folder called "skins" for skins folders. However, there are two drawbacks to sticking with this default location. First, if you ever decide to uninstall WinAmp and delete the WinAmp directory,

MORGAN COMMUNI... COLLEGE LIBRARY

you'll wipe out your entire skins collection. Second, since other players and other operating systems can all share a single collection of skins, it makes sense to keep them in a separate, sharable location (such as *C:\ DATA\SKINS*). You can change the skins directory by clicking the Change Directory button on this panel.

Tapping Alt+S will bring up the Skin Browser quickly.

Options → No Playlist Advance

When this item is selected and you're playing files via the WinAmp playlist, the next file in the playlist will not be played automatically when the current one is finished.

Options → Always on Top

This option affects the way WinAmp interacts with other applications. When selected, WinAmp will stay in the foreground even when another application has focus. In other words, it will let you type in your word-processing application even though the WinAmp window is front-most.

Playback → Previous/Play/Pause/Stop/Next

These entries are essentially just another way of accessing the normal functions of the player controls and the playlist. Note that each entry has an associated hotkey, so you can navigate and control your currently playing list without ever reaching for the mouse (knowing that you can quickly tap the V key whenever your phone rings is especially handy). The next six items in the list let you navigate with even more precise control. For example, you can jump forward or backward five seconds in the current file, which can be handy when trying to catch an obscure lyric, for example.

The last two items in the Playback menu let you jump to any arbitrary point in time or to any arbitrary file in your playlist. For example, if you want to jump to a point exactly 3:14 into the file, tap Ctrl+J, enter 3:14, and hit Enter.

Visualization → Mode

This item lets you control the graphical display representing the signal's visualization in the small box just below the time readout. Analyzer gives you a sub-band "real-time analyzer" or "equalizer"-style display, with peaks being represented at each of 20 frequency bands. Toggling to Scope mode will cause this display to appear similar to that of an oscilloscope, with a single horizontal line waving and peaking in sync with the signal.

Visualization → Misc

The rest of the Visualization sub-menu is occupied by dozens of options for customizing the precise behavior of the visualization, whether it be in Analyzer or Scope mode. Note also that additional options are given for customizing the behavior of the visualization when WinAmp is in WindowShade mode. If you find the visualizations distracting (because of their constant flickering and dancing), you can also turn them off completely. The Refresh Rate lets you specify how frequently the display should be updated. If you've got a lot of CPU clock cycles to spare, you may as well set this high to get the most accurate display possible. The bottom portion of this menu lets you enable, disable, or configure various WinAmp plug-ins. Plug-ins are covered in detail in Chapter 4.

 Click the region in the lower right of WinAmp's interface (usually demarcated by an icon but possibly blank, depending on the current skin) to access a tabbed dialog containing movie, credits, shareware registration information, WinAmp tips, and an excellent list of links to key MP3-related web sites. If your list of links appears blank or out-of-date, click the Update Links button to download an updated list from NullSoft. Really, despite all of the excellent MP3 "links" sites out there, this hierarchical list is one of the best and most complete you'll find anywhere—the cream of the crop.

Windows Media Player

www.microsoft.com/windows/mediaplayer/ While it's nothing to write home about in terms of features and appearance, your version of Windows may come bundled with a perfectly capable MP3 player in the form of the Microsoft Media Player, which gained MPEG support after the release of Windows 98, as shown in Figure 3-6. You'll find the Media Player in the Accessories → Entertainment program group. If Media Player gives you an error message when an MP3 file is dragged onto its interface, then you've got an older version. To update, go to the Microsoft URL listed earlier and download an update. Its controls are straightforward and easy to use.

Significantly, upgrading to a newer version of Media Player may install DirectSound3D onto your system, thus enabling supporting applications to share the sound stream.

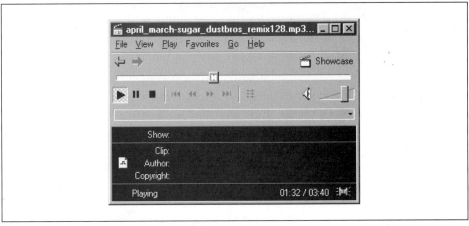

Figure 3-6. Later versions of Windows Media Player include support for the MPEG codec, and thus can play MP3 files

There is, however, one big gotcha to look out for if you use a recent version of Media Player and do most of your web surfing with Internet Explorer. Upon installation, Media Player will set itself up as the default MP3 handler without asking your permission. While you can easily take the association back through the preferences panel of another MP3 application, you'll still find that when you click a link to an MP3 file from within Internet Explorer, the file will be automatically streamed to Media Player, which means you'll get to listen to it immediately but won't be able to save the file for future use... or at least that's what Microsoft would have you think.* In reality, MP3 files streamed through MediaPlayer are indeed saved to your hard drive, though MediaPlayer gives you no indication as to where, and does not present any kind of download location file panel. The secret they apparently don't want you to know is that the downloaded file is kept in your cache. After listening to a file through MediaPlayer, open Windows Explorer and navigate to *C:\WINDOWS\LOCAL SETTINGS\TEMPORARY INTERNET FILES\ CONTENT.IE5* (that is, if you're using Windows 98 or IE5—the location for other versions of Windows/IE should be similar). You'll see thousands of small files representing all the HTML pages you've browsed with Internet Explorer that are still in cache. Sort this directory by Type and you'll be able to find all of the MP3 files in your cache. You can then move them to a more logical, and permanent, location.

A short-term work-around for this situation is to *right*-click MP3 links in Internet Explorer and choose "Save Target As..." from the context menu. The author has not been able to locate instructions for a permanent fix to this problem. Either you do all of your MP3 downloading with another browser, remember to use the right-click trick, or be ready to go digging through your cache for the goods.

---

* Downloads started through Netscape Navigator are not affected by this peculiar behavior.

Configuring the Default Handler for MP3 Files in Windows

All associations between filetypes and preferred applications are handled in Windows through Explorer's File Types panel:

Windows 95/NT4: In Explorer, pull down View → Options → File Types

Windows 98/IE4: In Explorer, pull down View → Folder Options → File Types

While one might expect to be able to locate a filetype directly, the arrangement of this panel instead sorts types by their current associations, which means you may find the MP3 entry under "MP3 File" if no player is currently associated with files ending in *.mp3*, or with the name of the current MP3 player, if you've set up associations through another program. In other words, the filetype you're looking for may be called "WinAmp Media File," "Sonique File," or something else entirely; thus, you can't necessarily just navigate through this panel for a definitive filetype. Instead, you need to know the name of the current association before you begin. If you don't already know the name of the filetype Windows is currently giving to your MP3 files, navigate through Explorer to an MP3 file, make sure Explorer is in Detail view, and find the name under the "Type" column. With any luck, a future version of Windows will correct this backwards state of affairs.

Once you've located the correct filetype, double-click its entry and you'll be facing a panel from which you can change that type's icon, descriptive name, MIME type, default extension, and associated actions. The actions that concern us here are "open" and "play." Double-click "open," click Browse, and navigate to the location of the MP3 player of your choice. Click OK, then re-open the "open" option, where you'll see the path to the executable surrounded in quotes. After the end of the quotes, add a space and the string "%1" (including the quotes). Thus, a correct entry in this field might read:

```
"C:\Program Files\MediaScience\Sonique\Sonique.exe" "%1"
```

if you want Sonique to be your new MP3 player. *%1* indicates that the program is able to accept filenames as arguments passed to it from the Windows shell. Click OK and then OK again to make your changes stick. While all of this is the "official" way to establish filetypes in Windows, most mature MP3 players include some kind of mechanism for establishing themselves as the preferred handler programmatically. In most cases, life will be easier if you simply dig around in your favorite player's options or preferences and let the app set up associations for you.

Remember that if you use Windows Media Player and Internet Explorer, you'll have an unbreakable association between the two. See the MediaPlayer section previously for workarounds.

Media Player, naturally, is also capable of playing Microsoft's challenger to the MP3 format, WMA/ASF (part of the Windows Media package). The ASF format is covered in Chapter 9, *Competing Codecs and Other File Formats.*

Linux

Linux is a tremendous server-oriented operating system working very hard to become an excellent desktop/workstation OS as well. Linux may not be an ideal platform for audio, but it's stable, flexible, and the hacker culture that embraces it means there's no shortage of MP3 options for those willing to roll up their sleeves and get their hands dirty. In addition, there's a natural affinity between the open source culture of the Linux community and the prevailing winds of "share and share alike" in the MP3 world.

Fortunately, the simplest of Linux players are a piece of cake to set up and start playing with. Unfortunately, if you want to get the really cool Linux players happening on your machine, you may have to do a bit of tweaking first (but hey, that's why you use Linux, right?). Due to its command-line underpinnings, there are many very effective players available that work from your favorite shell. In fact, these players tend to be the most efficient, so if you've got a slower machine or just aren't an X fan, you're all set. Many (but by no means all) of the GUI players for Linux function simply as graphical front-ends to command-line players such as mpg123. Thus, if you plan to experiment with a variety of Linux players (and you should), it's highly recommended that you get at least one command-line player running first.

mpg123

www-ti.informatik.uni-tuebingen.de/~hippm/mpg123.html One of the most basic, and yet most flexible, command-line MP3 players for Linux is the free mpg123. Installation is as simple as the usual routine:

```
./configure
make
make install
```

after which you should be able to type `mpg123 filename(s).mp3` from any prompt. Make sure that mpg123 is in your path, especially if you plan to use it as a back-end to a graphical frontend later. mpg123 can take a ton of command-line options; for a quick listing of possible arguments, type `mpgeg123 --help`. For complete usage details, type `man mpg123`. Here's a rundown on a few of the most useful/common arguments.

To have mpg123 report back with additional details as your MP3s are being played, use the −v switch (for verbose), as in:

```
mpg123 -v file.mp3
```

This will let you know the bitrate, frequency, channel status (mono or stereo) and, interestingly, an ongoing frame count as the file progresses. Of course, it's not often that you want to play just a single file. More likely, you've got hundreds or thousands of files, which may or may not be referenced from a playlist (see Chapter 4 for more on playlists). If you've already got a playlist, feed it to mpg123 with the −@ flag:

```
mpg123 -v -@ /path/to/playlist.pls
```

The same switch with a single trailing hyphen can be used to feed the decoder a list of files from standard input. Combined with your friendly neighborhood find command, you can play everything in a given directory structure with a simple command like:

```
find ~/shacker/mp3/ -name \*.mp3 | mpg123 -v -@ -
```

The value of using the **find** command over **ls** here is the fact that it will find everything in all subdirectories of the named parent directory automatically, whereas **ls** will list only the files in the named or current directory. Playing MP3 bitstreams over the Internet is covered in Chapter 4.

 If you have an older machine and CPU cycles are at a premium, you can force mpg123 to use a different frequency ratio with the −2 (2 to 1) or −4 (4 to 1) switches. For example, a standard 44kHz stream will be played at 22kHz if run with −2, or at 11kHz with −4. Both options degrade sound quality noticeably, and the latter option will probably cause output quality to diminish to unacceptable levels. A potentially more satisfactory solution would be to use the −m switch for "singlemix," which will cause stereo streams to be played back in mono, again reducing processor resource consumption. Owners of relatively modern machines won't need to worry about these options at all, unless you're using mpg123 to feed an icecast server (see Chapter 8).

To stop mpg123 (as with any command-line program), tap Ctrl+C. Note, however, that if you're playing more than one file at a time (and you usually are), this will only stop the current file, and mpg123 will move on to the next one. To stop all activity, tap Ctrl+C twice in rapid succession. On some machines, playback will not stop immediately, as the audio buffers must be flushed first (though this seldom takes more than a couple of seconds).

Output options. If your audio hardware is not supported by mpg123, you can send output to `stdout` (standard output), rather than to the default system audio device. Thus, if you have a bizarro sound card at */dev/somedevice*, you can tell mpg123 to output to the standard stream with the `-a` switch:

```
mpg123 -v -a filename.mp3 | /dev/somedevice
```

You can achieve some fairly interesting audio effects by speeding up or slowing down playback with the `-d` (doublespeed) or `-h` (halfspeed) switches, followed by a numerical factor. For example:

```
mpg123 -v -d 2 filename.mp3
```

will play your file twice as fast as normal, while

```
mpg123 -v -h 3 filename.mp3
```

will play the file at one-third of its normal speed. Negative values are not accepted. Note that these options merely chop out or double up on every nth frame, rather than changing the pitch of the currently playing file.

There are a large number of command-line MP3 (and general audio) players for Linux; mpg123 is only used here as an example. Most of them are fairly similar in their basic functionality, though their various switches and arguments may differ from one to the next. All should have documentation sufficient to get you up and running. In addition, most players come with source code you can tweak if you're in the mood, though most of the CLI players have already gone through quite a bit of evolution and are already well-optimized.

 In addition to the ever-popular command-line players, there are also dozens of GUI players for X Windows. However, configuring a fresh Linux distribution to be able to run some of them may require more effort than you expect. While some, like FreeAmp, will run right out of the box on a RedHat distribution (depending on the packages you chose when you installed Linux), others require additional libraries or toolkits to be installed before they can be compiled. Before you grab the source code, note that many players are distributed in both source and binary formats, so you don't necessarily have to worry about compilation at all, though you still may require additional libraries to get up and running.

FreeAmp

www.freeamp.org   Released as open-source software under the GNU Public License (GPL), FreeAmp is available for Linux and Windows (Figure 3-7), while development of versions for Mac OS, BeOS, and Solaris was underway at this writing. FreeAmp's development efforts are funded by emusic (*www.emusic.com*).

Programmers wishing to contribute source code to the FreeAmp development effort will find full documentation and details on accessing the FreeAmp CVS repository on FreeAmp's site.

 If you have trouble compiling FreeAmp, you may need to install the egcs-c++ package. If you use a distribution other than RedHat, you'll need to install glibc 2.07 or higher as well. If you run into problems during the make step, you may need the XFree86-devel package installed too.

Figure 3-7. FreeAmp is an open-source player that runs under both Linux and Windows

Usage is very straightforward:

```
freeamp file1.mp3 file2.mp3 ...
```

Of course, you can just use a wildcard to play a whole directory of MP3s at once, as in *freeamp /path/*.mp3*, or pass FreeAmp a playlist instead. You can navigate amongst the songs you've loaded from the command line by clicking the Back and Forward buttons in FreeAmp's interface. You'll also find two vertically positioned dials in FreeAmp's interface—the one to the left of the main display controls volume, while the dial to the right let's you "scrub," or skip through the tune. Note that you cannot close FreeAmp by clicking the close button in your X window manager—you must use the close button within FreeAmp's own interface.

 Another excellent audio player for Linux is Andy LaFoe's AlsaPlayer (*www.alsa-project.org/~andy/*). While AlsaPlayer is essentially a PCM player, it can work with plug-in modules that allow it to handle other formats. Unsurprisingly, an MP2/MP3 plug-in is included. Many Linux users appreciate AlsaPlayer for its low latency, variable pitch control, concurrent visual scopes, and multi-threaded design for better responsiveness.

Xmms

www.xmms.org One of the most popular MP3 players for the Linux platform is, perhaps unsurprisingly, a more or less identical clone of NullSoft's WinAmp, as shown in Figure 3-8. Xmms, which once went by the name x11amp, supports the vast majority of WinAmp's hotkeys, skins, and functions. And while Xmms also includes a plug-in architecture similar to WinAmp's, the specific plug-ins used with Xmms are, of course Linux native. Because WinAmp is covered thoroughly in the Windows section later in this chapter, see the WinAmp section of this chapter for usage details.

Figure 3-8. Xmms clones NullSoft's WinAmp more or less identically for the Linux platform

Xmms is also very keyboardable, and features the following hotkeys, as shown in Table 3-2.

Table 3-2. Xmms Hotkeys

Key	Function
z	Last (previous) song
x	Play
c	Pause
v	Stop
b	Next song
n	Eject (opens file requester)
Alt+S	Skin browser
Alt+O	Options
Alt+P	Preferences

Developers and hackers interested in contributing source code and modifications to Xmms will find complete instructions on accessing the x11amp CVS repository at Xmms' site and its mirrors.

XAudio

www.xaudio.com/ Bridging the gap between command-line and GUI players, XAudio can work in several ways—as a CLI-only tool (with switches similar to mpg123's), as an ugly-but-perfectly-functional GUI, or as a back-end player on top of which another GUI player can sit. To run XAudio from the shell, just use the standard syntax:

```
xaudio file(s).mp3
```

or invoke a playlist, like so:

```
xaudio -input=m3u /path/to/playlist.pls
```

To run the XAudio GUI, use the `mxaudio` command instead. The GUI interface is self-explanatory, and includes a very complete built-in help system, available from the Help → Help Browser menu.

Note that, at this writing, XAudio does not handle variable-bitrate-encoded files well at all, and you may hear a fair amount of "swishing" and skipping with downloaded files. While development of XAudio appears to have slowed down, the XAudio SDK (software developers kit) is still available for download, and does support VBR. The XAudio SDK, in fact, is used as the basis for a number of players and implementations, including MACAST, WindowsCE players, and embedded players in several small-footprint devices.

Mac OS

The venerable Macintosh has a long history as the favored platform for audio content creation and consumption, but that hallmark may be beginning to fade. Fewer MP3 encoders and players are available for Mac OS than for Windows or Linux, and the tools that do exist come face-to-face with limitations in the Mac OS that may make efficient playback difficult on some machines. Despite the excellent floating-point processor performance provided by the RISC chips in the PowerPC family, Mac OS utilizes a cooperative multitasking model, which puts much of the burden of CPU sharing on applications rather than on the operating system, as is done in pre-emptively multitasking environments such as BeOS, Linux, and Windows NT (Windows 95/98 uses a little bit of both). As a result, Mac OS version 8.5 and earlier does not multitask effectively, and interrupts being called by other programs or by the operating system may cause MP3 players to cut out momentarily, or worse, to crash the system. For example, the popular MACAST decoder works very nicely, and supports visualization plug-ins similar to those available for other platforms. But access one of MACAST's menus while a visualization plug-in is running, and the visualization will stop dead in its tracks until the mouse button is released. This is no fault of MACAST, but a limitation imposed by Mac OS itself. Fortunately, Mac OS X is scheduled to include much better interrupt handling, so all of this may be a moot point by the time you read this. The Mac holds its own in MP3 creation and playback, and the available players are of high quality.

 At this writing, there are no MP3 players that work on 68 K Macs, as the system requirements of decoding MP3 are simply too great for 68 K machines running Mac OS (although 68 K Amigas did have MP3 players, so this isn't strictly a hardware limitation). However, you can use a tool such as SoundApp (covered later) to convert MP3 files to AIFF, and then play the AIFF files. Note, however, that in doing so you will be obviating the compression advantages offered by MP3, since the resulting AIFF files will be around ten times larger than the MP3 source files.

SoundJam, SoundApp, and MACAST hew pretty closely to the general playback basics outlined earlier in this chapter. Both work via drag-and-drop—MP3 files can be dropped directly onto the application interface or into a playlist. MACAST has a much nicer interface and supports skins, while SoundApp is (at this writing) the more stable of the two players. And don't forget: QuickTime 4 handles MP3 files quite nicely as well, though it may not offer the range of features you'll get from a dedicated MP3 playback utility.

SoundJam MP

www.soundjam.com At this writing, Casady & Greene's SoundJam MP was the only complete, all-in-one MP3 solution for the Mac user, including encoding, playback, and visualization components into a single tool, as shown in Figure 3-9. In fact, most Mac users agree that SoundJam is the best MP3 solution for the Mac, period. If the default interface looks familiar, it's because the company has modeled it on the QuickTime 4 "brushed aluminum" look you've probably seen before. Don't like the appearance? SoundJam can be dressed up in skins—a sizable and growing collection is already available at SoundJam's site.

As with most Mac OS apps, playing files in SoundJam is a simple matter of drag and drop, and the interface controls are likewise intuitive. If you're a keyboard fan, note that SoundJam can be paused by tapping the Spacebar, or stopped by hitting the Apple Key. If you're entertaining at a party by playing music through SoundJam, you can run any number of visualization plug-ins, to provide a psychedelic light show in time with the music—tap Command+F to run your visualization plug-ins full-screen to complete the effect, and be sure to look for additional plug-ins on SoundJam's site.

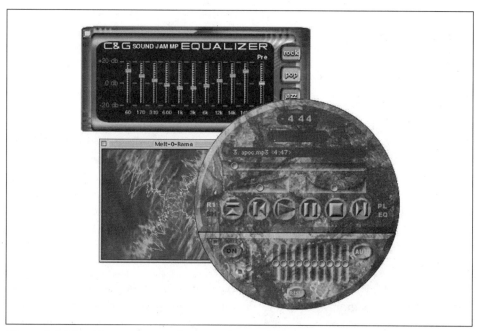

Figure 3-9. Most Mac users agree that SoundJam is the best all-around MP3 solution

SoundJam automatically maintains a "Master List" of all the tracks you've played, regardless where they live on your system, so once you've played a track in SoundJam, you'll never again have to remember where you've stored it (though SoundJam makes this easy, too, by automatically placing the files it encodes directly in the Music folder inside the SoundJam application folder*). If you don't want new files added to the Master List, you can disable this option in the preferences, and new songs will be added to a new playlist window instead. Of course, you're not limited to the Master List—just tap Apple+N to create a blank playlist window and drag your files into that instead. You can create as many custom playlists as you like.

SoundJam playlists will attempt to read the ID3 tags out of your files on the fly, so you'll get a nice, sortable database, with separate columns for artist, track title, album name, and so on. Click column headers to specify which ID3 tag to show in each column, then use the left-most column header to specify the sort order. Tap Apple+F in a playlist window and you'll be able to search through your database on the same criteria.

---

* While this default location for audio files may be convenient, it's a bad idea in general to store data files alongside application files; if you ever decided to delete the application folder, all of your data files are going to go with it. The makers of SoundJam really should know better.

When controlling the sort order via the picklist in the left column, pay special attention to the Play Order view—it's the only view that will let you drag songs up or down in the list, giving you manual control over playback order.

Like many MP3 players, SoundJam is fully "skinnable" (see Chapter 4 for more on skins). As you can see in Figure 3-9, SoundJam skins can have completely irregular shapes, and are not limited to a standardized layout, as are WinAmp skins. This is great from an aesthetic perspective, but does mean you may have to relearn the user interface a bit each time you try a new skin, as skin designers have the ability to move the main controls around, or even leave them out altogether. In fact, the default SoundJam skin doesn't even include a volume control. Instead, use the "Preamp" slider on the SoundJam equalizer for volume control when using the default skin.

SoundJam's built-in equalizer is similar to equalizers for other players (though one should take with a grain of salt the documentation's over-hyped claim that the equalizer delivers the software equivalent of $2,000 worth of equalization hardware). The equalizer does, however, include a neat handful of EQ presets, including Arena, Classical, Hall, Hip-Hop, Jazz, Latin, Lounge, Piano, Pop, Rock and Vocal. You can even tweak these presets to custom values and save them to your hard drive for future use. See Chapter 4 for more on equalization techniques.

When you install SoundJam, it will automatically become your default CD player, which is absolutely fine by most people, since it has so many more features than Apple's built-in CD player. If you don't want this association made, you can undo it after the fact by using Apple's Monitors and Sound control panel. Conveniently, SoundJam can also play QuickTime 4 audio files, though it won't create a default association with that filetype, since the chances are you'll want to retain the QuickTime player itself for that. In addition, SoundJam will automatically associate itself with *.M3U* and *.pls* files so you can stream music down from Internet radio stations and sites such as MP3.com (see Chapter 8 for more on that). You'll find details on ripping and encoding from CD with SoundJam in Chapter 5.

MACAST, MACAST Lite

www.macast.com/ @soft offers MACAST in two versions, which are similar in appearance and function but differ in the number of additional features offered. For example, the full version includes a graphical spectrum analyzer, an equalizer, complex skins, visual plug-ins, and is a closer competitor to NullSoft's WinAmp (Figure 3-10), while MACAST Lite (a.k.a. MALT) provides only basic playback functions. Both versions support MP2 and MP3 files (MP2 is favored by some owners

Setting MP3 File Associations in Mac OS

For better or for worse, Mac OS has this peculiar notion that files "belong" to particular applications. That means that rather than having a collection of thousands of MP3 files that can be launched in your system-wide preferred MP3 player, each MP3 file will be launched in the MP3 player associated with that file. Typically (but not always), this will be the last player that handled that file. Thus, you may have three MP3 players on your system, and the files in your MP3 collection may all be launched in different players when double-clicked. If you're a ResEdit jock you may be able to modify your system's Finder application to associate all MP3 files with a single application. But working with ResEdit is not for the faint of heart, and we recommend that you always make a backup copy of any file you intend to modify, and do enough research so you know what you are doing. Your best bet for changing the application associated with an individual MP3 file is either to open the file using the "open" command in a given application's File menu (which will set the type to that application), or dig around in your favorite MP3 player's preferences panels and look for an option labeled something like "Set type on playback" or similar (in MACAST, the option is labeled "Set Types/Creators"). Then simply drag your MP3 files into the player and let it handle the filetyping for you, without your having to resave the files. There are, of course, several third-party utilities that offer custom filetype control in one form or another. File Buddy (*www. skytag.com/FileBuddy.stuff/FB_home_page.shtml*) is a good place to start.

Mac users may also find that Netscape Navigator automatically wants to play MP3 files via QuickTime. If this is not what you want, pull down Navigator's Edit → Preferences menu. Click on "Navigator," and then "Applications" to reach the helper apps configuration panel. Scroll down to audio/mpeg, audio/x-mpeg, or "QuickTime Audio MPEG" and double-click. In the "Suffixes" field enter .mp3, and click "Application," then "Choose." Navigate to the MP3 player you want to be associated with MP3 downloads. Set the "File Type" to "MPG3," and click OK to dismiss all of the dialog boxes.

---

of older Macs, partially because there were no decent MP3 encoders for the Mac until later in the game), as well as CD audio, variable-bitrate-encoded (VBR) files, and a range of other common audio file formats.

MACAST can be extended through the use of "engines," of which there are two types: some engines bring additional file format support to MACAST (e.g., MIDI), while others provide additional visualization support. You'll find a small collection of engines already installed in the Plugins folder inside the MACAST folder; downloaded engines should be placed here as well.

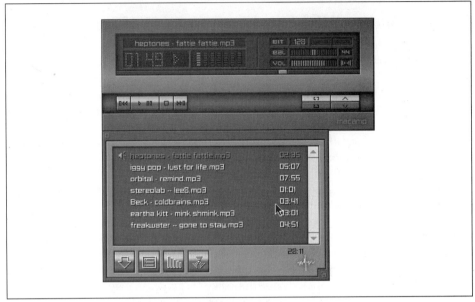

Figure 3-10. @soft's MACAST was once one of the most popular MP3 players for Mac OS

MACAST Performance Tips

If you own a non-PowerMac machine and have trouble hearing any sound at all, make sure you don't have any other audio applications open in the background—they could be hogging the audio channel. PowerMac users should not encounter this problem. If you suspect that an MP3 file is corrupt, grab the MusicVac utility from *musicvac.MACAST.com*, which will analyze MP3 files for unnecessary filename extensions, stray version resources, or ID3 comments where they shouldn't be. If you have a slower Mac and want to minimize MACAST's performance impact on your system, there are two important things you can do: Don't display the graphical spectrum analyzer, and select "Low CPU Mode (no equalizers)" in MACAST's Preferences → Toggles panel. You may also want to make sure that MACAST is allocated at least 10,000 K (10 MB) in the minimum memory size box located in the application Info panel (select the MACAST application icon with a single click and tap AppleKey-i).

SoundApp

www-cs-students.stanford.edu/~franke/SoundApp/ While not as, pretty as MACAST, Norman Franke's free SoundApp utility plays seemingly every known audio file format under the, sun, not the least of which is MP3. As previously mentioned, SoundApp is also known for being a rock-solid stable performer, and may prove more reliable for some users than other offerings, as shown in Figure 3-11. In addition, SoundApp works on 68 K Macs, though it does not decode MP3 on those machines—you'll need to use its built-in utility to convert MP3 to another format first. SoundApp also supports AppleScript, so you can create your own custom solutions (for example, you might create a script that jumps straight to a certain point in a certain file and plays a three-second segment every time a given event occurs on your system).

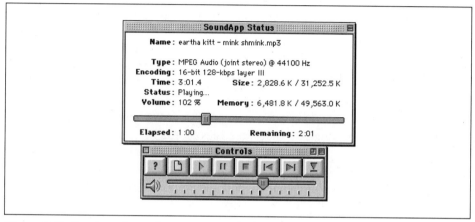

Figure 3-11. Simple and true (not to mention free), SoundApp is a trusty, reliable audio player that handles a huge list of audio file formats

SoundApp usage is very straightforward, and its controls are simple. Note that you can "scrub" through tracks as they're playing by dragging the progress slider. To get more information on a currently playing track, option-click the Get Info button in SoundApp's Controls palette.

BeOS

The Be Operating System may be an underdog in terms of total number of users, but it deserves a place in this book for one big reason: BeOS is optimized from the ground up for handling audio/video streams like nobody's business, and is quickly becoming a new focal point for the digital audio community. More germane to this book, Be, Inc. has stated that they intend to make BeOS the best platform for MP3 creations and playback, bar none. If you're not acquainted with BeOS, cruise through their web site, at *www.be.com*, or head straight for their "User Explanation Track," at *www.be.com/products/beos/user-info-track.html*. You may also find the author's own *BeOS Bible* from Peachpit Press a useful reference.

So what can you do with MP3 in BeOS that you can't do in other operating systems? Digital audio enthusiasts will appreciate the fact that BeOS is capable of addressing audio hardware with extremely low latencies. For example, where a

Windows application might require 20–30 milliseconds to get a response back from the sound card, a BeOS application on the same machine can address the same audio hardware with 2–6 ms latency, making the system very attractive to audio application developers and high-end users alike. BeOS includes an mpeg codec in the operating system as a "media node," which means users can save MP3 audio directly out of any audio application, including the system's built-in CDPlayer and SoundRecorder apps. Because the BeOS filesystem functions much like a database, users can copy ID3 tags into "attributes," so they can organize and query on custom collections of MP3 files in ways that aren't possible in other OSes, without using special tools. Unlike Windows' Explorer or the Mac OS Finder, Be's Tracker talks directly to the Internet's CDDB and displays audio CD tracks directly as intelligently named WAV files, so there's no need for BeOS encoders to "rip" files prior to encoding. Because the system incorporates a unified sound architecture, users don't need to jump through hoops to play lots of MP3 tracks simultaneously, or to create impromptu MP3 mixers. Meanwhile, the BeOS user can start playing half their MP3 files at +323% speed, or −227%, run a few movies, play tracks from audio CDs backwards, and so on. Thanks to BeOS' fine-grained multithreading, the rest of the system stays responsive, whereas Windows users will start to notice the OS and applications reacting slugglishly long before this point.

In case you're wondering, BeOS is every bit as easy to use as Mac OS. At the same time, the system offers a bash command-line shell for those who want it. The power of Unix, the grace of the Mac OS, and media-optimized from the ground up. What more could an MP3 hound ask for? At this writing, there are three primary MP3 players for BeOS, one bundled with the operating system and two provided by third-party developers.

SoundPlay

www.xs4all.nl/~marcone/be.html The definitive MP3 player for the BeOS is Marco Nelissen's SoundPlay, a full-featured, highly customizable audio player that handles a broad range of audio file formats (Figure 3-12). SoundPlay is one of the few MP3 players in the world that can not only play MP3 files backward and forward, but can play them at up to +400% or −400% of the original speed, not to mention being able to play as many as a dozen MP3 files at once (and note that CPU usage isn't the issue here—SoundPlay is very efficient—it's the physical act of accessing so many disparate points on the hard disk that slows things down when you start trying to play more than 12 files at once).

Because BeOS audio applications address audio hardware with such low latency, don't be surprised if you find you can do things like "scratching" your MP3 files DJ-style with a far greater sense of responsiveness than you can under Windows

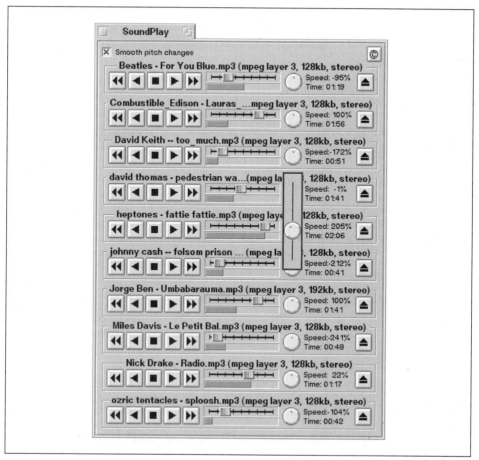

Figure 3-12. SoundPlay can take several other forms; load it up with multiple MP3s simultaneously for an impromptu multitrack console

on the exact same hardware. Try grabbing the blue progress indicator in Sound-Play and dragging back and forth quickly; it's not quite a turntable, but it's not a bad simulation. To increase the degree of control you have over scratching effects, try checking and unchecking the "Smooth pitch changes" checkbox. Keeping the box checked will give you snappier, crisper pitch changes, while checking it will make the sound more "rubbery."

When dragging audio files onto SoundPlay's interface, note a subtle but important distinction: If you drag your files into the lower part of the control panel, the dropped files will play in sequence. If you drop them into the upper portion, the files will all be played at once. The interface will change before the mouse button is released to let you know whether the dropped files will play sequentially or simultaneously.

Interface options

In addition to the default layout, SoundPlay also has several other masks. From the BeOS "Be menu," select Show Replicants, then drag the small red handle at the lower right of a SoundPlay window. As you drag, an outline of the application will follow your mouse. Release over the Desktop and Sound-Play will be embedded in the Desktop itself. As with any BeOS Replicant, you can now close the SoundPlay application, and the player will keep on chugging, even between reboots. When SoundPlay is running as a Replicant, it adopts the color of the Desktop behind it and all of the window borders disappear. SoundPlay will now appear to be built into the operating system itself, as an integral component. Only its controls will be visible, floating in the Desktop.

Since SoundPlay also handles "BMessages" from BeOS color utilities, you can drag a color swatch from the color palette in just about any BeOS paint, graphics, or color manipulation program (Becasso, ArtPaint, and Nelissen's own ColorSelector are all good examples).

Finally, SoundPlay fully supports WinAmp skins, so you can keep on using the collection you've built up while experimenting with other MP3 players. By default, SoundPlay looks for your skins collection in */boot/home/config/settings/ skins*, though you can customize this location via the Preferences panel. To access your installed skins, pull down the Skins menu and select either a WinAmp skin or the default BeOS look and feel. When in WinAmp mode, just click in the lower-right corner of the interface to access the same menu.

Crossfade Settings

Pull down Settings → Preferences and you'll be looking at a panel filled with options, most of which are self-explanatory. One of the most interesting options here is a button labeled "Crossfade Settings." When playing files sequentially (as when playing from a playlist or a collection of dropped files), SoundPlay will fade one file's volume down when it's a few seconds from completion, and simultaneously fade the next file's volume up. The fadeout start, fadeout duration, and next file start time can all be configured for all file sequences by selecting the Default Fade Setting entry in this panel and entering times for these parameters (though the defaults are quite good).

But if that sounds cool, hang on, because it gets better. The BeOS filesystem supports "attributes" of arbitrary size and type. Attributes are simply data that is associated with a file but is not a part of the file itself. SoundPlay takes advantage of filesystem attributes in several clever ways, and one of them is to let you drag any MP3 file into this panel and custom-set its crossfade settings. If these crossfade attributes are found on a currently playing file, they'll be used instead of the default settings, which lets DJs and other serious audio heads tweak out playlists to a level of customization not possible in any other player on any other operating system. Custom crossfade attributes can be removed by selecting a file and clicking Clear Settings of Selection.

Crossfade settings can also be accessed by right-clicking the title of the currently playing song and selecting Special → Crossfade from the context menu. It's important to note that crossfade settings are independent of particular playlists, and will apply regardless of which playlist a particular song happens to show up in.

Media Player

Naturally, Be includes a Media Player application with the system, capable of playing any audio or video stream that has a corresponding codec installed, as shown in Figure 3-13. Since BeOS understands MPEG natively, the MediaPlayer is capable of playing MP3 files. Media Player is nothing fancy—just a simple progress indicator/scrub bar and a set of standard controls. If you're downloading MP3 files from the Internet, MediaPlayer will snap into action automatically as soon as the download is complete, as long as you haven't associated your MP3 filetype with another player (see sidebar, "Associating MP3 Files with BeOS Applications"). You can of course, also drag MP3 files onto Media Player or navigate to them via the Media Player's File → Open menu.

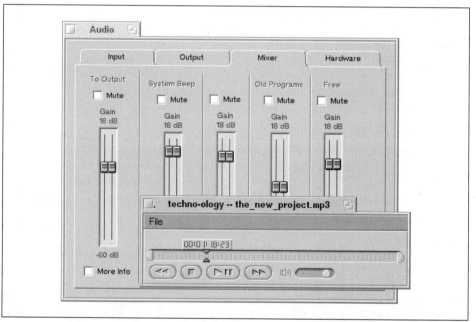

Figure 3-13. The BeOS Media Player application can play any audio/video media stream for which an installed codec is found, including MP3

CL-Amp

www.be.com/beware/ Claes Löfqvist's CL-Amp is a very capable MP3 player very similar in form and function to NullSoft's ever-popular WinAmp. CL-Amp (Figure 3-14) is intended as a free WinAmp clone for BeOS—it doesn't take advantage of native BeOS performance and UI features like SoundPlay does. CL-Amp is fully compatible with the thousands of skins available for free download (Chapter 4), so you can customize CL-Amp's appearance 'til the cows come home. Playing MP3 files with CL-Amp is a simple matter of dropping them onto its icon or directly into its interface or playlist window. Alternatively, drop a pre-existing playlist onto CL-Amp.

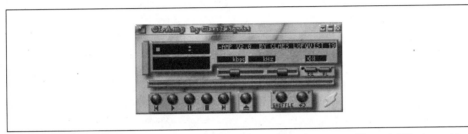

Figure 3-14. CL-Amp for BeOS: A freeware MP3 decoder fully compatible with WinAmp skins

To access CL-Amp's dozens of configurable behaviors, right-click anywhere in its interface. Items in the menus are self-explanatory, but here's a quick rundown:

Double mode
> Double mode (Alt+D) will cause CL-Amp to spring to twice its usual size, which may make it easier to access some of the less-visible interface controls. You may also appreciate double mode if you run your monitor at a very high resolution.

Skin selector
> Accessing the skin selector launches a small menu listing a combination of all skin folders found either in the Skins subdirectory, CL-Amp's installation directory, or in */boot/home/config/settings/skins*. The latter location makes it possible for CL-Amp to share a collection of skins with SoundPlay (this chapter) or other skins-compatible players for BeOS.

Drag and Drop
> From this menu you can control whether files dropped onto CL-Amp are added to the currently playing playlist or *become* the playlist.

Spectrum Analyzer Mode
> Like most Amp-oriented players, CL-Amp presents a graphical display of the current signal levels as your music is playing, much as you would see on some audio equipment. This mode menu lets you control the appearance of this graphical display.

If you use BeOS, Linux, and Windows on the same machine, why duplicate your skins collection on multiple drive partitions? Since BeOS can read and write to Windows partitions as easily as to its own BFS filesystem, and can read Linux ext2fs and Windows NT's NTFS filesystems natively, you can simply make your BeOS skins directory a link to your Windows skins directory. Mount your Windows partition by right-clicking the Desktop and selecting it from the Mount submenu. Right-drag your Windows skins folder into */boot/ home/config/settings* on your BeOS partition, and choose Create Link from the context menu. Rename the symlink to "skins" and you're done. Note, however, that you'll need to make sure your Windows volume is always mounted when you're in BeOS. Choose Settings from the Mount submenu and choose All Disks in the Boot section of the Mount Settings panel.

Speed Button Snap to 100%

CL-Amp will let you play audio streams at anywhere from 50% to 200% of their original speed, either temporarily or throughout the course of an entire track. When this option is selected and you manipulate the pitch bender, the speed will snap back to 100% as soon as you release the mouse. With it deselected, the pitch will stay "bent" until you select another speed or select this menu item.

MP3 and the Tracker

Speaking of attributes, the BeOS filesystem lets you do some pretty amazing things when it comes to organizing, sorting, and querying for data associated with your MP3 files. Every time SoundPlay encounters an MP3 file without custom attributes, it writes the file's total playing time and bitrate to two new attributes.

In addition, a number of BeOS utilities are capable of extracting the song's Title, Artist, Album, Year, and Comment information from its ID3 tag information (Chapter 4) and writing this data to five additional attributes. The result is the ability to use the BeOS file manager, the Tracker, to sift, sort, edit, and organize your files along criteria Windows, Mac OS, and Linux can't even dream about (Figure 3-15).

To enable this functionality in BeOS, download *tag2attr* and *attr2tag* from *www. be.com/beware/* and install them in *~/config/add-ons/Tracker*. Select any collection of MP3 files in the Tracker, right-click your selection, and choose *tag2attr* from the Add-Ons submenu. Of course, you can also edit your tag information directly in the Tracker as well. Want to make your customized attribute data stick, so that the file's *actual* ID3 tag data will be converted as well? Just edit your attributes as you would anything else in the Tracker and then run the *attr2tag*

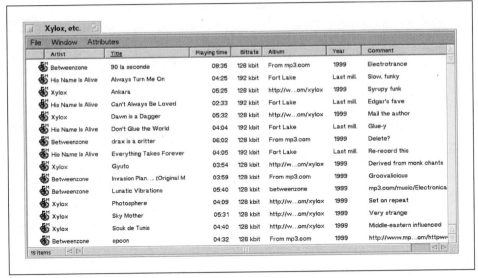

Figure 3-15. Tracker windows are like a customizable MP3 database

Add-On. Move the file to another operating system, open it in an MP3 player, and you'll see that the changes you made from the Tracker in BeOS will have been transferred right into the file itself.

If you prefer to work from the command line, download id3attr from *www.bebits. com* and install the id3attr binary in *~/config/bin*. Launch a Terminal window, cd to a directory containing MP3 files, and type:

```
id3attr *.mp3
```

All ID3 tags for all MP3 files in the current directory will be copied to corresponding attributes in the file system.

Simply copying ID3 tags to attributes will let you sort and sift through fields in the Tracker, but if you want to be able to run sophisticated system queries on ID3 data, you'll need to make sure these attributes are being added to the system index as they're created. While you can do this manually if you like, make things easy on yourself and download a copy of Jonas Sundstrom's MP3 AI, which will automate the creation and management of indexes and attributes. Sundstrom also makes available MP3 Mix, MP3 Flashlight, and the add-ons mentioned earlier. Taken together, they're an unbeatable MP3 management system for BeOS.

Obtaining MP3 Files

Before you begin building up your MP3 collection, it's important to understand the basic legal issues behind the distribution of what is the intellectual and creative property of artists and the recording industry. As with most technologies, MP3 has

Associating MP3 Files with BeOS Applications

Of course any MP3 player for BeOS will accept any file dragged onto its interface, but how do you get an MP3 player to come up in your favorite MP3 player automatically when double-clicked? BeOS uses an expansion of the Internet's MIME-typing convention to give all files appropriate types, and lets users associate these types with any capable application, either globally (system wide) or locally (on a file-by-file basis).

To set the global association in BeOS, open the Preferences → FileTypes panel and navigate to the Audio → MPEG Audio File entry, then use the Preferred Application picklist to select from any of the MPEG-capable players on the system. Double-clicking any MP3 file will now cause it to be launched in that application, *unless* you've overridden the preferred app for that file at the local level. To change the preferred handler for an individual file or group of files, select it or them in the Tracker, right-click the selection, choose Add-Ons → FileType, and select the preferred application.

Note that two different MIME types are commonly used for MP3 delivery on the Internet: *audio/x-mpeg* and *audio/mpeg*. Technically, the former is more correct, though there are plenty of the latter type out there as well. In any case, you may need to make the changes above for both filetypes when setting your global preferences.

both legal and illegal applications. Despite the excitement surrounding the prospect of the public undercutting the traditional distribution mechanisms of the recording industry, and no matter how you might feel about the moral rectitude of the profit-mongering of these traditional music supply chains, the mere fact of an MP3 being available to you does not automatically make it legal to help yourself. It's easy to steal candy bars, and you may feel they're too high-priced, but that fact doesn't make it legal to steal. Keep these points in mind as you begin to build up your collection:

- For the same reason that it's legal to make backup copies of software that you've purchased (so you still have access to it in case the physical media is damaged), it's perfectly legal to create and listen to MP3 copies of music that you've purchased. It is not, however, legal to make these copies available to other people via the Internet, through portable devices, or on any other storage media. You bought the rights to own a copy of that music—you didn't buy the rights for the rest of the world to own a copy as well.

- Many artists and record companies make their music available for download from the Internet (either for free or for a small fee) as a way to promote themselves. There are many sites that legitimately distribute hundreds or thousands of these tracks, and it's perfectly legal to download and listen to them. At the same time, hundreds of thousands of ordinary Joes make their MP3 collections available over the Internet for other people to download. It is illegal for them to do this, and it's illegal for you to download and come into possession of these tracks. If you're in doubt about whether music you're about to download is being legally distributed or not, poke around on the site in question looking for the fine print. If the site is distributing legal music, it will say so, or will be clearly endorsed by the artist or the label. Sites distributing music illegally will generally say nothing, or may even be brazen about their illegality.

You can read much more about all of the legal bits surrounding MP3 are discussed in detail in Chapter 7, *The Not-So-Fine-Print: Legal Bits and Pieces.*

Via the Web

Most MP3s distributed online are accessed by simply clicking a link to an MP3 file, as illustrated in Figure 3-16. Click a link to an MP3 file in your browser and a panel similar to (1) should appear. Select a location on your hard drive and the download will proceed (2). Once complete, launch WinAmp (3) or your favorite player and drag the file onto its interface, access its file panel to navigate to locate the downloaded file, or through command-line options (see the rest of this chapter for details and examples). Turn up the speakers and close your eyes.

Depending on the way your browser and preferred MP3 player are configured, downloads may be streamed directly to your MP3 player without being saved to a preferred location first. The most common culprit of this problem is the Microsoft MediaPlayer. After installing a recent version, clicking links to MP3 files in Internet Explorer will result in direct playing of the file, thus making it difficult to save the file for later use. To sidestep this situation, try *right*-clicking MP3 links instead, and choosing the "Save Target As..." from the context menu instead. In Netscape Navigator, you can always hold down the Shift key when clicking any link to force the file to be downloaded to a preferred location rather than being sent to a helper application.

Streaming MP3

Increasingly, many sites are dishing up MP3 as streaming broadcasts, rather than as direct downloads. In these cases, the preferred MP3 player will always receive the audio stream directly—saving to disk is not an option without resorting to clever hacks (some of which are in Chapter 4 and elsewhere in this book). You'll generally know if you're visiting a streaming/broadcast site because it will clearly say so. A good way to tell before clicking a link is to hover your mouse over an MP3 link and glance at the browser's status area (generally in the lower-left corner of the

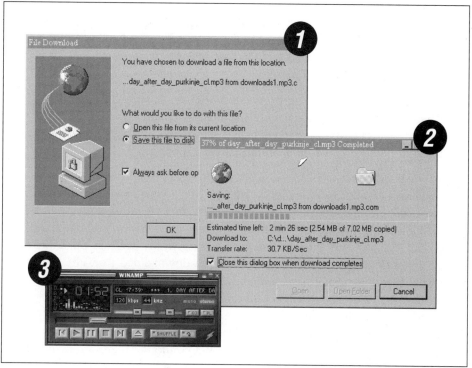

Figure 3-16. Your basic download

browser window). If the URL is of the form *http://www.somesite.com:8000* (has a
port address appended to the end), or includes some heinous combination of port
addresses, IPs, and domains, and includes pls extensions:

> *http://www.somesite.com/cgi-bin/playlist.pls?addr=219.147.18.44:*
> *9000&file=filename.pls*

then you know you're about to access a broadcast stream. See the section "Working with MP3 Streams" in Chapter 4 for more information.

Via FTP

FTP, or file transfer protocol, is the Internet's most basic means of making files
available for transfer between a server and a client, and predates the world wide
web by a couple of decades. It's important to note that pirated files are often made
available via FTP, so be careful. If the files are being provided legitimately by an
artist or label, the chances are very high that they'll offer them through a standard
web site, not through an FTP server. In addition, pirate FTP sites generally have
very brief lifespans, so links and messages pointing to them are often out of date
by the time you try to access them. Trying to hunt down a working FTP site can

be a time-wasting wild-goose chase, and often leads only to poorly recorded encoded songs that don't match your own taste. The best way to find MP3 FTP sites is to scan Usenet groups. In particular, *alt.music.mp3* often carries many listings (although, again, you'll find that the vast majority of them are dead and gone by the time you try to access them).

If you're serious about building up a good MP3 collection, you'll probably have much better results downloading from legitimate web sites and by encoding your own tracks. That said, there *are* legitimate instances of MP3 files being made available through FTP sites, so a basic introduction is in order.

FTP sites will be made available either on a pre-established domain, or on a specific machine's IP address. In other words, an FTP address may take the form *ftp.somesite.com* or something like *103.241.10.98*. An FTP address given as a URL will be the machine's address prepended by *ftp://*, as in *ftp://ftp.somesite.com*. Such a URL can be accessed through most browsers, which will set up a browser-specific interface onto the site, and files can be downloaded from the site in the usual way. However, you'll have much more control and flexibility over your FTP session by using a dedicated FTP client. Most importantly, FTP clients will let you download multiple files, or even entire directory structures at once. Good, graphical FTP clients include WS_FTP or CuteFTP for Windows, Fetch for Mac OS, Igloo for Linux (Figure 3-17), and NetPenguin for BeOS, though there are many, many more options than these. Check your favorite software library for options.

FTP sites will either be set up for anonymous access, in which case you can simply log in with the username "anonymous" or "ftp" and use your own email address as a password, or will have a specific username/password pair set up by the site's maintainer, which should be provided on the site or in the message providing access to the site.

 If you can't find a username/password pair listed and anonymous access doesn't work, try entering the word "mp3" for both the username and password.

Once logged in, files can generally be dragged from the remote server to your local machine. Some clients require navigating directory structures on both the remote host and the local client and then pressing a transfer button of some kind.

To use them, just open a shell or Terminal window, type `ftp address`, enter your username and password, and use the `cd`, `ls`, and `pwd` commands as you would on your own machine. To retrieve a file, type `bin` to make sure you're in binary mode, `hash` to make sure you see a progress indicator as the transfer proceeds, and `get filename` to retrieve a specific file. Typing `mget` will let you retrieve

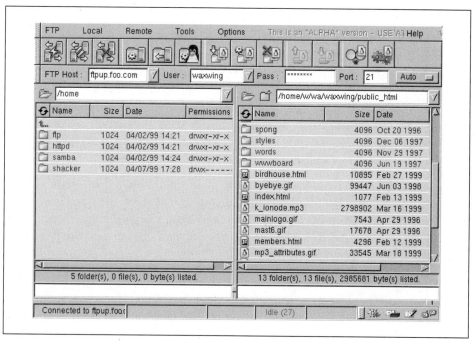

Figure 3-17. Igloo for Linux is one of many graphical FTP clients that make it easy to transfer files en masse from a remote server to your local machine

multiple files at once. For example, `mget *.mp3` will let you retrieve all MP3 files in the current directory. However, to make this option useful, you'll want to turn off prompting before downloading, so that you aren't asked for confirmation before transferring each file. Type `prompt` to turn off prompting, and optionally type `prompt` again later to turn it back on. Transferred files will end up in the directory from which you started the session. To change the download directory on your local machine, type `lcd pathname`.

Download Managers

If you've got a slow Internet connection, or if you'd like to download a lot of files from a lot of different sites while you sleep, you may want to get yourself a good download management utility. These will let you copy (or even drag in) links to files you want to download from any number of different web and FTP sites. Establish a download directory, fill the queue with URLs, and let 'er rip.

Windows users should check out ReGet (*www.reget.com*), while Linux and BeOS users should have a copy of wget. With wget installed in your path, just create a simple shell script consisting of wget lines followed by URLs. Save the script in your path with a name like "hoover," change to your preferred download directory, and execute hoover. Go to bed. If wget isn't on your system already, you'll be able to find it easily at your favorite software library.

Via Usenet

One of the least convenient ways to download MP3 files is via Usenet. Because Usenet is text-based, it's not possible to post binary attachments directly into a Usenet message. To get around this, a system called uuencoding is used to transform binary files into raw text. To humans, uuencoded binaries appear as a lengthy stream of ASCII garbage, and a tool called a uudecoder must be used to transform this stream back into its original binary state. Fortunately, most modern newsreaders include the ability to decode uuencoded messages with the click of a button. Consult your news client's documentation for details.

If you want do it by hand, you'll need a uudecoder installed on your system. Linux and BeOS users will find this tool already installed on their systems, while Windows and Mac OS users will need to download a separate uudecoder. Save the message in question to a text file on your system, giving it a name such as *filename.uu*. From a shell prompt, type:

```
uudecode filename.uu
```

A new MP3 file should appear in the same directory. Again, note that Usenet is a terrible way to distribute and access binary data in general. Use it if you need to, but I don't recommend wasting your valuable time when other distribution mechanisms are readily available. If you want to uuencode your own files for posting to Usenet, note that there are two subtle variants of the uuencode command floating around out there. On some systems, you'll simply be able to type:

```
uuencode filename.mp3 > filename.uu
```

However, some versions of uuencode require you to specify an additional filename, to be written into the file's header. This name will become the name of the resulting binary when the user decodes the file on their end. For example, if you want the recipient to end up with a file called *grotto.mp3*, you would use this syntax:

```
uuencode filename.mp3 grotto.mp3 > filename.uu
```

Roll Your Own

There are a number of advantages to encoding your own MP3 files. First, you don't have to deal with hunting around and waiting for lengthy downloads, and all bandwidth questions simply vanish. Second, you don't have to sift through other people's musical tastes—just encode what you like from the albums you already own and build a perfect collection with no dreck. Third, you have complete control over the quality of your encodings. You can set a bitrate with a higher quality than the de facto standard of 128 kbps, clean up your recordings in audio manipulation software prior to encoding, and so on. Finally, by encoding your own tracks you have 100% assurance that your entire collection is legal. With the quality and speed of some of the MP3 ripper/encoder packages out there, you can encode an entire album in a fraction of the time it would take to actually listen to it—the process really is a piece of cake. Ripping and encoding is covered in detail in Chapter 5, but here's the bullet-point brief:

Ripping

> If recording from CD, download and install a "ripping" utility that will let you access the real audio data on your CDs, rather than the 42-byte *.cda* handlers that normally appear when an audio CD is viewed through your file manager (only Windows users will see *.cda* handlers). If recording from another source, install audio software capable of saving the incoming audio stream to WAV, AIFF, or RAW audio format.

Encoding

> Download and install an MP3 encoding utility, which will take the audio data you've ripped or saved and run it through the perceptual coding algorithms covered in Chapter 2, spitting MP3 files out the other end of the process.

While that's the basic process between all ripping and encoding, most people use tools that handle both processes for you behind the scenes, so you can rip and encode at the same time and never worry about the intermediate step. With the right tools, the entire process becomes a no-brainer, It's really that simple, though there are still many options and caveats to consider if you're looking for excellent results.

Why Is It Called "Ripping?"

The practice of extracting music from an audio CD to a digital audio file on your hard drive is called "ripping." Why? Because, as you'll see in Chapter 5, audio CDs don't use a filesystem corresponding to that of any particular operating system. Your OS's file manager can't see the tracks like it sees normal files on a data CD, so you either need to trick your operating system into seeing the tracks' file "handles" as actual WAV or AIFF files, or use a special utility to read the raw data from the audio CD and turn it into a WAV or AIFF file. Because special techniques or tools are required and you're not doing a straight file copy, another name for the process was required. No one seems to know where the term "ripping" originated, but it sounds intuitive and has been floating around in the computer vernacular for many years.

Don't worry: ripping is a very simple process, and many tools completely hide the process for you, so you may not need to think about it at all.

Organizing Your Collection

Before your collection starts to grow, it's worth giving a bit of thought to establishing file naming conventions and an organizational system. While you can always use Explorer/Finder/Tracker to organize your collection later, you may find it useful to think a bit about filenames and directory structures a bit before you start downloading and encoding, as a number of variables enter the process. You'll be happier later on.

Naming Your Files

When encoding your own files, you should have total control over the way your files are named, although many players do impose some limitations in this department, such as disallowing spaces in filenames even for those who choose to use them. Dig around in the options and you should be able to find controls for choosing among many possible formats (more on that in Chapter 5). If you're downloading files from the Internet, however, it's a different story—files arrive with whatever naming convention was used by the person or organization who posted the file to begin with. Many files you'll find out there are simply named after the song, e.g., "Blue_Jay_Way.mp3". Would it make more sense to name a file with the artist's name as well, e.g., "Beatles-Blue_Jay_Way.mp3"? That depends on how anal you are. First off, keep in mind that the name of the artist is usually—but not always—stored in the file itself, in the form of its ID3 tags. Thus, even when the artist's name isn't in the filename, it will appear in the MP3 decoder's player's interface as the file is being played. However, there are files floating around out there with no information whatsoever stored in ID3 tags (Figure 3-18), so if you don't give your files a meaningful name when you download them, you may never discover the actual artist or track name.

The second question to consider is whether to allow spaces in your filenames. While all modern operating systems allow filenames with spaces in them, spaces can present certain difficulties in some operating systems when working from the command line. For example, Unix/Linux/BeOS shell environments treat spaces as separators between distinct commands or filenames. You might tell the Linux decoder mpg123 to play three files in a row with the command:

```
mpg123 file1.mp3 file2.mp3 file3.mp3
```

But trying to play the file from the previous example in this way:

```
mpg123 Beatles - Blue Jay Way.mp3
```

would cause mpg123 to hork, since it would look for files called "Beatles", "-", "Blue", "Jay", and "Way.mp3". There are two possible solutions to this situation: Surround the actual filenames in quotes:

```
mpg123 "Beatles - Yellow Submarine.mp3"
```

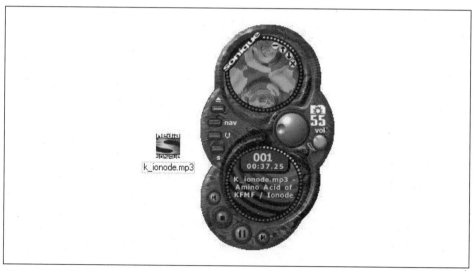

Figure 3-18. The artist's name and song title is embedded in the file itself, eliminating the need for their mention in the filename

or Simply replace all spaces in the filename with underscores and separate the artist from the track title with single or double dashes, e.g., "Beatles--Yellow_Submarine.mp3". For this reason, you'll find that many popular MP3 download sites, such as MP3.com, offer files for download with underscores in place of spaces. Whether you choose to replace these with the more aesthetically pleasing spaces or not is up to you and your needs. As a general rule, users who plan to play or manipulate files from the command line may prefer to retain the underscores. This is especially true if you plan to use scripts to organize, sort, or create playlists/indices for your MP3 collection, as pre-existing scripts may assume that no spaces are present in filenames.

Building Logical Directory Structures

Users intent on building up a large collection—especially collections including complete or partial albums—may want to create a directory/folder structure that makes it easy to group and organize artists and their albums. For example:

```
c:\data\mp3
c:\data\mp3\albums
c:\data\mp3\albums\Beatles
c:\data\mp3\albums\Beatles\Magical_Mystery_Tour
c:\data\mp3\albums\Beatles\Magical_Mystery_Tour\Blue_Jay_Way.mp3
c:\data\mp3\albums\Beatles\Magical_Mystery_Tour\I_Am_the_Walrus.mp3
c:\data\mp3\singles
c:\data\mp3\singles\Rolling_Stones--Paint_It_Black.mp3
```

Notes on Numbering

If you're encoding your own albums, it's a good idea to include track numbers from the CD in the filenames themselves. Without them, the files will appear in the encoding output directory in alphabetical order, rather than in album order. But an album is a complete entity, not just a pile of singles. Artists put a great deal of effort into determining the ideal order in which tracks should be heard. If you choose to respect this prerogative of the artist, have your encoder prepend track numbers to the filenames so they appear in Explorer/ Finder/Tracker in the proper order. When you drag the folder onto your MP3 player, you'll hear the album as it was meant to be heard, not willy-nilly. And remember: If there are more than 9 tracks on the album, you'll need to make sure the encoder uses "01" rather than simply "1," etc.—otherwise, your computer will order track 10 before track 1, and so on.

These are DOS/Windows-style paths, but the same principle of organization applies equally to Mac OS or Unix users. Note that in this example, songs stored under the albums hierarchy are named after song titles only, but songs stored in the singles directory are given both the artist and song name, since artist names in filenames are redundant if the directory structure is logically organized. In addition, some users may want to further subdivide their hierarchy into musical genres. For example:

```
c:\data\mp3\albums\rock\Beatles
c:\data\mp3\singles\jazz\Miles_Davis
```

After much experimentation with various organizational hierarchies, I've finally settled on a scheme that works well for me. Rather than separating out albums and singles, I realized that most of the time I only encoded portions of albums, and that as I gathered singles, a lot of them were by the same artists. My hierarchy now looks like this (BeOS/Linux-style paths used here):

```
~/mp3/artists
~/mp3/artists/Captain Beefheart/Trout Mask Replica
~/mp3/artists/Captain Beefheart/Trout Mask Replica/11 - China Pig.mp3
~/mp3/artists/Captain Beefheart/Trout Mask Replica/20 - Ant Man Bee.mp3
~/mp3/artists/Captain Beefheart/Lick My Decals Off/09 - Petrified Forest.mp3
~/mp3/artists/Hank Williams/...
~/mp3/encode
~/mp3/downloads
~/mp3/moonshine
```

Because each artist has a directory of their own, it doesn't matter whether I'm storing singles or albums—when I want to hear a particular artist, I just drag their folder onto my MP3 player. I don't even bother making playlists for artists anymore. However, if you tend not to encode complete albums very often, it may not make sense to create album subdirectories under the artist names—you may want instead to just include the album in the filename and put all tracks by a given artist into a single directory. Some users also like to store the source's format in the filename, designating whether the track came from an LP, CD, 7-inch single, etc. The *encode* directory is, obviously, used as a container for tracks currently being encoded in the background. Because I've configured my encoder always to create artist and album subdirectories if they don't exist, I can easily drag the newly created folders into the artist hierarchy after I've listened to the encodings and determined that their quality is satisfactory. The *downloads* directory is used as a temporary holding bin where downloaded tracks live until I've decided whether to keep or delete them. Finally, the *moonshine* directory is used to store miscellaneous tracks. As soon as there are two or more tracks by the same artist in moonshine, I create an artist folder for them in the artists hierarchy.

However, it may not be necessary to organize this tightly, since (as you'll see in Chapter 4), you can always create custom playlists based on artist, genre, and other arbitrary criteria. Tools are even available that will help you to generate custom playlists on specific criteria by hoovering ID3 tag information out of your files, thus treating your entire collection as a queryable database. Nevertheless, as your collection grows, you'll find that you appreciate having a well-kept directory hierarchy more all the time.

In the end, how you choose to organize your collection is completely up to you and your personal preferences. If you're the type who stacks hundreds of CDs up in random piles throughout your house, you may be perfectly happy with a single giant directory containing thousands of individual MP3 files. If, on the other hand, you're in the habit of meticulously organizing your LP/CD collection by genre and artist, you'll probably want to do something similar for your digital music collection.

Storage Requirements

While the average MP3 file is a mere one-tenth to one-twelth the size of its corresponding uncompressed raw audio track, don't think for a moment that the size of your collection won't add up faster than your last grocery receipt. At roughly 1 MB per minute, expect a typical album to occupy 40–70 MB of disk space. At that rate, a one-foot stack of CDs will hoover up about a gigabyte, and if you opt to encode your MP3s at a higher-than-average bitrate* than the average in order to achieve better audio quality, you can expect that space to be consumed even more quickly.

---

* Remember: Bitrate is a measure of the amount of storage space that will be allocated to each second of audio, and is measured in kilobits per second, or kbps. Higher-bitrate files sound better and consume more disk space, and vice versa.

Table 3-3 demonstrates the results of a real-world test to determine the relationship between file size and encoding bitrate. Of course, audio quality corresponds directly to file size, and the files encoded below 128 kbps carried enough audible compression artifacts on our test system to be not worth keeping, and the very low bitrate files sounded like total dookey. It's worth noting, however, that there are legitimate uses for very low bitrate encoding, notably in the field of voice recording (as opposed to music), where fidelity is of less importance. Voice recordings—lecture notes, for example—may also be very lengthy, which further encourages the use of low bitrates to minimize disk space.*

Table 3-3. MP3 File Size is Directly Related to the Bitrate at Which It's Encoded (File Sizes and Compression Ratios Have Been Rounded)

Bitrate (kbps)	Filesize (megabytes)	Compression Ratio
Original file	40.08	1:1 (none)
16	0.46	87:1
32	0.92	44:1
64	1.83	22:1
96	2.74	15:1
128	3.64	11:1
160	4.55	9:1
192	5.46	7:1
256	7.28	6:1
320	9.10	4:1

In Table 3-3, a sample file of 3:52 in length (Jorge Ben's "Ponta de Lanca Africano," a.k.a. Intel's "sock monkey" song) was converted to WAV format, creating a (more or less) exact bit copy of the data on the audio CD, and weighing in at a hefty 40.08 MB. The WAV file was then encoded at various bitrates using Music-Match Jukebox with default settings. As you can see, even when encoding is done at the highest possible bitrate, thus delivering a file indistinguishable in quality from the original CD, the MP3-encoded file is less than a quarter the size of the original (though it still gobbles 9.1 MB of disk space). At the Internet's de facto standard bitrate of 128 kbps, the resulting MP3 file is only one-eleventh the size of the original. Using lower bitrates achieves even more impressive file sizes, though audio quality degrades quickly below 128 kbps. If you're going to be encoding your own music, this book strongly recommends using bitrates equal to or higher than 128 kbps. More details in Chapter 5.

---

* But keep in mind that MP3 is not the ideal format for voice recordings; if you do a lot of this, you may be better served by going with RealAudio rather than MP3.

Clearly, if you're going to get serious about MP3 collecting, you won't be storing everything on your machine's hard drives for long before a more flexible storage solution is in order. While hard drives just keep on getting bigger and cheaper, having more storage available tends to lead people to just start encoding more—the author purchased a 36 GB drive just for MP3 storage, and had it one-quarter full in three weeks after going on a marathon encoding binge. Fortunately, a plethora of external and removable storage options have become relatively affordable in recent years. Don't bother with Zip or other 100–200 MB solutions—at the rate those fill up, you may as well just use the original audio CDs, as you won't gain any advantages in shelf-space consumption or the convenience of access. Think instead about compact disks and cartridge media such as the Iomega Jaz or the even higher-capacity and less-expensive Orb drive from Castlewood Systems (*www.castlewoodsystems.com/*). There are also a handful of tape storage units on the market that offer far faster access than the pokey data tapes of yore, and which can be accessed as a normal drive volume on the system. While tape storage often offers the lowest cost-per-megabyte ratio of any medium, their relatively low market saturation compared to other removable media means that MP3s stored on tapes may be harder to transfer to other machines if necessary.

Perhaps the best single solution for long term, affordable MP3 storage is the recordable CD-ROM. These units are available in either write-once (CD-R) or write-many (CD-RW) alternatives, and buy you 640 MB or more of disk real estate for a buck or two (not counting the cost of the drive mechanism itself). Recording to CD is covered in Chapter 5.

Equipment Considerations

This book assumes that you already have basic audio working on your machine, but since you may be about to start listening to real music through your computer on a regular basis, you may want to invest a little time and/or money into making sure you're getting the highest quality possible from your system.

Sound Cards

Most computers sold today ship with sound cards preinstalled and configured, but the cards in many discount and mid-range machines leave something to be desired from an audiophile perspective. Because the sound card is a fundamental bridge between what goes on in software and what ends up in your ears, it pays to make sure you've got a good one—overall quality can be drastically affected by the quality of your audio device.

While any recommendations on specific cards would quickly go out of date, keep in mind that better sound cards will also include digital signal processing chips (DSPs), which can take some of the computing load off your machine's CPU.

Good DSPs can go a long way toward minimizing the performance impact of MP3 playback, particularly if you've got a slower machine. If you intend to do any serious recording and/or mixing, look for a "full-duplex" card, which is capable of handling incoming and outgoing audio streams simultaneously. If you want to interface your card with external devices such as high-end digital-to-audio Converters (DACs) or home theater systems, look for a card with digital output jacks as well as the standard analog outputs.

When hooking up your speakers, most sound cards offer two analog outputs: one that is pre-amplified and is suitable for connecting directly to a set of unpowered computer speakers or headphones, and another that is unamplified, and is thus suitable for being connected to an external amplifier, such as a powered satellite/subwoofer system or your home stereo. This latter jack, labeled simply "Line," may offer a cleaner signal due to the fact that it hasn't been run through the sound card's (usually) suboptimal amplifier. If you're playing MP3 through a high-quality system, use the Line jack for output: the difference in quality could be noticeable.

There are many more nuances and subtleties between the many sound card flavors available out there. If you care about such things, it pays to do some research online before plunking down your money for a sound card.

Speakers

Since speakers are the last link in the chain, and because they vary so radically, speaker choice is crucial to ensuring the best MP3 experience. If you can afford it, avoid the cheapo plastic speakers sold in many discount stores and catalogs at all costs. If possible, look into a powered satellite/subwoofer combination, which will let you keep small, compact (but relatively high-quality) midrange tweeters on or near your desk, while putting the bulky subwoofer beneath it, or elsewhere out of the way. Because it's very difficult to locate bass frequencies in space, the placement of the subwoofer is nearly insignificant. It's a different story with midrange and high frequencies, however, and speaker placement can be very significant for your satellite speakers. Note that if you have a four-speaker setup, you will probably require additional operating system support to get sound out of all four speakers. Under Windows, for example, you'll need DirectSound3D installed. This support should come along with drivers supplied with the sound card, though you may need to download it separately from Microsoft.

 Note that merely getting four speakers up and running does not automatically give you true spatialized sound with all forms of audio. MP3 provides only standard stereo separation though the MPEG-4 standard will support multi-channel audio (see Chapter 9).

Speaker placement

While it can be difficult to place speakers optimally in cramped or cluttered quarters, the same rules that apply to home stereo speaker placement apply to your computer's sound system. Divide a room into imaginary thirds and place your speakers at the dividing lines. Keep speakers at least six inches away from walls to avoid bass response anomalies,* and angle your speakers slightly toward the center of the room, as illustrated in Figure 3-19. Experiment with this "toe-in" to achieve the best quality positioning of instruments in space. Keeping speakers away from side walls will help to avoid soundstage distortion, and it's important to make sure you leave adequate clear space between the speakers. At the very least, try to place your speakers on either side of your sitting position so that stereo effects will be perceptible.

Of course, in a computer-at-desk situation, you may be sitting closer to the speakers than the optimal listening position shown in Figure 3-19. In this case, it may not make sense to spread your speakers out to the 1/3 points of the room. Instead, aim for the more general rule of creating an equilateral triangle between the listening position and the two speakers.

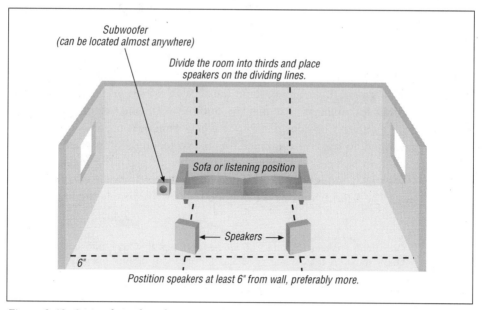

Figure 3-19. Optimal speaker placement

---

* However, note that some speakers are designed to placed against a rear wall, and these, of course, should be. Consult your audio dealer if unsure.

Connect your computer to your stereo

If your computer is near your home stereo, you can easily direct your computer's audio output into your stereo. You'll need a special adapter and a length of RCA cable long enough to bridge the distance. The adapter should have a 1/8" male jack on one side to plug into your sound card's line out jack, and two female RCA jacks on the other. Connect your RCA cable into the adapter's female jacks, and run them into the Auxiliary input on your home stereo's amp or pre-amp (actually, any input on your stereo besides Phono will suffice, but Auxillary is often the only input available). Turn your amp or pre-amp's input selector to Aux, and you're all set. If your sound card has digital outputs and you have an external DAC, DAT deck, MiniDisk unit, or home theater system with digital inputs, go for the all-digital connection to bypass the DAC built into the sound card (in most cases, the DAC in your digital amplifier or other device will be of a higher quality than the one built into the sound card).

Headphones

If you work in an office or other environment where you can't disturb others, or if you want audiophile sound without spending big bucks on computer speakers, it's possible to get high-quality headphones very affordably. While any set of headphones can be hooked up to your sound card's output, you may be amazed by the radical improvement in audio quality you can get by spending $50 or more on a decent set of ear goggles. Go to your local audio store and ask to audition models in your price range. Take along some music with which you're well familiar, and listen closely for nuances that may be audible with one set of headphones that aren't with another. Consider comfort as well—some headphones (even some with tremendous audio quality) can chafe, or start to feel tight after many hours. If you've got some extra bread to spend and want to go for the highest possible quality, get yourself a dedicated headphone amplifier and a pair of true audiophile "phones." The sound you can get through these is absolutely breathtaking.

 One thing to keep in mind about headphones if you're into bass-heavy music is that, while good headphones can deliver great bass, you'll miss that bodily experience of having your guts rumbled, as you would at a live show or with speakers that move a lot of air.

If you're new to auditioning either speakers or headphones, keep in mind that it's easy to be fooled by aspects of the sound that jump out at you. Speakers that overemphasize certain frequencies may sound more direct, punchier, or brighter than more subtle speakers. While these characteristics may sound impressive in an audio showroom, they may grow fatiguing and unnatural-sounding after lots of listening time at home. Remember: A brighter light is not necessarily a better light, and a brighter speaker is not necessarily a better speaker. The ideal playback system does not add to the incoming signal in any way—it merely passes it on in the most neutral and natural way possible. While playback equipment *always* colors the sound stream in some way, look for equipment that minimizes the effect, particularly if you listen to music with lots of subtleties (rock fans may appreciate a more direct sound, for example).

There are, of course, other ways to get MP3 audio out of your home stereo than just hooking it up to your computer. Increasingly, MP3 audio is finding its way into dedicated, external players that can be connected to your home stereo just like you would connect a CD player or other component. In addition, home CD players capable of playing CDs that store MP3 files are beginning to appear. We'll cover that ground in Chapter 6, *Hardware, Portables, Home Stereos, and Kits.* Finally, you can always use your computer to burn regular audio CDs that will play in any CD player (though you'll lose MP3's compression advantages in the process). We'll cover that in Chapter 5.

4

Playlists, Tags, and Skins: MP3 Options

The stock $35 SoundBlaster-compatible card, driving a pair of $25 plastic desktop speakers, has become a de facto standard throughout the '90s. But as computing power increases in accordance with Moore's law,* media production and playback functionality takes a more central role in the consumer computer. With the advent of audio cards like the SoundBlaster Live! and the increasing popularity of satellite/subwoofer systems and computer-to-stereo connections, quality file-based audio becomes a realistic possibility for millions of users. MP3's natural home may be the wildlands of the Internet, but its reach is quickly being extended into other domains as well. As homes embrace the "convergence" model, computers, stereos, and televisions are blending together into all-in-one, networked infotainment centers, and stereo component manufacturers are introducing hardware-based MP3 players. Sales of portable units such as the Diamond Rio and Creative NOMAD are skyrocketing, and more and more cars are being fitted with MP3 playback units as well. As a result of all this, it becomes more important than ever to think beyond the simple task of encoding and playing MP3 files. Increasingly, people need to move large amounts of data between their computers and their playback devices, optimize the quality of their MP3 collections, maintain a well-organized filing system or MP3 database, make sure all of their files are tagged with useful meta-data for future reference, parse meaningful playlists out of collections extending into the gigabytes, and extend the reach of their MP3 players to handle unusual situations.

---

* See the glossary for definition and more information.

MP3 Options and Considerations

Once you've mastered the basics, you'll want to expand your horizons a bit and start checking out the many advanced capabilities, cosmetics, playlist generation techniques, ID3 tagging tools, plug-ins, and other toys available. There's a lot out there, and we'll only have space to touch on a handful of examples of useful "peripheral" software here. Do some searching through your favorite MP3 site or software library and you'll find hundreds of tools not discussed in this book.

Before we get to the goodies, however, we'll discuss some of the issues affecting the quality of MPEG audio. Because the compression format discards some data, MP3 already stands on shaky ground from a fidelity standpoint. That's not to say the quality of MP3 stinks, as some critics claim—but there are some things you can do to optimize the quality of your MP3s during encoding and during playback.

On the lighter side of things, MP3 players can often be dressed up in "skins"— small collections of bitmap images that sit on top of your player to give it a customized appearance. You can download skins from the Internet or create your own, although the process is admittedly a bit tricky. Don't worry—we'll show you how to create your own skins from start to finish.

Two of the most important "peripheral" technologies you'll meet in this chapter are ID3 tags and playlists. We discussed ID3 tags in a technical vein in Chapter 2, *How MP3 Works: Inside the Codec*; they're the extra space in MP3 files that let you store "meta data" about a file, including the artist, album, and track names, as well as genre, year, and personal comments. An up-and-coming modification of the ID3 specification, called ID3v2, is much more powerful, and lets you store a nearly unlimited amount of additional information (up to 256 MB). We'll check out the many ways in which ID3 tags can be created or edited, either directly through your MP3 player or via separate software.

One of the most enjoyable aspects of building a large MP3 collection, and one of the things that makes it so different from building a tape or CD collection, is the fact that you can mix and match songs into a customized sequence at a moment's notice. These personalized "albums" are called playlists, and consist of simple text files referencing the locations of tracks scattered across your system. Playlists can be created by dragging tracks one at a time into an MP3 player's playlist editor, by dragging entire directory structures onto your MP3 player, by trawling your disk with scripts, by running command-line queries, or by scanning through your collection with a database-like solution like Helium.

Ensuring that your files have solid ID3 tag data (accomplished either while encoding or after downloading) can be very important later on when you want to start creating playlists based on query criteria, such as "Create a playlist of all songs on all of my disk volumes by either Neil Sedaka or The Carpenters written between 1971 and 1975 that don't have the word 'schmaltzy' in the comment field."

The functionality of many MP3 players can be extended by installing plug-ins, much as you would for Netscape Navigator or Adobe Photoshop. A bewildering variety of plug-ins is available, which will let you do everything from controlling your MP3 player via infrared remote control to applying sound effects to displaying wild visualizations of the music as it plays. We'll take a look at a few of the more popular plug-ins later in this chapter as well.

An increasingly popular way to listen to MP3s is not to save them to disk or to encode them, but to listen to them in real time as they're broadcast out over the Internet. While the process of running your own Internet broadcast is covered in Chapter 8, *Webcasting and Servers: Internet Distribution*, we'll show you how to tune into the two main types of streamed MP3 (broadcast and on-demand) in this chapter.

Finally, you'll want to make sure your system is well-tuned for MP3 encoding and playback, so we'll talk about the hardware requirements—what kind of processor you need, sound and video (yes, video) card interactions, disk speed issues, and the like. We'll also show you how to benchmark MP3 players and encoders in case you have an older machine and want to make sure you're not dragging down the rest of your system's performance.

Equalization and Sound Quality

While true audiophiles may never accept lossy compression formats as a home standard just for the convenience factor, most of us *do* place a very high priority on the many conveniences offered by the MP3 format. So we're left with a question: How do we make sure we're getting the most from our MP3 collections?

Can Quality Be Measured?

Before even *thinking* about evaluating standards of quality, it's critical to understand that "this way lies madness." Audiophiles have wrestled for decades to achieve "objective" measurements that would fairly represent the quality of a recording. And while there are many objective measurements that can be made for any given signal, it's important to understand that the mathematics of audio measurement and the subjective experience of quality are two different animals. Furthermore, the mechanics of lossy compression (discussed in Chapter 2) more or less nullify the validity of just about any objective criteria. In other words, the only tests that matter for MP3 audio are subjective tests, i.e., real-world listening tests. Your ears don't lie. Even so, it's possible that the file you encode to your own standards today could end up being played on much better equipment tomorrow, so it pays to shoot for quality a little above your own thresholds.

The most important thing to keep in mind when testing for MP3 quality is that your computer probably isn't the best place to do it. How's that? Unless you've invested a fair sum in high-end computer audio equipment, chances are that your home stereo sounds a lot better than your computer. And if you're planning to keep your MP3 collection around for a long time, your home stereo may very well be the ultimate destination for your MP3 files. Because your sound card and computer speakers may mask a whole lot of subtlety, it's important to eliminate those components from the testing chain so that you can tell which limitations are introduced by your hardware and which are introduced by the MP3 encoding itself. In other words, you want to isolate the encoding as much as possible and give it an optimum environment in which to be tested.

Conducting listening tests

Since "CD quality" is our benchmark here, you want to get your MP3s onto an audio CD. To run this test, you'll need access either to a CD burner or to a dedicated MP3 playback device. Find a couple of songs with which you're well-familiar, preferably ones that include a wide range of instruments, including those from the brass and strings families. It's often easier to detect limitations in the MP3 codec with non-electronic music, and the brass and string families do an especially good job of putting the codec to the test. However, it's also important that you choose music you enjoy personally. To be well rounded, you might want to choose one each of your favorite jazz, classical, and rock tracks, for example.

 If you have a portable or home stereo MP3 player, just patch it into your stereo as described in Chapter 3, *Getting and Playing MP3 Files*, and load it up with encodings created as described in the next section. The same principles described in this section apply whether you're working from a test CD or from a dedicated playback device.

Next, you'll need to save a reference track for each song, meaning you should rip uncompressed versions of each track to your hard drive (typically in WAV format, though Mac OS users will want to use AIFF format). See Chapter 5, *Ripping and Encoding: Creating MP3 Files*, for details on ripping tracks directly from CD without encoding them. For the actual compression, you'll want to use the highest quality encoder you can find (again, see Chapter 5),* and encode each track a

---

* The test described here can also be used to test various encoders against one another. The only difference is that you'll want to encode the reference track at the *same* bitrate, but with different encoders. In fact, you may want to encode at various bitrates with each encoder in your test, so you can determine whether a given encoder excels at low bitrate encodings but falls down at higher bitrates, for example.

number of times, at different bitrates. As you encode, give each file a descriptive name, including its bitrate. For example, you might use the following scheme:

```
Improv.Spacious.64.mp3
Improv.Spacious.128.mp3
Improv.Spacious.160.mp3
Improv.Spacious.192.mp3
Improv.Spacious.256.mp3
```

Automating Test Encodings

If the process of encoding the same track over and over again sounds tedious, it is. Here's a script you can use under Unix/Linux or BeOS to automate the process, assuming you have the LAME encoder somewhere in your path. This should be very easy to modify to work with other encoders:

```
#!/bin/sh
FileName="$1"

# Start a loop and encode once at each bitrate specified
for i in 64 96 128 160 192 256; do
        echo Creating "$FileName".$i.mp3
        lame -ms -b$i "$FileName".wav "$FileName".$i.mp3
        echo
done
```

If you're on a DOS/Windows machine, here's a batch file that will achieve the same effect:

```
Echo off
rem example
set filename=%1

if not exist %filename%.wav goto error
rem The following must go on a single line -
rem We had to wrap it to two lines for this book
for %%B in (64 96 128 160 192 256) do lame -ms -b%%B %filename%.wav
%filename%-%%B.mp3
goto exit
:error
  echo File %filename%.wav does not exist
  goto exit
:exit
```

Whether you're running the the bash or the DOS version, save the script as a file in your system's path with a filename like "TestEnc" and then run:

```
TestEnc filename
```

assuming your input file is called `filename.wav`. Of course, these scripts assume that LAME can be found in your system path as well.

Once you've encoded each sample at a variety of bitrates, you'll need to translate them *back* to WAV format and burn the resulting tracks to an audio CD (although your burning software may take care of this conversion for you; see Chapter 5 for details). Because the filenames won't be present on the audio CD, take care to print out or write down the track numbers and the corresponding bitrates so you'll have a reference sheet later on. Once your audio CD is complete, find the highest quality stereo you can (yours or a friend's), grab your reference sheet, dim the lights, relax, and listen through the CD. While you may want to skip back and forth between the reference tracks (which will sound identical to the original CD audio tracks) and the encoded tracks later on, you should first listen to the disc all the way through. Don't be too quick to flip back and forth between tracks, as that will only lead to schizophrenia and ear fatigue. The idea is to internalize the "flavor" of the tracks relative to one another. Evenings may produce the best listening environment, as you'll likely get less ambient noise and less sensory competition from vision (assuming some darkness). If you've been listening to loud music or noises during the day, save the test for another day—your ears will already be fatigued. Self-run audio tests using your own hearing as a "benchmark" should always attempt to isolate variables and incorporate a best-case scenario, against which everything else should be measured.

If your home stereo or entertainment system includes an on-board digital-to-analog converter which offers settings for surround sound or for various room effects (concert hall, small room, etc.), it's important to disable these options and make sure your system is set on the defaults. If you use an equalizer or other audio "enhancing" device, disable it or run it flat (unless it's a "set-and-forget" processor carefully tuned to neutralize a particular room). You're testing your encodings here, not your equipment. Artificial interferences in signal flow will compromise the integrity of the test.

As you listen, take note of the most subtle sounds in the reference track, and try to determine whether those sounds are still present in the various encodings. Can you hear the clarinetist taking that breath just before his solo? The sound of the guitarist's hands gliding over her strings? What about the sense of space (soundstage expansiveness)? Can you pinpoint the location of various instruments in the recording studio as accurately with files that have gone through the MP3 process as you can with the reference track? What about dynamic range? Are you detecting certain subtleties of the high and low ranges being chopped off or smeared out? Perhaps most importantly, do the MP3 encodings have a sense of "presence?" Can you close your eyes and imagine that the performance is taking place there in your living room? Does a given encoding make the performer sound sort of "mechanical" or "electronic?" Does the performance seem to be more or less intense with any of the encodings? Do any of them do a better job of making you want to tap your foot or sing along or dance, or do any of them make you feel edgy, or bored? Do the MP3 encodings sound "hollow" or "swishy" to you? Chances are, you'll be amazed to discover just how much quality has been lost in the 128 kbps and lower encodings.

The bitrate at which you literally cannot tell the difference between the reference track and the MP3 encoding is the bitrate at which you should start encoding your MP3 tracks, provided you're willing to part with the extra disk space this will consume (of course, if you'll be burning a lot of tracks to writeable CD for permanent storage, this may be less of an issue). To be really safe, and to make sure your tracks will sound great no matter what playback system they end up on one day, encode at a bitrate *higher* than the one at which you couldn't tell a difference.

If you don't have access to a CD burner, then your next best bet is to connect your sound card's line-out jack to one of your home stereo's inputs, and try similar tests. However, keep in mind that unless you use a fully digital transfer system (i.e., using digital coax or optical cable from the sound card to your digital receiver or external DAC), you'll be hearing the limitations of your sound card's digital-to-analog converter.

Digital to Analog (and Back)

As you know, computers store and manipulate information—including audio information—digitally. But your ears are analog devices, and so are speakers.* Somewhere in the process of getting information out of your computer and into your ears, the signal must be converted from digital to analog. The device that affects this conversion is called the *digital-to-analog converter*, or DAC, and its role is crucial. The quality of the DAC plays a huge part in the overall quality of the resulting audio pouring from your speakers or headphones.

In the case of most stock sound cards, the DAC is a part of the card's chipset. However, some higher-end sound cards offer digital outputs, which can be hooked up directly to the digital input of a digitally equipped stereo receiver or pre-amplifier. If your receiver or amplifier doesn't have digital inputs (they'll be clearly marked), you can purchase an external DAC or use the DAC built into a DAT deck, Minidisc player, or DCC, which will then sit between your computer and your receiver/pre-amp. The quality of external DACs is often directly related to their cost; a very high quality DAC can cost $1,000 or more, though you should be able to pick up a suitable model for a few hundred bucks.

---

* Or, at least, most of them are; completely digital PCM speakers are beginning to appear on the market.

Audio Test Checklist

To set up a test like this in a hurry (actually, it's best not to hurry when doing things like this), remember these simple steps:

1. Choose a reference track from your collection with which you're familiar. Look for a reference track with a wide variety of instruments and not too much density. A wall of guitar distortion is not a good choice, though you'll get mixed results with straight electric guitar under various encoders. Well-recorded acoustic guitar, vocals, strings, and brass will show you more limitations in the MP3 codec than hard rock. Rip the reference track to uncompressed WAV or AIFF format.

2. Using the best encoder you can find, encode the reference track at a variety of bitrates, using default settings in the encoder. Alternatively, test various encoders at the same bitrate.

3. Decode the encodings back to WAV or AIFF (see Chapter 5 for details).

4. Burn the reference track and the decoded encodings to an audio CD. Keep a list on paper of all the tracks going onto the CD.

5. Find the best stereo you can, relax, close your eyes, and just enjoy the music. Don't start analyzing carefully or paying special attention to subtleties and nuances until after you've relaxed into the music.

In any case, by turning the job of conversion over to a dedicated unit, you can bypass the typically poor quality built-in DAC on most sound cards, and get a far better resulting sound stream out of your system.* When purchasing a sound card, make sure it has digital outputs in addition to the standard line out. If you're serious about quality, do some research online to find out which cards have the best on-board DACs. If you're really, really serious, consider a high-end outboard (external) DAC.

On the flipside, the reverse process—*analog-to-digital conversion* (ADC) may also come into play, depending on your needs. If you plan to encode music from analog sources such as tapes, LPs, or microphones, you'll also appreciate the extra input quality you'll get by making sure your source signal is stored in the computer after having passed through a high-quality ADC (either onboard or outboard), rather than the one built into your average sound card.

---

* Of course, the rest of your system should be of high quality before you go spending money on a DAC. Putting an external DAC in a system with poor speakers, for instance, probably won't result in noticeably better sound.

Equalization

Most GUI MP3 players include some sort of equalization mechanism, typically accessed by clicking a button on the player's interface labeled "EQ." Bringing up the equalizer usually displays a row of sliders (most often 10, though there could theoretically be any number of them). So, what exactly is equalization, and what does it get you? The simplest way to conceptualize equalization is to think of the bass and treble controls on your home stereo, and imagine that you had a separate knob for each of many much finer slices of the frequency spectrum, affording you much tighter control over the resulting output signal.

Why equalize?

The point of equalization, of course, is to make the resulting audio sound better. EQ can be applied to compensate either for poorly recorded audio, for limitations in your speaker quality or design, or for the speaker placement or acoustics in the listening room. The ultimate objective of equalization is to obtain a "flat" frequency response (hence the name "equalization")—one in which the signal does not sound "colored" by the signal processing chain, storage media, or playback equipment.* Equalization can also be used to eliminate audio artifacts stored in the original recording. For example, you may be able to partially correct a recording with an annoying 60Hz hum, or to partially remove some of the scratchiness of encodings taken from LPs (though the latter can be pretty tricky, since scratchiness typically crosses many different frequencies, and you don't want to throw the baby out with the bath water).

Despite these advanced capabilities, many (if not most) people use equalizers not so much to correct for anomalies as to boost the frequencies they like and to diminish the ones they don't. For example, hip-hop fans may want to pump up the bass frequencies, while classical listeners may want to "sweeten" the strings.

Before you go tweaking your equalizer's sliders with wild abandon, consider the equalizer as something to be experimented with gently and systematically. Listen carefully to the resulting sound after each adjustment, and pay attention to how manipulating one sub-band affects your perception of others—diminishing one sub-band can cause others to sound more prominent. Note also that if you find you have to equalize heavily to compensate for room acoustics, poor speakers, or a poor sound card, you should consider addressing these problems directly. Equalization is a band-aid, not a panacea. Be aware of the potential for over-equalization, and of the limitations of EQ principles in general:

---

* Note, however, that many recording studios use equalization to *add* color, not to remove it—a fact which drives some audiophiles nuts.

- Without a lot of expensive test equipment, you have no concrete goal to aim for—you're just tweaking until something in the sound "feels" better for one reason or another.

- EQ bands come in predefined widths and slopes, but your equalization needs don't—they're typically more "fuzzy" than the usual set of EQ bands allows for (it's kind of like trying to apply mascara with a hairbrush... and no mirror).

- Analog equalizers can introduce distortions, especially phase distortion. Digital equalizers can minimize some of these effects.

It's easy to confuse louder and brighter sound for better sound. Optimum quality is achieved when music sounds as natural as possible—equalize with an ear toward a natural sound atmosphere. Over-equalization can easily degrade sound quality. In other words, the answer to the question, "Why equalize?" is often "You shouldn't, unless the situation demands it." It's easier to ruin the sound than to improve it. Experiment with your EQ, but don't overdo it.

Artificial Audio Enhancers

Every now and then, you'll come across a product that claims to improve the quality of computer audio dramatically. Typically, these products (QSound's iQ, *www.qsound.com,* being an example) work by running a series of proprietary algorithms over the outbound audio stream and applying digital effects to the stream just before it heads for your sound card. Much like the sample effects that come with some sound card drivers, or the presets found in some home theater amplifiers, these products create the illusion that the sound stage extends out beyond the edge of your speakers, generating a 3D sound stage on the fly. These products can also take a monophonic sound stream, such as you'll typically get when listening to SHOUTcast or icecast streams, and "turn them into stereo."

Do these products work? Well, there's no question that the effects are quite dramatic, and you'll most certainly notice a difference over normal playback. But the fact is, these products are creating a signal that isn't present in the source by playing auditory tricks with channel shifting and phase relationships (bouncing sound waves against one another). What these products do is unnatural and unrealistic, and while they may make a cheap computer sound system sound more dramatic, they certainly won't bring you any closer to the artist's vision of how the music was intended to sound.

If you choose to experiment with products like iQ, keep in mind that the signal you'll be hearing is not "true." This may or may not matter to you, depending on your perspective. My position is that effects like these are best reserved for use with games, but should be disabled when listening to music.

The Fletcher-Munson curve

While you should, of course, equalize as necessary to hit the sweet spot that works for a given situation, there's one commonly used configuration of which you may want to be aware: The classic "Fletcher-Munson" curve, which takes advantage of the fact that the ear is not as sensitive to low and high frequencies when music is being played at low volumes. Thus, boosting these frequencies somewhat above normal can help music to sound more natural at lower volumes (Figure 4-1).

Interestingly, the function of the loudness button on your receiver is similar; apply an Fletcher-Munson equalization curve to the music makes it sound more natural at lower volumes.

Figure 4-1. Fletcher-Munson curve, for use in low-volume situations

Note that many MP3 equalizers, such as WinAmp's, let you store equalization curves as presets, which can be loaded up again later without painstakingly re-creating them. Depending on your player, it may also be possible to store a prime equalization curve directly in the MP3 file itself, so you can optimize all of your songs' equalization curves independently. This capability is dependent on the fact that the ID3v2 specification allows for a huge array of meta-data storage capabilities in MP3 files; in other words, you must be using an ID3v2-compliant decoder capable of storing EQ presets. At this writing, this capability remained purely theoretical, though it should become a realistic possibility as the ID3v2 spec builds more momentum. See the ID3 section of this chapter for details.

Working with EQ presets

Because different tracks may require different equalization curves, WinAmp lets you associate an EQ preset with any given track. Here's how to associate an EQ curve with a track:

1. Play the track normally, and press AUTO in the EQ interface.

2. Dial in your EQ curve.

3. Click the Presets button and navigate to Save → Autoload Preset.

4. Allow WinAmp to associate the current track's filename with the current EQ curve.

After creating an association between a track and an EQ curve, the association is stored by WinAmp in a file named *winamp.q2* in the WinAmp installation directory (the file cannot be edited by hand). Any time AUTO is enabled in the equalizer and that track is played, the preferred EQ curve will snap into action.

Uncooking Bad Transfers

Every so often, you may end up with an MP3 file that's been corrupted during transfer somehow, usually by being transferred in ASCII mode rather than binary. If you should encounter one of these, search the Internet for *uncook. exe*, Uncook95, or OK Uncook, all of which do essentially the same thing— repair the damage that was done to the file during transfer and make it playable again. Linux and BeOS users may want to keep a copy of mp3asm (*www. ozemail.com.au/~crn/mp3asm.html*) around for the same purpose.

If you're using a recent browser and the web server you're accessing has been set up properly, this should never happen, though it's nice to know there are tools available to correct the situation if it does.

 In most cases, the equalizers built into MP3 players will have no effect on the audio stream when playing audio CDs, since CD audio is often routed directly from the CD player to the sound card without moving through software first. In this case, the MP3 player is just used as a convenient interface onto the CD transport's control buttons. However, there are plug-ins available that will "steal" the CD audio signal and route it through the MP3 player (the NullSoft CD/ Line Input plug-in for WinAmp, with the "sampling" option enabled, for example). See the "Plug-ins: Extending Your Reach" section in this chapter for details. Once the CD plug-in has been enabled, you should be able to use the equalizer and various visualizers to interact with CD audio.

ID3 Tags and Playlists: The Virtual Database

ID3 tags and playlists are two of the most important extended topics for people who take their MP3 collections seriously. Taken separately, both technologies are important in their own right, but taken together, these two functions can complement one another in very powerful ways, giving you the means to sort, store, organize, name, and build highly customized virtual collections. Because these two technologies are so synergistic, and because many tools exist to help you organize both of them simultaneously, we'll treat both of them together in this section.

What Are ID3 Tags?

Every MP3 file has the ability to store "meta-data" related to the track in the file itself, in the form of what are known as "ID3 tags." For example, a file's ID3 tags may store the song's artist, album, year, genre, and comments in ID3 tags. Many MP3 players have the ability to read ID3 data out of your files, and to display this information in the MP3 playback interface. Thus, giving your MP3 files descriptive names isn't the only—or even necessarily the best—way to identify the tracks in your collection.

Conveniently, ID3 tag information can either be included in the file at the time it's encoded or added in later. Most of the better encoders will provide a number of options to let you control whether and how ID3 tag data should be written to the file. While some MP3 players include the ability to edit, as well as to display ID3 tag information, you may want to download and install additional utilities that specialize in ID3 manipulation, for maximum control. We'll look at some examples of ID3 tag editors later on.

ID3v1 vs. ID3v2

It's important to understand that there are two basic flavors of the ID3 specification, conveniently named ID3v1 and ID3v2. Of the two, ID3v2 is vastly superior, for three reasons:

- Unlike ID3v1, ID3v2 imposes no arbitrary limitations on the amount of storage space available for meta-data, which means there's plenty of space for storing images, complete lyrics, performance notes, equalization presets, et cetera.

- ID3v2 data is stored at the beginning of the file, rather than at the end. This means that ID3v2 is much better for use in streaming situations, where it's important that users be able to see and use the meta-data while the song is being played, rather than after the download or broadcast is complete.

As useful as it can be to have ID3v2 data appear at the beginning of the file, this state of affairs also presents a problem—especially for older players. A player built to the ISO spec should simply skip over the ID3v2 data that it doesn't understand, and move ahead to the valid MP3 data. But exactly how far should the player seek through the file for an MP3 header frame before giving up and deciding that it's not currently dealing with an MP3 file after all? Unfortunately, the ISO spec is vague on the matter, which leaves the door open to interpretation by developers. Some believe that a player should seek forever (after all, ID3v2 data can occupy as much as 256 MB of space), while others feel that a player should give up after a certain number of bytes and assume that they're not dealing with a valid MP3 file after all. The user could have innocently tried to play a giant AVI movie through his MP3 player, for instance, which would cause a player that seeks forever to basically hang. Since the spec is not clear on the matter, the debate may never be resolved. The best solution may be store this data separately, in a hypothetical, centralized MP3ID database, for example, although that's just one of the ideas being floated around.

- The ID3v2 spec is open-ended and flexible, meaning it can be extended in the future to accommodate as-yet-unseen needs. Users may even be able to develop their own custom solutions, given the availability of future ID3v2 tag editors and management solutions. For example, the built-in "Popularimeter" field could be used to let users rate all of their tracks on a scale of 1 to 100, and then create custom playlists based on a scale of favorites.

The number of possible applications for ID3v2 data is staggering. Right off the bat, it gives artists and labels a place to store copyright information, terms of use, and proof of ownership. There are even possibilities for cryptographic security being embedded in MP3 files, thanks to ID3v2. For the end user, ID3v2 means the ability to store full-size, color scans of album covers, complete lyrics (even synchronized lyrics, for use in Karaoke situations), multiple URLs for further information, music reviews, extended information on the recording session, and so on.

 While users of ID3v1 players sometimes discovered that the spec, with its 32-character limitation, didn't even give them enough space to store very long artist or album titles (such as Stereolab's album "Cobra and Phases Group Play Voltage in the Milky Night"), the ID3v2 spec allows for a maximum of 256 *megabytes* of additional tag storage space, meaning users won't bump into arbitrarily imposed limitations. Of course, if you fill a file with 256 MB of ID3 data, don't expect many users to want to download it from your site.

Because a surprising number of older players are *not* ID3v2 aware, and because of the problem mentioned earlier regarding the length of time an older player should seek for MP3 data before giving up, problems do arise. For example, if you use MusicMatch Jukebox to embed an image of an album cover into an MP3 file using Jukebox's ID3v2 tag editor, you'll find that the file will no longer play in the command-line mpg123 player, while Xmms may be able to play the file but won't show any ID3 tags for it.

Despite these issues, ID3v2 is a spec with huge potential. One of the most popular applications to take a stab at the ID3v2 space is MusicMatch JukeBox. At this writing, ID3v2 support in MusicMatch was limited to a minority subset of the total frames available (although these were the most significant ones). In addition, MusicMatch was taking a proprietary approach to storing some categories, including tempo, preference, and mood, which some feel could have been better handled had MusicMatch gone with standard ID3v2 frames. Finally, MusicMatch's implementation of the Content Type frame was still incomplete, and resembled ID3v1 more than ID3v2. Still, somebody had to be first on the dance floor, and the company's commitment to driving the standard forward should be appreciated. However, there's a lot of work remaining to bring their product into full compliance with the specification.

So how do you tell which ID3 spec is in use on any given file? There's no way to get this information just by looking at a file; the best way is to open the file in a tag editor capable of reading both versions of the spec, and looking to see where in the editor's fields information shows up. Any older MP3 file can be "upgraded" simply by opening it in an ID3v2-capable player or editor and adding extended information to it. In fact, some utilities will automatically migrate all ID3v1 data to equivalent ID3v2 fields. Opening an ID3v2-enhanced MP3 file with an older player will probably result in you seeing nothing in the ID3 info fields. The file itself, however, should still play properly. If it doesn't, you should consider changing or upgrading your MP3 player software.

Having accurate information in your files' ID3 fields is important for several reasons. If you ever edit or screw up your file's names, you can always just open the file in an ID3-capable player, read the author and song title, and rename the file accordingly. Some tools will even do this for you, automatically and programmatically, so you can assign ideal file names to every MP3 track on your system. ID3 tags are displayed in many playlists, so that you can display only song names, only artists, or only the comments. ID3 tags are commonly used by hardware MP3 players such as portable "Walkman"-type devices and home MP3 units. And some programs and utilities will let you treat the ID3 info in your files collectively, as if your entire collection was a huge, multi-field database.

For more information on the ID3 spec and its evolution, see the ID3 Standards Group web site at *www.id3.org*.

What Are Playlists?

After all the talk about how the MP3 revolution represents a rebirth of the "custom cassette" revolution of the '70s and '80s, the arena of playlists is where you finally get to see that promise become a reality. In their simplest form, playlists are simply text files containing paths to MP3 files on your system—one line in the file for every track referenced. The beauty of playlists is that they can be constructed to reference arbitrary tracks, rather than being limited to entire directories. For example, you might have a playlist referencing only the tracks in your collection in the Free Improv genre, or all tracks by The Carpenters, or all tracks you're temporarily storing in a holding bin until you decide what to do with them. There are many ways to construct playlists. Most users will create them by simply dragging tracks (or entire directories) out of the system's file manager (Explorer/Finder/ Tracker, etc.) and into an open playlist window, then saving the new playlist to the hard disk. However, playlists can also be constructed from the command line by way of scripts, or from database searches. As you'll soon see, real playlist flexibility comes into play when you use your files' array of ID3 tags to search on specific criteria, then save the resulting found set as a playlist file.

Because they're constructed with such simplicity, playlists are nearly universal; for the most part, a playlist created with any method will work in any MP3 player (on the same operating system). Of course, the exact format of the lines comprising a playlist depends on the path style on your operating system. For example:

```
DOS/Windows - C:\DATA\MP3\ALBUMS\CAN\DELAY\PNOOM.MP3
Mac OS - Main HD:Data:MP3:Albums:Can:Delay:Pnoom.mp3
Linux - /usr/local/home/shacker/data/MP3/Albums/Can/Delay/Pnoom.mp3
BeOS - /gorgonzola/home/data/MP3/Albums/Can/Delay/Pnoom.mp3
```

So while a playlist will work on any MP3 player on your operating system, it wouldn't on another OS. (This really isn't much of an issue though, since people organize their collections very differently and it thus makes little sense to share your playlists with others, unless you're trading around data CDs full of MP3 files). Even if you're a Linux or BeOS user storing your MP3 collection on a Windows partition and then accessing it from Linux or BeOS, the paths to the files on the Windows partition will still appear differently, so you won't be able to share playlists between different OS partitions.

It's worth noting that most users will seldom see the actual text of a playlist file. While you can open a playlist in any text editor for viewing or hand-editing, it's almost always easier to view and manage your playlists directly in your MP3 player's built-in playlist manager, since these typically give you drag-and-drop, shuffle, sort, total playback time, and other MP3-specific features you probably won't find in a text editor. Playlist manager/editors generally do not show you the full paths to your MP3 files, displaying only the actual track names. In many cases, playlist editors will read the ID3 tags out of each file in the list and display those (if found) rather than the filenames. As you'll see in Chapter 8, playlists may also contain the URLs to MP3 files on the Internet, so that you can stream known favorites "out there" directly to your MP3 player.

 Because most MP3 players can accommodate multiple audio file formats, including WAV, RealAudio, AAC, and others, there's no reason you should restrict your playlists to referencing MP3 files alone. If you've been collecting multiple audio file formats on your system and your player supports them all, feel free to create playlists referencing multiple file formats. If such a playlist does get fed through a player that doesn't understand some of the referenced formats, it should gracefully skip those files (assuming it's well-designed).

Playlist formats

The form of playlist described above is known as an M3U list,* and is named as *playlist.m3u*. In some cases, you may also encounter playlists with a *.pls* extension. These files are virtually the same, with a couple of internal differences. They begin with an identifying block marking the file as a playlist, precede each track with a numerical identifier, and close by listing the total number of tracks referenced. *.pls* files don't always reference the *full* path to each track, so if you move a playlist to another directory, disk volume, or hard drive on the same system, it won't work. *.pls* files are often dished up by streaming MP3 SHOUTcast/icecast servers, since the *.pls* format allows for the distribution of meta-data.

 When creating playlists on your own machine, you'll almost always want to stick with .M3U for maximum compatibility with a wide variety of MP3 players. If you do need to create a *.pls* file, you'll find the option in the "Save Files as Type" picklist in the file panel when you access your playlist's Save function.

---

* For "MPEG Layer 3 URL"; the URLs contained by these files can be either local files on the user's system or remote files "out there" on the Internet. The MIME type for M3U files is *audio/x-mpegurl*.

Finally, there are a few applications that create their own custom playlist formats. A good example of this is the Apollo MP3 player for Windows (*apollo.mp3-2000. com*), which combines an MP3 player and sophisticated playlist manager into a single application. While Apollo offers a number of cool playlist features that others do not (such as ID3v2 support and the ability to create lists from arbitrary ID3 criteria), its playlists are only useful with Apollo itself.

Loading and manipulating playlists

Playlists can be loaded into your MP3 player in several ways, depending on the platform and the specific player. In most cases, the easiest way to load a playlist is to simply double-click its icon. If it's been properly associated with your MP3 player, it will launch the player with that list preloaded. Playlists can usually be dragged onto your MP3 players' interface, or loaded from the File → Load button in the player's playlist editor. If you're a command-line junkie, you can usually load a playlist by typing:

```
<path to player> <path to playlist>
```

WinAmp users can right-click a playlist file in Explorer and choose Enque from the Context menu. If a playlist is already playing, this one will start playing when the current one has finished. You can queue up a pile of playlists to play sequentially in this way.

Most playlist editors include a number of functions designed to let you sort the order of tracks by song name, artist, length, and other criteria, though "Randomize" seems to be far and away the most popular means of "organizing" playlist tracks. If you're using Windows and are dropping files into a playlist editor, note that a peculiarity of Explorer could end up frustrating your attempts to get them to appear in same order you selected them in. However, if you select the last file first in Explorer, hold down the Shift key, and then highlight the first file; you can drag the whole block into your playlist editor and have the selections appear in the right order. In other words, the order in which you begin your selection in Explorer is the reverse of the order in which the selection is passed to other applications. You gotta love it.

Most playlist editors include a set of buttons (or a pull-down menu) separate from that of the MP3 player itself. WinAmp's playlist editor, for instance, includes buttons that will let you add entire directories or URLs to the playlist window, remove all selected files or all "dead" files (i.e., references to files which no longer exist at the specified location), sort your playlist by a variety of criteria, or save your playlist. To access the ID3 info for any file in WinAmp, select it in your playlist and tap Alt+3.

You can also generate HTML playlists directly from WinAmp's play-list editor. With the editor open, click Misc Options and select Generate HTML Playlist (or just tap Ctrl+Alt+G). The current list will be sent directly to your default browser. You can then pull down File → Save in the browser to store the resulting HTML document for future reference.

ID3 and Playlist Editors

There are seemingly infinite numbers of ways to create interfaces onto ID3 tag data (Figure 4-2), and we can't hope to cover a fraction of them in this book, but here are a few examples of the creative ways ID3 tags can be accessed, displayed, used, and edited, in various operating systems.

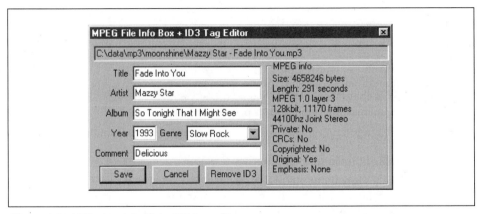

Figure 4-2. A WinAmp's built-in ID3 tag editor

Windows

MP3 collections are becoming larger, and large projects lend themselves well to database-like solutions. Since the array of all tags in all of your MP3 files, considered together, pretty much amounts to a database, the real trick is in building a good interface onto that database, letting you view and edit ID3 tag data, rename files based on existing ID3 tags, see the collection of all ID3 tags in a database-like manner, search that database on custom criteria, and generate playlists from the results. If you want to do all of these things, you have two choices. You can scan your favorite software library for individual tools that serve one or more of these functions (and probably get it all done for free, but create a lot of busy work for yourself), or you can grab an all-in-one tool like Helium (*www.citymob.rit.se/helium/*). While most of the all-purpose tools will probably cost you a few bucks, they'll more than pay for themselves in the time they'll save you in the long run. Since, at this writing, Helium is one of the best all-purpose ID3/database/playlist tools available, and because it covers the general principles involved in performing all of these tasks, we'll focus on Helium in this section. Note, however, that there will likely be other, perhaps better, tools available for your operating system by the time you read this.

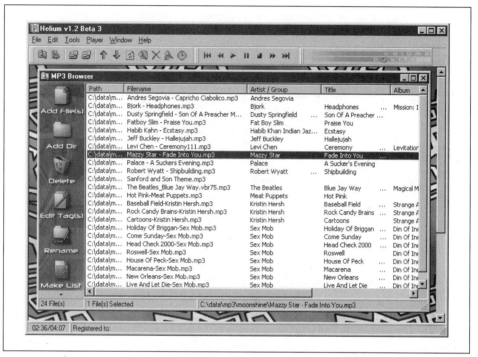

Figure 4-3. The main Helium window

The main Helium window plays host to any number of what are known as "Browsers," where a browser is simply a table of MP3 files: a sort of fancy playlist (Figure 4-3). To create a new browser window:

1. Double-click on the Helium background. Point the empty browser to an MP3 directory or collection of files by clicking the Add Files or Add Dir buttons on the left.

2. All MP3 files in that directory and its subdirectories will appear in a table, along with any ID3 tags stored in those files. If the referenced files don't include MP3 tags and you want to give them some, select those files in the browser and pull down Tools → Edit Tags (or tap Ctrl+E).

3. An ID3v2 tag editor will appear for the first selected file, offering tons of fields, picklists, and text boxes into which you can type or paste lyrics, select genres, and so on (Figure 4-4).

4. When finished editing a file's tags, click Save, then Next to move to the next file in your selection.

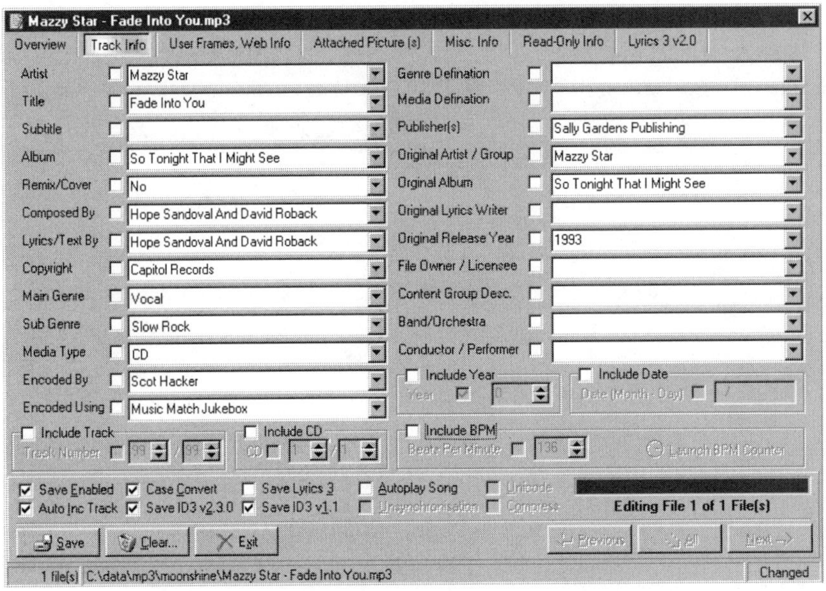

Figure 4-4. Helium's tag editor offers the majority of ID3v2 frames; buttons along the top let you navigate amongst major classes of allowable ID3v2 data

Helium is also capable of renaming files singly or in batches, based on the contents of their ID3 tags (though the version we tested did not offer special character or blank space substitution, which we feel should be a mandatory feature). To access the renaming function, select a file or files and pull down Tools → Rename Files. As with other ID3 renaming tools covered in this section, you have partial control over the format of the filenames that will be created, via a template function accessed from Helium's Output Editor. Conveniently, Helium lets you store as many naming templates as you like. A couple are built in, but you'll probably want to create your own as well. Click the New button, and then the Tag Help button to see a list of all allowable field strings. Artist/Group is represented by the symbol *%00*, Title by *01%*, Album by *05%*, and so on. So if you've got a file called *file1.mp3* and its ID3 tags specify that this is "Blue Jay Way" from the Beatles' *Magical Mystery Tour*, you could set up a template of the form:

%00%05%01

Renaming your file with this template selected will result in a file called:

```
BeatlesMagical Mystery TourBlue Jay Way.mp3
```

That, however, is probably not what you want. To add separators between the fields, enter them in the Prefix and Suffix fields.

Helium is capable of exporting lists in two ways. Before you do, however, you'll probably want to use some of Helium's filtering and sorting capabilities—here's where the real power of a database begins to come to light. Let's say you've got hundreds of folders full of MP3 files scattered around on your hard drive, and you want to make a playlist of all songs with their Genre tag set to "Booty Bass." If you haven't already assigned Genres to your tracks, use the Tag Editor to do so. You'll also need to make sure the Genre column is showing in the Browser table—you can enable this from Helium's preferences panel. Now pull down Edit → Search, type in "booty," make sure the "Copy matches to new window" checkbox is selected and click Search. All songs in the main browser window that are tagged as Booty Bass songs will appear in a new Browser. Now all you have to do is pull down File → Save Playlist, select either the *.M3U* or *.pls* format, and save. Bingo—instant custom playlist.

In addition to playlists, Helium is capable of generating HTML or text documents from its browsers, so you can keep documents on your desktop that list your entire collection of MP3 files, or any custom subset thereof. Select a set of files or create a new browser containing customized search results, and click the List button. The output format of Helium's list generator can be completely customized by specifying HTML or other header data, and then inserting ID3 tag symbols into the Main List section of the List Generator.

Because of the inherent power of database-driven tools, you'll find that applications like Helium become increasingly indispensable as your MP3 collection grows larger.

One-click master list

How would you like to be able to double-click a single icon on your Desktop, have it scan your system for MP3 files, generate a master playlist, and launch that playlist into WinAmp or another MP3 player? A batch file (that's DOS-ese for shell script) like the following one can make this easy. To do this, you'll need to invoke the ancient masters of your early DOS training.

Generating a playlist from the DOS command line (i.e., DOS prompt) is a matter of constructing a command that will find all files ending in *.mp3* in a specified directory and all of its subdirectories, that will not spew out all kinds of extra data you don't need, and that won't list directory names themselves. Here's what you want:

```
dir c:\data\mp3\*.mp3 /s/b/a-d > c:\data\playlists\thislist.m3u
```

If you scatter MP3 files all over your system (which wouldn't be very good house-keeping), you can change the initial path to simply *C:*. In case you're curious about those switches, */s* tells *dir* to recurse down through subdirectories. */b* tells *dir* to output only a simple list of pathnames, without file sizes, or foreshortened filenames. */a* tells *dir* to handle special attributes, as specified in its subsequent arguments. *d* is one of the attributes */a* can handle, and since we precede it with a - instead of *:*, we're telling *dir* to ignore directory names themselves (directory names in playlists will simply be ignored by most players, but they're still messy). The > symbol is a redirect, and tells DOS to dump the output of the command to a new file. Of course you'll need to substitute in the path to your collection of MP3 files, as well as the preferred path to and name of your generated playlist file.

If you want to do this sort of thing in a batch file, so you can simply double-click an icon on your desktop to have the whole thing run automatically, you'll want to create something like this:

```
@echo off
echo.
echo Creating playlist from d:\data\mp3 ...
:: Remember to edit the paths below to match
:: those on your machine! The second line is optional,
:: and shows how you can have this batch file scan through
:: multiple drives and directories and append the results
:: to the same playlist file. Note that if any of your directory
:: or filenames are longer than 8.3 you'll need to surround
:: them in quotes so DOS doesn't get confused.
dir d:\data\mp3\*.mp3 /s/b/a-d > "d:\data\playlists\alltracks.m3u"
dir e:\hold\music\mp3\*.mp3 /s/b/a-d >> "d:\data\playlists\alltracks.m3u"
echo.
echo Launching the new list in WinAmp...
:: The next line can be the the full path to any MP3 player
:: on your system that accepts a playlist as a command line
:: argument. WinAmp handles this just fine.
start "C:\Program Files\Winamp\winamp.exe" "d:\data\playlists\alltracks.m3u"
exit
```

To test your new system, double-click the batch file in Explorer. Did it work? Good. Unfortunately, you will have noticed that a DOS shell is launched automatically when you run the batch file, and doesn't close itself when you close WinAmp. The trick to fixing this annoying behavior is to click the small Properties icon in the DOS shell's menu bar and check the "Close on exit" checkbox (you may also want to select "Run: minimized" to keep the DOS window from flashing briefly on screen). Close the Properties panel, and a *.PIF* file will be created in the same directory as the batch file, appearing as a standard Shortcut file. Drag this shortcut to your Desktop or wherever, and from now on you can just click that to launch your script. The DOS shell will close as soon as WinAmp launches.

Do it with Perl

Search the Internet and you'll find tons of homebrew playlist solutions created by ordinary people, using free tools. One of the most common and useful such solutions is the Perl-based playlist creator, such as the one created by Patrick Hearon and available at *www.owlnet.rice.edu/~patrickh/playlist.html*. Point the script at a directory tree and it will "walk" through its contents, taking note of any MP3 files it finds in the path. When finished, it will generate either a plain text *.M3U* playlist file, suitable for use with any MP3 player, or a collection of HTML files, one in each directory, each listing the contents of that directory. Because each file automatically links to the others, you can browse through your MP3 collection easily, or post the HTML documents on a web site for others to peruse.

Perl junkies may also want to search CPAN (*www.perl.com/CPAN/*), a.k.a. the Comprehensive Perl Archive Network, for all sorts of useful Perl modules. At this writing, MP3.com was in the process of contributing some of their own modules into the CPAN database, including modules to give Perl built-in ID3v2 and MPEG Layer 3 info support (a less complete module already exists).

Because Perl is available for nearly every platform known to humankind, these scripts can be easily tweaked to work with your platform (though all you'll have to change are the magic cookies pointing to the Perl interpreter, and the path style used on your system).

Mac OS

Most of the popular MP3 players for the Mac include built-in ID3 tag editors, and usage is straightforward, as you might imagine. In MACAST, for example, make sure the playlist is showing, select a track, and click the Info button. Fill in or edit the fields as desired, then click Save to save your changes directly into the file, as shown in Figure 4-5. At this writing, MACAST supports only ID3v1 tags, though ID3v2 support may be available by the time you read this.[*]

Do not attempt to edit ID3 tags in a currently playing track. MACAST will issue a warning and offer to move to the next track in order to make changes to the current track, but in our experience this froze the Mac.

---

[*] In fact, a Lyrics field was available in the ID3 tag panel in the version of MACAST we looked at, and lyrics are officially a part of the ID3v2 spec. However, ID3v2 offers a much broader array of options than just lyrics, so we consider this to be only a partial implementation of ID3v2 support.

Figure 4-5. A MACAST window's Info button produces fields to fill in or edit; just fill in the fields and close the MATE window to save your changes

More powerful than the built-in tag editors is a piece of freeware called mp3tool, which will scan a specified folder for MPEG files and let you edit ID3 tags in any files it finds along the way. While mp3tool won't create playlists from the files it finds, it offer very straightforward tag-editing capabilities. Search your favorite Mac OS software library for mp3tool.

Since Mac OS doesn't have a command-line environment, it's not possible to create scripts that perform similar functions to the DOS batch file above or the Unix shell script below. However, if you're familiar with AppleScript, it should not be difficult to store references to your MP3 files in a commercial database (such as FileMaker Pro) or spreadsheet and extract the results of database searches to a plain text file. Alternatively, you can use the Finder's Find panel to scan your system for all MP3 files, then drag files in the resulting list onto the Desktop or into a folder. From there, you can drag files directly into your MP3 player. However, because you can't drag files directly out of the Find panel and into a player, this process essentially means moving your MP3 files around, which is probably not what you want to do. However, you *can* drag files out of the Find panel and onto the MP3 player application icon. In the end, you're probably better off using the MP3 finding tools built into the players themselves.

Linux

The power of Unix-based operating systems is often at the command line, and ID3 handling is no exception. One of the most popular tools available for handling ID3 tags under Linux is id3ren (*tscnet.com/pages/badcrc/apps/id3ren/*), a multi-purpose tool that can not only read and write ID3 tags, but can also rename files based on the ID3 tags those files contain. While id3ren is most popular under Linux, note that BeOS and Windows ports of id3ren do exist, and can be found at your favorite software library. The real power of a tool like this is in its ability to be embedded in shell scripts and run over batches of files at once.

To see the tags currently attached to `filename.mp3`, type

```
id3ren -showtag filename.mp3
```

To rename a file with the default (built-in) naming template, just type:

```
id3ren filename.mp3
```

If the file's Artist tag was "Beatles" and the Title tag was "Taxman," `filename.mp3` will be instantly renamed to `[Beatles].[Taxman].mp3`. Don't ask me where that goofy default format comes from, but fortunately, you can easily change this by means of the `-template` argument. Templates in id3ren are a means of defining the naming structure of the files to be renamed, where the following identifiers are available.

Tag	Identifier
%a	Artist name
%c	Comment
%s	Song name
%t	Album title
%y	Year
%g	Genre

So, for example, if your file's Artist tag is set to "Beatles" and the Title tag is set to "Taxman," you can have the file renamed as *Beatles--Taxman.mp3* with the following command:

```
id3ren -template="%a--%s.mp3" filename.mp3
```

 If you always want to use the same template, and don't want to have to specify it every time, create a text file called *.id3renrc* and place it in your home directory (see id3ren's documentation for more on allowable locations). In this file, specify the same template parameters, but leave out the quotes. id3ren will now always use your preferred template, unless you use the `-nocfg` flag in your command. Windows users will need to replace the % symbols with $ in the template examples here.

The simplest way to add to or change the tags associated with a given file is to type:

```
id3ren -tag filename.mp3
```

You'll be prompted to enter a string for each of the possible tags. Alternatively, you can add multiple tags at once with a single command, like this:

```
id3ren -tag -song "Mink_Shmink" -artist "Eartha_Kitt" filename.mp3
```

You'll then only be prompted for any tags you don't enter in the command (including -comment, -genre, and -year). If you don't want to be prompted for other tags, add the -edit argument. If all you care about are the Artist and Title tags, and don't want to be prompted for others, use the -quick flag. If you don't want the file to be renamed, and only want to edit tags, use -tagonly. To simply remove all tags, use id3ren -striptag filename.mp3. You get the idea. There are many more options available, but they all follow this basic model—just use id3ren -help to see them all.

The real power of id3ren, of course, comes into play when dealing with batches of files at once. In any of the example commands, wildcards or variable names can be used in place of filename.mp3. Thus, you can easily run through an entire directory of files at once. Since a directory might very well represent an entire album, you'll probably want to specify the artist and album names in the initial command, so you don't have to type them in over and over again. For example, let's say you just ripped and encoded all of *Magical Mystery Tour*, but the MP3 files you've created have been given names like *Track1.mp3*, *Track2.mp3*, and so on. The following command will give the files appropriate names, add the Artist and Title tags, and prompt you only for the song titles, skipping the year and comments:

```
id3ren -tag -artist "Beatles" -album "Magical Mystery Tour" -nogenre \
-nocomment -noyear -template="%a-%s.mp3" *.mp3
```

id3ren will prompt you for the name of each song in the current directory, write the song, album, and artist tags to each file, and rename each song as *Beatles-Taxman.mp3* and so on. If you don't mind being prompted for the genre tag with each song as well, you could use the -quick flag for a somewhat shorter command.

The following script can be used to sift through all of your MP3 files for just those files whose ID3 tags match criteria you specify. This sample script looks for matches on the Artist tag, though you can tweak it to search on the Genre tag, for example, "find me all songs that are filed under the Genre ('Gangsta'). Further adjustments could yield a script that searches on two criteria at once ("all Soul tracks from 1971"), or just about anything else you can imagine:

```
#!/bin/sh

# Get the artist name passed in from the command line
Artist="$*"

# Edit the next line to equal the full path to your main MP3 directory.
# To search your whole system, you could even make it " / ",
# But the more specific you are, the faster the script will be.
MP3Path=~/mp3
```

```
# Set this to the location in which you want your playlist files
# to appear. This universal HOME variable should work on all
# Unix-based systems, though you'll probably want
# to customize it.
PlayListDir=${HOME}

# Now we'll get a list of all MP3 files living in the MP3 hierarchy.
# The list will be saved to a temp file for further parsing.
find "$MP3Path" -name *.mp3 > $PlayListDir/.id3-tmp

# Now we're going to open that temp file and examine each track
# it references, trying to determine whether its Artist tag matches
# the one the user specified on the command line. We have to do
# a little fancy work with grep and sed to get just the info we need
# and nothing else.
{
while read ThisFile; do
    ThisArtist=$(id3ren -showtag "$ThisFile" | grep "Artist\:" | sed s/Artist\:\
//)
        if [ $ThisArtist = "$Artist" ]; then
            echo "$ThisFile"
        fi
done

# Input is the temp file, output is the final playlist
} < $PlayListDir/.id3-tmp > $PlayListDir/$Artist.m3u

# Remove the temp file
rm $PlayListDir/.id3-tmp
exit
```

BeOS

There are a number of tools for BeOS ID3 tag display and manipulation. All of the major MP3 players support normal ID3 display within their own interfaces, but BeOS also supports some ID3 manipulation not possible on other platforms. Because the Be file system supports "attributes" (data associated with a file that is not a part of the file itself), ID3 tags can be read out of MP3 files and displayed directly in the Tracker (the BeOS file manager), as shown in Figure 4-6. This provides an excellent database-like interface you can use to sort, query, and organize your MP3 tracks along user-selectable criteria.

One of the most useful tools you'll find out there is a collection of Tracker add-ons and applications by Jonas Sundström (see *www.be.com/beware/*). Install Tag2Attr and Attr2Tag in your */boot/home/config/add-ons/Tracker* folder, then right-click any MP3 file or collection of MP3 files and select Tag2Attr. All of the selected files will be examined for embedded ID3 tags, and attributes will be written to the file system. You can now enable the MP3 attributes you want to view from the Tracker's Attributes menu, and edit your attributes directly in the Tracker. Because other operating systems don't recognize BeOS attributes, you'll want to make sure

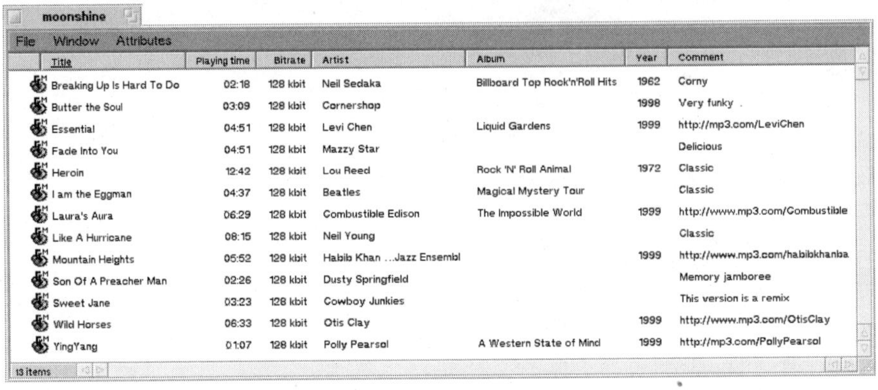
moonshine
File Window Attributes
Title Playing time Bitrate Artist Album Year Comment
Breaking Up Is Hard To Do 02:18 128 kbit Neil Sedaka Billboard Top Rock'n'Roll Hits 1962 Corny
Butter the Soul 03:09 128 kbit Cornershop 1998 Very funky
Essential 04:51 128 kbit Levi Chen Liquid Gardens 1999 http://mp3.com/LeviChen
Fade Into You 04:51 128 kbit Mazzy Star Delicious
Heroin 12:42 128 kbit Lou Reed Rock 'N' Roll Animal 1972 Classic
I am the Eggman 04:37 128 kbit Beatles Magical Mystery Tour Classic
Laura's Aura 06:29 128 kbit Combustible Edison The Impossible World 1999 http://www.mp3.com/Combustible
Like A Hurricane 08:15 128 kbit Neil Young Classic
Mountain Heights 05:52 128 kbit Habib Khan ...Jazz Ensembl 1999 http://www.mp3.com/habibkhanba
Son Of A Preacher Man 02:26 128 kbit Dusty Springfield Memory jamboree
Sweet Jane 03:23 128 kbit Cowboy Junkies This version is a remix
Wild Horses 06:33 128 kbit Otis Clay 1999 http://www.mp3.com/OtisClay
YingYang 01:07 128 kbit Polly Pearsol A Western State of Mind 1999 http://mp3.com/PollyPearsol
13 items

Figure 4-6. BeOS lets you store ID3 tag info as filesystem "attributes," which can then be displayed and edited directly in the Tracker

these attributes are written back into the file itself if you edit any of them (and plan to make them available to users of other OSes); hence, Attr2Tag works exactly the same, but in the opposite direction.

While this pair is excellent for batch jobs, you may find you want more control. Sundström is also the author of TagWorld, which is also a Tracker add-on, but lets you examine and edit the collection of tags for each file individually (see Figure 4-7).

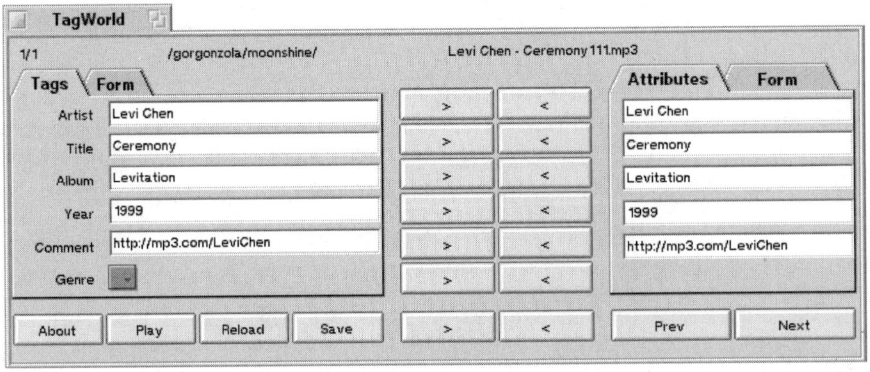
TagWorld
1/1
/gorgonzola/moonshine/
Levi Chen - Ceremony 111.mp3
Tags
Form
Attributes
Form
Artist
Levi Chen
Title
Ceremony
Album
Levitation
Year
1999
Comment
http://mp3.com/LeviChen
Genre
Levi Chen
Ceremony
Levitation
1999
http://mp3.com/LeviChen
About
Play
Reload
Save
Prev
Next

Figure 4-7. TagWorld lets you copy ID3 tags to attributes and back again

In order to query your BeOS system on ID3 data, you'll need to tell the filesystem to maintain an index of the ID3 attributes. Sundström also provides MP3 AI to help you create and manage the necessary indexes, as well as MP3 Flashlight, which makes finding MP3 files even easier than it is from the system's Find panel. Taken together, Sundström's collection of tools exploits native BeOS features to gain functionality similar to that found in Windows with tools like Helium (covered earlier in this chapter). Many BeOS encoding tools will write ID3 tags to attributes as they're encoding, and can even create custom folder layouts based on GUI templates. More on that in Chapter 5.

 If you prefer to work from the bash shell, or if you'd like to script some of these behaviors, download a copy of Ari Pernick's id3attr from *www.be.com/beware/*. Once installed, you can copy ID3 tags to attributes by launching a Terminal and typing:

```
id3attr *
```

The author also keeps this alias in his *~/.profile*:

```
idren='id3ren -template="%a - %s.mp3" -space=" "'
```

By using the `id3attr *` command followed by the custom `idren` command, he can "database" and give ideal names to a batch of freshly downloaded MP3 files in seconds.

Once your MP3 files have attributes attached, there's almost no limit to the ways you can create custom playlists. For example, if you want a playlist consisting of all the MP3 files in your collection written in 1971, just do a normal system query (pull down the Be menu and select "Find") on "MP3 → Year contains 1971." Select All in the query results window and drag the selection into an open playlist window. Save the new playlist, and you're done. Of course, you can extend the same principle to create playlists of any complexity. For example, you could create a playlist in three seconds flat consisting of all Neil Sedaka tunes that have a Comment field including the word "smarmy." Pretty cool, huh?

Of course, if you want to get more hands-on from the command line, you can also use bash shell scripts like the one shown in the Linux section earlier in this chapter, though the BeOS query function gives you the same functionality directly in the GUI, but without the need to edit configuration files.

Skins: Dressing Up MP3 Players

As shown throughout this book, WinAmp and other MP3 players can be "costumed" with alternate interfaces called "skins." Because skins are merely collections of bitmap images with pre-specified names and sizes, skins are not tied specifically to WinAmp, or even to Windows. While WinAmp is by far the most common place to find WinAmp skins in use, you'll also find MP3 players for Mac OS, BeOS and Linux that wear WinAmp skins. In addition, there other MP3 players out there with even more radical interfaces (such as Sonique and K-Jöfol) that also wear skins. Note, however, that these players don't wear WinAmp skins; see their sites for availability of skins for those players.

How to Get WinAmp Skins

There are a number of large skin repositories on the Internet. The definitive collection is on WinAmp's own site, at *www.winamp.com/skins/*. There you'll find nearly 3,000 downloadable skins made by WinAmp users like yourself, categorized into groups like "Computer," "Game," "Stereo," "Anime," and even "Ugly" (and believe me, some of them deserve their place in that category). You'll probably find the highest quality skins in the "Best Skins" category, a group that has been selected by WinAmp employees for their finesse and professional look. There are (at this writing) three other notable skins sites out there: *www.1001winampskins.com* is a site run by WinAmp fans for other fans (not connected to NullSoft), while *www.skinz.org* and *www.customize.org* offer skins for dozens of products, not just WinAmp (though their WinAmp skins collection is smaller than that of the other two sites).

Each skin collection arrives as a single zip file, and becomes accessible to WinAmp simply by living in the skins directory specified in the WinAmp preferences (which by default is in *C:\PROGRAM FILES\WINAMP\SKINS*). If you have an older version of WinAmp, you'll need to unzip each collection into a subdirectory of the skins directory. For example, a skin archive called "Evo" might need to be decompressed in *C:\PROGRAM FILES\WINAMP\SKINS\EVO*. However, if you're using WinAmp 2.04 or higher, you don't need to unzip the archive at all, since WinAmp is smart enough to unarchive the files it needs on the fly (there is no noticeable performance penalty for doing this).

If you do choose to decompress your skins, note that many skin authors carelessly zip up their collections without also zipping the parent directory, which means you can easily overwrite skin components of the same name if you don't manually create an appropriate subdirectory first. If you use WinZip, a good way to do this is to right-click the zip archive and select "Extract To…" from the Context menu.

Once installed, skins can be activated by right-clicking anywhere in WinAmp's interface and choosing Skin Selector from the context menu (tapping Alt+S will also bring up the Skin Selector). A panel will appear listing all installed skins. Single-clicking an entry will cause WinAmp's interface to instantly adopt the new look. After donning a new skin, try enabling the WinAmp playlist and equalizer functions. Depending on how the author created the skin, these modules may or may not also take on the theme of the new skin. If skin components for these modules were not provided, they'll appear with the default WinAmp look and feel.

Please note that some skins are distributed as shareware, rather than as freeware. You should find a file called *readme.txt* in each skin's directory. If the skin is shareware, it will say so in this file. If you like the skin and decide to keep it, pay the author his or her due.

 If you have multiple operating systems installed on your computer, there's no need to store the same skins collections multiple times. For example, since both BeOS and Linux can read Windows partitions, you may want to store all of your skins on your Windows partition and just create a symlink in your BeOS or Linux MP3 player directory called "skins" pointing to the location of your Windows skins directory. Of course you'll need to make sure your Windows partition is mounted automatically at boot time if you want this technique to work transparently.

WinAmp Easter Eggs

Like most heavily evolved software, WinAmp has a few "Easter Eggs" tucked away—non-obvious "features" that one might only stumble upon by accident... or if one read about them in a book. Try these:

- Right-click in WinAmp's interface and choose "NullSoft WinAmp" to bring up the About panel.

- Click the WinAmp tab to see the animated WinAmp character.

- With that animation running, hold down Ctrl+Alt+Shift and click on the copyright notice at the bottom of the panel. The character will be overlayed with a bitmap of WinAmp's original developer, Justin Frankel.

Older versions of WinAmp had additional Easter Eggs, though these seem to have disappeared after NullSoft was acquired by AOL.

Creating Your Own Skins

If you really want to call yourself a WinAmp pro, using other people's skins won't cut it—you've got to create a few of your own. While creating original skins can become tedious, time-consuming work—especially when you get into customizing regions and colors—the payoff can make the effort worth it. The only software you need is a good image editor, such as Adobe Photoshop, Paint Shop Pro, the GIMP (Linux and BeOS only), or something similar. You can even create skins in Microsoft Paint, though you'll probably find Paint underpowered for the job.

Next, you'll need to understand the purpose of each of the *.bmp* files in a skins directory. While you can use any skin as a starting point, the definitive collection of templates can be downloaded as *Base.<version>.zip* from *www.winamp.com/ skins.* You'll also find a skin-creation tutorial at that site. Unpack *base.zip* and you'll find three type of files inside: *.bmp* files, which are the actual graphics that will comprise your skin's interface; *.cur* files, which are standard Windows cursor files to be activated when the user's mouse hovers over different parts of the interface (ignored when the skin is used by another operating system); and *.txt* files, which can be customized to specify the colors of non-graphical elements and transparency behaviors.

 You do not need to edit—or even include—a version of every single file in this directory. The behavior of elements for any files you don't include will be supplied by WinAmp itself. In other words, the default WinAmp interface is always present behind your creation.

Skin graphics

Open the various *.bmp* files in your image editor, and the purpose of each will become immediately obvious—you'll see fragments of familiar interface elements in each one, while each file's purpose is also declared by its file name (Figure 4-8). For example, *volume.bmp* displays a column of colored horizontal glowing strips, representing the colors of the volume slider as you move it right and left. *Titlebar.bmp* likewise shows all possible incarnations of the WinAmp titlebar (e.g., as it appears when maximized, when in zoom mode, and with and without the visualizer enabled). All you have to do is edit these graphics to your liking, taking care to preserve their dimensions and division lines precisely. Because many of the elements, such as the fonts in *text.bmp*, may appear very, very small, you'll probably want to get familiar with your image editor's zoom (magnifying glass) function.

Because just creating new bitmaps for every possible interface element in WinAmp can be a huge job, most skin creators call it a day after finishing the graphics portion. If you really feel like gettin' jiggy wid' it though, you'll want to dig into the *.cur* and *.txt* collections as well.

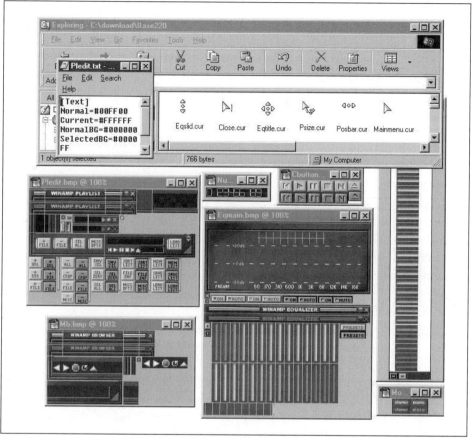

Figure 4-8. Bitmaps, base configuration files, and Windows cursors, all with specific filenames that must not change

Cursors and control files

The *.cur* files used by WinAmp are standard Windows cursor files, and can be generated in any number of Windows shareware programs designed for the purpose. You may want to look into the excellent Microangelo (*www.impactsoft.com*) for some serious cursor customization action. You should be able to determine the purpose of each cursor file by its filename; for example, *eqslid.cur* is the cursor that goes into effect when the mouse is using the equalizer's sliders, while *volbar. cur* takes hold when adjusting WinAmp's volume.

Manipulating fonts and colors

The most technical aspect of skin creation (and again, this is totally optional) may be the configuration of specific aspects of WinAmp appearance and behavior from the text-based configuration files *region.txt*, *viscolor.txt*, and *pledit.txt*.

The easiest to edit of these files is *pledit.txt*, which lets you control the fonts and font colors used in the playlist panel. All values are expressed in hexadecimal, a format that will be familiar to most web developers. If you need a good reference of hexadecimal color values, search the web for "netscape colors" or "hexadecimal colors." You'll find both web pages and applications that will help you look these up easily. The format of *pledit.txt* is simply:

```
[Text]
Normal=#00FF00
Current=#FFFFFF
NormalBG=#000000
SelectedBG=#000080
Font=Arial
```

Where **Normal** is the font color of most song entries, **Current** is the color of the selected track, **NormalBG** is the color of the playlist background, and **SelectedBG** is the background color for the selected track. If you specify fonts here, keep in mind that your users may not have this font on their system. If the specified font is not found, the default font will be used.

Manipulating the visualizer

viscolor.txt lets you control the colors being used by the WinAmp visualization module. Unlike *pledit.txt*, colors here are expressed as RGB triplets (one value each for the red, green, and blue color values). You can use Windows' built-in color manager (right-click on the Desktop, choose Properties, select the Appearance tab, and click Colors → Other) to determine RGB triplets. There are 24 lines in this file, each of which corresponds to an audio level threshold. Experimenting with this file is probably the best way to get a feel for which entries take effect at which audio thresholds. If you want to keep track of your changes, you can succeed each line with a comment:

```
24,33,41, // This corresponds to mid-volume signals
```

Manipulating skin regions

Perhaps one of the most interesting interface controls you have as a skin developer is afforded by *region.txt*, which lets you use masks to "carve out" regions of WinAmp to be considered invisible. By using a system of X,Y coordinates, you can tell WinAmp only to draw specific sections of the interface, and to leave the rest transparent. The results can be dramatic. Working with *region.txt* is somewhat more complex than working with the other text files. The principle here is that you specify the shapes of polygons by telling WinAmp how many points each polygon has, followed by a series of X,Y coordinates for each polygon. Since WinAmp's dimensions are 275×116 pixels, the X coordinate values can range from 0 to 274, and the Y values can range from 0 to 115. In order to determine the exact coordinate points you need, you'll want to find the tool in your image editor that reports the exact coordinates beneath the mouse cursor. (In Photoshop, pull down Window → Show Info.) WinAmp simply draws all regions that fall within the polygons you've defined and leaves the rest invisible. Open *region.txt* in the base skin collection and you'll see lines like this:

```
;NumPoints=4
;PointList=0,1, 275,1, 275,14, 0,14
```

Any line beginning with a ; is ignored, so to enable any series of sample coordinates, just uncomment those lines, save, and load the skin to see the effect. Of course, you'll probably want to define more than one polygon, but for ease of development, just work on perfecting one polygon at a time (comment out your perfected polygon and start a new one). Once all polygons have been perfected, you'll need to conjoin them all into a single line, like this:

```
; NumPoints = 4, 4 ; In other words, define two squares
; PointList = 0,1, 275,1, 275,14, 0,14,   3,15, 272,15, 272,113, 3,113
; The space between the two sets makes the coordinate series easier to read.
```

See the comments in *region.txt* for further details. If you don't want any transparency in your skin, just delete *region.txt* or make sure all of its lines are commented out.

Mac users! MACAST supports a skin format that is incompatible with WinAmp skins. Fortunately, this also means that MACAST users are not limited to the size and shape constraints of WinAmp skins. If you do want to use WinAmp skins with MACAST, you can download a tool called SkinConverter from *www.solsticetechnologies.com/skin-converter/* that will do the job nicely. If you use SoundJam, you'll find a copy of SkinConverter in the SoundJam installation directory—just drag WinAmp skins onto the SkinConverter icon and they'll be transformed into SoundJam skins and placed automatically in SoundJam's skins folder, ready for use.

Plug-ins: Extending Your Reach

Just as the capabilities of programs like Adobe Photoshop or Netscape Navigator can be extended through the addition of third-party extensions called "plug-ins," so can many MP3 players. The beauty of the plug-in model is that the developers of the MP3 application get to have their product's capabilities extended indefinitely by the contributions of the larger developer community, and a cottage industry can be established for plug-in programmers. As a user, you'll find that your MP3 player may actually be far more capable than it originally appeared, thanks to these additions. While skins let you customize the look and feel of your MP3 player, plug-ins let you extend its actual functionality. Unlike skins, however, which are generic enough to work across multiple operating systems and players, plug-ins must be written specifically to work with each MP3 player. While you must have programming experience to write plug-ins, anyone can use them. Some are free, some are shareware, and some are available only by paying a fee up front.

Some MP3 players, like WinAmp, are built modularly, around the very concept of plug-ins. Because much of these programs' functionality is derived from the presence of certain crucial plug-ins, you should *not* delete the plug-ins that come with the WinAmp distribution. You may very well end up disabling your player's ability to export any sound at all.

There are a seemingly infinite variety of third-party plug-ins available, but they all fall into a few overarching categories:

Input plug-ins
Allow your player to play audio file formats that are not built into the player itself, or to accept signals from external devices such as keyboards or stereo components.

Output plug-ins
Allow your MP3 player to export signals to other audio file formats.

DSP/Effects plug-ins
Let you apply any number of audio special effects, such as distortion, echo, reverb, and more.

Visualization plug-ins
Perhaps the most popular of the lot, let you "see" your music in displays far more sophisticated and psychedelic than the simple visualizers built into most MP3 players.

Other plug-ins
Let you do things that aren't easily categorized, such as handling incoming signals from universal remote control units.

The best place to find plug-ins for your MP3 player is usually at that MP3 player's web site. You'll also find a good cross-platform plug-in collection in the Software section at *www.mp3.com* and other popular MP3-related web sites. While the specifics of plug-in installation and configuration differ greatly from one player to another, you'll almost always need to install plug-ins in a subdirectory of the MP3 player's installation directory called "plug-ins" or "plugins." In most cases, you should *not* create a new subdirectory for each downloaded plug-in under the *plugins* directory (yes, this is inconsistent with the skins installation model). WinAmp plug-ins are stored in *dynamically linked libraries*, or *.DLLs*. To access or activate a given plug-in, try right-clicking your M3 player's interface or looking for a Plug-ins menu. In WinAmp, just tap Ctrl+P to bring up the Preferences panel and expand the Plug-ins section of the hierarchy. To configure any individual plug-in, double-click its entry in this panel, as shown in Figure 4-9. Because most plug-ins are actual programs that run in conjunction with the MP3 player itself, most of them sport their own configuration interface.

Before starting to download and install third-party plug-ins, you should spend some time experimenting with the collection of pre-installed plug-ins, just to familiarize yourself with the huge number of options already at your disposal.

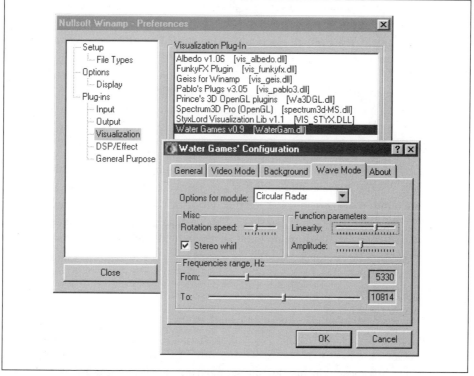

Figure 4-9. Double-click any entry in WinAmp's Plug-ins preferences panel to launch a configuration panel specific to that plug-in

Without question, the greatest number of plug-ins are available for WinAmp; at this writing, there were more than 140 WinAmp plug-ins available at *www. winamp.com/plugins/*, with more being added on a regular basis. That site, by the way, also includes a category called "Best Plug-ins," containing those deemed by WinAmp's staff to be of the highest quality or usefulness. You may as well start there. Let's look at a few of the most popular WinAmp plug-ins available, keeping in mind that plug-ins for other players and other operating systems perform similar functions but aren't available in such large number or variety.

Input Plug-ins

This category includes plug-ins designed to let your MP3 player handle arbitrary file formats and signal types as input. You'll find input plug-ins that let WinAmp handle MIDI, MPEG, Waveform, and CD/Line input, for example. Double-click any of these for further options relating to the way these input streams are handled. Most important for MP3 players is, obviously, the MPEG input plug-in. Owners of older machines and crappy sound cards will find a number of options here that let you adjust the performance of the MPEG decoder to use fewer resources. All users will appreciate being able to customize the way song titles and artist names are displayed as they're read out of each file's ID3 tags. If you have a very slow or eternally busy hard drive, you may get better MP3 performance by setting the Full File Buffering size to a number higher than the default of 128 K (a buffer here is simply a space in program memory dedicated to holding audio data before it's processed; by using a larger buffer, you guard against the possibility of skipping audio due to the hard disk's read head not being able to gather data from disk fast enough to satisfy the player). Streaming Data Buffers will be covered in Chapter 8.

If you start looking around for third-party input plug-ins, you'll find enablers that let you play obscure formats like sound tracks ripped from video games, plug-ins that let you watch AVI movies, plug-ins that work in conjunction with radio tuner cards, listen to high-quality AAC or VQF files, Amiga SoundTracker files, or the ever-popular RealAudio file format. Each of these will come with its own documentation and unique preferences/settings panels.

Output Plug-ins

Output plug-ins function as a sort of bridge that sits between the MP3 player and its output, controlling exactly how that output manifests. For general playback, the basic WaveOut plug-in (for WinAmp) is the only one you'll need, and you probably won't need to mess with its default settings unless you've got an older sound card (such as SoundBlaster 16), or need to perform some fancy footwork, like reversing the left and right stereo channels.

Decoding vs. Playback

Throughout this book, you'll see the terms "decoder" and "player" used pretty much interchangeably. Technically speaking, anything that plays MP3 audio is a decoder, since it's basically running the codec in reverse, re-assembling intelligible audio from a pile of bits in accordance with the MPEG specification. However, the term "decoder" is sometimes used specifically to refer to any process that takes an MP3 bitstream and converts it back into an uncompressed PCM audio file such as WAV or AIFF. Whether the MP3 file is converted to audible signal or to an uncompressed file, the exact same processes are in use.

Converting MP3 to WAV files

One of the most useful alternative outputs offered by the Output Plug-ins collection is the NullSoft DiskWriter, which lets you transform your outgoing MP3 signal into WAV files on your hard drive, rather than to audible signal. All you have to do to enable this function is double-click its entry, select an output directory on your system, and click Close in the WinAmp preferences panel. Playing MP3 files will now result in them being written to hard disk as WAV files. You will *not* hear output from WinAmp while this is happening, since only one output plug-in can be active at a time, and selecting the Disk Writer plug-in disables the WaveOut plug-in by definition. Of course, the resulting WAV files will be 10–12 times larger than the MP3 files they originate from. Remember to change back to WaveOut when you're done exporting to disk! You'll probably use this option a lot if you decide to burn audio CDs from your MP3 collection.

Use Microsoft Audio optimizations

If you want your system to be able to play sounds from multiple sources at once, or if you want to launch multiple instances of WinAmp simultaneously, you'll need to take advantage of capabilities offered only in later versions of Windows, or installed with upgrades to the Windows MediaPlayer. The technology that allows this is called DirectSound, and WinAmp must be told specifically to take advantage of it. Select the DirectSound output plug-in rather than WaveOut if you want to mix multiple audio streams down into a single output, or if you just want to see what it's like to play a bunch of MP3s simultaneously. Keep in mind that Windows may still balk if you tax its audio system too hard, since the operating system is not inherently optimized for this kind of maximum audio throughput.

Cross-fading your files

There aren't a ton of third-party output plug-ins floating around. The most popular is Justin Frankel's Crossfading output plug-in, which lets you start one MP3 file playing while the previous one is on its way out, with the first one's volume going down while the next one comes up. In other words, a cross-fade plug-in can make your MP3 audio stream sound as if it were coming off a DJ's mixing bench. Cross-fade timing is controlled by adjusting the size of the buffer, measured in milliseconds (i.e., a 5,000 ms buffer will give you a 5-second cross-fade). Note that using a larger buffer will help prevent skips on slower machines, but consume more memory.

 BeOS users: You can attach cross-fade settings to attributes of individual MP3 files, or to entire playlists at once, without needing a plug-in. Just click and hold on any currently playing track and select "Crossfade settings" from the context menu to adjust the settings for that file. If a playlist is currently being played, just select all tracks in the list and make your fade-out/fade-in changes, then click "Apply to Selection."

Linux users: If you use Xmms and have a multiple-CPU machine, try downloading the XAudio output plug-in from *www.xaudio.com* and using that instead of Xmms's default output—you'll feel the difference in performance!

DSP/Effects Plug-ins

This sophisticated (and often complex) breed of plug-in lets you apply digital signal processing and other effects to the audio signal. While you may enjoy simply tinkering with some of the amazing effects you can produce with these, many of them are geared specifically toward the more high-end user: radio stations, DJs, and sticklers for absolute quality and customization.

Virtual DJ

One of the most amazing DSP plug-ins available is Leif Claesson's PitchFork, which will literally let you treat your MP3 collection as if it were a pile of vinyl records, to be cued up, nudged, and synchronized. Pitchfork's controls are rather complex, and you'll definitely want to step through the included tutorial if you want to get the most out of the program. Of course, you'll need to be running at least two instances of WinAmp simultaneously, which means you'll need to be using the DirectSound output plug-in. If you really want to do it right, you'll want to have two sound cards installed in your computer, both of them running their line outs into an external mixing board. Needless to say, PitchFork's hardware requirements are a little beefier than your usual plug-in (but not overwhelming)—you'll need at least a Pentium 200 and 64 MB of RAM.

If you're serious about DJing with MP3 files and want something more than a plug-in, check out virtual dj at *www.virtualdj.com*, a complete playlist organization/automation system that handles MP3 files (along with other formats). Linux users may want to check out DigitalDJ, at *www.nostatic.org/ddj/*. BeOS disk jockeys use FinalScratch (*www.n2it.net/finalscratch/*), which uses physical turntables and special records containing nothing but microsecond timing marks—the system depends on Be's extremely low audio hardware latencies to let DJs "scratch" MP3 files in SoundPlay from the helm of actual turntables.

Normalizing playback

More down-to-earth is another of Claesson's creations, called AudioStocker. This gem provides a solution to the annoyance of having to reach for the volume control between tracks to compensate for the fact that MP3 files often demonstrate substantially different volume levels. Since most MP3 files are encoded digitally, without signal tweaking by the person doing the encoding, this artifact is due to the fact that different audio engineers and different recording labels tend to record albums at different levels to begin with, for whatever reason. You've probably noticed this effect before on your home stereo, but with MP3, where you're often jumping quickly between tracks extracted from different albums, the effect becomes much more noticeable.

The general term applied to the process of making multiple volume levels peak at similar thresholds is called *normalization*, and this is exactly what AudioStocker does. AudioStocker's controls consist of a set of push buttons that let you control the thresholds of the plug-in's intervention in the output signal. Tell the plug-in how much it's allowed to amplify a tune, how much frequency balance (equalization) can be applied, and a degree of audio compression (not to be confused with file compression) that can be applied. With a little tweaking, you should be able to get all of your tunes coming out of WinAmp at virtually the same perceived volume.

However, it's worth pointing out that this normalizing process is bound to result in some degradation of quality. Normalizing usually relies on the fact that the whole track can be examined in advance in order to establish peak levels. Normalizing on-the-fly, though, doesn't enjoy the luxury of a complete pass—it has to work by trimming the peak volumes and boosting the volume of quiet sections. The final output will therefore differ somewhat from the original by definition. While this is unavoidable in some situations, keep in mind that you'll always be better off doing your normalizing during the encoding process (from a quality standpoint).

In the future, it may become possible to store relative volume levels in a file's ID3v2 tags. Players would then be able to examine that data and adjust volume dynamically for each track. No known players were capable of working with ID3v2 tags in this way at this writing.

Other DSP/Effects

Take a look around and you'll find a number of simpler DSP/Effects plug-ins available for many MP3 players, including modules that let you bend the pitch of the current signal up or down (without speeding up or slowing down the track), modules that let you apply standard effects like chorus, reverb, flange, or echo, and even modules that let you "stack" multiple plug-ins on top of one another, so that you can create cumulative effects.

While not technically a plug-in, WinAmp does offer a cool little output feature that will let you generate pure tones for testing purposes. Turn down your system's volume control so you don't accidentally hurt your ears or speakers, then tap Ctrl+L (for Open Location) in WinAmp and enter *tone://1000*. WinAmp will play a 1kHz tone until you press the Stop button. Of course, you can substitute any frequency you need. If you'd like to save the tone to disk as a WAV file, enable the DiskWriter plug-in in WinAmp's Output Plug-ins section.

Visualization Plug-ins

This variety of plug-in is probably the most popular because they're the most fun. If you thought WinAmp's built-in visualization module was cool, you ain't seen nothin' yet. B-b-b-b-baby, you ain't seen nothin' yet! These modules analyze the signal flowing out of the player and into the system and run spectrum analyses, mapping changes in frequency and volume to rules that control a visual display. Because there are infinite numbers of ways to construct these rules, the appearance of these visualizers is virtually unlimited. Some of them are soothing, offering effects as subtle as drops of waters landing in a pool, while others can only be described as seizure-inducing, with wild psychedelic light shows emanating from every delta point. While some visualization plug-ins run in small or resizeable windows, others will optionally run full screen, which is perfect for use at parties, or late-night, low-light zombie sessions.

The screenshots shown in Figure 4-10 are of visualization plug-ins for WinAmp, but there are visualizers available for many different MP3 players, and for virtually all operating systems. These screenshots don't do justice to the experience of seeing these for yourself—you've just got to download a few and play with them. While all visualizers come with good default settings, most of them also include settings or preferences panels that let you customize the colors, responsiveness thresholds, and visualization forms. Dig around, turn the knobs, push the buttons, check and uncheck the checkboxes, and drag the sliders around. If you're a customize-a-holic, be prepared to set aside several hours of twiddle time.

Some visualization plug-ins are very CPU-intensive, and can have a noticeable effect on system performance. You probably won't want to run visualizers as a matter of course, reserving them for times when you're not trying to do other tasks in the background while listing to MP3 files. Not to mention the fact that many of these are wild enough to completely distract you from getting any real work done while they're running!

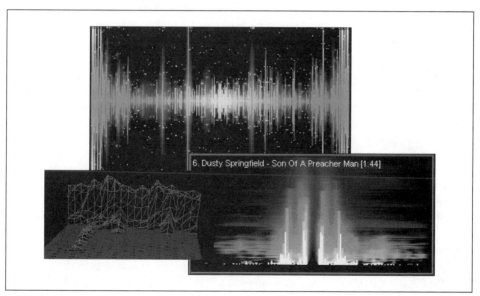

Figure 4-10. A few of the many visulization plug-ins available for WinAmp

General Plug-ins

The category "general" is really just a nice way of saying "miscellaneous," referring to plug-ins that do odd-jobs around the house. Did you know, for instance, that you can control WinAmp with a standard, $25 universal remote control? You'll need to purchase a separate infrared receiver to connect to your computer, and then install a corresponding IR plug-in to process the invisible signals it generates. This is the kind of connectivity that people are talking about when they refer to "convergence"—the computer becoming the center of the home infotainment system. See Ampapod (*www.v.nu/core/ampapod/*) or Irman (*www.evation.com/irman/*) for more information.

Other general plug-ins let you output your current playlist to an HTML file for use with SHOUTcast or icecast, some let you operate WinAmp controls from the Windows TaskBar tray, or even control WinAmp over a local area network (LAN).

Listening to MP3 Streams

MP3 files don't have to be downloaded to your hard drive, necessarily. In many cases, you'll be able to play them back in your favorite MP3 player directly from the server on which they're located. As you'll discover in Chapter 8, there are several ways in which MP3 webmasters can dish up files for "streaming." As an end user, you won't need to worry much about the particular streaming technique in use, though it's interesting to know the difference. In some cases, you may have to tweak a few settings in your browser or player to make sure streamed files are handled by your operating system properly.

Types of Streaming

There are two primary ways in which MP3 files can be streamed to users without being downloaded: MP3-on-demand and MP3 broadcast.

MP3-on-demand

In this form of streaming, control of the download is in the hands of the MP3 player, rather than the browser. Because this capability is built into most MP3 players, users can choose at any time to listen to an MP3 file directly from a web server, without saving it to their hard drives first. Of course, this assumes that the user has sufficient bandwidth to listen to the file in real time without it skipping or halting, but we'll get to bandwidth issues later. If you have a fast Internet connection, look around in your player's menus for an option labeled something like "Open Location" or "Play URL" and enter the URL of any MP3 file on the web. The easiest way to get this information is to right-click a link to an MP3 file in your browser and choose "Copy Link Location" from the context menu, then paste the URL into the Open Location dialog in your player.

In addition, MP3-on-demand can be forced by the webmaster, so that clicking a link normally will cause MP3 files to be pulled down by the player and played directly, rather than saved to hard drive as with a normal download. To do this, the webmaster creates an "M3U" (MPEG URL) playlist file, which is a plain text document containing the full URL to an MP3 file (or list of files) on a web server. Because the text file is tiny, the browser can download the M3U file to the user's hard drive nearly instantaneously. The web server sending the M3U file should (if it's configured correctly) dish it up with the MIME type *audio/x-mpegurl*. This MIME type should, in turn, be associated in the user's browser or operating system with a preferred MP3 player capable of handling MP3 streams.

Once the M3U file is downloaded, it's launched in the preferred MP3 player, which reads URLs out of the file and takes over control of the actual download.

Note the difference here: when you download an MP3 file normally, the browser itself handles the entire download, and users have to then launch the MP3 file in an MP3 player manually. The MP3 file is stored on the user's hard drive for future use. With MP3-on-demand, the MP3 player handles the download, not the browser. The MP3 player plays the file *as* it's being downloaded, not later on. And unlike a standard download, the MP3 file is not present on the user's system after they've finished listening to the track.

The advantages of using the MP3-on-demand technique are:

- The user does not have to wait for the download to complete before beginning to hear music.

- The user has more control over playback than with real streaming (e.g., the user can skip around between songs or fast-forward through songs at will).

- The webmaster has a degree of protection against MP3 files being stored permanently on the user's system.

- The publisher or webmaster does not have to set up any special MP3 serving software by having the MP3 player "suck" the file down. A plain vanilla web server running on any operating system is capable of serving up MP3-on-demand.

Because MP3-on-demand offers so much flexibility to both the webmaster and to the user, it may eventually become more popular than true MP3 streaming if and when all of us have lots of bandwidth. As long as our bandwidth is limited, however, true streaming solutions will continue to outweigh on-demand systems in popularity.

An important aspect of the MP3-on-demand technique is that it's "asynchronous," or outside of time. In other words, it doesn't matter what time of day the user accesses the file—he'll hear it from the beginning. This is very different from TV, radio, or MP3 broadcast, where you get whatever is being broadcast at the moment in time when you tune in to the channel. For this reason, the MP3-on-demand technique is also sometimes referred to as "pseudo-streaming."

A good example of MP3-on-demand can be found at MP3.com. Access any artist's page and access one of the Hi-Fi or Low-Fi links. Rather than being prompted for a download location, your favorite MP3 player will be launched and the file should start playing immediately.

See Chapter 8 to learn how to set up your server for MP3-on-demand.

MP3 broadcast

In contrast to pseudo-streaming, MP3 broadcasting (or real streaming), is "synchronous," and thus more akin to TV and radio broadcasting. In this case, the user tunes in to a channel or station which is playing an MP3-encoded bitstream much like a radio station, sometimes complete with live announcements and commercials. The person running the MP3 server is running the show in real time, and the listener only hears the portion of the show currently being dished up. When you tune in to an MP3 broadcast, you can't just pick an arbitrary tune from the show, any more than you can with radio.

Running an MP3 broadcast station is a fairly complicated matter, and you'll learn all about that in Chapter 8. As a user, however, listening to streamed MP3 is rarely more than a matter of point and click. To find MP3 broadcasts, check out sites such as *www.shoutcast.com*, *www.icecast.org*, *www.radiospy.com*, *www.mycaster.com*, *www.greenwitch.com*, or *www.live365.com* and you'll find dozens—or hundreds—of ongoing broadcasts. If your system is configured properly, clicking a link to a stream in progress will cause your MP3 player to be launched and (after a short delay) for that stream to begin playing. If it doesn't, see the following section, "Configuring Your System to Handle Streaming MP3."

 Real MP3 streams are usually sent as *.pls* files (MIME type `audio/x-scpls`), rather than *.M3U*. The difference between these two playlist types is described earlier in this chapter.

The advantages to real-time MP3 streaming are:

- Much greater control for the webcaster (voice, live mixing, etc.)

- Webmaster can send a stream to many people without needing tons of band-width on the playback machine (though they still need access to a server with a fast connection)

- Difficult for user to save MP3 bitstream to hard drive

- Optimization of bitstream for various client bandwidths

Of bandwidth and buffers

To receive MP3 streams from MP3 broadcasts or pseudo-streams, your player must be capable of managing downloads and buffering streams over the Internet on its own. The vast majority of popular MP3 players are stream-enabled—even many of the command-line players for Unix/Linux.

The biggest concern for most users, of course, is the speed of their Internet connections. If you're on a slow connection and the stream being served up (or pulled down) carries more bits per second than your modem is capable of delivering, you'll experience choppy, halting playback.

This can be mediated somewhat by two solutions. On the client (user) side, a process called *buffering* can be used. In the buffering process, the MP3 player grabs a good chunk of data before it begins to play, and continues to read ahead in the stream. The music being played is thus delayed by a few seconds. The slower the connection, of course, the larger the buffer required. Theoretically, one could utilize a buffer so large that the entire song was downloaded before a second of music was played. This would guarantee perfect playback over even the slowest connections, but would undermine the advantage of listening to streams.

Most users, however, require more modest buffer settings. If you find that your MP3 streams are skipping or pausing as they're played, dig around in your player's options and preferences for something like "Streaming Preferences." In WinAmp, tap Ctrl+P to bring up the preferences screen and navigate to Plugins → Input → NullSoft MPEG Audio Decoder. Click the Configure button and select the Streaming tab, where you'll find an array of buffering options. Most likely, you'll just want to change the numerical value for kilobytes of prebuffered audio (try increasing it by 25% or 50% for starters). You can also control how much of a track will be grabbed before a single byte is played.

On the server side, webmasters can do a number of things to make things easier for their modem-connected users, including downsampling MP3 files to lower frequencies, encoding files at lower bitrates, and sending mono, rather than stereo, streams over the Internet. All of these, of course, degrade sound quality, but are necessary to deliver acceptable streams to modem users. A sophisticated MP3 server will offer high-bandwidth and low-bandwidth options so users can select the best possible quality for their connection speed (such as the Hi-Fi and Low-Fi pseudo-streaming options found at MP3.com).

Technically speaking, on-demand servers are capable of doing some of the things that broadcast servers do, such as downsampling MP3 audio on the fly. For the technically inclined, this would be a matter of creating a CGI interface that would invoke a downsampling program when the user accesses a link on the server, and sending the output of that program to the user rather than the actual file. This is really a CGI implementation, rather than an MP3 issue. While there aren't many sites doing this currently, the technique would have certain advantages for some users, since it wouldn't require the installation and configuration of special broadcast software. More on this in Chapter 8.

Configuring Your System to Handle Streaming MP3

Regardless whether you're accessing real MP3 broadcasts or pseudo-streams, the ideal is to have your browser, your operating system, and your MP3 player all configured to interoperate correctly so that accessing a link to an MP3 player automatically results in the right thing happening—your player gets launched and begins to play the stream with no further intervention on your part. In most cases, simply installing an MP3 player capable of handling MP3 streams is all it takes to set things up properly, but it's possible for the necessary associations to become broken if you fiddle around with a lot of software or tweak your browser settings. In addition, you may at some point want a different player associated with MP3 streams.

The easiest way to create an appropriate association is to look in the options and preferences of the preferred player for something like "Make preferred for all types." Better players will let you establish associations on a per-filetype basis so that you can, for example, make Sonique your preferred MP3 player for regular MP3 files, and WinAmp the preferred player for streamed *.M3U* and *.pls* files.

If you have multiple MP3 players and browsers on your Windows system, the easiest way to establish associations may be to download the MP3Fix utility from *help.mp3.com/help/diagnosis/*. Although MP3Fix is packaged in a Windows InstallShield package, running it will not in fact install anything on your system. Rather, it will scour your system for known MP3 players and allow you to make one of them the preferred player for all browsers.

Netscape Navigator/Mozilla

> If Netscape Navigator is your primary browser, you can tell the program exactly how to handle any incoming MIME type (file type) by pulling down Edit → Preferences → Applications (this may be slightly different in various versions of Navigator). Scroll through the list of known file types for something like MPEG Audio File or WinAmp Media File and click the Edit button. To change the associated MP3 player, click the Browse... button and navigate to the location of your preferred MP3 player. If you don't find an entry in the list for the file type you want to associate, you can create a new one by clicking New Type... and filling in a description, file extension (e.g., MP3), a MIME type (e.g., *audio/x-mpeg*), and the path to an MP3 player.

Internet Explorer

> If you use Internet Explorer as your browser, remember that Explorer is integrated into Windows itself. Therefore, it does not use a separate MIME association database. Instead, it uses the operating system's FileTypes panel. To change an association manually, open Windows Explorer (not Internet Explorer) and pull down View → Folder Options → FileTypes. Navigate to the Playlist file type (which may be called, for instance, "WinAmp Playlist"), click Edit, and use the resulting dialog to change the description and program association. More details on this procedure can be found in the sidebar "Configuring the Default Handler for MP3 Files in Windows" in Chapter 3.

Performance Considerations

The average consumer machine of today is much more efficient than it was a few years ago, and most people have gobs of underutilized computing horsepower to spare. Nevertheless, there are still plenty of older machines hanging around out there, and owners of those machines will want to make sure they've got the most efficient decoder available. And, of course, true geeks will want access to the most efficient decoder whether they need it or not. Here are a few techniques you can use to determine the efficiency of your MP3 player. The same techniques apply to MP3 encoders, by the way.

Benchmarking Decoders

As mentioned in Chapter 2, MP3 decoders have a lot less work to do than encoders, since the task of MP3 playback is far less CPU-intensive than encoding. All the decoder has to know is how MP3 files are structured, and how to reconstruct a coherent signal from the combination of audio data and "side information" stored in the files' frames. In days of yore, when a Pentium 90 was considered top-of-the-line and most people were using 486-based computers, playing MP3 files was proportionally intensive enough to be cause for concern, and many experienced a significant impact on system responsiveness when MP3s were playing in the background.

However, modern CPUs have so much processor bandwidth to spare that decode speed isn't much of an issue for most users. For example, playing an MP3 stream on a Pentium 233 with the average decoder for Windows will generally consume only 5% of your processor speed.

If you're experiencing a noticeable performance impact when playing MP3 files, you might want to do a little benchmarking of your own. CPU/resource monitors are available for most operating systems, either as part of the system itself or as a separate download. A few of the more popular options are listed in this section. If you can't find a CPU monitoring app for your system that breaks up CPU usage by task (as opposed to giving you an overall rate), just note CPU consumption with and without your MP3 decoder running, then calculate the difference.

Once you've got a resource meter up and running, try several different MP3 players and take note of how many system resources (CPU and memory) they consume. Keep in mind, however, that even if a particular MP3 player consumes less resources than another, it may do so at the expense of sound quality or important features. You'll have to establish your own criteria for the compromises you're willing to make.

Windows 95/98

Windows 95/98 both ship with a resource meter bundled in the system. If *C:\ WINDOWS\SYSMON.EXE* is present on your system, you're all set. You may find a shortcut for Sysmon pre-installed in Start → Programs → Accessories → System Tools. If not, go to Control Panel → Add/Remove Programs → Windows Setup → Accessories and add it. Sysmon's default display shows the percentage of total CPU available being consumed by all currently running tasks, but does not tell you exactly how many resources are in use by each individual process. The large spikes in Figure 4-11 occurred when launching applications, and resulted in WinAmp skipping. The flat areas represent straight MP3 playback. Several other applications were open, but no work was being done. Sysmon reports approximately 15% processor consumption, but gives no indication of exactly how much of this is being consumed by MP3 playback. For a more specific breakdown or resource consumption, download Microsoft's "Kernel Toys," right-click *top.inf*, choose Install, then click Start → Run, and type *wintop*.

Popular third-party resource meters for Windows include L-Ement and sysmeter, both downloadable from *www.skinz.org*.

Windows NT

Windows NT 4.0 has a similar performance monitor built into the operating system. To access it, tap Ctrl+Alt+Del, click Task Manager, and select the Performance tab. Alternatively, use Start → Programs → Admin Tools → Performance Monitor.

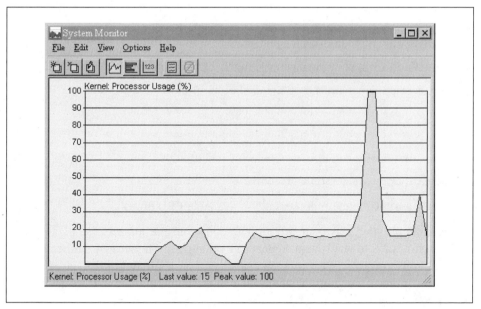

Figure 4-11. Using Sysmon to track CPU resource consumption as various tasks are performed

Mac OS

Search your favorite Mac software library for a utility called Process Watcher by Hugues Marty, which will allow you to view information on all currently running processes. However, Process Watcher will not show you a breakdown of CPU activity *per application*, so its ultimate usefulness is somewhat limited. You'll find a copy at *perso.magic.fr/suli/pw.html* if you want to check it out. Users may also want to experiment with Process Monitor or Process Spy, though this utility suffers the same limitation.

Linux

There are dozens of options for Linux users. Typing *top* at any prompt will give you a detailed overview of resource consumption, broken down by process. By default, top will update its report once per second, which may be too rapid to study properly. If you want a better view, use:

```
top -d 5
```

to have top update itself every five seconds. The problem with top is that it isn't always easy to figure out exactly how much CPU a given application is consuming, because many apps do their work in worker threads that may be difficult to identify. Fortunately, you can launch an app through the "time" utility. The operating system will calculate the total time the app was running and report the total number of seconds of processor time consumed in system space and in user space. From that, calculating the percentage of available CPU consumed by that app time's syntax is pretty simple:

```
time /path/to/mp3player /path/to/Song.mp3
```

As soon as mp3player finishes playing the song, close it and you'll get a report like this:

```
real  1m42.708s
user  0m9.427s
sys   0m1.769s
```

To calculate CPU usage, use this formula:

(user + sys)*100 / real = percentage of available CPU time

In this example, the player in question is consuming around 10.9% of available CPU resources. Note that these figure will be slightly off because launching the app will consume extra CPU time, but it gives you a pretty good idea of what's going on. There are dozens of alternative resource monitors available for Linux. Search your favorite software archive for GUI resource meters such as xosview.

BeOS

In addition to the Pulse application built into the system (which shows CPU load indicators for each detected processor), there are quite a few third-party tools available, downloadable from *www.be.com/beware/*, such as the graphical process controllers TManager and ProcessWatcher. The "top" and "time" utilities described for Linux are also available for BeOS, and function identically.

System Requirements

A few MP3-related hardware issues were covered in Chapter 2. To summarize and put it all in one place, here are the most important things you need to consider when contemplating hardware upgrades for your MP3 playback machine.

CPU speed

While you can theoretically use a 486 for MP3 playback, the experience is likely to be painful, as even the comparatively low-resource act of decoding MP3 is going to consume a good deal of horsepower that you'll probably want to give to the operating system itself. Trouble-free MP3 playback really demands a Pentium-class computer or better, where processor consumption may be around 5–10%, rather than 50–75%. Mac users, similar deal: Anything slower than a PowerMac or Power-Mac clone is going to give you problems with MP3 playback, if you can even find an MP3 player that works on your machine at all.

Encoding is another matter altogether. Because encoding requires so much math, you'll be happiest with the fastest machine you can get your hands on. While fast encoders running on a modern Pentium can encode a song faster than it would take to play it back, you'll hear absolute horror stories from users who try to do their encoding on an antique machine. An old 386, for example, may take 12 hours or more to encode a single 3-minute song.

Memory

MP3 encoders and players aren't huge memory hogs, but they do require more memory than, say, a simple text editor. The process of encoding will benefit more from extra RAM than will playback, but unless you already feel your memory subsystem could use a shot in the arm, don't go running out to buy more memory just to improve the MP3 experience. At the most, getting into MP3 probably means you'll be running one additional application in the background most of the time, and a relatively lightweight application at that.

Sound cards and speakers

Again, this is a critical area. Most people have traditionally thought of their sound cards as a vehicle for games, or for listening to streamed news broadcasts. But as you get more involved in MP3, you'll start to think of your computer as a cousin of your home stereo in some ways, and will want to get the best quality you can. Do some research online to find out what the audiophiles are recommending this month as the best-sounding card at an affordable price. In the sub-$100 range, top cards from CreativeLabs and Yamaha were among the most popular cards among MP3 buffs at this writing.

Chances are, the speakers that came with your computer aren't of the best quality. Again, look around online for recommendations. Get yourself a nice set of powered subwoofer/satellites, connect them to your new sound card, and be prepared to be blown away by the difference they make over the default audio hardware that probably shipped with your computer, as shown in Figure 4-12. Because the system has a built-in amplifier and runs on standard wall power, you don't need to rely on the amplifier built into your sound card. If you're going speaker shopping for your computer, you'll get better results by going to an audio store and telling them you want speakers for use with your computer than by going to a computer store and telling them you want high-quality computer speakers.

Of course, you can always route audio signal from your computer directly to your home stereo by purchasing a length of RCA cables and a simple adapter. See Chapter 6, *Hardware, Portables, Home Stereos, and Kits* for details.

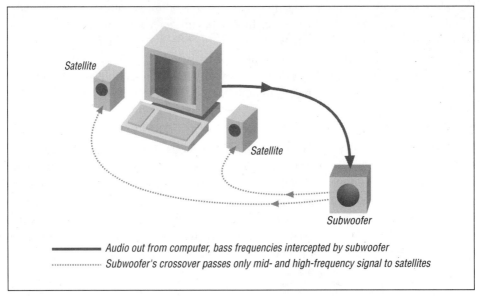

Figure 4-12. Mid-range and high frequencies are handled by satellite speakers

Disk speed and space

People sometimes wonder whether their hard drive is fast enough for good MP3 playback, or contemplate going with a high-end SCSI adapter/disk to optimize their systems for MP3 use. For the most part, this is piffle. At the default bitrate of 128kbps, a mere 16 K is being scooped from disk every second—even the lowly floppy drive can keep up with that. All of the work is going on in the CPU. The fact that MP3s are so highly compressed not only means you save on disk space, but that the hard drive has to do very little work.

However, there are some caveats to this point. If your all-IDE system has more than one hard drive and one CD-ROM drive, you'll end up putting two devices on a single channel with IDE. But IDE, unlike SCSI, cannot transfer data back and forth between two devices on the same bus or channel simultaneously—IDE accesses are serial. Therefore, you can end up with your MP3 player requesting data from a storage volume while the operating system is requesting data from the boot volume simultaneously, which can potentially lead to skips or pops in the audio stream. But IDE disks are so much more affordable than SCSI that most users in this position will simply have to deal with it. If you need to run several IDE devices and want to ensure optimum performance, you might want to consider purchasing inexpensive IDE controller cards for the additional drives, so that each one gets a channel all to itself.

Note also that IDE disks are more CPU-intensive than SCSI disks, which can have an impact on low-performance systems. If you have UDMA IDE drives, make sure they're running in UDMA mode to lessen the processing impact on the CPU.

Once you start on the task of encoding your entire collection, or downloading lots of tracks from the Internet, you'll likely find disk space being chewed up faster than you ever dreamed possible. Suddenly those 30 GB drives on sale down at the local computer superstore don't seem obscenely huge after all. Of course, it won't be long before you're looking for some kind of external storage solution, and most people start burning data CDs full of MP3 files to deal with the space issue. See Chapter 5 for more on that.

When playing MP3 files from CD rather than from your hard drive, you may experience skipping, or "halting" playback, especially if you're using an older or cheapo CD-ROM drive. This is probably not happening because the CD-ROM drive isn't fast enough, but because it isn't accurate enough and has to do a lot of error correction to grab data accurately. You may be able to correct for this by increasing the "buffer" or "preload" size in your MP3 player. Dig around in the options and look for a control that will let you establish the size of the "preload" or "buffer" size, and turn it up until the problem goes away. By doing this, you're telling your MP3 player to read data from disk in larger "gulps," which gives the drive more time to retrieve data from CD successfully before the amount of music stored in RAM is exhausted.

Sound/video card interactions

One of the most frequently encountered hardware-related problems users find is that even very fast machines can "skip" or "pop" MP3s when switching tasks, scrolling windows, or doing other things that require a lot of screen redraw. This typically occurs for users with PCI graphics cards, because some card manufacturers have attempted to increase card performance by letting video cards take control of the entire PCI bus when necessary, which can prevent an even stream of audio data from reaching a PCI sound card at an adequate rate. Many people have noted that this does not occur with AGP graphics cards or ISA sound cards (since they're on a separate bus), which you may want to keep in mind when shopping for new hardware. If your audio and video cards are both on the same bus, you may be able to tweak some of the video card's driver or BIOS settings to disable or lessen this effect, though possibly at the expense of some graphics performance.

5

Ripping and Encoding: Creating MP3 Files

Sure there's tons of free music available on the Internet. But are you able to find the music you're actually looking for? Chances are that the music you seek is out there somewhere, but servers go up and down every day, and you'll quickly discover that the MP3 search engines don't always deliver the goods. When you do find the track you're looking for, you may find that it's poorly encoded. Most of the time, you won't even know what bitrate has been used in the encoding until you've already got the file in question on your hard drive. And, of course, there's the fact that most MP3s available for download are pirated, which means many users end up depriving the artists they respect out of income to which they're entitled.

There's one meta-solution to all of this: Spend your energy on encoding your own CD/LP/DAT/8-track collection, rather than trying to download someone else's. If you don't redistribute the files you encode, you won't run afoul of legal hassles, you'll have complete control over quality issues, and you won't have to wait for lengthy downloads. Of course, if you're an artist, you'll also want to know how to create MP3s from your own original music.

General Encoding Principles

Creating MP3 files is generally a two-step process: Extract your audio from the original source medium into an uncompressed format stored on your hard drive, then run that uncompressed audio through an MP3 encoder. However, many tools exist to help you rip and encode through a single interface, in a single pass. Before taking a look at the tools and processes, you may want to read these notes and suggestions on ripping and encoding principles.

Achieving Optimum Quality

As described in Chapter 2, *How MP3 Works: Inside the Codec*, MP3 is a "lossy" compression format, meaning that some audio information is discarded in exchange for smaller file sizes. The big question you have to face when encoding your own MP3 files is *how much* information do you want to discard. The more you throw away, the worse your files will sound and the smaller your MP3 files will be. The more you keep, the better they'll sound and the larger the resulting files will be. Only you can decide where on this spectrum you want to sit, but again, always remember that your computer may not be the only place where you play your MP3 files. Next year you may purchase an MP3 playback component for your home stereo, a better sound card, or better computer speakers. All of a sudden, you may discover that the MP3 files you once thought sounded just fine don't sound so hot after all. Always aim for a threshold higher than your current tolerances, and remember that disk space and blank CDs just keep on getting cheaper. Unless you'll be listening to MP3s in a noisy environment such as a car, or will be dealing with limited storage space (as you might with a portable MP3 player), you can probably afford the larger file sizes incurred by going with a higher bitrate. I recommend setting 128 kbps or approximately 50% VBR (VBR is explained later in this chapter) as your lower threshold, and going for 160 kbps, 192 kbps, or higher if you're serious about this stuff. Music with a lot of smooth, or synthesized tones (such as techno) will far better at lower bitrates. Note, however, that no matter how high you set the bitrate, Garth Brooks will still suck lemons.

 Remember: Quality can always be reduced later from the original source material, but it's extremely difficult to significantly improve on the quality of an existing recording. At this writing, encoded MP3 files cannot be altered at all without decoding to WAV and then back to MP3. However, even though it's a very difficult task, never say never—this may become possible in the future. In any case, "Garbage In, Garbage Out" (GIGO) has been the motto of programmers for decades, and it applies very well to recording and encoding considerations as well. Think of it as if you were cutting your hair—you can always chop more off later, but if you cut too much, you have to suffer the consequences.

Pre-encoding optimizations

So what can you do prior to encoding to optimize the quality of the final results? The answer to this relies on the fact that encoding is always a two-step process. First the source signal is transferred into an uncompressed file format such as WAV or AIFF, and then that uncompressed file is encoded to MP3. Even if you use "all-in-one" software such as MusicMatch Jukebox (covered later in this chapter), that software still has to take this intermediate step, even if it's transparent to the user. So... while your audio is still in this raw, uncompressed, and highly editable state, you can open it in a sound editing/mastering tool of your choice and perform any necessary equalization, de-hissing, de-popping, and de-scratching. You can cut the silent bits off the beginning and end of your files, add effects, alter the levels, and more. There are many such tools available for various operating systems, and you should be able to find them at your favorite software library.

 Technically speaking, you can *only* perform these sorts of functions on uncompressed audio, not on MP3. However, there are increasing numbers of tools that will appear to let you work directly on MP3 audio, such as CoolEdit 2000 (*www.syntrillium.com/cooledit/*) or GoldWave (*www.goldwave.com*). However, these tools are actually decoding MP3 to PCM audio behind the scenes, and then recompressing when finished, so they're not actually editing MP3, even if they make it seem like they are. If you want to edit an existing MP3 file, your only option is to decode it to WAV or AIFF (this chapter), run your voodoo on it, and then re-encode it. However, this process of going back and forth between formats will probably degrade the file's quality enough to outweigh any gains you might achieve. Your best bet is usually to re-encode the original source material.

While the possibility of "re-mastering" your original source material is always there whether it was originally stored on CD, LP, cassette, etc., you'll probably find that this option is really only interesting/useful when trying to clean up old or damaged non-CD material that you simply can't get into MP3 format any other way.

You may also find dedicated audio-editing tools useful for creating "unusual" MP3s. For example, you may want to create an audio collage out of snippets of sound sources, or create psychedelicized versions of your favorite songs by running flange, echo, reverb, and reversal effects on them in an audio editor. Save the results of your auditory mangulations back to WAV format and encode them to MP3 just as you would any other track. Popular sound editing tools include CoolEdit Pro and SoundForge for Windows, Deck or Peak for the Macintosh, XWave for Linux, and Pebbles or 3dsound for BeOS.

 A true audiophile will recommend not preprocessing prior to encoding, reason being that encoding directly from the source material will give you the most neutral signal possible—you can always alter the signal somewhat with your MP3 player's built-in equalizer later on. However, this admonishment doesn't take into account situations where you just want to remove blank space from the beginning or end of a file, mix your signal with other sources, or do other things you can't easily do after the fact with an MP3 file.

Samplerates

The quality of uncompressed audio is in large part determined by its *samplerate*. This is a measure of how many times per second the audio signal is digitally represented in the final stream (whether it be "live" or stored on disk), and is typically described in Kilohertz. A samplerate of 22kHz means that "slices" of the audio stream are represented 22,000 times per second. As with bitrates, the higher the samplerate, the better the quality and the larger the resulting file.

All consumer compact disks are sampled at a rate of 44.1kHz, 16 bit (16 bit meaning there are 65,536 possible values—i.e., 2^16—for each sample), and you're well-familiar with compact disk audio quality. However, the next generation of digital audio hardware, particularly in the high-end and professional audio recording space, will be built to handle 24-bit audio at 96kHz, more than doubling the number of samples per second and greatly increasing the number of possible values for each bit. The result will be much higher fidelity and much less of the "cold," "brittle," "mechanical," or "grainy" effect that audiophiles typically associate with CD audio. Utilizing this higher samplerate on your home computer will require both a 96kHz-capable sound card and upgraded software that can handle the higher data throughput. Note, however, that MP3 can't handle anything higher than 48kHz; if that's your bag, you'll have to turn to a codec like AAC or MPEG-4.

For detailed comparative analyses between MP3, RealAudio, and MS Audio encodings, see *david.weekly.org/audio/*.

For most MP3 users, that's neither here nor there. More likely is the possibility that you'll want to *decrease* samplerates prior to encoding. You might want much smaller file sizes at the expense of fidelity when working with the spoken word—for encoding class lectures, for example. Even more likely is that you'll want to start running a SHOUTcast or icecast server, streaming MP3 audio from your home computer to the Internet at large. In streaming situations, decreasing the samplerate of your outgoing signal is the easiest way to decrease the bandwidth necessary for listeners to hear your broadcast without skipping and without huge buffers.

Lower samplerates are, by the way, the main reason why streamed MP3 typically sounds worse than standard MP3 downloads, though broadcasters will often decrease both the samplerate *and* the bitrate. Lowering the samplerate results in less resolution, while lowering the bitrate results in poorer dynamics.

Samplerates can be controlled in two ways. You can open your uncompressed audio files in any audio editing software prior to encoding, downsample it to a lower rate (see your audio editor's documentation), and then encode. If you're broadcasting MP3 streams from your machine, you can tell SHOUTcast or icecast to downsample your existing MP3 files "on-the-fly." More on that in Chapter 8, *Webcasting and Servers: Internet Distribution.*

Speed vs. Quality

It's hard to imagine another area in the software industry where similar applications differ so radically in terms of performance. While encoders may all share the same basic functionality, the degree to which the underlying source code has been optimized for speed differs *radically* from one encoder to the next. To throw yourself for a loop, rip a WAV file from your favorite CD, then download as many encoders as you can find for your platform. Use each encoder in turn to compress the WAV file, using identical encoding options if possible, and carefully time the process in each case. You'll be amazed to find that some encoders are as much as ten times faster or slower than others.

The reason for the disparity is simple: Some developers and vendors feel that encoding speed is of the utmost importance when it comes to pleasing the general public and in making the MP3 phenomenon viable. Thus, you'll find that some of the big commercial MP3 encoders, such as MusicMatch Jukebox and Real-JukeBox are able to encode faster than real time (e.g., a 3-minute song may be encoded in 90 seconds). Meanwhile, some freeware encoders, such as BladeEnc, may require 25 minutes to encode the same song.

 Again, speed and quality may or may not be directly related. For example, early tests of the LAME patches against the ISO sources showed that it was capable of producing bit-by-bit identical output to that of BladeEnc, but 2.5x faster.

As you might guess, not all of the speed delta is achieved through simple optimization of source code and by taking advantage of floating-point CPU extensions—some of it comes from *cheating*—discarding frequencies that the developers felt just weren't as important (although this only shaves one-twentieth of a second from encoding time, and doesn't affect the quality of encodings at 128 KB or lower). Purists may prefer to stick to brass tacks and wring every possible drop of quality from their encodings, but in most cases, you can great results with fast encoders—don't automatically assume that fast means bad. If you do decide to work with a slower encoder for whatever reason, you can always let your encoding process chug along merrily in the background as you work, or to set up batch encoding jobs to crunch as you sleep.

While not 100% applicable, the general rule of thumb is that the encoders you pay for, especially those from large companies, are based on either Xing or the later versions of the Fraunhofer coder MP3ENC, which at this writing were the fastest in the biz. While some freeware encoders may be faster than others, few can begin to approach the speed of these two, with the Fraunhofer coder edging out Xing in most tests, both on speed and on quality. In fact, after a long period of dominance, some major vendors (such as MusicMatch) were beginning to shift away from Xing in favor of Fraunhofer. Note also that many speed advantages come from MMX processor optimizations.

Because MP3 encoding is so math-intensive, PowerMac users may enjoy faster encoding speeds than x86 users. In fact, a PowerMac G4 with a fast, DAE-accurate CD-ROM drive (see the "Notes on manual track separation" section later in this chapter), is the fastest ripping/encoding solution available to consumers at this writing. G4 users have reported being able to rip and encode tracks up to ten times faster than the playback speed of the track in question. Current advances in x86 technology—such as the AMD Athlon processor and Intel's Merced architecture—should even the score here. But remember: it's not all about raw processor speed; the real question is how well-optimized the CPU and the encoding software are at handling floating point and FFT functions. x86 encoders such as GOGO (covered later in this chapter) do an exceptional job at taking full advantage of special processor instructions such MMX, SSE, and 3DNow!, and at working with multiple processors if present.

Normalization

One bugaboo that often crops up when creating mixed song collections is the fact that the original source materials are all recorded at slightly different levels, leaving you with MP3 files of varying volumes. This isn't much of an issue when playing entire albums, but can get annoying with mixed collections and random playlists. The solution is to use a *normalizer*, which will boost the overall signal of weakly recorded tracks and diminish levels for loud ones. See the "Plug-ins: Extending Your Reach" section in Chapter 4, *Playlists, Tags, and Skins: MP3 Options*, to learn about the AudioStocker normalizing plug-in for WinAmp. Many encoding applications also have normalization functions built in, as do some CD burning applications; see your encoder's or burner's documentation for details.

Most normalizers let you control the "threshold" of normalization. If you normalize at 100%, all tracks will have the same average volume, whereas 95% normalization will allow for some distinction to be made between loud and soft tracks, which is probably what you want in most cases.

Normalizing downward (decreasing the volume) can degrade the sound quality of both PCM and MP3 audio because of the linear distribution of sample levels. Not a ton—but enough to be noticeable to some people. You may want to do your normalization in your MP3 player rather than at encode time, so you judge for yourself whether quality has been audibly degraded, and not have to re-encode your files if it turns out you don't like the results. If you normalize during the encoding process, those files will be normalized forever. If you normalize at playback time, you can always make adjustments in the equalizer or volume controls to accommodate different listening environments. However, some people feel there are more advantages to normalizing at encode time, because you only have to do it once, and you won't be consuming extra processor cycles with every playback. Go with the solution that works best for you.

The Venerable CDDB

Surprisingly enough, compact disks do not include a simple table of contents listing the names of the tracks they contain.* As a result, ripping and encoding tools have no easy way to give your extracted files reasonable file names. By default, ripped tracks will end up with names like *Track01.wav*, *Track02.wav*, and so on.

However, it *is* possible to extract a unique identifying string (called a CDDB-ID) from any audio CD by summing the lengths of the tracks on a disc and running a quick mathematical algorithm on it to generate a unique identifying number. The chances of this ID number for any two audio CDs being identical are very small.

 Conversely, it is not always the case that there is only one unique CDDB-ID for a given *album*. Because pressing plants may press different batches of the same album with different techniques in different months, and because of variants in promotional CDs and remastered versions of original albums, the same artist/album can potentially generate multiple valid CDDB-IDs. Some encoding tools will even show you the results of an ambiguous lookup if they encounter a disc they can't be sure about.

Thanks to this capability, one of the Internet's great collaborative efforts has arisen: The *Compact Disk Database*, or CDDB (*www.cddb.com*), is populated by normal

---

* Although they do contain a "reference table" that allows CD players to discover the byte offsets where tracks begin. In addition, the CD spec actually does allow for a text listing of audio tracks, though it has seldom been used by the industry. Sony now takes advantage of this capability, under the name "cd-text." Others may follow.

users with the track listings of just about every CD ever made (only the most obscure recordings have not been logged—see if you can stump it!). While you can search for track listings directly at the CDDB web site, the primary use of the database is as a back-end to supporting CD players and ripper/encoder tools, as shown in Figure 5-1.

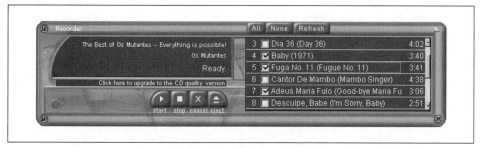

Figure 5-1. MusicMatch JukeBox uses the CDDB to extract CD-specific information

Any ripping/encoding tool can extract a CD's unique identifier string, look it up in the online CDDB, and return a plain-text table of contents, including artist name, album name, and track listing. It can then use this table of contents to give your ripped or encoded tracks reasonable file names, or even output files to directories and subdirectories named for the artist and album. In addition, this data can be used to embed meaningful ID3 tags in your files as they're being encoded, so you don't have to do it manually later on. Note that ID3 tag creation isn't always enabled by default. Look around in your encoder's settings panels for an ID3 options checkbox.

Of course, taking advantage of the CDDB requires online access, at least as the ripping session begins. But even if you don't enjoy a permanent Internet connection, rippers and encoders that know how to speak CDDB will save you tons of file-renaming time, and it's worth the effort to make the connection. Most operating systems also maintain a database of audio CDs that have already been looked up, so the next time you insert the same CD you won't have to run the lookup procedure again. Most of the tools covered in this chapter support CDDB connections, or interface with other tools that do.

If you're using ID3v2 tags and are looking for lyrics to associate with your tracks, there's no better place to search than the International Lyrics Server, at *www.lyrics. ch*. However, legal actions taken in 1999 forced the site to put all lyrics into Java applets, which prevents users from simply copying and pasting them into other applications. You'll have to manually type the lyrics into your ID3v2 tagger.

Alternatives to the CDDB

Escient, who owns and maintains the CDDB, imposes certain requirements on developers of applications who make use of their database. For example, their license requires that such applications display the CDDB logo, and that those applications do not make use of any competing database. Some developers—especially those in the Open Source community—feel that these requirements are unfair and overly restrictive. What, for example, would this mean for the developer of a command-line-only CDDB lookup tool which can't display the logo by definition, or for a CDDB-savvy filesystem, such as the one built into BeOS?

In response, a couple of alternatives to CDDB have arisen, without these restrictions. You may find some tools configured to point to freedb (*www.freedb.org*), rather than CDDB by default, and you can of course edit your encoder's preferences to point to freedb instead. Another alternative, cdindex (*www.cdindex.org*) intends to offer a superior technique for identifying CDs, fuzzy lookups, and instant web-based submission of new albums. The only disadvantage to these alternatives is that their databases are smaller, so you may not get successful lookups on some more obscure CDs. Since most encoders will let you select multiple databases to check, you can tell your tool to look at freedb or cdindex first, and then to look at CDDB only if the CD isn't found.

Other Encoding Options

While all encoders include some tool, widget, picklist, or command-line flag to let you select the bitrate at which your files should be encoded, bitrate selection is where the similarity ends in terms of available options. While it would be impossible to catalog all of the encoding options made available by all available encoders, here are descriptions of the most commonly found encoding options. If you don't find these options in your encoder's interface or described in the documentation, it may be time to look for another encoder (assuming these options are important to you).

As a general rule, you'll probably find that some or most of these options are absent from the majority of encoders aimed at the general public, while the more arcane options are often found in command-line and less-popular encoders. More options means more complexity and possibly a more intimidating interface. To be perfectly frank, however, most of the more unusual encoding options are simply not useful to most of us most of the time. If all you want to do is encode your collection with reasonable quality and a minimum of fuss, you'll probably never need to think about most of these possibilities. If your encoder's interface does have these options, the chances are they'll already be set to reasonable defaults, and you can leave them alone.

MPEG-1 vs. MPEG-2

Some encoders may let you choose between the various MPEG classes, as described in Chapter 1, *The Nuts and Bolts of MP3*. When creating MP3 files, you always want to make sure this is set to MPEG-1.

Layer

Some encoders are capable of creating Layer I, II, or III files. Unless you're encoding audio that's destined to be embedded in an MPEG movie or want to create MP2 files for any other reason, you want to make sure this is always set to Layer III. Since Layer III is the most complex, this setting will always take the longest, but you can't make MP3s without it.

Stereo/Joint Stereo/Dual-channel/Mono

You'll probably encounter few occasions where you'll actually want to create monophonic MP3s, unless you're encoding the spoken word or preparing your files for Internet broadcast and want to save on file size. For most purposes, leave this set to stereo. Remember that a 128 kbps MP3 file actually stores left and right channels separately, allocating proportions of the data dynamically to account for the needs of the respective channels (one may be dynamic while the other grows quiet, resulting in a 65%/35% split, for example). You can enable joint-stereo if you want to save a little space by storing high frequencies monophonically (since very high frequencies are difficult to locate in space), but this capability only goes into effect when the "intensity stereo" option is enabled… which, by the way, destroys phase information and makes the file unsuitable for some applications. The M/S (middle/side) option is not subject to the same limitations as intensity stereo.

Dual-channel was designed to allow for transmission of independent content in either channel—for example, you might want to put an English track in one channel and a Japanese track in the other. Of course, this means that each channel will be restricted to half the bitrate it would otherwise get, so quality will be degraded.

In general, you'll find that joint stereo encoding options work better at lower bitrates.

Psycho 1/Psycho 2

If this option is present (and you'll only find this in ISO-based encoders), you may be able to toggle between two different psychoacoustic models in order to optimize your encoding for various types of music. Psycho 1 is available only when encoding Layers I and II, while Psycho 2 works with Layer III, and is a more complex algorithm, delivering better quality at the expense of slower encoding.

Emphasis/De-emphasis

This option is only useful for files that have been run through a noise-reduction processes in an audio-editing application prior to encoding. If enabled, you can choose between two modes: *50/15 microseconds* or *ccit j.17.* Enabling these options does not trigger a change in the encoding, but merely sets a flag in the MP3 file which can be read back by the MP3 decoder so that corresponding noise reduction can be undertaken by the decoder.

Private/Protection/Copyright/Original

These options set corresponding bits in the MP3 header frame, and do not affect audio signal. They may be used by specific MP3 players to display ownership attributes of the file. Very few MP3 players read or display these bits, and the MP3 world basically ignores them. This kind of data becomes much more important in "secure" formats such as those proposed by SDMI, but not in straight MP3. Artists encoding their own music who want some measure of ownership stated in the file will probably want to set these bits, but note that simply enabling these options will not automatically make your file secure— you'll still need to adopt a complete security system for that, and straight MP3 probably won't be it—you'll probably want to look instead towards Liquid Audio, Windows Media, or any of the other secure formats discussed in Chapter 9, *Competing Codecs and Other File Formats.*

 It is possible that the additional meta-data storage area offered by ID3v2 may allow for true security mechanisms to be built into straight MP3 files. While no such implementations were available at this writing, this book strongly recommends investigating the possibility. Avoiding proprietary formats such as Windows Media will help to keep digital music distribution a fair and open game, accessible to users of any player and any operating system. Supporting open formats helps keep any one company from becoming "landlord" over digital music distribution. Fighting MP3 piracy may also help artists and labels from being cautious of utilizing the format.

VBR

As described in Chapter 2, increasing numbers of encoders and decoders support "variable bit rate," or VBR encoding techniques. These allow denser musical passages to use a higher bitrate (and hence more disk space) and sparser passages to use a lower bitrate. This allows for a maximum storage space/quality ratio. VBR thresholds are adjustable not in specific bitrates, but are specified as percentages. The downsides to VBR are that not all MP3 players support VBR-encoded files (though most do), and that you really need to do a lot of careful listening tests to the get the most out of the option. Different types of music respond differently to different VBR thresholds.

Finding the Best Encoder

At the rate the MP3 industry moves, any recommendations on specific encoders would surely become outdated in six months. Nevertheless, almost all encoders are originally based either on the Fraunhofer or the ISO source code bases. Because Fraunhofer has always looked to MP3 as an "Internet radio" solution, their codec is optimized for lower bitrates (at or below 128 kbps). When encoding at 160 kbps or higher, look instead to encoders based on the ISO sources (such as BladeEnc or LAME). Encoders based on the Xing or later Fraunhofer codecs will generally be five to seven times faster than either of these, but Xing suffers some when it comes to the nuances and details because it works in long "blocks" and therefore has trouble with some transient signals.

Didn't Fraunhofer put together the ISO reference sources? If so, why are we discussing them here as separate entities? The reason they are treated separately is because Fraunhofer publishes an encoder under its own umbrella that is separate from the original reference sources. Later versions of the Fraunhofer encoder are better optimized for both quality and speed. Technically speaking, all encoders available are descendants of the original ISO source code, though many (if not most) have evolved along divergent paths as their developers worked on independent and often proprietary optimizations.

You'll see a lot of talk out there about the supposedly poor quality of Xing-based encoders, because Xing established an early reputation for getting high encoding speeds by cutting corners at higher frequencies. You should know, however, that more recent versions of the Xing encoder do not cut as many corners, and most people find their quality quite good. Only the most extreme audiophiles still shy away from Xing encoders, while many former critics of Xing have seen the light and been converted by later editions of the Xing encoder, which works all the way up to 20kHz. Many real sticklers and purists still swear by BladeEnc as offering the absolute highest quality, but its reputation is fading as the later Fraunhofer encoder soaks up more attention, and the development pace of the LAME encoder continues to improve both its quality and its speed.

 If you're using a command-line version of the Xing encoder, you can force it to use the old 16kHz cut-off by adding the –N switch to your command.

You'll see the "What's the best encoder?" question asked frequently on MP3 mailing lists and Usenet groups, and will probably be asking yourself the same question before long. Unfortunately, there is no simple answer to this question, and every time the question comes up, you'll see a dozen different people offering a dozen different answers. You need to evaluate your own needs and priorities, try a bunch of them, determine whether you can hear the differences in the quality of their output, and decide whether speed, quality, or convenience is the most important factor.

Improving the Quality of Existing MP3s

Once you start playing with an audio editing tool, you may get inspired to start tweaking on some of your existing MP3 files. Before you get too excited, be prepared for disappointment; no audio editor under the sun will let you change the sound of an existing MP3 file. It just doesn't work that way. The complex algorithms involved in compressing and decompressing audio to MP3 and back make live MP3 editing impossible. In addition, the "bit reservoir" aspect of the MP3 spec means that each frame may depend on knowing something about the frame that comes before and after itself; if you start cutting up MP3 files, you're going to end up with audible glitches at every edit point (this limitation does not apply to MPEG Layer II, since it doesn't use the bit reservoir). Your only option is to decode your MP3 tracks to WAV or AIFF, edit those, and then re-encode them. Again, going back and forth like this is going to result in an overall degradation of quality, and you'll probably find it isn't worth the bother.

Your best bet when dealing with MP3s of poor quality is to do what you can with your MP3 player's built-in equalizer. In other words, make adjustments in the way your computer handles the output stream, rather than trying to change the MP3 file itself. Of course, that will only get you so far, and won't help to eliminate that "hollow" or "swishy" sound you get with some badly encoded files. If at all possible, just re-encode the file again from the original source.

While you can't edit the actual audio signal stored in an MP3 file, you may be able to cut a few seconds from the beginning or end of a file that starts or ends with "dead air" or other unwanted audio cruft. At this writing, only a couple of tools were known to be capable of this. MP3Trim and MP3 Cutter are both capable of very simple edits to MP3 files (Windows only). Linux and BeOS users may be able to use a tool called mp3asm to clean up "broken" MP3 files, finding and discarding illegal header frames, and even assembling multiple MP3 files into a single new one.

Again, the best solution is usually to just go back and re-encode the file. Use a better ripper, clean it up with aftermarket audio manipulation tools while it's still in WAV, RAW, or AIFF format, and re-encode it. Really and truly, this is the only way to guarantee high quality.

General Ripping Principles

Before you can encode a single bit, you've got to get the music you intend to compress into your computer. This may be accomplished by piping the signal directly into your machine through your sound card's Line In jack (either from a mixing board or from home stereo components) or by extracting tracks from compact discs by way of your machine's CD-ROM drive in a process known as "ripping."

Ripping from Compact Discs

When you insert an audio CD into your machine's CD tray, then try to view its contents through your file manager (such as Explorer), you'll notice that all you see is a collection of 1 KB tracks labeled "Track1.CDA," "Track2.CDA," and so on. Drag one of these tracks to another location, and you'll find that you haven't copied that track's audio data to your system at all. This is because CDA (Compact Disc Audio) tracks aren't actually audio tracks—they're just "handles" that tell the operating system where on the CD to find the actual audio bits. Technically speaking, what you see when you view a folder full of CDA files is the CD's "table of contents," which tells the CD player at which byte offsets to find corresponding PCM data on the disk. By default, most operating system's file managers will only give you access to CDA handles and not to actual audio data, so you need to find a way around the situation if you want to encode those tracks.

You could take the long, cumbersome route and play the audio CDs through your machine's CD player application, then record the sound stream to disc as it plays, but that would grow very tiresome very fast and degrade quality, since the audio stream would be passing through a superfluous set of digital-to-analog and analog-to-digital conversion routines.* The real solution is to use "ripping" software, which is specially designed to read CDA files, find their associated audio data on the CD, and transfer that data to your hard drive as an uncompressed WAV, AIFF, or RAWS file. In other words, rippers let you get around the barriers the operating system throws up in your face, and gives you direct access to the actual audio data living on the CD. There are exceptions to this, as you'll see later on in the chapter.

Don't, however, let this mislead you into thinking that CDs store audio data in WAV format—they don't. They actually store it in a format called *pulse-code modulation*, or PCM. However, PCM, WAV, and AIFF are all slight variants of the same thing: raw, uncompressed, unfiltered audio data.† All of these formats are essentially the same, and none sound any better or worse than the others; they just

---

* This is how most people ripped audio from CD before DAE-compatible CD-ROM drives became popular.

† Technically, the WAV format can support compressed audio—even MP3 audio—but that's an entirely different story. For all practical intents and purposes, WAV audio is uncompressed audio.

wear slightly different hats (technically, they sport different file headers) and are preferred on different operating systems for historical reasons.

There are literally hundreds of ripping tools and solutions available, covering every operating system under the sun, and they take on dozens of different guises. Some work from the command line, some offer nice graphical interfaces. Some serve multiple purposes, and also let you copy entire data (as well as audio) CDs. Some are capable of encoding to MP3 *as* they're ripping. Some are freeware, others will cost you. Nevertheless, the principles behind all of them are the same, and their usage is generally pretty intuitive. We'll look at some of the most popular ripping solutions for various platforms in the next section. Note, as always, that these are just *examples*—not necessarily recommendations. Check your favorite software library or search engine for other rippers, experiment, and stick with the one that serves your needs.

Notes on digital audio extraction

Ripping audio tracks from CDs is not just a matter of having the right software— your CD-ROM drive must also be capable of *digital audio extraction*, or DAE.[*] Fortunately, the vast majority of modern CD players are DAE-compatible. Very few users find that their CD-ROM drives are not capable of digital extraction. Even if you do have a DAE-compatible drive, note that some drives are simply better at the process than others, and some ripping software is more "paranoid" (careful) about ripping quality than others.

Ideally, you want to find and use ripping software that does its own error correction, so that if bits aren't sucked off the disc perfectly the first time, redundant passes will be made until the bits being output exactly match the bits on the CD. The process is not as simple as copying normal files through your file manager— the hardware and the software must all cooperate to ensure perfect rips. Look around on the web sites or in the documentation of hardware and software you intend to use to find out whether they perform any kind of CRC checks, redundancy, or error-correction. You may also want to ask online to find out which brands and products produce good results for other users. If in doubt, just rip the same track from a CD a few times and check their exact byte sizes. If any of them differ by even one byte, then you'll know that you're either not using an error-correcting ripper or your CD-ROM unit doesn't do perfect DAE.

---

[*] It is possible to rip from audio CDs without a DAE-compatible drive, but this requires going through the analog stage of the sound card, with a concomitant reduction in sound quality. You'll lose a minimum of 20dB to noise in the process, and it's just not worth it. If you're shopping for a new CD-ROM drive, make sure it's DAE-compatible (most are).

When purchasing hardware, keep the following notes about CD-ROM devices in mind, but remember that quality is not always a function of cost; an inexpensive IDE drive *may* outperform a more expensive SCSI drive in the final analysis.

 If you have problems creating error-free rips, try slowing down the rip speed. Take it all the way down to 1x if necessary—whatever it takes to eliminate *all* pops and glitches. You may also want to increase the buffer size.

SCSI

The SCSI-1 specification had no standards for audio operations. SCSI-2 introduced audio playback operations, but in a very limited way. SCSI-3 is much more complete and defines a complete set of audio related operations, including playback, audio seeking (a.k.a. fast-forward and rewind), and digital audio extraction. Good SCSI drives include Pioneer, later Yamaha CD-RW drives, and especially some of the newer Plextors, which set the bar for DAE quality. Plextor drives do offer a Windows utility to let you view your CDA tracks directly as WAV files, though files are "blocked" when in use, so you can't play multiple CD tracks simultaneously or cross-fade your CD tracks, as you can in BeOS with the cdda-fs driver. Plextors do excellent error correction.

ATAPI

ATAPI employs a variant of SCSI-3 over the IDE bus to achieve similar capabilities. ATAPI devices are basically inexpensive clones of their SCSI progenitors; their firmware is not as reliable, though some are quite acceptable. Many Toshiba drives produce excellent results, while those from Acer, Cyberdrive, and TAEIL have developed less-than-sterling reputations as audio performers.

 If you have trouble getting a ripper to work at all with your CD-ROM drive and you're sure it's DAE-compatible, look around in the options or preferences for ASPI and MSCDEX ripping methods. If one doesn't work, try the other.

Ripping and Encoding Tools

Depending on the tools you use, ripping and encoding may either be a one-step or two-step process. The traditional path is to rip first and then encode. However, increasing numbers of tools that perform both steps in one pass are beginning to appear. We'll cover rippers, encoders, and combination tools together in this section, which is broken down by operating system. Many of these tools have been ported to various platforms, with operation virtually identical for each port.

Windows

As is usually the case, there are far more ripping and encoding options available for Windows users than for any other platform. The following are just a few.

HyCD's HyCD

www.hycd.com HyCD is a well-rounded, multi-purpose tool designed to handle every facet of your CD ripping, encoding, and CD copying needs. Users looking for a way to clean up pops and scratches from LP and other noisy recordings will also find an excellent Effects processor included in the HyCD package. While most of the HyCD tools include an interface dedicated to the task at hand, its built-in ripper/encoder is somewhat oddly designed. Rather than launching a separate application, just navigate through Windows Explorer to the location of an audio CD track or tracks you want to rip. Right-click on those tracks and choose *HyCD Copy* from the context menu. A dialog will appear, asking whether you want to "paste" the files into the selected folder in WAV or MP3 format. In other words, do you just want to rip the selected tracks, or do you want to rip and encode them all in one step? If you think you'll need to pre-process or clean up your WAV files prior to encoding, then you'll just want to rip. Otherwise, choose Encode to go straight from PCM to MP3.

The biggest disadvantage to HyCD's ripper/encoder combination is that it offers no connectivity with the CDDB, so you'll have to manually rename and add ID3 tags to your tracks later. Despite this design limitation, HyCD offers a great collection of additional tools that anyone serious about building a quality MP3 collection will find useful, including a "Sampler" that will turn MP3 files back into WAVs in preparation for burning your own CDs (covered later in this chapter).

Xing's AudioCatalyst

www.audiocatalyst.com One of the most popular all-in-one tools available for Windows is Xing's AudioCatalyst, a very fast combination ripper/encoder with CDDB support, a zillion encoding options, ID3 support, and excellent normalization features, as shown in Figure 5-2. AudioCatalyst also comes bundled with an MP3 player of its own, though power users will probably want to use one of the more sophisticated players outlined in Chapter 3, *Getting and Playing MP3 Files*.

Usage is intuitive and documentation is detailed. Just be sure you check the settings before you begin to make sure ID3 support is enabled, and remember to click the CDDB button before starting so your tracks end up with reasonable filenames.

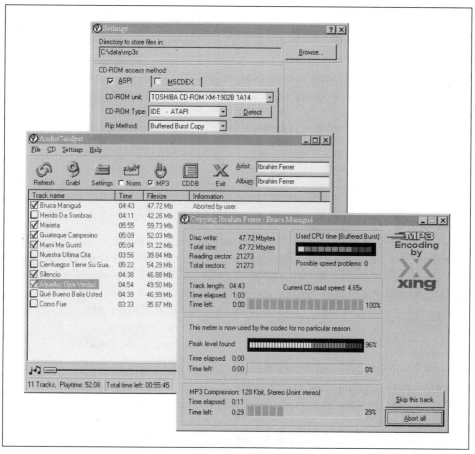

Figure 5-2. AudioCatalyst has it all: a fast encoding engine, a no-nonsense interface, and tons of features and options

 AudioCatalyst has trouble detecting some CDs accurately, especially those in laptop computers. If you have a non-SCSI CD-ROM drive and get mysterious error messages as you start to encode, enter the Settings panel and change the drive to "ATAPI – IDE," which should work with the vast majority of drives out there.

AudioGrabber

www.audiograbber.com-us.net A popular cousin of AudioCatalyst is AudioGrabber, which works similarly. If the two seem to have eerie similarities, it's because Xing licensed some of the AudioGrabber code for use in AudioCatalyst. One of the great things about AudioGrabber, though, is the fact that it can work with alternative encoders that have been compiled into Windows .DLLs, essentially treating encoders like plug-ins. At this writing, the LAME encoder (covered elsewhere in this chapter) had just become available as an option for AudioGrabber users, alongside Xing, BladeEnc, Plugger, and Fraunhofer encoders. The nice thing about this system is that it makes it easy for users to test the comparative speed and quality of various encoders without having to switch to an entirely different system.

MusicMatch Jukebox and Real Jukebox

Two of the easiest-to-use encoding tools on the market are MusicMatch's and RealNetworks' "Jukebox" products, both of which combine ripping/encoding and playback tools into a single interface. Both products are covered in Chapter 3.

CDFS.VXD

Ah, the wonders of the Internet. Somewhere out there, a pretty smart programmer figured out a way to do what Windows—for whatever reason—doesn't offer automatically: Display the tracks on your audio CDs as WAV files directly in Explorer, allowing you to completely bypass the need for third-party ripping tools. This file, which simply replaces your existing Windows CD-ROM driver file, is distributed anonymously, and has no central homepage. No one seems to know where the file originated. Just search the Net for "cdfs.vxd" and unzip the package.

In Explorer, navigate to *C:\WINDOWS\SYSTEM\IOSUBSYS* and rename *CDFS.VXD* to *CDFS.VXD.OLD* (**not** *CDFS.OLD.VXD*). Then drop the downloaded version of *CDFS.VXD* into this folder, restart your machine, and insert an audio CD. You'll see all of the usual CDA files in the root of the drive as usual, but you'll now also find subdirectories named for stereo and mono variants, 8- and 16-bit bit-depths, and a variety of samplerates. For most purposes, you'll want to navigate to stereo, 16bit, 44,100Hz, where you'll find the highest quality WAV files. However, if you're doing any kind of Internet streaming or need low-size, lower quality WAVs for any other purpose, they're all there waiting for you. Note that *CDFS.VXD* works only under Windows 95 and 98, not Windows NT.

CDFS.VXD does not, unfortunately, do CDDB lookups.

BladeEnc

home.swipnet.se/~w-82625/ Hard-core command-line users may want to look to the legendary BladeEnc. BladeEnc was developed by a programmer who was dissatisfied with the quality of the typical 128 kbps MP3 file, and wanted to ensure the best quality he could for his own encodings. BladeEnc was once hailed as being one of the best quality encoders available, though this claim is now widely disputed. While BladeEnc was originally based on ISO sources, its encoding engine was later optimized for speed as well, eventually making it 50–100% faster than the original ISO source (although BladeEnc is still no speed demon—in our tests, it was slower than virtually every other encoder available). BladeEnc's author feels that his encoder surpasses its Fraunhofer competitors in quality at around 160 kbps.

Usage of BladeEnc is pretty straightforward. A simple:

```
bladenc *.wav
```

Will encode every WAV file in the current directory at the default rate of 128 kbps, while:

```
bladenc -160 *.wav
```

will do the same, but at 160 kbps. If you want to specify the output directory, just use the -output flag:

```
bladenc -192 -output c:\data\sounds\mp3 track*.wav
```

If you're not comfortable with the command line, the Windows version of BladeEnc will also let you drop your uncompressed files onto *bladenc.exe* (or a shortcut to it) and have 128 kbps files output automatically. Note that even though the program opens a DOS shell to do its business, BladeEnc is not in fact a DOS-based program—it's a true 32-bit Windows application that just happens to run in a DOS shell.

There are also many graphical "frontend" programs that will let you operate BladeEnc through a GUI. Consult your favorite MP3 software site for details.

MP3ENC

www.iis.fhg.de/amm/download/mp3enc What may constitute the definitive encoder—the one coming directly from Fraunhofer themselves—is also paradoxically one of the more seldom-used (at least by individuals and casual MP3 collectors). The biggest reason for this is that MP3ENC (sometimes referred to as FhG, after its creator) is expensive. At this writing, it cost $199 to purchase Fraunhofer's very high quality encoder (a demo version limited to outputting 30 seconds of MP3 is freely downloadable from the URL above). And for that price, all you get is a command-line tool with no graphical user interface (which, many feel, is a blessing, not a curse).

While this tool may be both more expensive and more difficult to use than the popular encoders available from large vendors, it will give you some of the best quality you're liable to find anywhere, and offers all possible encoding options. Even if you don't think you'll be able to afford a registered version of MP3ENC, download the demo and run some listening tests against other encoders—you'll probably be able to hear the difference.

While the command-line switches are simple to use, you'll need to know at least a few of them before beginning—be sure to read MP3ENC's documentation thoroughly. Assuming you've already ripped or created a WAV file, basic usage is:

```
mp3enc -if filename.wav -of filename.mp3
```

where −**if** represents the input file and −**of** represents the output file. The default bitrate is an assumed 128 kbps. If you want to output a different bitrate, you'll need to specify it in bits per second, not kbps. In other words, use:

```
mp3enc -br 160000 -if filename.wav -of filename.mp3
```

to generate a 160 kbps MP3 file. Because MP3ENC does not spit out a progress report to the command line by default, you'll probably want to use the −**v** flag (for verbose) most of the time. MP3ENC also takes a −**qual** flag with a value of 0 to 9, which lets you control the balance between encoding speed and quality by toggling various aspects of the algorithm on and off. To generate the best possible MP3 files without worrying about speed or filesize, use something like:

```
mp3enc -qual 9 -br 320000 -if filename.wav -of filename.mp3
```

Yes, it will be slow, but the quality will be unparalleled. Conversely, set the quality to 0 and watch how fast it whips along.

MP3ENC is available for Windows 95/98/NT, Linux, Solaris, SUN OS, IRIX, and Alpha/OSF1.

Bypassing Protection Schemes

If you want to save audio streams moving through the system to which you don't have direct access (such as Internet broadcasts that your playback application won't let you save), search the Internet for the Wave To Disk, or WTD driver. This driver masquerades as an audio driver, so that any audio signal normally headed for your sound card is stored in a WAV file rather than being played. Some music pirates use the WTD to bypass copyright protection mechanisms, though it doesn't work in all versions of Windows. If you just want to encode RealAudio or G2 RealMedia files into MP3 format, search the Internet for the $30 Ra2Wav utility, which supports file format conversion either singly or in batches.

MacOS

It's a toss-up: For a long time there, the most popular ripper/encoder solution for MacOS was Xing's AudioCatalyst, usage of which is virtually identical to the Windows version of the product—just set your encoding options in the preferences and drag audio files into the encoding window (see the previous section for details on using AudioCatalyst).

SoundJam

www.soundjam.com The advent of SoundJam MP for the Mac (see Chapter 3) has presented a serious threat to the dominance of AudioCatalyst, thanks to its extreme ease of use and neat integration with the SoundJam playback system. The Sound-Jam "Converter" (Figure 5-3) is capable of converting WAV or AIFF files, tracks from CDs, or even QuickTime movie soundtracks to MP3. To convert from CD, insert a disc and choose Audio CD from the Window menu. Select the track numbers you want converted, and click the "Add to Converter" button. Alternatively, you can drag tracks directly from the Finder—or even the whole CD icon on the Desktop—into the Converter window. Click the Configure button and establish preferences for the usual range of MP3 output options: bitrate, mono/stereo, sampleplate, and (very important) whether or not to use ID3 tags. Click the Start Converting button and let 'er rip.

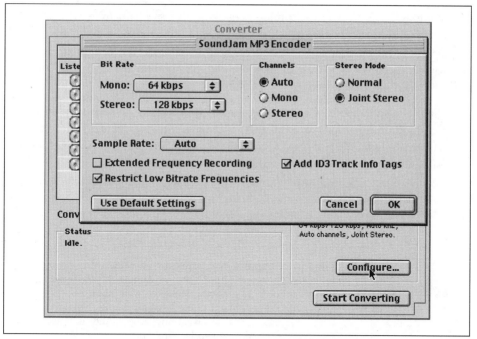

Figure 5-3. Before encoding with SoundJam, be sure the "Add ID3 Track Info Tags" option is enabled

Audiophiles take note: By default, the SoundJam encoder discards frequencies above 16kHz, for faster encoding. While this is fine for most purposes, people who intend to listen to their MP3 collection on systems other than their computer speakers should select the "Extended Frequency Recording" checkbox, which will cause the SoundJam encoder to reproduce frequencies all the way up to 22kHz. Note, however, that doing so will subtract from the amount of data space per frame available to storing information in the more audible lower frequencies. Therefore, you should only use this option when encoding at higher bitrates, or you'll end up with worse-sounding MP3 files, not better. On the other end of the spectrum, you can save additional disk space by selecting the "Restrict Low Bitrate Frequencies" checkbox, which throws out additional data at the high end *only* when you're encoding at 96 kbps or lower.

Oddly enough, the Converter's preferences panel does not include an option for setting the output folder into which encoded MP3 files will be placed. By default, all MP3 files will be dumped into the Music folder inside the SoundJam application folder. However, you can change the default location for all SoundJam files from the main preferences panel.

SoundJam is also capable of converting source files to AIFF, which may be useful if you're preparing to burn an audio CD and have an older version of Toast that doesn't convert from MP3 to PCM automatically, or if you want to be able to open your MP3 files in an audio editing application for tweaking. MacOS users may also want to check out Fraunhofer/Macromedia's SWA Plugin for SoundEdit 16, as well as the independently developed Mpecker (*www.anime.net/~go/mpeckers.html)* encoder/decoder combination and a shareware utility called TrackThief.

Developers of the once-popular, free Mpecker encoder were contacted by Fraunhofer/Thomson Multimedia in August of 1999, in search of their royalty fees. As a result, Mpecker was taken out of public distribution until an agreement could be reached. By November of the same year, the situation was unchanged and it was unclear whether Mpecker would ever surface again.

N2MP3

www.n2mp3.com Mac audio pros gravitate toward another all-in-one ripping/encoding solution for the Mac called N2MP3, which many feel generates superior quality encodings to those generated by SoundJam. The encoder built into N2MP3 is based originally on the LAME encoder, with additional proprietary optimizations.

The company calls their version, "Proteron." N2MP3 sports a very clean, logical interface, all of the power options you would expect, full integration with the Finder, plus VBR, CDDB, and ID3 support.

Linux

There are two rippers for Linux that bear mention: cdparanoia and cdda2wav. This, however, does not mean there are only two ripping *solutions* available for Linux. Since anyone can build scripts around these two core tools, or GUI interfaces on top of them, there are zillions of ways to turn CDA tracks into WAV or MP3 files from within Linux. And of course, these aren't the only rippers available for Linux—just the most popular. As far as encoders go, users generally consider LAME to render the highest quality, although again, there are a multitude of choices out there.

cdparanoia

www.xiph.org/paranoia/ Of the two, cdparanoia is the more popular (though cdparanoia began life as a series of patches to cdda2wav before branching off in its own direction). The tool is so-named because of its author's unflagging attention to detail. Just read cdparanoia's FAQs to see what I mean; cdparanoia corrects for every possible glitch that can crop up during the digital extraction process. To preserve optimal sound quality, cdparanoia is insistent about always retrieving data in digital form, never ever letting audio data near the sound card where it might be converted into analog signal during processing. Given a clean CD, your rips are guaranteed to be 100% accurate, with no skips or pops due to data transfer errors.

To compile cdparanoia, grab the sources from *www.xiph.org/paranoia/* and type:

```
./configure
make all
```

Once installed, you can test the tool by inserting an audio CD and typing:

```
cdparanoia -Q
```

This will query your CD-ROM device and return a listing of all tracks. To rip a single track, use:

```
cdparanoia 4
```

to rip track 4, for example. An ASCII progress indicator will give you a readout of the ripping process, while a series of symbols will inform you if errors are encountered (see cdparanoia's documentation for details on these symbols). When complete, a file called *cdda.wav* will be dumped in the current directory. Of course, there are zillions of command-line options you can use for more precise control. To specify the output filename, use:

```
cdparanoia 4 ~/yourname/testoutput.wav
```

To do batch encodes, use the -B flag, followed by a directory name (remember to append the directory name with a trailing slash, or you'll get unexpected results). The -B flag, in turn can be handed arguments to specify a series of tracks. For example:

```
cdparanoia -B 3- ~/waxwing/music/mp3/
```

will output every file from track 3 to the end of the CD to *~/waxwing/music/mp3/*. cdparanoia is also capable of extracting specific portions of tracks. To grab just the audio between time points 1:32 and 3:47 in track 8, use:

```
cdparanoia "8[1:32]-8[3:47]" output_file
```

Here's a command sequence you can use to simultaneously rip and encode tracks 1–10 on the current CD at 160 kbps, using cdparanoia in combination with the l3enc encoder (not covered here, but similar to other tools described in this section):

```
for i in 1 2 3 4 5 6 7 8 9 10
    do cdparanoia $i $i.wav
    l3enc -br 160000 $i.wav $i.mp3
# Comment out the following line if you don't want
# the wav source files deleted after encoding.
rm -f $i.wav
done
```

Because of all the error checking and extreme "paranoia," cdparanoia will always run at a maximum of 1x speed. If you're wondering why your 36x CD-ROM drive is ripping so slowly, add the -Z flag to disable paranoid checking and get the full speed out of your drive.

cdparanoia was available for Linux and BeOS at this writing, with xBSD, IRIX, and Solaris next on the "to-do" list.

cdda2wav

Available at nearly any Linux software site. If you prefer speed over accuracy, you might want to try the somewhat faster cdda2wav, instead. Don't leap to the conclusion that your rips are going to be full of errors if you use cdda2wav; rips made from the vast majority of drives with scratch-free audio CDs are going to come out fine. You just have to ask yourself how paranoid you are about these things. cdda2wav functions very similarly to cdparanoia, with a few exceptions in its command-line syntax. See the included file *HOWTOUSE* for details.

When compiling cdda2wav, note that the default Makefile generated by *./configure* will point to a SCSCI CD-ROM device. If you have a SCSI CD-ROM, make sure the appropriate line in the Makefile is pointing to the correct device before compiling. If you have an ATAPI device, comment out the SCSI line and uncomment the line beneath it, pointing to *./dev/cdrom*. Save the Makefile, then run `make` and `make install`.

LAME

www.sulaco.org/mp3/ Widely considered to render the most consistently high quality of the available encoders, LAME (Lame Ain't an MP3 Encoder), is not an encoder in and of itself. To get around issues surrounding encoder licensing issues, LAME is, as its name says, not an encoder. By itself, it is incapable of producing an MP3 stream. Instead, it's a set of patches against the ISO reference sources. In other words, it gets by on a technicality. Its authors have put a great deal of work into making LAME faster and of a higher quality than the ISO sources, and the work shows. The sources compile on GNU/Linux, Unix, Windows, MacOS, BeOS, AmigaOS, and OS/2.

Once installed, you can discover all of LAME's command-line options by typing `lame` with no arguments. The following are some basics.

Encode a WAV file to a 192 kbps MP3 file called `funky_popsicle.mp3`:

```
lame -b192 funky-popsicle.wav ~/funky_popsicle.mp3
```

Do the same, but use a VBR setting of 7 instead (when using VBR with LAME, remember that the −V parameter specifies an allowed threshold of distortion, so −V1 is better than −V7). Note that here we're using both a VBR setting and specifying a bitrate—if you specify a bitrate, the bitrate will never drop below that bitrate, even in totally silent passages:

```
lame -V7 -b128 funky-popsicle.wav ~/funky_popsicle.mp3
```

Do the same, but specify that the input source is 22kHz and was ripped on a Mac and therefore needs its bytes swapped from big endian to little endian (the **x** flag takes care of that):

```
lame -x -s22050 -V7 funky-popsicle.wav ~/funky_popsicle.mp3
```

Later versions of LAME even include some ID3 tagging features, so you don't have to use id3ren separately:

```
lame -b192 --tt "Funky Popsicle" --ta "The Jaw Droppers" \
--tl "A Day in the Factory" -ty 1964 funky-popsicle.wav ~/funky_popsicle.mp3
```

LAME also has a "fast mode" option which lets the encoder run at up to 2.5x its normal speed, with some quality degradation (though not as much as you might expect). Still, I recommend reserving this −f option for use only with spoken word, broadcasts, and very badly recorded music. To learn how the −f option works, see "GOGO-no-Coda" section, next.

GOGO-no-Coda

www.kurims.kyoto-u.ac.jp/~shigeo/gogo_e.html A high-performance variant of LAME called GOGO (available for Windows, Unix/Linux, BeOS, and other x86 platforms) had just appeared as this book was going to press, and was impressing the heck out of users with its blazing speed. GOGO is written to take explicit advantage of MMX (Enhanced), 3D Now!, and SSE instruction sets if your processor supports them. Many portions of the LAME code are also rewritten in assembly language. In addition, GOGO is the only encoder available (at this writing) that takes advantage of multiple processors. If you use a dual-proc machine, you'll definitely want to check this out. By default, GOGO is about twice as fast as LAME. With two processors, you'll get virtually identical encodings four times faster than LAME. The important thing to note about GOGO is that it achieves its speed not by cutting corners in the encoder, but by taking better advantage of modern processors, especially in the most math-intensive areas of the codec.

In addition, GOGO supports the command-line flag −nopsy, which disables the psychoacoustic model and speeds up encoding even more (way more). But how can you have a valid MP3 file that doesn't use the psychoacoustic model? The -nopsy option is the same as the −f (fast mode) in LAME. Recall from Chapter 2 that the MP3 codec computes masking thresholds between frequency sub-bands in order to decide how many bits should be allocated to each band. The −nopsy option causes the codec to stop computing the masks. Instead, it assumes a constant, predefined masking threshold for each sub-band, regardless of the content being encoded. So in essence, −nopsy is a hack. The psychoacoustic model isn't really being thrown out entirely as it is being cheated of its intelligence. This enables GOGO to encode at blazing speeds, with some loss of quality. Depending on your expectations, you may be surprised to learn just how good −nopsy encodings are, though I recommend avoiding this option for most purposes— quality should almost always be your paramount concern.

Get a Grip

www.nostatic.org/grip/ If you prefer to do things through a friendly, graphical interface, Grip is an excellent GUI interface onto either cdparanoia or cdda2wav (your choice), written by MP3.com employee Mike Oliphant. Grip doesn't stop with ripping, however. It also functions as an interface onto encoding tools such as BladeEnc (see the Windows section for BladeEnc coverage) and ID3 tagging

---

Grabbing Streams

Linux users may find this trick useful for stuffing any audio moving through the system into a raw audio file. The link */dev/audio* normally sends all audio signal straight to your sound card. By replacing this link with an actual file, all audio will end up in that file. Try this:

```
mv /dev/audio /dev/audio-bak; touch /dev/audio
```

Now start your favorite audio application, and anything it plays will be dumped into the file at */dev/audio*. You can later copy this to a new filename, replace the original link, clean up or edit the audio file in an audio editor, and encode it to MP3. Some users circumvent copyright-protected formats in this way, although the technique does not always work, especially if the audio stream is pointed at */dev/dsp* rather than */dev/audio*.

If you have a copy of the text-mode lynx browser on your system and want to capture an MP3 broadcast stream to disk, try this:

```
lynx -source http://ip_address:port/ > somefile.mp3
```

---

tools such as id3ren (Chapter 4). In addition to handling virtually every command-line option supported by these tools, Grip also supports CDDB connections, so your tracks will end up with reasonable filenames and ID3 tags right off the bat.

 Grip requires GTK 1.2 or later. See *www.gtk.org* for details, as well as the GTK installation notes in Chapter 4.

Before running Grip for the first time, su to root, since you'll need to have appropriate permissions to establish Grip's configuration details. Click on the Config tab to establish the path to your ripper executable, specify any command-line parameters you'd like to pass to it, the ripping file format, the CPU-intensiveness at which Grip should run (i.e., its "niceness"), the preferred output directory, and the paths to your MP3 encoder and ID3 tools. You also have complete control over the file naming convention and output directory. By default, Grip will create a new directory for every new artist and within that, a new directory for every new album you rip. You may want to begin by specifying some location within your home directory; otherwise, output will be placed in the current directory.

Once you've saved your configuration, return to the Tracks panel. If you're connected to the Internet and have an audio CD inserted, you'll find that the current CD has been properly detected and that all of its tracks are properly listed, as shown in Figure 5-4. You may want to click the pencil icon in the lower toolbar to display the Disc Editor, in case you want to change parameters such as Genre or Year. When finished, move to the Rip tab, click the Rip button, and cdparanoia or cdda2wav will kick into action. If you've also got an MP3 encoder installed and properly specified in the Config panel, your tracks will be simultaneously ripped and encoded.

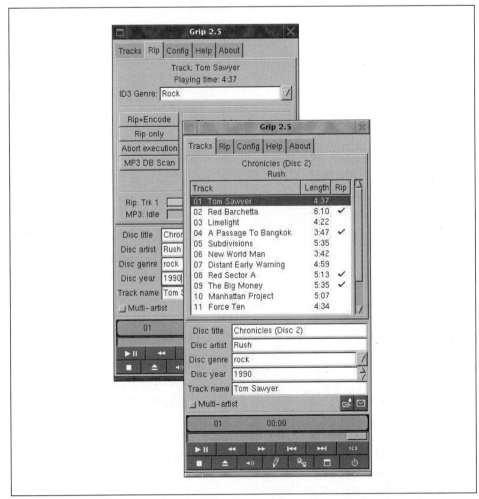

Figure 5-4. Grip for Linux serves as a GUI frontend to command-line tools

RipEnc

www.asde.com/~mjparme Following the same philosophy as Grip and other graphical front-ends, users who don't run X (or just prefer the command line) will appreciate some of the shell scripts out there that do a similar "all-in-one" job. One of the most popular and complete shell scripts for MP3 ripping and encoding on Linux is RipEnc—a monster of a script which interfaces with your choice of cdparanoia or cdda2wav for ripping, BladeEnc, 8hz-mp3, or l3enc for encoding, and the command-line CDDB lookup tool "cda." This makes for a complete, all-in-one tool comparable in power to Windows applications like AudioCatalyst, but consisting only of "glue" that holds the classic Unix "atoms" together. Oh, and like most Linux tools, RipEnc is free.

Getting RipEnc set up for the first time can be a bit tricky—you've got to make sure all of your ducks are in a row. First of all you'll need to make sure that at least one of the rippers and one of encoders discussed in this section are installed and in your path (actually, RipEnc can run without an encoder if you just want extract uncompressed audio).

If you want to save yourself the trouble of having to manually rename and add ID3 tags to your tracks, make sure you've got full CDDB support: Head over to *metalab.unc.edu/tkan/xmcd/xmcd.html/* and download the package appropriate for your platform, make the **install.sh** script executable, and run it. You'll be led through a series of questions regarding the CDDB servers you want to connect to and the make and model of your CD-ROM drive.

In RipEnc's launch menu, tell the program which ripper and which encoder you want to use. The first time you run RipEnc, be sure to check the path to the **xmcd** library on your system, which may not match the default path provided (use the **find** or **locate** commands to track this down). Once you start ripping, you'll be prompted to enter any ID3 fields that could not be determined from the CDDB lookup. If you opted not to encode the entire disc, you'll be asked which tracks to encode. The rest is gravy, baby... yeah!

RipEnc has also been adapted to work under BeOS, though it functions somewhat differently. See the BeOS section below for more on that..

BeOS

Users won't find many ripping tools available for BeOS, because it doesn't need any. Since the operating system supports alien filesystems with the addition of a single device driver module, Be provides a "cdda-fs" driver with every copy of the operating system. The cdda-fs driver basically creates a "front" for CDA tracks, making them appear to the operating system as WAV files. Insert an audio CD into your CD-ROM drive and it will appear on the Desktop just like any other mounted volume. Inside, you'll find two folders: One called *CDA* and another called *WAV*. The CDA folder contains the standard CDA handles described earlier, while the WAV folder contains actual WAV files, which can be played immediately without ripping them first. These WAV files can be used directly by the user or accessed from the command line or from within third-party applications, and can of course be dragged off the CD and into the Tracker. Performing this mapping of CDA to WAV incurs no delay; nothing is being translated. The filesystem driver is simply mapping the CDA pointers to actual audio data, granting you direct access. BeOS encoders can therefore encode to MP3 without having to rip tracks first.

This capability is useful for more than just MP3 encoding—you can also play these WAV files in any BeOS audio player. In fact, if you use a tool like SoundPlay (Chapter 3), you can even play three or four tracks simultaneously, backwards or forwards, at variable speeds, *directly off the CD*.

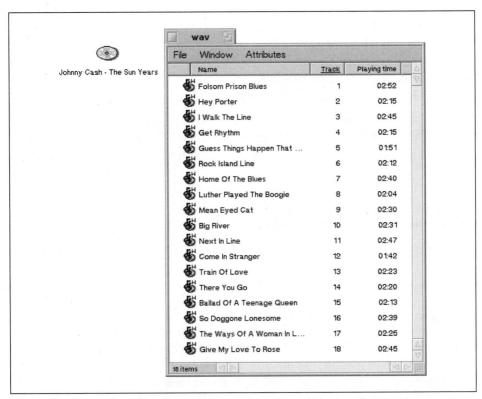

Figure 5-5. Tracks on audio CDs in BeOS appear to the Tracker as WAV files

As you can see in Figure 5-5, the cdda-fs driver doesn't just make the files masquerade as WAV files—it also works in conjunction with a small daemon called *cddblinkd*, which runs in the background and automatically makes contact with the CDDB (or other database) whenever you insert an audio CD (if you have an

Internet connection). The CD volume is then mounted with the artist and album name, and all tracks on the disc appear with their actual song names in the Tracker. This means that BeOS ripping/encoding tools don't necessarily have to do CDDB lookups of their own—they can just extract the artist, album, and track names directly from the filesystem.

If you want to be really hardcore about it, you can rip tracks from audio CDs without the help of cdda-fs, by using the system's built-in "play" command (which offers a "save track to file" option), or use the BeOS port of cdparanoia, described earlier in this chapter.

 Be has licensed the MPEG codec from Fraunhofer and Thomson, and includes MP3 encoders and decoders in the system. This means that, in addition to ease of ripping from CD, you can save directly to MP3 from any BeOS audio mixer/editor/sequencer application that works with the media kit.

CDPlayer and SoundRecorder

If you prefer to do this graphically, or just want to rip portions of tracks, the graphical CDPlayer application included with BeOS also has a built-in ripper and encoder. Just click the floppy disk icon in CDPlayer's interface, select a track number, and use the triangular sliders to select the portion of the track you want to rip (the default setting rips the entire track). Select an output format to save your selection as WAV, AIFF, RAW, or directly to MP3. Similarly, the system's built-in SoundRecorder application will let you crop arbitrary segments of audio from any track and right-drag them to the Desktop. Choose an output format from the context menu and you'll be cropping and encoding audio to MP3 simultaneously.

MediaPede's UltraEncode

www.mediapede.com The easiest to use of the BeOS ripper/encoder solutions is an all-in-one package from MediaPede called UltraEncode, which sports an intuitive interface and fast encoding thanks to Be's inclusion of an MP3 encoder in the system. Usage is straightforward: Establish your CDDB server, bitrate, and destination directory in the preferences, insert a CD, and its track names will appear in the Extractor Queue. Establish a genre and year for the CD from the Settings menu, and double-click any track name for which you want to edit details.

Check off the tracks you want to encode, or tap Alt+A to select all or Alt+D to select none. Click the Start button and ripping/encoding will take place simultaneously (UltraEncode is heavily multithreaded). You can show/hide any of the interface panels by clicking the "switch" widgets at the right of the interface (see Figure 5-6).

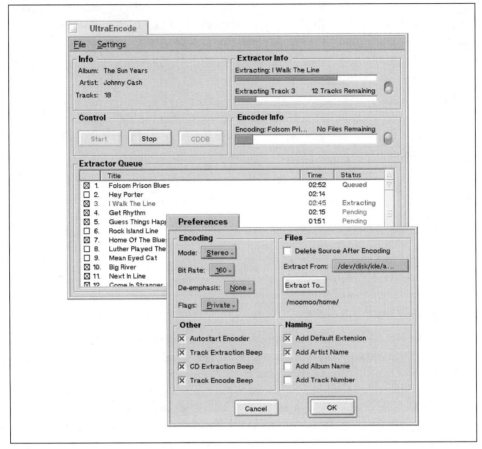

Figure 5-6. MediaPede offers an all-in-one ripping and encoding package for BeOS users

RipEnc

www.betips.net/software/ RipEnc for BeOS is a distant cousin of the Linux version mentioned above. The BeOS version (by this book's author) started life as a straight port of the Linux version, but was later gutted and rewritten from scratch to take advantage of cdda-fs. The BeOS version is therefore "ripless"—tracks are encoded directly as they appear in the Tracker, without being extracted from the CD first. Like the Linux version, the BeOS version is a "frontend" to a small collection of command-line tools, including id3ren (covered in Chapter 4), the GOGO encoder (covered ealier in this chapter), and a tool called id3attr, which copies ID3 tag information into BeOS filesystem attributes which can be queried on to create custom playlists quickly. RipEnc for BeOS also makes use of "folder templates" so that generated folders full of MP3 files are pre-organized in a customizable fashion, showing ID3 tags as attributes in the Tracker (as shown in Figure 5-6). RipEnc also supports optional manual track naming, a "play when done" option, variable bit rate mode, CD automounting, and other goodies.

The nice thing about using frontends such as RipEnc for Linux or BeOS is the fact that the user can choose their favorite tools to be used with the system. For example, you can choose to use a different encoder while still retaining the same overall encoding framework. And because shell scripts are easy to edit, users can dig in and make modifications if they wish.

Other popular ripping and encoding tools for BeOS include RipChord, KizunoMP, GOGO Gadget, 8hz, and KonaKoder. You'll find these tools and more at *www.be. com/beware/* or at *www.bebits.com.*

Ripping from Other Sources

Of course, the audio you want to encode isn't always going to originate on audio CDs. Many of us still have huge music collections stored mostly on LPs, cassettes, DAT, 8-tracks, reel-to-reels, and possibly other media. MP3 represents a great opportunity to finally create a permanent digital archive of these collections... or at least the best of them (most people would have to be horribly masochistic to dedicate themselves to the digitization of every track they own). The good news is that encoding your existing collection in this way is do-able. The bad news is that it's going to require quite a bit more manual labor than encoding from CD. Since you can't stick an LP into your computer and let it twirl, you've got to go to the extra step of patching your home stereo into your sound card and manually cueing everything up properly. And of course, there are no batch-ripping/encoding solutions available for digitizing 8-track tape collections. Finally, you may have to separate songs manually when encoding from analog sources—LPs don't have any real awareness of when one track ends and the next begins. Without special software (see the following section), you'll have to do all of that yourself in an audio application prior to encoding.

The term "ripping" doesn't exactly apply when talking about sources other than compact disc—nothing needs to be ripped since the source isn't hidden, as it is with .CDA files. We use the term "ripping" in a somewhat looser sense in this chapter, though it might be more accurate to refer to "extraction."

If you're a recording artist, you'll probably already have your repertoire stored on tape, DAT, or another medium, so this section applies to you as well. Of course, it's possible to connect a microphone or other instrument directly into your sound card and save the signal direct to disk, and you may even have a fancy-schmancy sound card that handles multiple inputs and lets you do all kinds of preprocessing with dedicated DSPs, etc. But even if you are a digital-friendly musician, you're still going to want to do all of your mixing and mastering in dedicated multi-track audio software, creating a final stereo mix before going to MP3. In other words, while recording live to MP3 is a possibility, it's not often done unless you're capturing a live performance—and even then, you'll probably want to store that unencoded first.

When recording from LP, cassette, or other analog sources that don't have the same crispness at the high end, try using an equalizer to boost the higher frequencies by a couple of dB before encoding. This can help to alleviate some of the "swishy" effects for which MP3 is known. However, increasing high frequencies on LPs and tapes will also result in more noise, so there's a trade-off here. As always, you'll get better results from analog sources by using higher bitrates.

Direct to Hard Disk

As described in Chapter 4, a lot of audio hardware, including most sound cards, deal with two possible input specifications: Line level and Mic level. Mic input is used for amplifying low level input, which mostly consists of that coming from microphones. Line input handles signal from audio equipment with line-level outputs, such as CD players, tape decks, tuners, and so on. Most sound cards offer two or more input jacks, one Mic and one Line. If you're not sure which input jack on your sound card is which, consult its documentation. Note that phono cartridges need a unique amplification stage that converts their output to line level.

There are two ways to connect audio hardware to a sound card. You can either connect an instrument, microphone, or a stereo component's output directly to the appropriate input jack on your sound card, or you can run a line from your stereo amplifier/receiver's output terminal to your sound card (if your amplifier has an output jack—not all do). With the first method, you'll have the very slight advantage of eliminating your stereo's circuitry from the recording chain for slightly better input quality, but have to deal with the physical awkwardness of yanking stereo equipment and placing it near your computer. The second method incurs a little extra circuitry, but may be more convenient. In all cases, you'll get better results whenever you can minimize the length of cable runs.

Record What You Hear

Note that most of the same techniques outlined above also apply if you want to record other audio streams moving through your system, such as those coming from Internet broadcasts (any format). The only difference is that rather than fiddling with cables and jacks, you'll need to set your system's audio mixer to trap all signals. Look for a setting labeled something like "Speaker Out" or "Record what you hear." This is different in every operating system, and some sound card utility installations override your system's default settings, so you may need to use your sound card's software rather than the operating system's mixer to establish this setting. In any case, it should be possible to save any incoming signal to WAV or AIFF, clean it up in an audio editing application, and encode the resulting audio file to MP3 normally. Some audio pirates use this technique to circumvent protection schemes built into Internet broadcast formats.

Alternatively, you can use the tape output jacks on your amplifier, which will let you use the amp's switching facilities (such as the Tape Monitor button). If you do this, the volume control on the amplifier won't affect the level of the signal being sent out, so you can change the volume of the music you're hearing without affecting the level of the recording being made.

Once you've got your equipment hooked up, you need to be able to save the signal coming into your sound card to hard drive. While most operating systems come with basic audio recording software, you'll probably find that this software isn't quite up to the task. Since you may need to edit out silent spaces at the beginning and end of various tracks, or apply noise-masking, equalization, or other effects to the tracks you record prior to encoding, I strongly recommend looking into the third-party audio software options available for your platform. Usage of general audio recording software is outside the scope of a book on MP3, but popular applications include CoolEdit Pro or SoundForge for Windows, Pebbles or 3dsound for BeOS, Deck or Peak for the Macintosh, and fOX Mixer for Linux. See the section "Encoding from Analog Sources" later for more information.

If you do want to encode directly to MP3 from audio input, some of the more complete tools—such as MusicMatch Jukebox—are capable of doing so. In MusicMatch, pull down Options → Recorder → Source and choose from Line In, Mic, or System Mixer. Set your encoding preferences as usual, hit Record, and you'll be encoding from that input.

About S/PDIF

If you want to make sure your transfers stay 100% digital, or if you need to get audio data out of digital devices such as DAT players, look for a sound card with a Sony/Philips Digital Interface Format (S/PDIF) port, which usually looks like a standard RCA jack and can be connected directly to the S/PDIF port on the device. You'll also need special software (generally supplied with the digital device) to manage the transfer. All transfers will be 100% perfect; none of the issues that make CD ripping sometimes problematic affect S/PDIF transfer.

Ripping from DVD

The audio tracks on most DVD disks are stored in the copy-protected VOB format to prevent ripping. If you should be in possession of a DVD disk to which you have legal copyright access, you can bypass this copy protection by going through the sound card—just plug the DVD player's output directly into the sound card and record from that channel with an audio-editing application. If you want to go for higher quality, run the S/PDIF output of the sound card into a digital amplifier, then from that amplifier's output to an external CD recorder. You can take the analog output from a DVD player, run it through analog-to-digital conversion to output a WAV file, and encode that. If you have a digital sound card, you can take the digital output from the DVD player, run it through the sound card's digital input, and generate a WAV from that.

The fact that a group of Linux hackers had succesfully unlocked the DVD security mechanism in late 1999 may mean that tools for getting signal from DVD to hard disk may become available by the time you read this; it was too early to tell at this writing

---

Encoding from Analog Sources

Many thanks to technical editor Bruno Prior for his contribution of this section.

There are two basic ways to encode from analog sources such as LP or tape: Either use an "all-in-one" solution to encode directly from the audio source to MP3, or record the source to an uncompressed audio file (WAV, AIFF, etc.), preprocess in a dedicated audio editor, and compress it with an MP3 encoder. While it may seem at first like all-in-one tools would be the easiest route, this often turns out not to be the case, for a variety of reasons. For the purposes of illustration, we'll look at one example of each type.

MusicMatch Jukebox

www.musicmatch.com We've already covered the basics of MusicMatch Jukebox in Chapter 3, but here we're going to take advantage of one of Jukebox's more advanced features—its capability of encoding from your sound card's line-in jack. To be more consumer-friendly, MusicMatch refers to encoding processes as "recording," so we'll use that term here, even though it technically isn't quite correct.

To enable the Recorder, make sure the "Show Recorder" option is selected under Options → View. To configure the Recorder for line input, navigate to the Recorder configuration page via Options → Recorder → Settings and select Line-in from the Recorder Source picklist. Select your Recording quality (bitrate) from the options on the left. Click the Songs Directory button and specify the folder and filename formats under which your recordings should be stored.

You may also want to click the Advanced button to specify whether tracks should fade in or out, which can be useful if the actual fade in or out on the source material is corrupted with vinyl crackle or tape hiss. You can also choose to offset the start of each track, (which is useful to account for gaps between tracks), and to normalize your recordings.

The MP3 encoding selection box will let you choose between Joint Stereo (the default), Stereo, and Mono. As described earlier, you probably want to select Stereo here, unless you want to keep file sizes down. This can be particularly important when recording from tape, since left and right stereo channels on some tapes can be slightly out-of-phase, especially with older music. Combining the lower frequencies of out-of-phase channels, as Joint Stereo does, can produce significant distortion—the only way to avoid this is to use simple Stereo encoding.

The most important section in Advanced dialog is the Auto Song Detect option, which is intended to let MusicMatch Jukebox detect gaps between songs so you don't have to stop and start recording for each track on an LP or tape. If you know the approximate or minimum length of gaps between songs you're recording, you can help MusicMatch make a better educated guess as to where songs begin and end.

You'll notice that the Jukebox recording interface now looks slightly different than it does when ripping from a CD. Sample album title and artist names will have been added, and only one track will be displayed, awaiting the name to be entered. Enter real album and artist names and give a meaningful name to the first track. With your turntable or tape deck attached to your machine as described earlier, start the music source playing and hit Start on the Recorder. If you chose the Auto Song Detect option, it will attempt to break the input into tracks wherever it finds a gap in the music. If it doesn't find gaps, Jukebox will output the entire audio stream until you press Stop.

There are a number of problems you may encounter when recording from an analog source. For example, Jukebox does not start recording immediately when you press Start. Instead, it listens for the start of the song before recording begins. This is fine if the song starts assertively, but if it fades in or starts with a quiet intro, you'll probably lose the start of the song. You can get around this by selecting the Delayed Record option in Recorder Settings and then specifying Start Immediately. The side effect of this technique is that you'll have to stop and start recording for each track, whether or not you have selected Auto Song Detect.

Regardless whether you have Start Immediately enabled, Auto Song Detect may introduce other problems. For instance, ASD simply looks for gaps longer than the specified Gap Length which do not contain sound levels above the specified Gap Level. Unfortunately, most analog sources contain quite a bit of noise, so you'll have to specify a fairly generous Gap Level—probably at least 10%. But if your music encompasses a significant dynamic range, you may end up with split tracks, as Jukebox may mistake quiet passages for song gaps (try recording Queen's "Bohemian Rhapsody" from vinyl for a splendid example of this). Fade-outs may also be prematurely truncated.

Even if you can get past these gotchas, you'll still have some work to do when recording is complete. You now have a series of MP3 tracks, but only the first one will have a meaningful name, while the remaining tracks will have names like "Line-in track 2," etc. You're going to have to rename the files and edit the ID3 tags by hand for them to be of any use. With any luck, a future version of Jukebox will offer a more intelligent interface for handling this in advance of recording.

While Jukebox does a pretty good job as far as it goes, you may end up deciding that you need a more sophisticated tool for reasons like this. LineRipper, for example, may be better suited to meet your needs.

LineRipper

leo.worldonline.es/mpicarth/ LineRipper exists for the sole purpose of encoding from Line-in (although it is also capable of conventional encoding from WAV files, and supports a variety of encoders, including LAME and GOGO. Conveniently, LineRipper lets you specify track names for all the tracks to be recorded beforehand. More importantly, LineRipper lets you specify different artists for each track, which gets around problems commonly encountered by encoders trying to deal with compilation albums. For the real power user, LineRipper can separate tracks either by listening for gaps or by reading a table of track lengths input by the user before encoding begins. While this takes more effort up front, it offers a better chance of accurate track separation.

LineRipper is clearly superior to Jukebox for the purpose of encoding from Line-in, but it has its own weaknesses. Even if you do type in track lengths beforehand, some slippage is still likely to occur due to differing gap lengths. If you use the auto-detect option, there's still no way to avoid the problem of truncating tracks that fade in or out when there's significant noise in the signal, and there's no way to avoid noise from sources like vinyl or tape unless you preprocess the output. This is no fault of LineRipper, but a fundamental weakness in the process of encoding from analog sources in general.

Notes on manual track separation

It may seem like a lot of effort, but in the end, the traditional route of recording to one giant WAV file, processing and splitting the WAV, and then encoding the processed tracks can be the most effective technique for creating MP3s from your tape and vinyl collection. Not that this process is not without its problems either.

The first difficulty you're likely to encounter is the fact that the audio-editing facilities which come standard with your system may not be adequate for the job. Sound Recorder (the bundled Windows recorder), for instance, can only handle around two minutes of music, which won't get you very far (the audio recorder bundled with BeOS, however, is extremely well suited for tasks like this, and can output directly to MP3; there are a number of third-party utilities for MacOS and Linux that will do the job, though I wasn't aware of any that could save directly to MP3). For most purposes, you'll need a program to record audio from Line-in. If you have a Creative Labs sound card, you should have a program on your system called Wave Studio, which goes far beyond the capabilities of Windows' Sound Recorder. Other sound cards often come bundled with similar audio editors.

To really get all the power features, you'll have to lay out the cash for a pro or pseudo-pro sound editing program. Unfortunately, the leading contenders, such as Sound Forge and CoolEdit Pro are not cheap, at several hundred dollars each. Fortunately, cheaper contenders are starting to emerge. One attractive option is CoolEdit 2000 (*www.syntrillium.com/cooledit/*) which currently costs a more reasonable $69. An optional Audio Cleanup plug-in for CoolEdit 2000 is also available, which includes the features you need for reducing clicks, crackles, and hums from analog audio. However, the plug-in is extremely slow, and doesn't offer a visual preview. A popular and even cheaper alternative is GoldWave (*www. goldwave.com*), a $40 shareware audio editor. GoldWave includes noise reduction, but click/pop/crackle removal still has to be performed by an external program.

Remember that these giant WAV files are going to consume large amounts of disk space. One 30-minute album side will take up around 300 MB at the standard 44.1kHz, 16 bit (and you probably don't want to go lower than that for your quality MP3 collection). A reasonably fast hard drive can also be useful when dealing with lots of uncompressed audio.

Notes on noise reduction

Assuming the recording process goes well, you're left with a 300 MB, crackly, hissy uncompressed audio file. The next step is to lose the crackles, hisses, etc. In CoolEdit 2000 (or other, more expensive editors like CoolEdit Pro or Sound Forge), you can probably pass the file through the included Audio Cleanup process. If your editor doesn't include such a feature, a wide variety of programs are available to do this. Some of the better ones are:

Sound Laundry (www.algorithmix.com)
> The Compact Edition offers limited functionality but has the easiest interface of any of these programs, while the full version has a confusing interface but is very flexible and powerful.

Groove Mechanic (www3.bc.sympatico.ca/badgerbytes/groove/)
> Very good output with the default values, but not as flexible as most.

Dart Pro 32 (www.tracertek.com)
> Highly configurable but slightly confusing user interface and somewhat sensitive to source file format.

Regardless of the program you choose, play around with the options for reducing click/crackle and noise/hiss until you're getting the cleanest sound possible without removing any of the actual audio. Keep in mind that it's very easy to throw the baby out with the bathwater here—remove too much signal and you'll affect the ambience of the whole piece. Then pass the file through the filter or filters and save the clean output as a new file.

A good way to make sure you're removing only the noise and not the signal (if your program supports it) is to listen to the sound being removed, rather than to the audio that remains.

Splitting large files

The next step is to chop up the clean file into its constituent tracks by selecting the in-point and out-point of a track, copying the selected area to the clipboard, and pasting the results into a new track. Most editors offer a visual image of the file, so it's easy to see the song gaps as "troughs" on the display. Jump to the gap points, zoom in, and listen carefully to make sure you're selecting exactly the right in- and out-points for each track.

Once you've got a set of clean, uncompressed tracks, all that's left is to encode them to MP3 by passing the files through your favorite encoder. Most encoders will not offer the option to tag the resulting MP3s, as they can't interface raw audio with the CDDB and therefore do not have the information they need. You'll have to insert your ID3 tags manually with a separate ID3 tagger or through your favorite MP3 player, if it includes its own tag editor.

If you named the files sensibly, try a tool such as id3ren (see Chapter 4), which can extract track title, artist, album, and other data from the filename and use that to create the tags automatically.

If splitting and encoding files manually sounds like a lot of work, a tool that will help to do this in one step is LP Ripper (*www. cfbsoftware.com.au*). Tell the program how many tracks are on the recording and it will split the file for you by checking for perceived gaps. You can adjust the start and end times of each track to a sensitivity of 0.1 second, and you can enter track titles beforehand, which LP Ripper will use to name the files. Some basic manual editing (such as removing leading and trailing noise) is advisable before passing the file to LP Ripper, but this tool can save a good deal of time and effort when dealing with giant WAV files. LP Ripper's greatest weakness is that it won't let you jump to the end of a track to adjust the end time. If you want to edit the end time of each track precisely, it's probably quicker to do it manually.

Roll Your Own Compact Discs

When compact discs first appeared, they were "black boxes"; unlike LPs or cassettes, few people understood how they worked. In the mid-'90s, writeable CDs appeared for the first time, enabling anyone to create their own audio or data CDs at home... as long as they were sufficiently wealthy. By the end of the '90s, however, the cost of CD-R (the "R" is for "recordable") devices had fallen to well within the casual user's reach, and the cost of blank CDs dropped to the point where CD-R had a lower price-per-megabyte than any other storage medium.

MP3 collections typify the kind of problem CD-R was meant to solve: What happens when the amount of data you want to keep around exceeds the amount of storage space available on your system's hard drives? True, the price of hard drives has plummeted as well, but no matter how big a hard drive you install, it won't be long before your MP3 collection is even bigger.

However, relying on compact discs as a primary storage medium probably isn't the way you want to go either. With the price of hard drives continuing to go down, some people are surprised to discover that storing large MP3 collections on hard drives is actually *cheaper* than storing them on compact disc. Let's do the math. At this writing, 28 GB hard drives could be had for around $8/GB. Assuming you encode at 128 kbps, you'll need around one megabyte per minute of music. Now let's assume a baseline price of a CD-R drive at $200 and $1 for each disc. One 28 GB disk will cost around $224 and hold around 470 hours of music. Storing the same number of MP3s on CD-R will require around 44 discs, at a cost (including the drive) of $244. Storing the same number of tracks in CD audio format will require around 380 discs, at a cost (including the drive) of $580. So to store approximately 500 hours of music, hard disk is the best cost option. On the other hand, if you double this (i.e., 1,000 hours of music), then storing MP3s on CD-R looks like the best option. But by then, the inconvenience of having to search through 90 CDs to find the track you want will probably outweigh the marginal cost benefits.

If cost is all that counts, then the balance point (where CD-R overtakes hard-disks in terms of value) is currently at just over 500 hours of music. But unless you absolutely require portability, having all your tracks on CD-R as opposed to hard disk is going to be extremely inconvenient. And remember that CD-R is not editable. Keep these considerations in mind before devoting a ton of energy and money into building a giant collection of hand-rolled compact discs.

CDA vs. Data

There are two ways to approach MP3 storage on compact disc:

Keep your files in MP3 format

Advantages
> Assuming 128 kbps, you can store 650 MB of MP3s, or about 10 hours of music on a single CD.

Disadvantages
> You can only listen to the stored music through an MP3 player, which usually means on your computer. However, increasing numbers of dedicated MP3 hardware devices are appearing on the market, and some of them will let you play data CD-ROMs full of MP3s.

Transform your MP3s into CD audio format

Advantages

Can be played on any CD player (and most DVD players) in the known universe (and possibly in alternate universes as well, excepting those comprised of antimatter).

Disadvantages

Doing so means uncompressing your MP3s, so they take up 10 times more space. You're back to the 74-minute storage length of regular audio CDs. And doing that often means more manual labor to burn each CD.

How you approach this dilemma depends completely on your needs, and which end of the convenience spectrum you want to land on. If you do most of your MP3 listening at the helm of your machine and just want to free up some disk space, you'll want to burn normal data CDs. If you want to create standard audio CDs you can play in the car or on your home stereo, you may want to go the distance and start burning audio CDs.

Hardware/Software Requirements

In order to create CDs of any type, you'll need a CD-Recording device of some kind. Inexpensive models, as of late 1999, could be had for as little as $200, while professional models (and CD duplicators) could set you back more than $1,000. Most people should find the base models more than adequate for their needs, however. If you want to do some detailed research on CD recorders, take a look at CD Media World (*www.cdmediaworld.com*).

You'll also need to decide whether to get a straight CD-R device or go for CD-RW. The latter type is capable of writing to a blank CD multiple times, just like you would with a hard drive. However, blank media for CD-RW is considerably more expensive than blank CD-Rs, and may not provide as much added convenience as you might imagine, primarily because CD-RW discs have a lower reflectance than standard CDs and thus can't be played back in many standard audio CD players. This makes them more suitable for data storage than for audio storage (although many late-model audio CD players are CD-RW-compatible). At a buck or two a pop, CD-Rs are cheap enough to make occasional mistakes with, even if you can't go back and correct them later on.

Burning Notes

The actual process of burning CD-ROMs is completely dependent on the burning software used. While almost all CD-R and CD-RW burners come with some kind of burning software, it's often possible to use software other than what comes with your unit, in case you don't find it up to snuff. Some users with exacting demands, for instance, find that the Adaptec software that comes with many CD-R drives is not configurable enough, and has trouble with some scratched CDs. Many "pro" users turn to Goldenhawk's CD-recording software instead (*www.goldenhawk. com*). In any case, the process is usually pretty intuitive, and most CD burner applications come with complete documentation and wizards to guide you through, should you need assistance. In general, the process consists of nothing more than telling the software whether you intend to burn an audio or data CD, then dragging your tracks or files into a window.

If you want the audio CDs you burn to be playable both in computers and in stereos, you must remember to "close" the disc when the burn is complete. You should find an option for this somewhere in your burning software.

When shopping for a CD burner, don't get overly excited about speed without asking around online about burning quality first. While not universally true, some people find that the faster the burner, the higher the chance of bad burns, or of pops and glitches in the final CDs. With a high-quality drive such as a Plextor or Yamaha, however, fast burns can still be error-free (the author hasn't toasted a CD yet with his 8x SCSI Plextor burner). The better drives from Panasonic and Pioneer also get good marks among users for bit-perfect DAE. Also, make sure you get a drive capable of "Disk at Once," or DAO technology. This lets you burn disks without a two-second delay between tracks (not generally an issue for mixed collections, but possibly annoying for live shows and for creating segues).

When shopping for blank disks, don't lunge immediately for the 100-pack at the super-mongo discount price. The chances of bad burns (which wastes both time and money) is much higher with cruddy CDs than with good ones. Unfortunately, there are no blanket rules for determining which of the dozens of available brands is going to work best for you. Buy your CDs in small quantities until you find a brand with near-perfect, reliable results. Again, check around online for recommendations, and see *www.cdmediaworld.com* to learn all about the various dye colors and manufacturing plants.

If your CD-ROM drive is working but you're experiencing pops, glitches, or drop-outs regardless of which burning software you use, look for an option in the software that will let you decrease the burn speed or increase the buffer size. You may get more accurate transfers at slower speeds.

Making space

Depending on the CD burning software you're using and the kind of disk you wish to burn, you may need to set aside a big chunk of disk space for the process. If you're burning exact duplicates of existing CDs, this won't be an issue as you'll be copying data directly from one CD to another. If you're burning custom CDs consisting of various tracks from multiple sources, however, you'll need to make sure you've got enough temporary storage space to hold everything that's going to go on the CD. Since the capacity of a CD is 650 MB,* one of the best solutions is to create a 650 MB disk partition. Fill it to capacity with WAV or AIFF files (or MP3s, if you're burning a data CD) and you'll know exactly how much space you've got to work with. You can then just drag the entire folder into the burn window of your CD creation software, or create a "disk image" of the entire partition and burn the image to CD (images or "Disk At Once" options are especially useful if you have albums with songs that flow into each other smoothly, or anytime you want to eliminate gaps between the tracks). If you plan on burning images, however, note that you'll need twice the space, or 1,280 MB, since the image file will be exactly the same size as the total amount of data you intend to burn.

Since creating a new partition isn't a convenient option for all users, you may just have to keep an eye on the size of the folder you're storing source material in. You can learn this information in Windows Explorer by right-clicking a folder name and choosing Properties from the context menu, in the MacOS Finder or BeOS Tracker by selecting a folder and tapping Opt+I to Get Info, and in Unix/Linux by typing du <pathname>.

In addition, most graphical burning software will provide some kind of interface widget or status area reporting the total amount of space occupied and remaining on the pending CD by examining the contents of the burn list. Thanks to this feature, you can drag in files from anywhere on your system without needing to set aside a specific folder or partition. Your burning software shouldn't let you attempt to burn a CD with a burn list larger than the capacity of a CD.

Format Conversion

If you only want to burn data CDs, you can skip this section and just use the documentation that came with your CD-R unit. If you're burning audio CDs, read up. While some CD burning software, such as MP3 Maker for Windows, Toast for MacOS, and CDBurner for BeOS will let you drag MP3 files directly into the burner application and have everything decoded to PCM audio automatically, most CD

---

* Audio CDs have actually pushed this limit up to 750 MB.

Custom CDs vs. Portable MP3 Players

Some people wonder whether it's worthwhile buying a portable MP3 player after they start burning their own audio CDs. Why not just buy a portable CD player and be done with it? After all, most first- and second-generation portable MP3 players won't give you 72 minutes of music encoded at a reasonable bitrate without additional storage cards, and audio CDs don't suffer quality loss due to compression. A portable CD player can play your existing CD collection along with your custom CDs. CDs are universally compatible, and can be played anywhere you find a CD player. Offloading MP3s to CDs will save you tons of disk space. Finally, investing in CD-Rs gives you more flexibility for your money because you can use the same drive as a normal CD-ROM in your computer, and can burn CDs containing any type of computer data, not just audio.

If you're wondering by now why the recording industry isn't more freaked out about recordable CDs than it is about the Rio and similar players, remember that there's a critical difference here: You have to make a physical copy of the disc for every person you want to share your music with, and that's a serious barrier to piracy in comparison to the popular-but-usually-illegal "Upload once, distribute to the entire web population" model. In addition, portable MP3 players are much smaller than portable CD players, and have no moving parts. Portable MP3 players never skip, no matter how hard you exercise. And you don't have to burn a new CD just to get a new playlist!

---

burner applications will only accept uncompressed audio as input. That means you'll need to find a way to convert your MP3 files to WAV or AIFF before you can make an audio CD. There are many ways to do this, depending on your operating system and the tools you use. Here are a few of the most common methods; see your application's documentation if you use other tools.

Windows: WinAmp

Right-click on WinAmp's interface and select Options → Preferences from the context menu (or just tap Ctrl+P). Navigate to Plugins → Output and select Nullsoft DiskWriter. When you click the Close button, you'll be asked to specify an output directory. Now just play your MP3s normally. You won't hear anything, as all output will be dumped to WAV files rather than sent to the sound card. To decode batches of files, just set up a playlist and let it go to town. Don't forget to return to the Preferences panel and reset the output to WaveOut or DirectSound when you're done!

MacOS

Most MacOS users don't do format conversion directly. Instead, they use CD burning applications like Adaptec's Toast that convert MP3 to raw audio as files are dragged into the burning application itself. Creating audio CDs from MP3s with Toast is no different from creating audio CDs from any other source; the process is elegant and totally transparent.

If you do want to convert from MP3 to AIFF, use the Converter built into Sound-Jam MP. Open the Converter window, drag in your tracks, and change the MP3 option in the "Convert using…" picklist to AIFF. This may be especially useful if you have an older version of Toast that doesn't convert from MP3 to PCM audio automatically.

Linux: amp

Many command-line MP3 players for Linux include the ability to decode MP3 files to PCM audio; you'll need to check your player's documentation for this ability. Here's an example using the encoder mpg123—a simple shell script that creates a WAV file for each MP3 file in a given directory; you may need to change the initial command and flags on the second line to work with a different tool:

```
for i in *.mp3 ; do
    mpg123 -w $i ${i%.mp3}.wav
```

To burn CDs, most Linux users use cdrecord (*www.fokus.gmd.de/research/cc/ glone/employees/joerg.schilling/private/cdrecord.html/),* a command-line burner that works with the majority of CD recorders out there, and which has a ton of optional features. cdrecord's documentation is somewhat dense; be sure to look through some of the FAQs and HOW-TOs available on the cdrecord site. For a nice graphical wrapper to cdrecord, download a copy of xcdroast from your favorite Linux software library.

BeOS: SoundPlay

BeOS comes with a drag-and-drop CD burner as a standard component of the operating system—just drag MP3 files from the Tracker into the CDBurner window and click burn—an audio CD will be generated automatically. Third-party burning software is available as well, as is a BeOS port of cdrecord. If you just want to decode MP3 files to WAV without burning them first, drop the files you want to decode onto SoundPlay's interface, then click on the title of the playing file. From the Special menu, select "Decode to file." Tell SoundPlay whether you want to decode to RAW or WAV, single or all files in the current playlist, and specify the destination folder. Click OK, sit back, and you'll end up with a folder full of RAW or WAV files.

CDs vs. MiniDiscs

Some users prefer to store their music on the Sony MiniDisc format rather than recordable audio CDs, for a variety of reasons. First, and most obviously, Mini-Discs are much smaller than CDs, while storing the same amount of music (ten MiniDiscs require less physical volume than four conventional CDs). This also means MiniDiscs are great for joggers and other people who use a portable player heavily. By default, all recording on the MiniDisc is done with a proprietary, non-MP3 Sony format called ATRAC, which compresses audio at a ratio of 5:1.

It's possible to record to MiniDiscs 100% digitally, just by connecting a TOSLINK digital signal converter to your sound card's digital output (actually, this is a technique which should work with any kind of consumer-oriented digital audio device that comes with TOSLINK or S/PDIF output jacks). This means you can just play MP3 tracks through your favorite decoder and dump them straight to MiniDisc. Finally, MiniDiscs are re-writeable, like a CD-RW device. If you're thinking of buying a RAM-based portable MP3 player, you might want to consider a MiniDisc instead—you'll get a lot more playing time and flexibility.

On the other hand, CD-R blanks are quite a bit cheaper than MiniDisc blanks, so you can afford to just throw out the ones you don't like and not worry about it. Perhaps more troubling, you lose compatibility with the zillions of standard CD audio players out there (this problem is somewhat less substantial in Europe and Japan, where MiniDiscs are more popular than they are in the U.S.). Finally, recording to MiniDisc is quite slow—a 74-minute disc will take 74 minutes to record, which is far longer than the speeds you'll get with 2x, 4x, 8x, and even faster CD-R drives.

6

Hardware, Portables, Home Stereos, and Kits

Until recently, MP3 audio was a software-only proposition for most people. MP3 files were created on the computer and listened to on the computer. But that was before the appearance of the now-legendary Diamond Rio, which won the landmark court battle against the RIAA and, in so doing, legitimized a tidal wave of hardware-based MP3 playback devices. At this writing, there are at least a dozen portable MP3 players, and a whole genre of MP3-oriented home stereo devices is threatening to enter the consumer channel. Dozens of sites are available on the Web designed to help you build an MP3 player from scratch, and many alternatives for playing MP3 in your car are available.

This chapter covers the aspects of MP3 playback that escape the limited confines of the personal computer. Since many of the devices covered here involve connecting computers, home stereos, and custom devices, we'll start with an overview of analog and digital connection issues, before examining the field of MP3 portables and the quickly changing question of how best to store files for use with portables (including the advent of Lilliputian hard drives and removable memory cards). In a similar vein, you'll see how you can use a hand-held computer to play back MP3 files, assuming you've got a suitable PDA. We'll survey the landscape of MP3 equipment designed for use in home and car stereos, then move on to the tricky stuff: Do-it-yourself schemes for building your own MP3 hardware from prefab kits and plans, or, for the truly hardcore among you, from scratch.

Note that in most cases, the hardware mentioned here will not help you *create* MP3 files outside your computer—only play them back. The fact that commercially available hardware-based players are classified exclusively as storage devices—and thus do not contribute to piracy—is the essence of the landmark Rio suit and has completely shaped the MP3 hardware landscape.

Playing MP3 Through Your Home Stereo

There are basically two ways to listen to MP3 audio through your home stereo. Both methods have their advantages and disadvantages.

- Connect your computer's sound card to your stereo, thereby keeping MP3 decoding functions and playback control inside the computer.

- Purchase or build dedicated MP3 player hardware to occupy a permanent place on your stereo component rack.

Either way, you'll be hooking up your hardware either via analog ports, or through digital outputs in the playback equipment. The difference between these two types of connections is in the conversion process. As described in Chapter 3, *Getting and Playing MP3 Files*, digital bits need to be converted into analog signal at some point in the chain. The question is whether this job is done by a (usually) low-quality, built-in DAC (digital-to-analog converter) or by a higher-quality DAC in a digitally equipped amplifier, DAT, or outboard DAC.

Analog Connections

Since most people have neither amplifiers with digital inputs nor outboard DACs, connections are usually a simple matter of obtaining the right analog cables and connecting the right jacks.

Connecting your computer to your stereo

To make the direct connection, you'll need a special adapter and a length of RCA cable (also known as a "patch cord"). The adapter should have a 1/8" male jack on one side to plug into your sound card's line out jack and two female RCA jacks on the other, as shown in Figure 6-1.* Connect your RCA cable into the adapter's female jacks, and run them into the Auxiliary input on your home stereo's amp or pre-amp (actually, any input on your stereo besides Phono will suffice, but Auxilary is often the only input available). Turn your amp or pre-amp's input selector to Aux, and you're all set.

The necessary patch cord and adapter can be obtained inexpensively at most electronics parts stores, such as Radio Shack. You can also find prebuilt cables designed for this purpose at *www.musicmatch.com/get_gear/*.

---

* To relieve a little stress on your cables, you can get a 1/8" stereo plug attached to a soft cable, rather than the hard adapter pictured here.

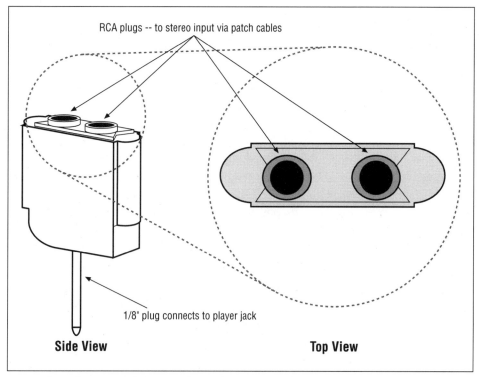

RCA plugs -- to stereo input via patch cables

1/8" plug connects to player jack

Side View   **Top View**

Figure 6-1. Obtain an adapter similar to this one to connect an external MP3 player or computer sound card to your home stereo

Do not purchase more cable than you reasonably need. In the ideal environment, your computer would be very near your stereo, so you can use 3' or 6' patch cords. Of course, this is seldom feasible in real living situations, where the computer is in a completely different room. But keep in mind that longer cables will pick up noise and increase impedance, which will cause high frequencies to roll off.

Connecting external devices

Virtually any external MP3 playback device (some of which are covered later in this chapter) can be used through your home stereo, in addition to functioning as a stand-alone unit. While connection options vary from one device to the next, the principle is generally the same. Home stereo MP3 components will have RCA plugs on the back which can be jacked into the Aux or any other free input on your amplifier (with the exception of Phono). Some car stereo MP3 units, such as the empeg, have a pair of RCA jacks as well, to make it easy to slide them out of the car and use them as a home stereo component. Future high-end MP3 players may include digital outputs as well, though we weren't aware of any at this writing.

Portable players such as the Creative NOMAD typically do not have RCA outputs, but rather a 1/8" headphone output jack. To play a portable device with these outputs through your stereo, you'll again need to obtain an appropriate adapter and cables. Some portable units come bundled with these. If not, you should be able to find one at your local Radio Shack or other electronics/stereo store.

Digital Connections

Digital input jacks have become increasingly common on amplifiers sold in the late nineties, and are the norm on amps built for use with home theaters. The advantage, again, is the ability to transfer the job of digital-to-analog conversion from the sound card itself to a device specialized for the task, such as a digital receiver, home theater system, or outboard DAC. The low cost and limited space available on a typical computer sound card means that built-in DACs are functional, but not optimal. Audiophiles often spend from $300 to $10,000 for a dedicated "outboard" DAC in order to handle all incoming digital sound optimally.

In order to use a digital connection, you'll need support for it on either end of the chain—in addition to support on the amplification side, you must also own a sound card or dedicated MP3 playback device with digital outputs. The Creative Labs SoundBlaster Live! is an exceptionally popular card with S/PDIF jacks, though the digital output comes on a "daughter card," not on the main sound card body. If you purchase the SoundBlaster Live! Value Edition, you won't get this daughter card.

 The SoundBlaster Live! is used as an example of a popular, relatively high-quality card here, not necessarily as a recommendation. Audiophiles will note that the Live! resamples signal up to 48kHz, even in the case of digital output, and thus introduces some quantization noise. This is not the case when using Turtle Beach or Guillemot ISIS soundcards, for example. The ISIS is even sold with an additional external DAC.

Connection types

Digital connections come in four flavors, though you're likely to see only one or two of them on the vast majority of consumer hardware. Remember—you must have the same connector type on both your sound card and on your amplifier or DAC. Adapters between some of these formats can be found at specialty retailers, but it will take some hunting.

While some people are able to hear the difference between quality cable and consumer cable (analog or digital), others are not. In the grand scheme of things, the differences between these connection types are small enough to be considered negligible. However, if you have very good stereo equipment and listen carefully, the differences *are* there. Like fine wine, it's often the subtle differences that take the most training and experience to detect, but that mean the most in the long run.

If you're purchasing cable for digital connections rather than analog ("digital coax"), be sure to get cable rated at 75 Ohms for S/PDIF connections, or 110 Ohms for for AES/EBU connections. Standard analog interconnects will do the job, but won't deliver optimal results. You can also use 75 Ohm video cable with RCA plugs for the job, and probably save some money in the process.

S/PDIF

Short for Sony/Phillips Digital InterFace, this connector looks like a standard RCA jack,* but one jack handles both left and right channels (if you see a pair of them on your equipment, they're for input and output, not left and right). Better home theater systems, outboard DACs, and digital-output-capable sound cards work with S/PDIF, while consumer-grade equipment is more likely to use Toslink (see the following entry). While you can use any standard RCA-type patch cable with S/PDIF connectors, most audiophiles purchase dedicated digital cables for the job. This cable type is typically referred to as *digital coax* in stereo stores.

Toslink

The most commonly available type of fiber optic connection is made over the comparatively inexpensive Toslink cable. Toslink jacks consist of a square-ish shield surrounding a small-diameter metal housing for the optical cable itself. Toslink does an adequate job of transferring digital signal, but does not tend to win accolades from audiophiles due to the fact that the fiber inside is plastic, not glass, and is therefore prone to internal reflections. Because the tip of the fiber must be kept perfectly clean, always replace the plastic shields that came with your Toslink cables when not in use.

AES/EBU

Found almost exclusively on high-end and dedicated equipment, this digital transfer spec moves through balanced cable—like a microphone—and usually terminates in XLR (3-pin canon-style) connectors. You'll most likely see this only on specialized equipment where quality considerations are paramount and long runs are necessary, as is the case in recording studios.

---

* Higher-quality equipment will use BNC connectors rather than RCA plugs for S/PDIF.

AT&T Glass

Expensive and uncommon, AT&T Glass is a fiber optic connection type which does not suffer the quality stigma of Toslink because the glass fiber is not subject to the internal reflection problems that affect plastic fiber. Only the most expensive, specialized equipment sports AT&T Glass connectors.

As with any cable type, make sure your digital connections are firm and secure, and keep cable lengths short whenever possible (though length is less important with optical connectors than with traditional cables).

Portable Players

MP3 took its first big step outside the realm of the computer when it entered the portable player market. In fact, the market is heating up so quickly that research firm DataQuest expects to see 155 million portable MP3 units sold to consumers in the year 2000. The devices are quickly becoming as ubiquitous as the portable cassette or CD player.

All of these units are based on the same basic concept as a portable CD or cassette player, but enjoy the advantage of having no moving parts, and therefore not being susceptible to skips caused by bumping or jogging. On the other hand, they have the disadvantage that they must be loaded up with music prior to use, which takes more time and effort than just throwing a few CDs into your backpack.

 There are many more portable devices on the market than are listed here, with more coming all the time. As MP3 becomes less of a geek toy and more of a killer app for the general consumer, expect portable players to become as popular as—or more popular than—portable CD and cassette players are now. What you see here is a brief survey of the field at this writing, focusing on features and flexibility. Think of this as a guide to the kind of functionality you should be looking for, not a complete menu of portable choices. Take a look at the Hardware section of MP3.com at *www.mp3.com/ hardware/* for more options.

You'll also want to give some thought to the type of computer connections offered by the device. Various portable brands and products connect to your PC over parallel, serial, or USB connections. I don't know about you, but I haven't had a machine with a spare parallel or serial port for some years now, and despite what anyone says about parallel pass-through arrangements, these have often caused me grief. The parallel port just wasn't designed for sharing (it *is* faster than serial, however), and increasing numbers of low-cost consumer computers ship with only one serial port, rather than two or four, as they did once upon a time. The real solution is USB, which *is* designed for sharing, and is much faster than either parallel or serial. Unfortunately, USB-compatible portables were somewhat rare at this writing (this situation should rectify itself in the near future).

To quickly compare the kinds of features you should be looking for in a portable player, see Table 6-1.

Speaking of connections, make sure you get a unit with its own desktop "cradle," as shown in Figure 6-2. Without a cradle, you'll have to manually connect your portable to your PC every time you want to transfer tracks. This becomes less important with USB connections, since you can just leave a USB cable dangling from a USB hub. Since a cradle stays permanently connected, all you have to do is drop the unit into its bay, fire up the software, drag a few tracks into the player's desktop software, and be on your way.

Figure 6-2. The Creative Labs' Nomad portable player in its cradle

Memory and Storage Issues

Most first and second generation portable units suffer from limited storage capacities, which means you get to listen to the same music (typically an hour or less) all day long. If you want to cram more music into a portable player, you have to encode at lower bitrates, which means decreased quality. The problem is being mitigated by the advent of next-generation, hot-swappable memory modules, tiny hard drives, and portable CD players that play MP3 data CDs. Just prior to press time, a new player called Personal Jukebox (*www.pjbox.com*) had announced an

MP3 player packing a 4.86 GB hard drive capable of storing around 100 CDs worth of music, in a form factor only slightly larger than a traditional MP3 portable.

By Christmas 1999, most portable MP3 hardware was slated to start being SDMI-compatible (see Chapter 7, *The Not-So-Fine-Print: Legal Bits and Pieces*, for more on SDMI). If you want no part of this scheme, you may do well to scan the online auction sites for an older portable.

Many of these units are also capable of operating as simple storage devices for data other than MP3 and other audio files. If the provided software allows (and in many cases it does), you can drag Word docs, images, spreadsheets, or whatever you like into the unit. If you purchase an additional cradle so you have one attached to both your work and home machines, you can take advantage of your fast Internet connection at work to download the latest huge browser upgrade, take it home stored in the portable's memory bank, then transfer it back to your home machine's hard drive for installation. Whoever said floppies were obsolete was right.

Memory to go

When shopping for a portable, *do not* underestimate the importance of getting a unit with as much memory as you can afford. Limited amounts of memory are the single biggest stumbling block to portables being truly viable. Vendors frequently overestimate the amount of playback time you'll get with 32, 64, or 96 MB of RAM in their marketing materials. If you don't mind swishy, warbly sound, sure you can fill up your portable with 96 kbps files and get a lot more playing time. But is it really worth it? If you care enough about your music to want to bring it wherever you go, then you care enough to have it sound decent.

Be cautious when a vendor tells you you'll get an hour of "digital quality audio" from your unit. What does the term "digital quality" really mean? Pretty much anything the vendor wants it to mean. In reality, such statements are often based not on 128 kbps audio, the quality of which is already questionable, but on 96 kbps or even 64 kbps encodings. They might be talking about mono, rather than stereo encodings. Or they might be talking about 22kHz, rather than 44kHz audio. At those rates, the quality is noticeably worse than AM radio or cassette tape—noisy and swishy. Who wants to disrespect the music they love that way? On the other hand, many of these units are capable of taking voice memos at very low bitrates (low enough to discourage you from trying to record live music concerts), and you *can* store several hours of acceptable-quality class lectures in 64 MB without difficulty.

One of the most viable near-term solutions to the storage problem is the portable, hot-swappable memory module. These are beginning to appear from a number of vendors, but the two leaders in the field are SanDisk (*www.sandisk.com*) with their Multi Media Card (MMC) (Figure 6-3), SmartMedia, and CompactFlash cards, and Sony, who are currently marketing their "Memory Sticks." Sony has a leg up because they also manufacture so many popular consumer electronics devices, including photo printers, car navigation systems, digital telephones, digital cameras, and personal computers compatible with the Memory Stick technology. Toshiba, Matsushita, and SanDisk have announced a partnership to eventually develop postage-stamp sized memory cards capable of storing up to 256 MB, and capable of up to 10 MB/sec of throughput. Most portable units that accept memory cards at this writing were using MMC cards of one flavor or another, though Sony was preparing to jump into the market with a portable player of their own, which would of course use Sony Memory Sticks.

Regardless of vendor, the principle behind these modules is the same—purchase as many memory modules as you like, load them up beforehand, and take them with you. This solves the storage problem quite nicely... if you can afford to buy a bunch of them.

Figure 6-3. The SanDisk Multi Media Card, commonly referred to as an "MMC" is barely the size of a quarter, and can be used as everything from a floppy replacement to an MP3 swappable storage solution

An industry specification called SSFDC (for Solid State Floppy Disk Card) represents an attempt for flash memory cards to adopt common mechanisms and interfaces to ensure interoperability across devices. For example, an SSFDC memory card will work as easily in your portable MP3 player as it does in your digital camera or even your cell phone. If this is important to you, check the manufacturer's web site for mention of SSFDC compliance.

Lilliputian hard drives

Meanwhile, IBM has developed its MicroDrive, a hard drive barely larger than a Susan B. Anthony, weighing less than an AA battery, and capable of storing 340 MB of data (Figure 6-4). Of course, the flipside of small drives is a return to moving parts, and with them a return to skippability and mechanical failure, so this may be one for those who don't exercise rigorously. Interestingly, physics dictates that inertia won't affect tiny hard drives as much as it does larger drives; it should take quite a blow to dislodge the read arm of a microdrive. And, of course, first-generation technologies are always expensive until they reach mainstream adoption.

Shortly after IBM introduced the drive, Diamond Multimedia, Clarion, Samsung, Sanyo, and Casio announced that they already begun receiving shipments of the $499 device for use in upcoming products. Diamond, in fact was the first to announce that their upcoming Rio II MP3 portable would include the MicroDrive. Meanwhile, i2Go (*www.i2go.com*) had just released a device called the eGo near press time, which was capable of working with two MicroDrives, for a total storage capacity of 680 MB. Things are about to get a whole lot better.

In my mind, that kind of storage capacity is the key to real usability for these units, and will obviate many of the hassles of carrying around additional flash memory cards and/or constantly updating the contents of MP3 portables. If you're an early adopter and just can't wait, get one of the available units now—they're loads of fun. But if this is a device you intend to use for a long time to come, hold off for better storage capacities; the scene is going to get a lot better than it was in early 2000.

Portable MP3 data CDs

Also new on the scene at this writing are portable devices that can read MP3 tracks from data CDs, which means you get a meaty ten hours of playback time. Unfortunately, it also means a potential return to the skipping problems that occur whenever mechanical devices and physical exercise come together. These skipping problems can, however, be mitigated by a good read-ahead caching scheme.

Figure 6-4. IBM's MicroDrive stores 340 MB of data and is small enough to be used in portable MP3 devices

If a unit can read a few minutes of music off the CD in one "gulp," it can then play that music from memory until the buffer expires, keeping the time spent reading data from disc to a minimum. See the section on the Pine player, later in this chapter.

Diamond Rio

www.rioport.com Diamond's Rio changed everything. With the advent of the Rio portable unit, MP3 files were freed from people's computers and suddenly became playable at the gym, on the subway, in the schoolyard, and while skydiving. The suit against Diamond by the RIAA (as covered in Chapter 7, *The Not-So-Fine-Print: Legal Bits and Pieces*) set a critical precedent and cleared the way for the future of similar devices and burgeoning competition.

Since the Rio was a first-generation device, it lacked many of the features now commonplace on portable units. However, subsequent editions of the Rio are much improved, with more memory, USB connections, a better-looking case, and a built-in equalizer so you can optimize the output for any given genre, as shown in Figure 6-5. While Diamond has big plans for the future, they're shipping both their original Rio 300 and the newer Rio 500 simultaneously through the first part of 2000. The price difference of $100 gets you a USB connection, more storage, a cooler case, a backlit display, and MacOS support.

Diamond has created an integrated software/web site solution called the RioPort, which is the name for both the companion software you get with the Rio and the site at *www.rioport.com*. While any MP3 user can head over to RioPort and download tracks from their growing library of signed (often "name brand" artists) for

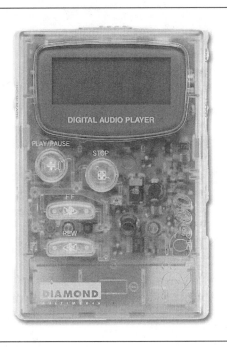

Figure 6-5. The Diamond Rio PMP500, in its cool translucent case

free or for a small fee, Rio owners have the advantage of tight integration between the site, the RioPort software, and your Rio player. The software, which is a combination music library, ripper/encoder, and sync utility, will automatically detect MP3 files on your system, regardless whether they come from the RioPort site or another site. The software also includes a built-in web browser that connects directly to RioPort.com and other popular MP3 sites, so you can find the files you're looking for quickly and easily. Once downloaded, songs become part of your music library, and can be synched with a connected Rio (or, in fact, any portable player) or played directly through the computer.

The Rio 500 has a cool bookmarking feature that lets you mark specific points in your files. This is particularly useful for saved news broadcasts, lecture notes, etc. To mark a point in a file, just press the Bookmark button. To access your saved bookmarks, use the thumbwheel on the unit to navigate through your bookmark collection.

Rio use on other platforms

While older versions of the Rio do not provide software or the proper connection type for MacOS users,* BeOS and Linux users are in luck, thanks to the presence of an Open Source version of the Rio filesystem protocol made available by The Snowblind Alliance. Linux users can download source for the Rio utility from *www.world.co.uk/sba/rio.htm*. After compiling and installing, usage is straightforward. You'll need to be running as root, since it accesses hardware directly. You'll also need to know the address of your parallel port (if your PC doesn't use the default) and specify it with the -p flag. Common memory addresses for parallel ports are 0x378, 0x3BC and 0x278. Then use:

```
rio -d
```

to display a directory of the files currently loaded on the unit. To upload a new file, use:

```
rio -g ~/data/mp3/somesong.mp3
```

to delete a song, use the -z flag instead. The utility is capable of many additional functions; see the included documentation for details.

BeOS users have it even easier. Rather than using the Rio utility directly, Be provides a version of the Rio filesystem as a dynamically loadable add-on, as shown in Figure 6-6. See Be's documentation on setting up the Rio.† Once mounted, the Rio appears in the Tracker just like any other mounted file system, and you can simply drag MP3 files into the Rio folder from elsewhere in the Tracker. In fact, you can even FTP files directly from the Internet into the Rio.

If you're a Mac user, you'll find that SoundJam (covered in Chapter 3) includes native support for later versions of the Rio over USB. You'll need to have USB 1.2 support installed—this comes with MacOS 8.6 and later. If you're using an earlier version of MacOS or a PCI USB adapter card, you'll need to download USB 1.2 or later from Apple's support site. You'll find an application in the SoundJam folder called RioPort SoundJam MP. Launch this and you'll be able to drag files into the player from the Finder, create folders within the Rio, delete files, reformat the Rio's memory module, and sort your on-board playlists exactly as you would a standard SoundJam playlist.

Rio: The next generation

While an exact release date was not available at press time, we were able to get a few projections on features to be included in a version of Rio to be released sometime in the first quarter of 2000. Diamond is looking closely at giving users a

---

* The Rio gained native MacOS connectivity with the advent of the Rio 500.

† BeOS support for the Rio was in "experimental" mode at this writing.

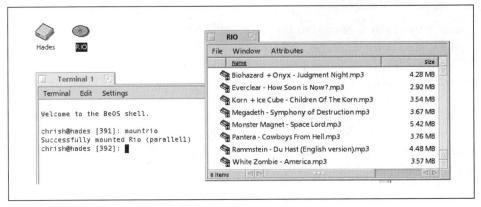

Figure 6-6. In BeOS, users mount the Rio as a normal filesystem

choice in the type of removable storage to be used. Users should be able to buy a base unit capable of playback, and expansion modules similar to those available for the Handspring Visor (covered in this chapter), so users can snap on an MMC module, Memory Stick module, or even an IBM Microdrive module. As the number of mini-storage options increases, this kind of expandability will become increasingly important, and users won't be locked into storage technologies if they should become obsolete.

The new Rio is scheduled to include support for Windows Media files, and Diamond is working with InterTrust to work out the details of a solid security model.

The company is working with outside design firms to find an optimum form factor; Diamond wants users to be able to operate the unit comfortably without even looking at it, which is important for use when driving or biking, for example. And of course Diamond wants the units to get even smaller, so users can stuff them into smaller pockets. They're also looking at ways to expand the size and quality of the display. Ultimately, it should be possible for users to view song lyrics stored in ID3v2 tags, or even to potentially display album cover art. Better playlist support is also on the table.

Meanwhile, Diamond is working on plans to launch a home stereo MP3 component, possibly similar to the Rio in ways, but in a home stereo component form factor and integrated into the home network. Diamond is beginning to see the writing on the wall here: many consumers have seen home networks as a geek toy without any real advantage for normal user. But everybody loves music, and once people see what they can do with a networked MP3 home, they'll be compelled to get those miniLANs up and running. No further details on the device were available at press time.

Creative Labs' NOMAD

www.nomadworld.com Creative Labs, progenitors of the widely popular Sound-Blaster and SoundBlaster Live! sound cards, has their own answer to the ubiquitous Rio: the NOMAD (Figure 6-7). The NOMAD I is available in both 32 MB and 64 MB models, both of which can take additional 32 MB flash ROM cards. The NOMAD II, on the other hand, has no built-in memory and relies instead on add-in memory modules, for greater expandability. The NOMAD II can accept any type or size of SmartMedia card.

An important point to keep in mind is that any unit that utilizes memory modules rather than built-in storage circumvents issues surrounding the ability to get files back out of the device (see Chapter 7).

Both versions of the NOMAD feature a built-in FM tuner and, more interestingly, built-in voice memo capabilities. If you have a sudden brainstorm, are fresh out of paper, or forgot your PalmPilot, you can just switch to Memo mode, hit the Record button, and speak directly into the device. When you're done speaking, your memo is encoded to MP3 (at an extremely low bitrate, judging by the quality of the results) and stored in the device's memory. When you later fire up the NOMAD I Manager software, you can save your voice memos to hard disk for posterity (note that, like all portable MP3 players, you *cannot* transfer music files out of the NOMAD I and back to disk; this would allow piracy and put the vendor afoul of laws outlined in Chapter 7).

Because the NOMAD II is fully programmable, the unit is designed to be "future-proof." By this, the company means that users can run Creative-provided software to update the built-in flash ROM, which will theoretically enable it to handle additional file formats or copyright protection mechanisms. This means you won't be left out in the cold if the industry decides to move in another direction. Like a computer, you'll just upgrade the software, rather than being left with an obsolete device.

You *must* set you parallel port to ECP to establish a connection with the NOMAD I. There's a good chance your BIOS is already set up this way. If you're not sure, enter you computer's BIOS screen at boot time and look for the option. Again, this problem could be easily circumvented by providing additional transfer ports.

Figure 6-7. The author in the great urban outdoors with the Creative Labs' NOMAD I

RCA Lyra

www.lyrazone.com While the Lyra doesn't break any real new ground, it does offer a few features that weren't available on other players at this writing. Perhaps most noteworthy, the unit is software-upgradeable, meaning you won't be locked out if one of the other excellent file formats discussed in Chapter 9, *Competing Codecs and Other File Formats*, comes into greater popularity. As shipped, the unit supports RealAudio G2 in addition to MP3, which could be especially beneficial for those wanting to listen to Internet radio shows on the train or bike ride to work. G2 files are uploaded to the unit through the same drag-and-drop interface provided for uploading MP3 files.

The Lyra also sports a six-line LCD readout-displaying track and artist names, folder name, track number (as stored in the unit—not the track number on the original CD), and the bitrate and elapsed time. The display is backlit, so it can be easily read in dimly-lit situations. It also supports a certain amount of on-board file management, so you can actually arrange your music in directory structures similar to those on your hard drive[*]—a capability I'd like to see in more portable players. To manage folders on the Lyra, just click the New Folder button and give the new directory a name. Files can be dragged into folders from within the Lyra management software, which is a modified version of RealJukebox (see Chapter 5, *Ripping and Encoding: Creating MP3 Files*).

---

[*] Up to 99 directories are supported, each of which can have up to 99 subdirectories.

Living with the NOMAD

I lived with a NOMAD I for several weeks, taking it virtually everywhere, from long bike rides over mountainous terrain to shopping trips in the car. The unit performed flawlessly, though I did have some qualms with certain aspects of both the hardware and software design. I found the unit's buttons well-located and easy to access, even when the its leather slipcover was in place. However, the buttons are not easy to distinguish from one another without looking at the unit, which made it very difficult to operate when biking.

With a pair of my own headphones, I found the audio quality of well-encoded MP3 files excellent.

I also really appreciated the magnesium case; many players out there come in plastic cases, lending them an air of, as Frank Zappa would say, "cheepnis." This unit, even though it weighs only a few ounces, felt rock solid in the hand, like a quality instrument. The NOMAD II is scheduled to move to a plastic case, which allow for more color options. This is unfortunate from an aesthetic perspective but not surprising—the company pointed to manufacturing issues with the magnesium cases.

So what are my complaints? For one thing, the NOMAD I is for some reason beholden to Microsoft's antiquated 8.3 filenaming restrictions. This doesn't affect usage of the player, but if you drag a file called "Bob Dylan—One More Weekend with You.mp3" into the NOMAD Manager, it will appear in the panel as "BOBDYL~1.MP3." If you have multiple files all starting with the same artist name, it becomes very difficult to tell which file is which. Yuck. Note, however, that this does not affect the unit's own display window, which properly shows ID3 tags. Why this couldn't be done in the Manager interface as well is beyond me. This issue should be cleared up with the NOMAD II, though it was too early to tell at press time.

Second, I found my patience worn a little thin by waiting around for transfers to happen. In my perfect world, the NOMAD cradle would have USB, FireWire, and Ethernet interfaces so I could plug in any of the high-speed connectors available to my system. The version of the NOMAD I tested had none of these (a problem the NOMAD shares with most of the first- and second-generation portable units). Oddly enough, even deleting files takes much more time than one would expect. If you want to delete a lot of files, your quickest bet is to click the "Format" button at the top of the NOMAD Manager window, rather than deleting files singly or in groups. Fortunately, the NOMAD II is scheduled to include USB support, so this should be a non-issue. Interestingly, the convenience of having a cradle becomes less important with units like the NOMAD II, since all you really need is a free USB cable to plug in—no more messing with parallel ports on the back of the machine.

I-Jam's I-Jam

www.ijamworld.com If small is your bag, the I-Jam is one of the smallest portable MP3 players of the bunch, and comes in a rainbow of case colors. Supporting both USB and parallel, MacOS and Windows, the I-Jam boasts a heckuva lot more power than other players, pumping out 60mW, rather than 5, as most players do. The I-Jam stores music only on SanDisk memory cards (Figure 6-3), and includes no built-in storage of its own. The unit also comes equipped with two output jacks—one headphone and one stereo output—which is a nice touch. Also included is a neck strap for those who don't wear belts (though a belt clip is provided as well).

Unlike other portables, the I-Jam comes with no dedicated upload or file management software. Instead, I-Jam provides a .DLL which allows the I-Jam JamStation (a sort of dock for your memory cards) to appear in Windows Explorer as a normal drive. Once mounted, all you have to do is drag files into or out of the drive letter, just as you would with any other drive. You'll know your unit is full when you get an "Out of disk space" error message. Not only does this capability free you from having to use dedicated software, but it also gives you the ability to organize your files in directories and subdirectories, and to store any type of data you like on the memory cards, rather than being limited to audio files—essentially treating the unit like an overgrown floppy drive.

Table 6-1 compares a variety of MP3 players. Features and specs for portable players vary from one to the next. While it may be impossible to find a single player that does everything, think carefully about your needs before purchasing. This table represents a brief snapshot of the market as of October 1999—options may be radically different by the time you read this.

Table 6-1. Portable MP3 Players Compared

	Diamond Rio 300	Diamond Rio 500	Creative Labs' NOMAD I	Creative Labs' NOMAD II	RCA Lyra RDD204	PONTIS MPlayer3[a]	I-Jam's I-Jam
Storage type	SmartMedia	SmartMedia	Flash memory	SmartMedia	32 MB or 64 MB flash cards only	MultiMedia cards	San Disk MultiMedia Card (16 MB, larger ones expected in the future)
Built-in storage capacity	Built-in 32 MB plus optional 32 MB add-in cards	Built-in 64 MB plus optional 32 MB add-in cards	32 MB plus optional 32 MB cards	None plus optional 64 MB cards	None plus optional memory modules	None plus two slots	In future models
Weight (in ounces, w/o batteries)	2.4	2.75	2.5	Unknown	4.0	3.5	2.5
Dimensions (in inches)	3.5×2.5×0.625	3.59×2.46×0.74	2.3×3.35×0.67	Unknown	4.5×2.5×0.875	4.36×2.75×0.8	3.375×2.0×0.875
Can record voice memos	No	No	Yes	Yes	No	No	No
FM radio tuner	No	No	Yes	Yes	No	Planned	Yes
Backlit display	No	Yes	Yes	Yes	Yes	Planned	Yes
Output connector types	Headphone	Headphone	Headphone plus stereo connecting cable	Headphone plus stereo connecting cable	Headphone	Headphone	Headphone and Stereo
Upload connection types	Parallel	USB	Parallel	USB	Parallel	Serial, parallel, or USB	Parallel or USB
Output signal strength?	5mW	5mW	5mW	Unknown	15–20mW	5mW	50mW

Table 6-1. Portable MP3 Players Compared (continued)

	Diamond Rio 300	Diamond Rio 500	Creative Labs' NOMAD I	Creative Labs' NOMAD II	RCA Lyra RDD204	PONTIS MPlayer3[a]	I-Jam's I-Jam
Case type	Opaque black plastic (teal or camoflage in some editions)	Opaque metallic gray or translucent teal or purple	Magnesium	Plastic	Metal	Plastic	Plastic (clear or opaque)
Cost (as of December, 1999, in U.S. dollars)	169.95	269.95	249.99	Under 400.00	249.99 for 64 MB with car kit, 199.99 for 32 MB	190.00	219.95
Software upgradeable	No	Yes; audible codec	No	Yes	Yes	Planned	Yes
EQ controls	4 presets	4 presets plus bass and treble	Yes, environments	Yes, environments	5 modes: Flat, bass, rock, pop, jazz	Bass and treble	Bass and treble
On-board file management	No. Displays numbers only, not filenames	Yes; Filenames displayed, play-lists possible	No	Unknown	Yes	Planned	Complete (shows up in Explorer)
Supports other audio file formats	MP3 only	MP2, Audible. com content	Windows Media (WMA)	Any formats are possible with software upgrade	RealAudio G2	Planned	Will support all audio formats
Can store normal data in addition to audio files	No	No	No	Yes (Smart-Media)	No	Planned	All data types

Table 6-1. Portable MP3 Players Compared (continued)

	Diamond Rio 300	Diamond Rio 500	Creative Labs' NOMAD I	Creative Labs' NOMAD II	RCA Lyra RDD204	PONTIS MPlayer3[a]	I-Jam's I-Jam
Copy protection mechanism	None	MetaTrust infrastructure present, not implemented w/o upgrade	No	Planning SDMI	Will have SDMI in future	Planning SDMI	Will be SDMI
MacOS support	No	Yes	No	No	No	Yes	Yes
Linux/BeOS support	3rd party	3rd party	No	No	No	Yes via open SDK	No
Comes with cradle	No	No	Optional	Memory dock	No	Optional	JamStation

[a] Not covered in this chapter; see *www.mplayer3.com.*

Hand-Held Computers and Other Devices

Necessity is the mother, and MP3 is a necessity for many people. But not everybody can afford to buy a dedicated portable, since they already spent this year's geektoy budget on a PDA or other hand-held device. Fortunately, the popularity of MP3 is driving the extension of some existing devices to support the format. The list here is short, but expect MP3 support to find its way into nearly anything that has a CPU and can conceivably play audio in the near future. In fact, Ericsson had just announced a cell phone with MP3 playback capability via an add-in cartridge at press time.

Utopiasoft's Hum

www.utopiasoft.com This one isn't actually a portable MP3 player, but, a skinnable software system for WinCE-based handheld computers that lets you play MP3 files directly through your PDA (Figure 6-8). Of course, most PDAs ship with a very limited amount of memory, and much of what's there is already occupied by the operating system, applications, and your data. That means Hum probably won't be useful unless you're using add-in CompactFlash memory cards, which are currently available in capacities up to 96 MB.

The Hum software utilizes a technology called AdaptivePlay. If your device has a slow CPU, or is busy handling tasks for other applications, or does not have high-quality media capabilities, audio processing is bumped down to 22kHz automatically. When more computing resources become available to the device, quality jumps back up to the normal 44kHz automatically.

Handspring Visor/InnoGear MiniJam

www.handspring.com / www.innogear.com As this book was going to press, lovers of the original PalmPilot and Palm OS were reveling in the news of the release of the new Handspring Visor, created by several of the original Palm team members and executives. While the Visor runs PalmOS (making it backwards-compatible with the thousands of Palm applications out there), it added the dimension of expandability, thanks to a new class of "Springboard Expansion Modules," one of which is InnoGear's MiniJam MP3 Player, a tiny hardware-based player that snaps into the back of the Visor. The MiniJam can use either power supplied by the Visor's internal batteries or be hooked up to an external power converter or to a cigarette lighter adapter. The unit ships with your choice of 0 or 32 MB of internal memory, and uses standard MMC (Multi Media Cards) for additional expansion. The company also plans to sell car cradles for the unit.

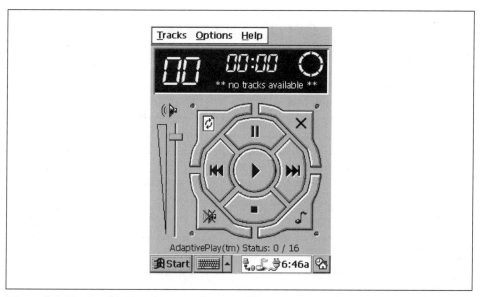

Figure 6-8. Utopiasoft's Hum lets you play MP3 files on your Windows CE-based hand-held computer

 In practice, the MiniJam has two MMC slots. One is on the back of the unit, and is inaccessible when the module is snapped into place; the other is on the front, so you can swap memory cards without removing the expansion module. By early 2000, the industry projects that MMC cards may be available in capacities up to 128 MB, which means you may be able to stuff 256 MB of music into your Visor. And because the Visor shares memory space with its expansion modules, you can store data from your PDA on the same MMC cards that hold your music.

Controls and display on the unit are fairly standard: Stop, Play, Rewind, Fast Forward buttons appear on the top of the unit. Display screens are provided for playlist, ID3 tag info, and equalization controls (four EQ presets are available, though users can modify and save additional EQ settings). Users can even store voice memos on their Visors via the MiniJam.

Internally, the MiniJam uses DSPs from Micronis, which some believe offer sound quality superior to that of the DSPs used in most units. Early testers were allegedly claiming that the MiniJam sounded better, and had better bass response than the Diamond Rio, though I was not able to confirm this. The MiniJam outputs a standard 5mW through its headphone jack.

Of PDAs and MP3s

As you can see here, there are both Win CE- and PalmOS-based Personal Digital Assistants (PDAs), or hand-held computers capable of playing MP3 files. If you've been thinking about getting a PDA anyway, should you consider going with an MP3-capable PDA instead? There are pluses and minuses here. Obviously, storage is the biggest limitation you'll be facing. But while PDAs traditionally have shipped with a paltry 2–8 MB of storage, the genre is beefing up as it matures, and hand-held computers are increasingly becoming more full-featured, and coming with larger complements of built-in RAM and hot-swappable storage options. The trend shows no sign of abating.

One advantage to using a single device for both purposes (besides the money you'll save) is the fact that you'll be able to use a single desktop cradle, minimizing the number of ports you'll need to take up on the back of your computer (not an issue for USB-connected devices, thankfully), and saving a little space on your desk. And of course you'll have one less device to cart around or clip to your belt.

On the other hand, a PDA isn't going to have the full complement of physical buttons on its case (unless you get an add-in hardware unit such as the InnoGear expansion module for the Handspring Visor, as shown in Figure 6-9). You'll probably need to operate everything via software running on the PDA itself, just like you do on your desktop computer. However, some MP3 software for PDAs may be capable of mapping simple stop/start/next controls to the normal operational buttons on the PDA itself—you'll need to do a little research beforehand to see whether this will be possible. Perhaps more importantly, your PDA may not have the horsepower to run an operating system and its applications while simultaneously decoding MP3 in the background. Custom DSPs in dedicated MP3 players take care of this job with no risk of skipping or drop-outs. The audio chipset in a PDA also isn't as likely to have the same level of quality you'll find in a dedicated player.

If MP3 is your life, there's probably no question you'll want to go with a dedicated MP3 unit. If you just want to listen to the occasional MP3 file in the background, give this option some serious consideration. The possibilities of having a well-integrated unit are only going to get better as time goes on.

The companion software shipped with the MiniJam is Real Networks' RealJukebox Gold (covered in Chapter 3), which is capable of searching your system for attached portable units. Behind the scenes, RealJukebox ships with Windows .DLLs containing connectivity code for various players. The MiniJam is one of them, so the unit shows up as a choice in RealJukebox's portables menu. Of course, the MiniJam does not require a separate cradle: it uses the Visor's.

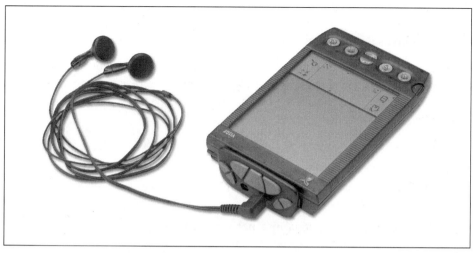

Figure 6-9. The InnoGear MiniJam is an expansion module for the HandSpring Visor PDA

Mac support should be available sometime in 2000, while Linux and BeOS users will be happy to learn that InnoGear is planning to distribute a developer's package (SDK), which will include all the source code needed to deliver MiniJam support for those platforms. The SDK should become available sometime in the first quarter of 2000.

One of the more unusual MP3 players scheduled to make the scene by the time you read this is Sony's VAIO Music Clip Personal Network Player, which quite literally comes in the form of a fountain pen (though it doesn't write). It's truly amazing to behold how many goodies Sony has packed into this little device: An LCD readout, a headphone jack, the standard array of control buttons, and—get this—a USB port. The device stores up to five hours of music and runs on a couple of AA batteries. Advantages: Slips easily into your shirt pocket so you don't have to deal with belt clips or long cords. Disadvantages: Non-expandable storage, limited battery life. Think of the Music Clip not as the most far-out product you've seen, but rather as a harbinger of devices to come: Unlimited by traditional constraints of shape or size, and capable of being streamlined into your lifestyle with near transparency.

Home Stereo MP3 Players

At this point, it practically goes without saying that MP3 playback hardware is bound to become a fixture of the consumer home stereo setup. Because most stereo component MP3 players will be linked to a computer somewhere in the home, these devices fit perfectly into the "convergence" scenario you've been hearing about for so long; the boundaries between computers, networks, and home entertainment systems eroding one piece at a time.

At bottom, these dedicated players aren't all that much different from portable devices, though they're packaged in standard home-stereo-size component cases and typically offer more flexibility and playback options than you get with portable players. Not to mention storage space up the yin-yang.

There are essentially four types of home stereo MP3 players:

- Devices similar in concept to a portable: Load it up from your PC via parallel, serial, Ethernet, or USB and treat it much as you would a home stereo CD player.

- Full-on miniature computers in a home stereo form factor and modified with LCD or LED readouts and remote control units.

- Modified CD players designed to handle MP3 data CDs as well as standard audio CDs.

- Noncomputer-based home stereo components dedicated to handling MP3 and other audio file formats.

... and of course we'll be seeing myriad variations and hybrids of these concepts.

Choosing the Best External Player

While the market for external MP3 players is still young, this is clearly going to become a huge field before long, and competition will undoubtedly create a bewildering array of choices for consumers looking to jump in. So what should you look for in an external player? Here are some criteria to keep in mind as you shop, which you will of course have to balance against your budget.

Storage

How much can it hold? If you have to load it up with new music every few days, you'll probably end up regarding the device as a hassle. If you've got a huge collection, you'll want to cram as much of it into the device as possible. If you're already in the habit of burning your own CDs, look for a unit that can play directly from MP3 data CDs.

Good connectivity

If you're looking for a unit that interfaces with your PC for file transfer, don't settle for archaic parallel or serial connections.* They're slow and they hog

---

* Actually, transfer speeds over parallel can be pretty good if ECP is enabled in the BIOS and the transfer software support is. But that doesn't get around the inconvenience of using the parallel port rather than USB.

ports that could be put to better use with other devices. If you have a home
network, look for a machine running a real operating system, with a real
Ethernet port. This way you'll be able to transfer files to it from any room in
the house via FTP or Windows Networking, or, if it's a Unix/Linux- or BeOS-
based machine, telnet in and manage the machine remotely. Failing that
option, don't settle for anything but USB or FireWire. At this writing, none of
the commercially available boxes allowed for Ethernet connectivity, though
several of them promised it for the future. However, potential legal consequences make it difficult to allow this kind of transfer commercially; you may
have to build your own machine if this is what you're looking for. The advent
of SDMI should make MP3 networking commercially possible without step-
ping on the toes of the legal suits.

Display

Look for a machine with a clear, multi-line LCD readout viewable from a distance. Make sure the unit is capable of reading ID3 tags, so you're not left
grappling with meaningless track numbers. Check to see whether the display
output can be redirected to a TV (most cannot, though it could be a nice feature, depending on your needs).

Software

The unit will probably come with some kind of companion software that can
be used for uploading tracks, creating playlists, and possibly even encoding
albums. Find out from existing users of the product what they think of the
software. Does it impose unnecessary or arbitrary limitations? Can you work
with tracks of any bitrate? Good companion software may be an important
aspect of your enjoyment of the device.

Playlists

Some of the early devices on the market were limited to playlists of a certain
size, or could only manage a single playlist. Music is largely about mood, and
you're going to want to be able to switch atmospheres with the press of a button. Check to see if the device or its companion software will let you create
query-based playlists. If you're going to have gobs of storage on the machine,
you better be able to organize it however you like, either on the machine itself
or from playlists created on your PC and transferred to the device.

Audio output

Does the device use a standard sound card for output to your stereo, a custom DSP, or a proprietary chipset? If it uses a sound card, find out what kind.
Overall quality may be heavily affected by audio chipset quality. If the device
is a sealed unit, you may void your warranty by trying to upgrade it yourself.
Ask around online to find out other people's impressions of unit before plunking down your cash. If you have a digital amplifier or DAC, look for a unit
with optional digital outputs.

Ambient noise

If the machine is based on standard computer hardware, it may also contain a fan or fans, just like your PC. Do you really want to hear the hum of a fan in the background when you're trying to listen to music? This may be unavoidable with some devices, but ask around to find out just how much noise is being generated by the fan before committing your money. If you have a choice in the matter (i.e., you can open up the case and replace parts without voiding the warranty, you might consider replacing the power supply and CPU fans with some of the ultra-quiet models available from a specialized retailer such as *www.pcpowercooling.com*. Also see the Silent Systems section of *www.molex.com*. If you're really hardcore about it, consider coating the inside of the case with acoustical foam, though this will almost certainly void your warranty and could introduce air circulation issues if your existing fans aren't moving enough air.

CD types

If the device has a built-in CD player, will it handle both audio and MP3 data CDs? And with the steady rise of recordable DVD, the possibility arises of storing gobs of MP3s on a DVD disk. You might want to make sure your unit is capable of handling these as well. Of course, you may be able to stick a DVD drive in the machine yourself at a later date, but will the unit's software be upgradeable as well? Most units based on computer hardware are software upgradeable, but make sure before spending your money.

Hackability

This one depends on your personality type. If you're a real do-it-yourselfer, you may want to make sure the machine is running an operating system you understand well, so you can make modifications if necessary. And again, you may want to give the device a larger hard drive, or monkey around with the controls. Will doing so void your warranty? Probably. That's a decision only you can make. If you're more the standard consumer type, you'll probably want to go with a slick, sealed unit much like your existing stereo components.

ReQuest's AudioRequest

www.audiorequest.com One of the most interesting and complete home stereo MP3 solutions out there is ReQuest's AudioRequest—a complex and unusual beast capable of just about everything your PC is capable of doing, MP3-wise. So why not just stick a computer next to your stereo and be done with it? First of all, it wouldn't look too hot, and to make it really useful you'd either have to have a monitor attached or install an LCD readout and control buttons. You'd want to rig up a remote control unit, and figure out how to connect your PC to your television

(AudioRequest lets you manage playlists and play synchronized animated video images via TV hookup). And you'd have to deal with the ambient noise created by the CPU and power-supply fans. Ambitious geeks could pull all of this off, sure, but by the time you were done you probably would have invested a lot of time and money, while the AudioRequest is ready to plug and play, and looks slick to boot.

AudioRequest includes hard drive options large enough to store 150 or 300 hours of MP3 audio—that means you can play it 24 hours a day for 2 weeks before hearing the same song again. And because the device is virtually a complete computer,[*] it won't be difficult to upgrade its software to allow support for other file formats. Windows Media files were about to become playable on the AudioRequest at this writing.

But it gets even better: In addition to hard drive storage, the AudioRequest (Figure 6-10) also includes a CD-ROM drive capable of playing either audio CDs or MP3 data CDs. In fact, you can even slide an audio CD into the tray and encode it's tracks directly to MP3, directly within the unit.

Perhaps the biggest difference between AudioRequest and a standard PC is that ReQuest takes great pains to enforce compliance with existing copyright laws. Unlike the Rio, AudioRequest most definitely *is* a recording device as well as a playback unit, and thus has to disallow the transfer of unprotected digital audio files back to your PC. Details on that arrangement are covered in Chapter 7.

AudioRequest's ECP parallel connection can be used both for transferring files from your computer to the device or for transferring from the device to portable players. Some form of USB networking is scheduled to be included on the unit in a future release. Analog inputs are also provided, so you can easily encode from cassette or LP.

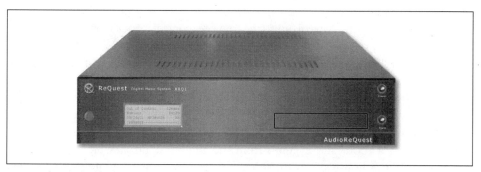

Figure 6-10. The AudioRequest prototype; the appearance of shipping units may differ

---

[*] At press time, ReQuest would not disclose what operating system the device runs on.

Lydstrøm's SongBank

www.lydstrom.com Occupying a rather unique niche in the file-based home audio scene is Lydstrøm's* SongBank (Figure 6-11). The SongBank is not specifically an MP3 unit, though it does handle MP3 files, alongside many other digital audio compression formats including Windows Media. Future versions of the SongBank will support the RealNetworks G2 and AAC formats as well—Lydstrøm is format-agnostic. Internally, the unit uses Lucent's EPAC format, for an optimum quality-compression ratio. To understand what the SongBank is and does, you have to first stop thinking in terms of computer-based devices. The SongBank is not a computer, nor does it interface with your computer. It's a home stereo component with an eye toward the convergence of digital audio, the Internet, and even some non-audio home-control functions (you can power up your coffee pot in the other room with this thing).

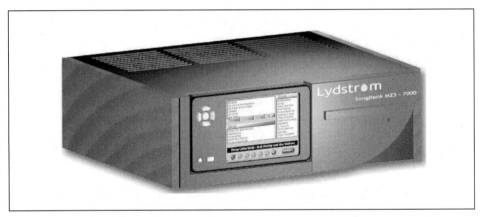

Figure 6-11. An artist's rendering of the futuristic Lydstrøm SongBank

The unit itself features very sleek Euro styling and a large and detailed LCD read-out/touchscreen remote control unit (the remote control "docks" into the face of the SongBank and doubles as the onboard control interface). Rather than a single output to your home stereo, the SongBank offers three separate analog output ports and three digital ports (Toslink, S/PDIF, and AES/BEU), connected to three separate software playback modules. Each playback module can be directed toward a separate output, so you can play different music in different rooms of the house, all from the same unit. Want to play blues in the kitchen and jazz in the den? Just select a room and a genre from the remote control, which is RF-based and can work in a house of up to 30,000 square feet in size. While the base unit already stores 6,000 songs, additional "slave" (external storage) units can be connected via FireWire for nearly infinite archivability. Current slave units are standard

---

* Pronounced "Ludstrum," where "Lud" is like "hood." It's a Swedish name.

external hard drives, but Lydstrøm will eventually support various types of removable cartridges, flash cards, PCMCIA units, etc. Other models available at this writing can store up to 14,000 songs without slave units.

How it works

So, how does this thing work again? You pop a standard audio CD into the player and it gets cross-referenced against an internally stored database (not the CDDB; Lydstrøm says their database is more flexible than the CDDB) and all of its songs are encoded to EPAC format on the internal storage. The contents of that CD are then made available for playback on the unit via the remote control/faceplate, even after you remove the CD itself. And if you insert a data CD full of MP3 files, the unit handles everything transparently—same deal. Because the internal database is not on the Internet, the device doesn't require a network connection of any kind. Every month, you receive a CD in the mail that updates the SongBank's internal database and upgrades the onboard firmware to make improvements or to enable new features and capabilities.

However, the unit *is* Internet-capable, and Lydstrøm plans to have a complete backend site online by the time you read this. Once that happens, you'll be able to optionally connect the unit through a modem or Ethernet connection (via DSL or cable modem) and have the database and firmware upgraded automatically. More importantly, you'll be able to browse Lydstrøm's site for music and purchase it for download, all through the remote control unit, which Lydstrøm claims is dirt-simple to use. Lydstrøm won't be alone selling music online, though. They're partnering with other vendors so you'll simultaneously be able to browse and purchase from collections put online by other online music retailers. The company couldn't disclose their partners at press time, but they're thinking big here: imaging being able to connect directly to a music label, or to an online CD retailer like CD Now! or Amazon.com. Or to more established existing MP3 distribution sites. Meanwhile, the online database will be intelligent. It will know where you live, and will be able to tell you that concert tickets for the same musician are available. You'll be able to buy tickets and sample songs simultaneously, through multiple vendors, all through a single account you maintain with Lydstrøm.

 Lydstrøm claims to have a patent pending on a technology that allows modem users to double their digital audio download speeds, though they were very tight-lipped about the specifics of this technique at the time of this writing. File this under "sounds too good to be true."

What happens when you want to get music out of the SongBank and into your computer? Well, you can't do that, for the usual legal reasons discussed elsewhere in this book, but Lydstrøm is working with Rio and other vendors to support export to portable units. When you do that, music will be moved to the device, rather than copied, to prevent unauthorized proliferation of digital music. And Lydstrøm is doing all of this with the computer completely removed from the loop.

New paradigms in distribution

The internal database used by the SongBank lets you create and manage playlists, of course, and also does some fancy tricks with the music itself. For example, the SongBank can keep track of the beat count and adjust the tempo of the next song (without changing the pitch), so guests dancing at your parties can keep right on jamming. You'll probably want to keep this option disabled most of the time—changing the tempo is pretty disrespectful to the artist, in my opinion, though DJs do it all the time for precisely the same reason.

Meanwhile, each SongBank owner gets a unique ID, and each unit has a serial number. This information is stored and transmitted through all online music purchases, so if your unit should be stolen or damaged, you can always retrieve the music you legally own without having to pay for it again.

 Lydstrøm is careful to point out that the SongBank is not a geek toy—they're not going after the technophile audience, but after the general consumer. They're selling a convergence device masked as a fancy CD player. Amazingly, the SongBank is not priced out of the ballpark. The base unit retails for $399, and the higher-end models still come in at under a grand. The day of the sophisticated consumer convergence device is here.

MP3 CD-ROM Players

While only a few MP3 CD players are mentioned here, this field is growing fast. Be sure and search the Internet for more options.

NetDrives' Brujo

www.netdrives.com/brujo.asp This one is basically a modified CD player designed to handle MP3 data CDs as well as standard audio CDs. Since there's no on-board storage, there's no need to interface this unit with your computer. On the other hand, you must have access to a CD burner, so the total cost of ownership is higher than advertised by NetDrives. If you've already got a CD burner and have been busy socking away massive archives of MP3 data CDs, you'll find this unit a dream come true, with one CD being capable of storing 10–12 hours at 128 kbps.

The unit includes both standard RCA and headphone outputs, and comes with a 31-key remote control usable at up to 8 meters away. The unit can handle up to 220 MP3 files, but oddly enough, playlists are limited to 63 tracks.

MacPower Peripherals' Mozart's Music Box

www.macpower.com.tw/ Despite the name of the manufacturer, this unit has nothing to do with the Macintosh, nor does it require that you own one. The unit is a very simple combo player that handles both audio and MP3 data CDs and jacks into your home stereo via standard RCA plugs. Unfortunately, the unit does not read ID3 tags, so all you'll see on the LCD readout are track numbers. While the version available at this writing required users to hook up different cables to play either audio or MP3 CDs, an updated version without this limitation should be available by the time you read this.

Mozart's Music Box is equally at home in car or home installations. See pictures of the Mozart in car environments at *www.mp3car.com*.

Pine's D'Music

www.pineusa.com Shipping with no on-board storage of its own, D'Music is a portable CD player capable of playing both audio and MP3 data CDs. If you don't already own a CD burner, this unit probably isn't for you, unless you buy a lot of data CDs from MP3.com or other sources. If you've been storing up a multi-gigabyte collection and burning the overflow to data CDs all along, this unit may be just the ticket. The D'Music comes with a ten-second anti-shock buffer, a remote control (useful for hooking the unit into your home stereo), and a built-in graphic equalizer. Although designed for use as a portable, there's no reason the unit won't work well in home stereo configurations as well.

Car Players

What better place to get deep into your MP3 collection than on a long car trip, or to switch off the endless commercials on the radio and drink in a few new downloads to pass the time while you wait for the gridlock to clear? Because the basics of MP3 hardware are compact, they can be crammed into a car stereo form factor and treated like any other in-dash or pull-out car stereo unit. They can be hooked up to high-quality car amplifiers and speakers, or to those ridiculous monster-bass kettledrum speakers that make even the best music sound like it's been blown out with a gas station air pump.

After reading this section, learn more on MP3 audio and cars at *www.mp3car.com*.

Remote Control

While most of the non-portable hardware discussed in this chapter comes with its own remote control system, some users will be happy to discover that they can save a ton of money and "virtually integrate" their existing computers into their home stereos by adding a remote control to the PC itself. A company known as Irman (*www.evation.com/irman/*) makes a small black box about the size of a cigarette pack that connects to an available serial port. One face of the box includes an infrared receiver capable of interfacing with virtually every remote control ever made.

Once installed, users can use any of a number of MP3 playback applications running Irman plug-ins, or otherwise modified to accept incoming signals from the Irman box. Hook up your sound card to your home stereo, attach an Irman box, and run WinAmp or X11Amp from a distance. If your computer isn't situated within line-of-sight of common areas in the house, you can place the Irman box anywhere—even in another room. Serial cables up to 15 meters in length have been tested and allegedly work perfectly.

Then again, you can approach the situation the other way around, spend a bit more, and have a transceiver on your computer broadcast MP3 audio right through the air to a receiver on your home stereo. Essentially, you end up with the same situation you would get by hooking your sound card to your stereo, but without the need for long cables. X10's MP3Anywhere includes transceiver and receiver units that operate at 2.4GHz, and can transmit right through walls (unlike standard IR signals, which are blocked by obstacles). X10 also provides a remote control designed to operate with a wide variety of common MP3 playback software, giving you capabilities similar to those of Irman. See *www.x10. com/mp3_x10/mp3_anywhere.htm* for details.

Car MP3 on a Budget

Before you get too excited, be aware that the first few generations of any new technology are always going to be expensive, and this genre is no exception. At this writing, dedicated car MP3 players were running $750–$1000. Some intrepid souls were creating their own solutions with soldering irons and home-drawn schematics, but that's just not something your Average Joe is likely to do.

Fortunately, there's a cheaper, and possibly more flexible way to go about it. Get yourself a standard portable MP3 player as discussed earlier in this chapter and jack into your car's audio circuitry. There are a number of ways to go about this. Check the documentation or web site of your portable's manufacturer—there's a good chance they sell inexpensive accessories to make auto hookup easy.

To keep things organized inside the car, you might want to attach a bit of velcro tape to your dashboard and to the back of your portable unit. Alternatively, go to a cell phone store and look at the car phone caddies. Some portable units and remote control devices fit neatly into some cell phone caddies.

Cassette adapter

These odd little units are shaped exactly like a cassette tape, and fit into the cassette slot on your existing car stereo. Plug the headphone output of the portable into the jack on the front of the "cassette" and you're in business. These units are a clever, inexpensive hack, but are a bit of a hassle—you've always got to keep the "cassette" handy and swap things around every time you want to play MP3s. But they do get the job done, and let you get more mileage out of your existing equipment. Note, however, that this technique is also the lowest-quality car MP3 solution you're going to find.

Auxiliary in

Some car stereos come with an auxiliary input jack right on the face plate, which makes hookup of portable devices a snap. If you're shopping for a normal car stereo anyway, be sure you get one with an Aux input, just so you've got the flexibility to work easily with a portable device sometime down the road.

Cigarette lighter adapters

If you want to save on batteries, you can get a cigarette-lighter adapter at nearly any electronics, hardware or department store. These usually come with a variety of connectors and/or a voltage switch. Portable players commonly run on 3V of DC, but check your portable's documentation carefully before running current through it. You almost certainly *do not* want to run your car's full 12V through your portable!

It is dangerous (and illegal in most regions) to wear headphones while driving.

Direct wiring

Unless you have Aux In jacks on the back of your receiver, or an equalizer or other external preamp (which also implies the presence of a separate amp), you'll need to jack your portable directly into the car's audio wiring via an "RF modulator," which accepts line-level input and outputs VHF or FM signal. However, this is not a job for the squeamish. If you're not already well-versed in car stereo wiring principles, talk to your local car stereo installation shop.

If you're not using a dedicated portable unit and want to hook up a laptop or dedicated computer in the trunk or under the seat, you'll probably want to get an inverter to transform the car's 12V DC into 120V AC. However, unless you purchase a very high quality inverter, you'll find that these generate additional noise. In addition, using a laptop raises other issues—how will you control the unit? Will it be sufficiently shock-proof? While many users initially get excited about the prospect of using a laptop computer as a car stereo, only serious hackers or those willing to spend time and money putting together a complete system should contemplate this seriously. In the end, it's going to be a lot easier and cheaper to just jack in a standard portable unit. If you do want to go this route, see the In-Trunk and Do-It-Yourself sections later in this chapter for additional tips, and start doing research at *www.mp3car.com*.

If you don't know what you're doing, let your fingers do the walking and head over to your local car stereo installation shop and let them take it on. In most cases, the job should be simple and inexpensive, but keep in mind that some cars make behind-dash access more difficult than it needs to be, and this fact may mean added labor charges. Still, you'll end up with a fairly elegant solution for less than you would pay for a dedicated car MP3 player.

In-Dash and In-Trunk Players

If you know you'll never be satisfied with the paltry 32 or 64 MB of RAM in your portable and are looking for a better solution, you'll want to go with a unit specifically designed for in-car use. Like standard car stereos, these come in two flavors: Pull-out units you slide into the dash, and trunk-mounted units operated from the driver's seat via remote control. Regardless, you'll still need a way to get MP3 files into the unit. Chances are, you'll have to take the unit into the house to load it up from your PC, unless your garage is very close to your office and you have a very long USB or Ethernet cable. The ideal solution, it seems, would be to use wireless networking technologies so you could FTP files into the unit from a computer in the house, right through the air. I haven't seen anything like this on the market, but it's only a matter of time.

empeg

www.empeg.com The amount of attention directed at the remarkable empeg unit in the year leading up to its release was nothing short of incredible. Audio buffs were excited. MP3 buffs were excited. And the Open Source software crowd over at Slashdot.org were positively jubilant, thanks to the fact that the empeg unit runs a superbly hacked version of Linux.

Developers and geeks may want to check out *www.empeg.mars.org*, a site dedicated to exploring the internals of the empeg unit at the source code level.

Make no mistake: This is not your mother's car stereo. Imagine the components of a laptop computer stuffed into a car stereo form factor, given a custom LED read-out instead of a monitor, and some neatly placed buttons instead of a keyboard or mouse. And rather than risking the "blue screen of death" right in the middle of your favorite track, make sure it's running one of the world's most stable operating systems.

Because the bootstrap code is stored in flash ROM, the empeg unit boots in a few seconds. The empeg includes a 220Mhz Digital/Intel StrongARM processor, 8 MB of memory, and a 6 GB hard drive (in the base model; a 10 GB model is also available, and even larger drives may be available in the empeg by the time you read this), and can be used as easily in the home as in the car, thanks to the presence of a pair of standard RCA plugs in addition to the car audio wiring. Digital to analog conversion is provided by custom DSPs built into the machine, which also handle bass, treble, and other audio output controls. And because the slimmed-down operating system takes up less than a megabyte of system memory, there's RAM left over to do read-ahead cacheing. The hard drive can grab around three minutes of music and store it in memory, so the read heads don't need to be in constant contact with the platter, saving both power and heat while further minimizing the possibility of pothole-induced playback errors.

The decoder software, based on XAudio, can handle MP2 and MP3 files, and since all decoding happens in software, it should be easy to upgrade the unit to handle other compresssion standards when/if they take off. Shock and vibration protection is provided by hard drives rated at 150G while running and 400G when not running.

Since 6 GB is a lot to transfer, the empeg mercifully comes with a USB port in addition to serial. You can load the hard drive to capacity in around an hour over USB. Oh, and it comes with a credit-card sized remote control, so your friends can operate the unit from the back seat (the driver uses buttons built into the front panel), as shown in Figure 6-12. The default faceplate is blue, though amber and green plates can be had for an additional surcharge.

The unit is loaded by connecting to your PC's serial (230,400bps max), or USB (12Mbit) ports, then firing up the bundled Emplode software (even though the empeg itself runs Linux, the desktop software is aimed at Windows 98/2000 users). Create new playlists by pulling down Edit → New Playlist, then drag tracks from

Figure 6-12. The empeg unit running through the author's home stereo

Explorer into that playlist. Space available on the unit is reported in the status bar at the lower right of the Emplode window (Figure 6-13).

 As noted in the instructions, be sure to launch the Emplode software before hooking up the USB cable. Otherwise Windows will get confused looking for driver support for the attached unit.

Playlists are created via drag and drop, then synchronized with the contents of the unit. When you've got everything arranged the way you like it, click the Synchronize button on the toolbar and the transfer begins. By the time you shower, eat breakfast, and drink your coffee, the unit will be ready to grab on the way out the door.

 Perhaps the only big minus for general consumers interested in going with an empeg unit is that since its case is tightly packed with computer parts, there's no place for an on-board amplifier. You *must* have an external amplifier in your car if you want to run the empeg.* In addition, demand was still exceeding supply at this writing, and potential buyers were queued up for months waiting for units to become available. It's likely that empeg will have ramped up production to a commercial level by the time you read this.

---

* Unless you're keeping your old cassette deck and or radio, in which case a cassette adapter or RF modulator should work. However, you would lose some quality in the conversion processes.

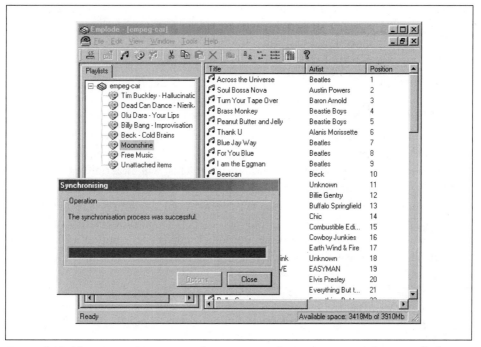

Figure 6-13. The empeg unit comes with its own transfer management software, called Emplode

Using the on-board controls

Navigating the empeg controls (see Figure 6-11) may take a bit of getting used to at first, especially as the buttons on the faceplate are unmarked. Pressing the bottom button on the faceplate will bring up a horizontal menu in the display, consisting of:

    Playlists | Source | Sound | Shuffle | Information | Visuals | Power Off | About

Use the left and right buttons to navigate this main menu, then press the bottom button again to select that entry; you'll get a submenu relating to that choice. For example, pressing the bottom button while Shuffle is selected will let you turn shuffle mode on or off, while pressing the same button while Source is selected will let you toggle between empeg (the unit itself), auxiliary input, and FM radio. Selecting the Sound entry lets you control the volume, balance, fader (front to back balance), and the built-in equalizer. Be sure and check out the Visuals menu—there are a ton of built-in visualizers from which you can select, from simple ID3 tag display to rather sophisticated histograms, dancing pixels, and warping lines in time to the music. Pressing the top button will always let you escape from any given menu or submenu.

To get the full effect from the built-in visuals, navigate to the Information menu and turn Information off. All available pixels will be used for visualization display.

Upgrading the empeg

Both the firmware on the unit and the Emplode desktop software are software-upgradable, and users (especially early adopters) should check empeg's Upgrades page frequently at *www2.empeg.com/upgrades/*. This will not only get you bug fixes to the firmware and/or the synchronization software, but important new features as well. If there are upgrades available for both the Emplode software and the player itself, install the Emplode upgrade first. With Emplode open, pull down Tools → Upgrade empeg-car software, then click the Browse button and navigate to the location on your system where the upgrade binary was stored.

 Always unplug the power cable from the unit before starting the upgrade. You'll be prompted to turn the power on later during the upgrade process. If you typically use the USB connection to synchronize with the unit, note that you *must* use a serial connection to apply the firmware upgrade (an appropriate serial cable is provided with the unit).

A progress indicator will inform you of the update's progress as the kernel and RAM disk are erased and reprogrammed. Finally, the MP3 data partition on the unit will be "pumped," which prepares the unit's database to work with its playback software.

 It's worth remembering, whether you're talking about the empeg or any other unit that's essentially a re-fashioned computer, that just because you build it specially to play MP3 files doesn't mean that the rest of the powers of a general-purpose computer suddenly disappear. Give your machine some connectivity, and you've got web access from your MP3 player. Give it a satellite uplink, and you can have a GPS system in your dashboard, giving you directions to anywhere you need to go, or even playing music appropriate to the scenery outside your window. Need some extra storage space to cart big image or video files around? There's no reason your car stereo, with its massive hard drive, can't also function as a gargantuan floppy disk, letting you cart media files between home and work.

Living with the empeg

I had the pleasure of borrowing one of the first units to roll off the empeg assembly line, and lived with it for a month before I sadly had to return it. Because I do not have an external amplifier in my car, I used the unit exclusively as a home stereo component, in a month-long MP3 fest.

The empeg's built-in DAC is excellent, and I found the audio quality to be fully equivalent to CD audio when listening to 192 kbps MP3 files. Still, I would have liked to have seen a digital output on the unit so I'd have the option of using my outboard DAC for its extra warmth. I also found that the remote control, which was clearly designed for another device, was not as intuitive to use as I would have liked, though I quickly learned its controls. My biggest beef with the controls in my evaluation unit was the lack of a radial volume knob; it was just too much work to get to the volume controls from the faceplate buttons. Fortunately, empeg hints at a big change coming in the future: "… a volume knob done one better." They didn't offer more clues, but hopefully you'll be able to get a glimpse of their plans by the time you read this.

With a 6 GB hard drive, space was a non-issue. I only reloaded it a few times, and that was mostly to add new test files. 6 GB gave me enough storage to play music several hours a day for weeks without repeating tracks. The unit's display was clear enough to read from across the room, and I enjoyed switching between playlists with the press of a button, and toggling between the many built-in visualization modes. I found the built-in FM radio perfectly functional. In a perfect world, this unit would optionally come in a case designed to be integrated into home stereos, and would have an Ethernet interface so I could transfer files via FTP from any machine in the house. Fortunately, empeg hints on their site that they intend to offer a version that allows remote logins in the future. I'll know the future has arrived the first day I can telnet into my home stereo.

Xeenon MP Shuttle II

www.xeenon.com/xeenonweb/product/product.htm/ A rather different approach is taken by the Xeenon shuttle products. Rather than sticking a complete computer in the dash, Xeenon puts a unit in the trunk, with the exception of a removable hard drive which slides in and out of the dash for quick portability and security. The brains of the machine are out of sight and out of mind. All potential thieves will see is an empty hard drive bay in the car—hardly tempting.

Rather than controlling the unit from buttons on the faceplate, the Xeenon utilizes an external keypad, which connects through the car's chassis back to the brains in the trunk, which in turn control the hard drive in the dash. The arrangement

sounds a little inelegant, but has its advantages. The removable hard drives in particular mean that loading the unit up with new music will be faster than with any
competing unit, and by locating the drive in the dash rather than in the trunk,
everything stays convenient.

In essence, the unit is functionally similar to the trunk-mounted PCs some users
build themselves, except the unit is ready to go—you don't have to scrounge for
parts and hack things together. Think of this one as a hybrid between a total do-it-
yourself tweak and a commercial implementation.

There are *many* more options for playing MP3 in the car, and don't
be surprised if the major car stereo vendors start presenting their
own models in the near future. Again, keep on eye on *www.mp3car.
com* for the latest dope.

Kit Players

If none of the commercial offerings available by the time you read this quite fit the
bill, if you think you can do it yourself cheaper, or if you're the type who has a
garage of tools dangerous enough to take off a limb, you're a good candidate for
an MP3 hardware kit. If you want something done right, do it yourself, right? Right.

Virtually all of the commercial manufacturers go to pains to remain
compliant with SDMI and other security considerations. If you'd
rather not be beholden to these laws and would rather be on your
own recognizance in terms of legal issues, building your own player
will give you the freedom to get tunes into and out of the unit without having to jump over security fences.

There are basically two approaches to building home- and car-based MP3 units:

*   Purchase all the parts and plans as part of a bundled unit. Spend an evening
    with the instructions, get out your razor blade and gluestick, and and start
    sticking Tab A in Slot B until you've got something resembling an MP3 player.
    This is the easiest approach, designed for those with little-to-no experience
    working with hardware and software at a low level.

*   Purchase, download, or otherwise procure plans—without the parts. Then
    hunt down the parts yourself at flea markets and electronics warehouses. With
    any luck, you'll actually be able to find the same parts specified in the plans
    and everything will just work. In all likelihood, you'll end up doing some
    improvising and further research to make it all happen.

Of course, if you're really intrepid you can always go it alone, without a plan. However, this option should only be considered by self-styled inventor/programmers ready to get themselves out of any jam they end up creating for themselves. And be warned: Projects like this inevitably run into obstacles.

If you decide to just go for it, be prepared to spend hours in electronics newsgroups or at the library, figuring out how to fool a motherboard into thinking it's got a keyboard attached when all it's really got are a few buttons made out of bottle caps. Clear a space on the workbench, fire up the soldering iron, and go for it. Seriously though, this approach can be both the most challenging and the most satisfying.

If you decide to go the do-it-yourself route, you should definitely subscribe to the mp3stereo mailing list. Send a message to *mp3stereo-subscribe@lists.gofast.net* with the word "subscribe" as the subject.

Ready-to-Build Kits

While there are a number of ready-to-build MP3 hardware kits floating around out there, you'll want to track one down that best suits your needs and sense of aesthetics. Some kits consist mostly of additional parts needed to hack an existing computer into a standalone MP3 player, while others are based entirely on custom parts. Unfortunately, few of the kits I've seen available on the Internet are things of beauty—most place function above form. If looks matter a lot to you, you might want to either rethink and go with a commercial unit after all, or be prepared to depart from the kit and devise your own case and/or readout.

CarPlayer

One of the best all-around informational sites for MP3 kit builders at this writing was *www.carplayer.com*, which offers both prebuilt units for the car and the home, and offers both ready-to-build kits and plans without parts. In addition, the site offers a lot of data up front, so if you think you can get by on your own ingenuity, you may be able to simply studying the available diagrams, pictures, and explanations.

TrackZ

If you want to make sure the build process is painless and you're on a budget, check out the TrackZ player at *www.mp3kit.com*. This unit can be purchased preassembled or as a kit. Both are available in a variety of configurations, giving you control over the quality of the display, whether or not you want an external enclosure for it, whether you need cables, etc.

TrackZ uses a proprietary operating system, so don't expect to be able to fiddle much with the unit's basic functionality.

Do-It-Yourself

While the prefab kits make the build process relatively painless, many people opt to go the distance and create their players from scratch, using readily available, cheap parts and either devising the schematics themselves or relying on the shared experience of others who have gone down that road before. While this isn't a book on hardware or operating system hacking, here's a basic outline of the kinds of things you'll need to think about if you go the DIY route. After reading this section, hit the Net and start doing additional research. There are dozens of sites set up to show off the projects other people have built, where you'll find plans, diaries, solutions to common problems, and perhaps most importantly, some of the software you'll need to make it all come together. You'll find a list of good starting points in the "More information" section at the end of this chapter.

Hardware and form factor

The first thing you've got to decide is how your unit will be housed. Most people building their own players from scratch go with a complete computer, using standard parts from the "PC organ bank." This approach avoids the necessity of crafting your own parts to fit into a custom form factor or to play a particular role. Of course, the ease of use is offset by the fact that computer-based players are generally going to be larger than players built to custom specifications (though very small computer cases and motherboards *are* available, if you know where to look). Another approach is to get an old CD player from the swap meet and gut it, saving only the chassis and case. Alternatively, save only the chassis and build your own case from custom-molded sheet metal, plastic, or carefully bent stainless steel mesh.

If you're lucky enough to have an old laptop laying around, you can always use that to cut down on the size, keeping in mind that you won't be able to mount a display in the front. One of the unfortunate things about laptop solutions is that their built-in audio chipsets are generally inferior to dedicated sound cards, and can't be changed out on a whim. If audio quality is paramount, avoid the laptop route. A better solution is to shop around for the smallest case you can possibly find and start from there. Meanwhile, ask around online and find out who's making the quietest power supplies and fans available. You don't want all that humming interfering with your enjoyment of the music. See the notes in the "Choosing the Best External Player" section earlier in this chapter.

Do not shop for computer parts with maximum performance in mind, as you might with your own home computer. Save money, keep things cool, and enjoy the quietude of smaller fans by going with the slowest Pentium machine you can find. For dedicated work like this, where you won't be doing anything but decoding MP3, you can get by with a Pentium 75 or 100 and 8 or 16 MB for RAM. You'll be amazed how cheaply you can purchase a machine like that at online auction sites. Nobody wants them but you.

If you're brave and willing to work with very small parts, you can always rip the guts out of a laptop and place them in a custom-designed case, and possibly even alter the audio path if you're skilled with printed circuit boards and soldering irons.

Another nice thing about building your own box is that you can decide which sound card goes into it. Since you're going to be interfacing with your home stereo, don't skimp on the sound card—get the best one you can afford. If you've got a digital receiver or outboard DAC, be sure to get a sound card with digital outputs to maximize quality. There are also a couple of manufacturers of dedicated sound cards for just this purpose, with MP3 DSPs soldered in place. These may also have RCA outputs, so you won't need an external DAC. See *www.interlog. com/~miclee/mp3.html/* for one such example.

If you've got a slower machine, or one that for some reason will also be busy doing lots of other CPU-intensive tasks, take a look at lp3, a dedicated MP3 hardware decoder that hangs out of the parallel port and talks to plugins for WinAmp and other players: *lp3music.com*. With one of these, you can use a machine much slower than a low-end Pentium or high-end 486—you'll probably get good results even with a 386.

Operating system

If you're building a computer-based system and depending on existing software, your machine will of course need an operating system. While many people use Windows 95 or 98 as a base because that's what they're most familiar with, it may not be the best solution for a standalone MP3 unit, for several reasons:

Long boot times

Granted, you may end up leaving your machine on most of the time, but when you do turn it on, you'll need to wait 30–90 seconds, depending on the configuration. If you do use Windows, make sure you aren't loading anything unnecessary in the startup group. Windows can, however, be configured to boot straight to DOS, which will save greatly on boot time. In fact, if you know you want to go the Microsoft route, try and get a hold of an old DOS installation, and don't even bother with Windows. Understand, however, that this may present other problems—most (but not all) existing solutions depend on the presence of WinAmp or other GUI Windows players.

Resource consumption

Because you'll probably be going with inexpensive, older, slower hardware, you want as much of your horsepower and memory as possible available to the task of playing MPEG audio, not being soaked up by the operating system. Even when running nothing at all, Windows consumes more resources than the alternatives.

Stability

When was the last time your CD player crashed? When was the last time Windows 98 crashed? Need I say more?

Hackability

Because you're creating a custom solution, it may be beneficial to be able to remove parts of the operating system that are unnecessary, or at least opt not to load them at boot time. If you think you may want to alter the operating system to suit your needs, Linux will be your best solution, as its source code is completely available and open to you. BeOS is less hackable than Linux, but you can get in at a fairly low level and choose not to load unnecessary components. Very few aspects of Windows can be altered by the end user at a low level. If you do intend to build your own Linux kernel or alter the operating system substantially, you will of course need some C or C++ experience.

While thousands of people have created Windows-based standalone MP3 players, you'll probably end up with a more satisfying end-product by going with a Linux- or BeOS-based system. Linux is the most flexible of the lot, and you'll find many tools already out there in the field that work with Linux-based systems. However, working with Linux also requires the greatest degree of technical/programming skills. BeOS has the advantage of being much easier to configure and use than Linux (even easier than Windows in many regards), and is media-optimized from the ground up—it's perfect for this kind of project.* Both Linux and BeOS have the potential advantage that they include built-in telnet servers; if you set up your machine on an Ethernet connection, you'll be able to telnet in from any machine in the world running any operating system and control them from a distance.

---

* You can find more information on BeOS-based stereo components at *www.betips.net/mp3box/*.

While it's certainly possible to use a Mac as a standalone MP3 player, this may not be the ideal solution for a variety of reasons. Macs take a long time to boot, MacOS is difficult to program for, cheap parts are not as readily available, and MacOS is not as stable as other platforms thanks to its cooperative multitasking and lack of a memory protection model. Of course, stability isn't usually an issue with units like this, which are just doing a single task for extended periods of time, but you're just not going to find much info out there on how to hack MacOS to output display data to an LCD, or to work via remote control. You could, however, probably create a Perl or other web-based system for controlling an MP3 player on a Mac from browsers on other machines in the house.

Display

Whether your unit ends up in the car or amid the home stereo components, it's highly unlikely you'll want to have a monitor taking up extra space. But you'll still need some way to get a readout of the currently playing song, browse your playlists, and monitor the state of the unit.

This is most often accomplished via an LCD or LED display. Since these don't attach to a video card, you'll need to connect them via another means, typically over a serial connection. You can connect the machine's outbound serial connection to a tethered LCD display in a miniature case, which can be mounted wherever convenient, or you can reroute the connection through the computer case to the front panel and mount the display in a free drive bay.

LCD readouts can be ordered from a number of electronics supply houses. Many people are very happy with the quality of displays purchased from Matrix Orbital, *www.matrix-orbital.com*, though nearly any display for which you can find a suitable driver is a good candidate. Users looking for an even more polished appearance may want to spend the extra money and get a VFD (Vacuum Fluorescent Display), which enjoy better clarity at a wider viewing angle than do LCDs. Of course, hooking up an LCD isn't as simple as rerouting the normal video display signal to the display unit. You'll need a special driver for your operating system and for your particular LCD. The driver must be capable of receiving data sent to it from a separate software module or from an MP3 player plug-in module. See the URLs listed in the section previously for more information. Precise implementations on various operating system/playback software combinations are very different from one another.

Input methods

Because your unit will probably not have a full keyboard attached, you'll need to find another way to control it. Perhaps the simplest solution is to get a cheapo numeric keypad—the kind with a standard keyboard connector but missing the rest of the keyboard. The nice thing about these is that you can just plug them into the standard keyboard port and be done with it. Unfortunately, they're not exactly elegant looking, and you may not want a separate module dangling from your home stereo.

A much more elegant (and stereo-like) approach is to purchase an infrared remote system, such as the Irman described earlier in this chapter. One of the great things about the Irman is that plug-ins for Windows and Linux already exist (the Linux source code should compile in BeOS without much reconfiguration), so no programming experience is necessary and a big part of the battle has already been fought for you. Setup should be a breeze.

If you want buttons on the front of the unit like normal stereo components, you're definitely going to have some more work to do, and will need some electronics skills. Some users have figured out how to split open a normal keyboard, remove the controller chip and its lead wires, then mount the chip inside the unit and connect the leads to the buttons on the front of the unit from inside the case. You'll need to do some sleuthing to isolate a set of wires, determine the signal they send, and map them to the buttons you install on the front of the unit. The other lead running out of the chip will remain connected to the motherboard where the keyboard normally connects. One thing to keep in mind is that poorly done buttons can easily make a nice case look like a hack job. If you go pure infrared, you can keep the case design very clean.

Software

Finally, you'll need to decide which MP3 player you'll be using in your system. Since the usual graphical interface isn't an issue, you should definitely consider command-line players, since these consume fewer resources and are likely to be easier to control from the keyboard, which is essentially what you're doing with any of the input methods described above. However, many GUI MP3 players can also be launched and controlled from the command line, or have plug-ins to enable keyboard control, so graphical players are not out of the question. As long as you can find a way to create an interface between your chosen input method and the software, you're sitting pretty.

If you're building a Windows machine based on infrared input, definitely check out the Ampapod and Irman plug-ins available at *www.winamp.com/plugins/*. Just specify the COM port through which your infrared receiver is attached, tell the plug-in which buttons on the remote should map to which WinAmp functions, and you're set. Linux users can use LIRC (Linux Infrared Remote Control; details at *fsinfo.cs.uni-sb.de/~columbus/lirc/*) in conjunction with the IRMP3 software (details at *www.fasta.fh-dortmund.de/users/andy/irmp3/*).

 If you're using Linux, you'll need to do some tweaking to get the operating system to boot directly into operational mode without prompting the user for a login. If you don't have much experience hacking Linux, ask around in the community for a custom init pre-configured to bypass the login sequence. If you want to do this yourself, there are a few gotchas to watch out for. You don't want to simply set up your system to boot into runlevel 1, because while that will put you directly into single-user mode, it will also prevent you from using some important services, like networking. The secret is to change a single character in /etc/inittab and the system will boot to root access without prompting you for a password. Specifically, you want to change:

```
id:1:initdefault
```

to:

```
id:3:initdefault
```

If your system boots straight to the xdm graphical login manager, change `id:5` rather than `id:1`. Note, however, that there are the usual risks associated with having the box running as root all the time, but this is a stereo component, not a public web server.

If you're working with keypad or button input, you'll probably have to create a custom solution (remember that the kit available from *www.carplayer.com* includes the software you need to do this, in case you don't want to create it from scratch).

Many projects use rxaudio (*www.xaudio.com*) for its flexibility and the ease with which it can receive control signals from scripts and custom programs, thanks to a companion utility called rxcontrol. IR support is also possible through rxcontrol. See *www.softlab.ece.ntua.gr/~sivann/rxcontrol/* for details. Xaudio is available for nearly all platforms.

Networking alternatives

At several points in this chapter, I've mentioned the advantages of making sure your MP3 player is networkable. While most of the commercial solutions available at this writing didn't have network capabilities, many of the devices being built by hobbyists and hackers do. The prospects of being able to load your MP3 player via FTP, to manage your playlists via telnet, or to select tracks through a web interface from another machine are all irresistible.

If you're building a Linux machine with networking capabilities and want to get really fancy, you can store all of your songs in a database such as MySQL and interface with it through a web server extension such as Perl or PHP. Myriad Perl modules are available so you won't have to create everything from scratch. See *igalaxie.com/ ltt/mp3/php3/* for more information on PHP solutions, and *www. cpan.org* for Perl modules. Once configured, you'll be able to bookmark a web page in a browser on another machine in the house, see available playlists, and select songs on your stereo just by clicking on them in your browser. Windows users can of course use Microsoft Access or other Windows database software that can be accessed from the command line or external programs to create custom solutions. If you're building a BeOS-based system, download MP3box from *www.betips.net/software/,* which does the same thing but uses the Be File System as a native database rather than requiring additional database software.

Even more irresistible is the prospect of *not* having to transfer files between your computer and your home stereo via FTP. If you're crafty and have an always-on home server or "convergence device," you can make this the central repository for all MP3 files in the home. The stereo playback unit or units would still have a sound card and Ethernet capabilities, but would be configured to stream MP3 from the server on-demand and in real time. The playback units wouldn't actually store any MP3 files at all. One could theoretically construct such a system so that multiple playback units in the house could all siphon down separate files or playlists, so each family member could hear the music they want to hear.

However, not everyone has a home network already in place, so these possibilities aren't always viable. If you don't have an existing network and are considering it, take a look at systems from X10 (*www.x10.com*). This company has long specialized in remote control of lights and alarms, and provides systems for automating many aspects of the home environment, from the simple to the complex. Responding to the desires of MP3 fans, X10 makes available a system called MP3 Anywhere, which lets you beam MP3 audio through the air or right through walls (using 2.4-gigahertz wireless signals), from a computer to the home stereo, without the need to run cables, install a network card, or purchase hubs. Because the system comes with a remote control, you don't need to be sitting at the PC to control the flow of music. The MP3 Anywhere system comes with send/receive units, a "MouseREMOTE" remote control, and software interfaces for talking to the most popular Windows MP3 players. This way, you can still sit at the couch in the living room, but control the playback by pointing the remote at a wall, toward a computer loaded with MP3 files in another room.

The disadvantage to MP3 Anywhere is that you don't have the complete flexibility of possible solutions that you have with a generic TCP/IP connection. On the other hand, you may not need to. Why transfer MP3 files from your computer to another storage unit in your home stereo if you can just beam them through the air as needed?

More information

This is a book on MP3, not on building hardware or hacking operating systems. Creating a custom system for MP3 playback can be very satisfying, but it's not something to be undertaken lightly. You'll definitely need to learn more than what's presented in this book. Here are some good starting points:

Convert your PlayStation into an MP3 stereo component
> *www.mp3psx.com/info.html/*

Information on BeOS-based stereo components
> *www.betips.net/mp3box/*

The InMotion car player
> *www.jarcom.com/inmotion/*

KarPC: Automobile MP3 stereos pre-assembled or in kits, for most operating systems
> *kpc.phester.org*

Kits and prebuilt players for home and car
> *www.carplayer.com*

LC-DAT
> *www.public.iastate.edu/~jmesterb/lcdat/*

Linux MP3 Players Project Page
> *www.ccs.neu.edu/home/bchafy/mp3.html/*

lp3: Dedicated MP3 hardware decoder unit
> *lp3music.com/*

MP3 Server Box
> *igalaxie.com/ltt/mp3/*

MP3-o-Phono: Plays MP3 CD-ROMs in a standalone Linux-based unit
> *www.softlab.ece.ntua.gr/~sivann/mp3ophono/*

MP3God: The Car MP3 Player
> *www.scott.kincaid.net*

MP3Hardware
> *www.mp3hardware.com*

Obsequieum: A networked MP3 Jukebox for Linux
obs.freeamp.org

PC104: Small, stackable motherboards for use in dedicated units of all kinds
www.pc104.com/

Wired remote control products for car players
www.mp3ondemand.com

XIMP
ximp.iscool.net

7

The Not-So-Fine-Print:
Legal Bits and Pieces

The legal side of the MP3 world can be either utterly simple or unbelievably complex, depending on how you approach and use the technology and how thoroughly you'd like to understand the inner machinations of the U.S. legal system (which is increasingly tied into the legal systems of other countries, thanks to the fact that "bits don't stop at the border"). Balancing the need to protect consumer rights with the rights of artists and the recording industry has opened up a Pandora's box of conflicting interests that may never be fully resolved. In this chapter we'll take a look at some of the common myths surrounding the transfer of digital audio files (The Rules of Engagement) and then examine some of the finer points of copyright law (The Players), along with several initiatives, technologies, and specifications that have come into play, including the Audio Home Recording Act, the Secure Digital Music Initiative, the No Electronic Theft Act, the Serial Copy Management System, the MP3 patent, and more.

This chapter represents our best attempt to summarize and put into plain language the myriad legal aspects surrounding the MP3 scene. As we are not lawyers, and because the scenery changes on a near-weekly basis, this chapter does not represent the final word. If you need to make critical legal decisions regarding MP3 usage, consult with an attorney specializing in copyright and digital issues.

The Rules of Engagement

Throughout this book I've said the same thing over and over again: You are entitled to create MP3 copies of the music you own for your own personal use. You are not entitled to make accessible digital copies of music to which you do not hold the copyright. While the ramifications of this are fairly clear (i.e., you can't just copy tracks from a CD and put them on your web site), there's a whole lot of misinformation floating around out there, and many people believe there are numerous exceptions to this rule. Let's try and set some of these common misconceptions straight. Some of the content in this section is paraphrased from the "Top 10 Myths" section of the RIAA's ancillary web site, *www.soundbyting.com.* Please see that site for the recording industry's perspective on artist and consumer rights in the digital arena.

 Everything in this section may seem like small potatoes to you. It may seem trivial and unimportant. You may think that your personal activities are too small and insignificant to be noticed. While that may be true, remember that if you are caught, copyright violation that involves more than 10 copies and a value exceeding $2,500 is *a felony* in the United States. OK, chances are pretty slim that you'll go to jail over it. Very few people ever see anything but a cease-and-desist letter, or have the plug pulled on them by their service provider. But it's important to realize the potential gravity of what you're dealing with here.

Copyright

Virtually everything in this chapter depends on a solid definition of copyright, so let's get that out of the way first. We'll focus on the aspects of copyright that apply to music copying and distribution.

In a nutshell, copyright and copyright law are means of making sure that the person or agency who creates a creative work has control over who gets to make copies or derivations of that work and how. Copyright is, quite simply, the right to copy, and the creator is the person who holds that right. Of course, the owner of a copyrighted work also has the right to sell the right to someone else. In the music industry, artists typically sell their copyright to the label that publishes their work.

In order for a work to be copyrighted, it must exist tangibly in the real world—not just in your head. A song you make up and hum to yourself is not copyrighted. A song you make up and write out on paper or record to DAT tape or post to Usenet *is* copyrighted. Computers and the Internet have somewhat complicated the notion of making copies. There are obvious copies, such as those created when you download a song from a web site to your hard drive, and less obvious copies, such as the copy of a song that's loaded into RAM from your hard drive when you go to play a song. But that sort of "ephemeral" copy is seldom of concern to anyone, as it's not likely to affect the artist's right to earn money from the work.

Copyright law differs in some specifics from one country to the next, but most of the world's countries have signed the Berne copyright convention, which specifies that a work becomes copyrighted the moment it's put into tangible form. Creators are not required to affix a copyright notice to their creation, though they do if they're wise—it can help in resolving disputes should they arise later on. But the important thing is, copyrights aren't like patents; artists don't have to file them with any legal bureau or do anything special. If you create something tangible, you just earned the copyright to that thing.

Of course, money is the reason most copyright holders want to retain control over their right to copy. If that right slips away, the creator is deprived of potential earnings they might make from controlling the right to copy. That's why digital music distribution is such a problem for artists—it grants them the opportunity to reach a wide audience, but simultaneously weakens their control over the copying process in a way that compact disc distribution (for example) does not.

 A great place to learn more about copyright is "Ten Big Myths About Copyright Explained," at *www.templetons.com/brad/copymyths.html/*.

Fair Use

The notion of "fair use" is an important element of U.S. copyright law, and allows some parties to use portions of some copyrighted works in a limited way in some situations, without obtaining prior permission. Fair use is designed to make sure that intellectual or artistic expressions aren't totally blocked from being entered into the public discourse by overly strict copyright enforcement that could limit the free flow of ideas. By necessity, fair use has always been the source of gray areas in copyright law. However, many people misunderstand the concepts of fair use and mistakenly think it means they can trade copyrighted MP3 files around freely.

When courts look at cases where the notion of fair use is brought to bear, they consider whether the property in question was used for commercial purposes, the length of the excerpt, whether the excerpt utilizes the most distinctive portion of the piece, how distinctive the original work was to begin with, and how the usage in question will affect the market for the original work. Courts will usually grant fair use protection when the excerpt is made in the context of commentary and criticism, or for educational purposes, although there are no hard and fast rules here. In any case, making available to the public an entire track of digital audio will almost certainly not qualify for fair use protection in almost any circumstance.

Personal Use

Do not confuse the terms "fair use" (described previously) and "personal use." The latter is a right granted specifically to users of digital audio recording devices to guarantee that they can make copies of the original work on other media. For example, if you have a CD player in the home but a cassette player in the car, "personal use" guarantees you the ability to listen the music you purchase on CD while you're in your car, since you can legally make a cassette copy. The line is still drawn at handing that music out to people who didn't purchase the music.

The devil's advocate will note that the cost of a blank cassette tape includes a small royalty that flows back to the recording industry on the assumption that a certain number of blank cassettes will be used to create illegal copies of copyrighted works. One interpretation of this is that even when you create a cassette copy of a work for personal use, you still pay the recording industry for it, albeit a small amount. But note here that no part of the price you paid for your hard drive flows back to the recording industry, so the situation is not identical.

Personal use derives from the Audio Home Recording Act of 1992, described later in this chapter. The important bit for MP3 users is the distinction between a computer hard drive and a digital recording device. Even though a computer can digitally copy, a computer is considered a "multipurpose device," not a recording device. Computers *are not* covered by the AHRA, which means that no royalties flow back into the recording industry from computer-created copies. Furthermore, the AHRA does not require that computers include SCMS protection (also covered later in this chapter). Because computer-based copying does not generate royalties for and offers no protection to the recording industry, creators of computer-based copies (i.e., you) do not enjoy immunity from suits over copyright infringement. However, this does not imply that copies you make of your own music, for personal use only, are infringing copies. It only means that if you are trafficking music you do not own, the AHRA won't protect you.

The short answer: If you made the digital copy on a computer, you do not qualify for the personal use clause of the AHRA.

Note that the limitations of personal use apply to people downloading MP3 files as well to webmasters—if you download a copy of a copyrighted song from another site, you can't hide behind the "personal use" clause, because the devices being used for the transfer are computers and therefore aren't protected by the AHRA.

Keep an Eye out for Bogus "Permissions"

When surfing for MP3s, it's not uncommon to find notices like these on Web sites offering MP3 downloads:

- Please support the artist and buy the CD.

- This site is for promotional purposes only.

- You must already own these CDs to legally download these tracks.

- If you download these files, you must delete them from your hard drive within 24 hours.

All of them are nonsense. Unless the webmaster owns the copyright or has explicit permission from the copyright holder, none of the above caveats make a wit of difference. The site is still illegal. As the RIAA says, "If you reproduce, offer to distribute and/or distribute full-length sound recordings without a license, you are violating copyright law." So how can you tell whether a site is legitimate or not? Unfortunately, it's not always so easy, and it's always possible that the webmaster of a site may be lying when he says you have permission to download a given file. You'll have to make judgment calls based on the appearance of integrity the site displays. One good technique you can use to determine whether a site is hosting legitimate downloads is to head over to an online compact disc store such as CDNow.com and search for corresponding artist/track titles. If you can find the same track on an existing CD, you can be fairly certain that the files being offered for download are illegitimate.

Using International Servers

Some people are aware that copyright laws are different in non-U.S. countries, and thus assume that if they host their files on a server located in another country they will have circumvented U.S. copyright law. There are two problems with this line of thinking.

First of all, if you upload or download to or from a machine located in the U.S., you'll still be in violation of the law. And no, sending removable cartridges or disk volumes by mail isn't going to get you around this issue. Second, copyright laws in many countries are very similar to those in the U.S. In some cases, they're more strict than U.S. laws, and in others they're more lenient. You'll need to do careful research into the laws of the country hosting the server to find out how any given country is handling the situation.

The Berne Convention guarantees that a copyright violation committed in one country will be subject to governing laws in another member country. The convention makes it much easier to prosecute copyright violations internationally, and virtually guarantees that member countries will cooperate to prosecute copyright violators regardless their country of citizenship and the country in which they commit the crime. Since most major nations of the world have signed the Berne Convention, attempts to work around copyright laws of one country by moving the base of operations to another country usually doesn't work.

The First Amendment

Some people believe that the First Amendment, which guarantees every American the right to free expression, will protect them from charges of copyright violation. Keep in mind, however, that copyright itself is even more fundamental to the Constitution than free speech; it was written before the Framers even got around to the first ten amendments. But more importantly, the First Amendment does not override the principles of copyright. Free speech does not give anyone the right to deprive an artist of their right to market their works on their own terms.

Linking to MP3 Downloads

What if you don't have any interest in offering pirated music for download, but do want to create an "index" site pointing to other sites where illegal files are available for download? Here we get into ambiguous territory. Linking-related legal questions have come up on the Internet again and again, and no hard-and-fast answers have come to the fore. In the case of MP3, the question revolves around the legality of linking to unauthorized MP3 downloads even if you don't take direct responsibility for hosting those files. The RIAA has traditionally taken the tack that such sites are guilty of "contributory copyright infringement"—kind of like being a willing accessory to a crime.

However, the RIAA has not (at this writing) made significant headway in enforcing this viewpoint. As you know, many linking sites are run by big-name companies that would stand to lose a lot if forced by law to stop linking altogether. The RIAA is only able at this point to say "we believe" that such sites are guilty of contributory infringement. The question may boil down to whether the linking site has "the right and ability to control the activities of the direct infringer and also receives a financial benefit from the infringing activities." Furthermore, "Liability may be imposed even if the entity is unaware of the infringing activities."

In other words, this one is technically up in the air. It's commonly done, there is to date no court precedent to settle any suits that might arise from the practice, and even some of the Internet's largest companies (such as Lycos) do it. Lycos, for their part, claims to act quickly when reports of copyright infringement are submitted, and deletes links to those sites from their database. Lycos also provides a complete and detailed disclaimer of liability (*mp3.lycos.com/disclaimer.html*), and makes it patently clear that they are not providing the content being linked to. The RIAA doesn't like it, but at this writing, there's no proven law against it. The Internet is just too fuzzy for the law sometimes. You'll have to draw your own bead on this one.

In late 1999, the International Federation of the Phonographic Industry (IFPI) arrested a 17-year-old Swedish citizen for maintaining a site consisting of links to illegal MP3 files. The youth was later acquitted on a technicality, though IFPI still maintained that he was guilty of complicity to crime against copyright law, i.e., contributory infringement. To date, there are still no known cases of people being prosecuted for linking to MP3 files, but it's probably only a matter of time before a precedent is established.

Not-for-Profit Sites

Some people believe that if they don't seek to gain any profit by offering copyrighted music for download, then their files are legal. This is most definitely not true. What this viewpoint fails to take into account is the fact that your site can potentially result in lost sales for the artist and the record label representing the artist. Whether you profit from it or not does not exempt you from the responsibility to respect the copyright holder's rights to do as they please with their own material. This stance is clearly laid out in the No Electronic Theft Act, which amended Section 506 of the Copyright Act.

Free Advertising

Some people believe that they're doing the copyright holder a favor by promoting their material for free. Who could argue with free advertising? The problem with this line of thinking is that it's up to the copyright holder to decide whether he wants free advertising or not. You can always ask the copyright holder whether you can advertise for him or not, but you can't make these kinds of assumptions on his behalf.

Of course, it can't hurt to ask; a little communication can go a long way. But if you want to distribute the works of a major artist, it's usually not going to do you any good contacting them directly, as the copyrights to their work are probably held by a record label. If the label is small enough, there's always the chance they may say yes... but don't count on it. If you're talking about a major label artist, your chances of getting permission to redistribute works by their artists are nil to zero.

The Players

As soon as you start trying to look into the current state of MP3 law as it pertains to copying, distributing, digital devices, and patents, one thing becomes immediately apparent: The whole situation is a mess and a minefield. Dozens of laws, acts, protocols, specifications, and precedents come into play. Most of them are interdependent in some way, and some of them come close to contradicting one another. One of the reasons why most people are so lackadaisical toward MP3 copyright issues is because it's all so difficult to figure out. While several sites exist for the purpose of explaining it all to the layman, many of those sites also have their own interests at stake, and may not give you the straight dope. And God help anyone who tries to go straight to the laws as written. The author of this book has determined that trying to make sense of all that legalese can cause brain damage.

The best you can do is to start sifting and sorting through the various published opinions and summaries presented out there and try to piece it together for yourself, keeping in mind that many documents conceal their own hidden agenda. Here, then, is a quick guide to "the players"—the most significant laws, acts, recommendations and specifications that affect the legality of MP3 copying and distribution.

Again, keep in mind that the law is a fluid thing, and may very well have changed by the time you read this.

The Audio Home Recording Act (AHRA)

www.hrrc.org/ahra.html/ The AHRA was passed in 1992 and is based on the recording industry's assumption that many digital audio recording devices are used for the copying and distribution of pirated music. While the industry had once feared that the cassette tape would kill music sales (clearly, this did not turn out to be true), the advent of Digital Audio Tape recording/playback devices and units like the Sony MiniDisc rekindled those original fears. However, this time the industry was able to make a better case. Unlike the analog cassette tape, digital devices give the user the ability to spawn a potentially infinite chain of copies where every copy enjoys the same audio quality as the original. Where cassette copiers had to keep making copies from the original source in order to keep audio quality decent, it was now suddenly possible to make copies of copies of copies of copies ad infinitum without ever sacrificing quality.

In an attempt to balance the threat to the recording industry of digital copying techniques with the need for individuals to retain the right to make their personal copies, a compromise was reached regarding digital recording devices. The AHRA requires that all digital audio recording devices include a mechanism or system that will allow first-generation copies to be made, but not further generations. The AHRA thus requires digital devices to be incapable of spawning the infinite copying chain. You would, for instance, be able to make a first-generation copy and send it as an email attachment to your sister in Poughkeepsie. But if your sister then tried to transfer that copy onto her own DAT player, she would be unsuccessful. The system works by setting a "copy bit" in the file's header to the "on" position. Any AHRA-compliant device looks for this bit, and refuses to allow a copy to be made if the bit is found to be switched on. This serial-copy prevention mechanism, found in all DAT, MiniDisc, and legitimate home stereo or portable MP3 *recording* devices is known as Serial Copy Management System (SCMS).

The AHRA doesn't stop there. The act also requires that vendors of such devices register with the Copyright Office, and that 3% of the cost of blank digital audio media be collected as a "tax" and turned over to the RIAA. This tax was intended as a means for the recording industry to recoup some of the losses they expected to incur as a result of rampant piracy.

But there's a *really* big problem with the AHRA tax: It operates on a presumption of guilt. Even if you're adamantly in favor of recording industry and artist rights, even if you're a recording artist yourself and never, ever try to copy a file illegally, you have to pay the tax anyway, because the industry has convinced Congress that you're probably a pirate. Possibly even worse, there are tens of thousands, perhaps millions of legitimate MP3 files floating around out there that are not attached to any particular label. All of the songs downloadable from MP3.com, for example, are placed into the public sphere by the artists who created them. Those artists *want* you to copy their songs around. They *want* to use the power of the Internet to get their music into as wide a distribution net as possible. They have blessed the limitless copying of their own music. But certain aspects of the AHRA make this difficult, because the RIAA has convinced Congress that most MP3 files are pirated, totally ignoring the completely legitimate distribution of thousands of works of art by the artists on their own terms.

In exchange for their agreement to abide by the terms of the AHRA, hardware vendors gain legal immunity from any lawsuits that might arise from any illegal copying done for noncommercial purposes using their equipment. This does not mean that all copying suddenly becomes legal, only that manufacturers of the devices cannot be held responsible if their customers use the devices for illegal copying.

So, what are the specific ramifications of the AHRA for MP3 users? First of all, the act includes a provision that allows users to *space shift* the music they own. Just as television users have the right to "time shift" programs, i.e., tape programs to watch them later, digital audio users have the right to make copies of the music they own in order to listen to them in other locations: in the car or at the beach, for example. Space shifting may necessitate the creation of multiple copies of a track in different formats; i.e., the user uses a cassette deck at the beach and a DAT player in the car. This is a key consumer right, but it's also the very right most often abused, leading to a tendency to make personal copies public.

It's important to understand that the act applies only to certain types of devices. No analog devices or analog transfers are covered, so this has nothing to do with standard cassette players, for example. The analog clause, by the way, opens the door for manufacturers to create MP3 devices that accept analog input. More importantly, "general-purpose" devices such as computer hard drives and CD-ROMs are not covered by the act, so the AHRA has no bearing on users who burn audio or data CDs of audio material originating from MP3. And since these devices are not covered, the AHRA provides no immunity to makers of CD burners.

Where the AHRA does make contact with MP3 is in the realm of devices specifically designed to record MP3 files. This was the crux of the RIAA's suit against the Diamond Rio portable MP3 player in 1999. The RIAA tried to make the case that the Rio was a recording device and therefore subject to the terms of the AHRA. Since Diamond did not implement SCMS or pay royalties back into the industry, the RIAA felt that Diamond was flouting the law. However, Diamond was able to make the case that the Rio is not in fact a recording device, but rather a simple storage and playback device. The Rio doesn't make digital audio, it just stores it and plays it back. Diamond even went as far as to implement security measures that would prevent the transference of audio files out of the Rio and into other devices. Diamond rightfully won their case on these grounds.

However, it is entirely possible that future portable MP3 players may gain the ability to record from external input, or from a built-in radio tuner. In this case, the AHRA would clearly apply to vendors of these devices, and those vendors would need to implement other anti-copy mechanisms to stay legal. At the moment, no such portable devices exist. But there are an increasing number of home stereo MP3 components that can both play and record MP3 files.

AHRA in the real world

To give you an example of how the act applies to a real life vendor of an MP3-recording device, let's take a look at ReQuest's AudioReQuest (see Chapter 6, *Hardware, Portables, Home Stereos, and Kits*). The machine is capable of accepting an audio CD and generating a pile of MP3 files for playback. This means several things for users of AudioReQuest (and similar devices):

- If a CD has its copy bit set to "high," only one digital copy can be made, and that copy is encrypted and marked so that it cannot leave the device.

- If a CD has its copy bit set to both high and low, the device recognizes the disk as a digital copy, and will refuse to encode its tracks. It will, however, play the CD normally.

- The AHRA states, "As long as the copying is done for noncommercial use, the AHRA gives consumers immunity from suit for all analog music copying, and for digital music copying with AHRA covered devices." To respond to this clause, AudioReQuest's Line-in jack is analog. Music entering through the analog port is digitally encoded, but by this time it has already gone through an analog phase and has therefore lost a (very) small amount of fidelity in the conversion process, thus responding to one of the fears the AHRA intends to address. Future versions of AudioReQuest will have digital ports, and those ports will comply fully with the Serial Copy Management System described later in this chapter.

- When you copy digital files from a PC to AudioReQuest, it becomes an "interface device" as well as a recording device. Since MP3 itself doesn't have SCMS capabilities, AudioReQuest will play it safe and assume that the files are copies and will encrypt them. This potentially saves AudioReQuest's butt, but note that this practice unfairly assumes that the user is guilty of piracy even if the files in question are not pirated. If you're the artist who created the MP3 files in question, you're unfairly disadvantaged.

- Even more significantly, all files transferred from a PC to AudioReQuest are moved, rather than copied. That's right—the files will be deleted from your computer's hard drive after copying, again because ReQuest has to assume the worst to stay on the good side of the law. This saves AudioReQuest from functioning as a digital recording device in this case, and avoids "serial copying"; the transfer becomes analogous to carrying a CD from your house to your car. If you don't want files deleted from your hard drive, your only choice is to make backup copies of them first.

All of this is messy, but necessary from the vendor's perspective. Either they expose themselves to lawsuits, or they comply with AHRA and enjoy its immunity clause. Simple as that. Note that some of the points above could change when SDMI (discussed later in this chapter) is finalized.

The Digital Millennium Copyright Act (DMCA)

www.digmedia.org/DMCAexp.htm/ The DMCA, signed by Bill Clinton in 1998, is a portion of the Copyright Act that implements a pair of international treaties from the World Intellectual Property Organization (*www.wipo.org*). The act has two main components: 1) To make it illegal to circumvent technologies created to protect copyrighted works, and 2) To define the terms by which Internet Service Providers may or may not be responsible for copyright infringements.

The DMCA makes it a crime to create, sell, or use technologies that can be used to circumvent copyright protection software devices. This applies equally to things like digital watermarks, encryption techniques, and even firewalls. However, the DMCA also takes care to provide an exception to its anti-circumvention rules:

> ...a person may develop and employ technological means to circumvent a technological measure, or to circumvent protection afforded by a technological measure... for the purpose of enabling interoperability of an independently created computer program with other programs, if such means are necessary to achieve such interoperability, to the extent that doing so does not constitute [copyright] infringement.

In other words, the DMCA wisely allows for the possibility that it may be necessary for copyright techniques to be used to protect a consumer's right to make copies of legally purchased works. For example, if you purchase a song in a secure format that cannot be played on another computer, what does this do to your right to play music you own on multiple devices? A copyright circumvention tool may be necessary to guarantee that copyright protection mechanisms don't interfere with your right to create multiple personal copies of a given work.

The DMCA also entitles webcasters to a "statutory license" to perform copyrighted sound recordings over the Internet, and an exemption to let webcasters make a single copy of a recording (an "ephemeral" recording) and a statutory license for storage on servers for the purposes of webcasting. The DMCA also launched a two-year study on how current law regarding making copies of audio music should apply to the Internet (the Internet, as you know, changes everything).

The DMCA provides for the notion of "safe harbors" for ISPs. In particular, a service providers' liability is limited when the ISP is acting as a "mere conduit" for the data in question, when such data is just being cached (so long as the caching mechanism is designed to meet copyright owners' rights), when the ISP does not know that their equipment was harboring illegal copies, when the ISP does not benefit financially, if ISPs respond "expeditiously" to notifications of illegal activity, and when search engines provided by ISPs unknowingly link to illegal material (so long as they then "respond expeditiously" to the offending material). These protections ensure that ISPs are not legally saddled by circumstances outside their control, but they still place a burden on ISPs that didn't exist just a few years ago.

Webcasting

The exact implementation details of the DMCA as it applies to webcasting have yet to be worked out at this writing, and will ultimately be the product of lengthy negotiations between DiMA (The Digital Media Association), who represents webcasters, and the RIAA. Both sides see the value and the intractability of webcasting, but there is some disagreement over how licensing issues should best be decided. It is likely that webcasters will be able to obtain a license to broadcast files over the Internet by paying a single fee and deal with a single point of contact. This will help to avoid the impossible situation of webcasters needing to work out royalties with the label of each artist whose work they intend to broadcast, which is technically the situation at this writing (though few, if any, independent webcasters are bothering to actually do this).

After five months of talks, the RIAA and DiMA were unable to reach an agreement, and talks had officially stalled. Meanwhile, heavyweights such as America Online, broadcast.com, Eclectic Radio Corporation, MTV Networks, NetRadio, RealNetworks, SonicNet, Spinner.com, Tunes.com, and Westwind Media had signed on with DiMA. As the stalled talks moved inevitably toward arbitration, DiMA was stating that they wanted the following goals recognized:

- Webcasting provides promotional value to new artists.

- Webcasting allows for the creation of partnerships with the recording industry; users will be able in some situations to purchase the music they're currently listening to.

- Rate models already exist in the marketplace (such as in traditional radio) and that the Internet should not be considered categorically different from existing markets.

- Undue restrictions or requirements on webcasters will impose hardships that are not imposed on traditional broadcast models.

In any case, you'll need to pay royalties to ASCAP and BMI if you want to run a legal webcasting operation. BMI requires a base rate of $264 per year if your site garners less than $12,500 per year in revenue. ASCAP appears to have lowered their rate from the $1,000 per year they once charged, though the exact amount was not available at press time. See *www.bmi.com* and *www.ascap.com* for details. Also unclear at this writing was how artists not covered by those organizations were to be compensated. A good deal of useful information on the subject can be found at *www.kohnmusic.com*. If your webcasting operation is for-profit, note that ASCAP and BMI have a reputation for vigorous prosecution. If you're a small or non-profit operation, you're probably safe, though that doesn't mean you're legal without going through the proper channels.

The No Electronic Theft Act

Passed by the House of Representatives in late 1997, the NET Act amends copyright law to:

> define "financial gain" to include the receipt of anything of value, including the receipt of other copyrighted works. Sets penalties for willfully infringing a copyright: (1) for purposes of commercial advantage or private financial gain; or (2) by reproducing or distributing, including by electronic means, during any 180-day period, one or more copies of one or more copyrighted works with a total retail value of more than $1,000. Provides that evidence of reproduction or distribution of a copyrighted work, by itself, shall not be sufficient to establish willful infringement.

How's that again? Quite simply, the NET Act means that pirates who make money from their practice—whether that money comes from selling files, advertisements, or any other related means—can be sent to the clink for three to five years. In addition, it means that if the total value of the files posted exceeds $1,000, you can go to jail even if you don't directly profit from having made the files available.*

Those are strong words, and appear to be a strong tool the recording industry can leverage against pirates. Of course, enforcing the law is a more difficult matter, and so far we haven't seen a whole lot of pirates prosecuted in accordance with the terms of the NET Act. But that's not to say there haven't been any. In August 1999, a 22-year-old University of Oregon student pleaded guilty to charges of criminal infringement of copyright law thanks to a collection of MP3 and other illegal files he had made available on his web site. The perp faced 3 years in prison and a $250,000 fine. While this was the first actual arrest under the NET Act, it most certainly will not be the last. Don't let anyone tell you the industry isn't serious about this stuff.

The First Sale Doctrine

This doctrine comprises the section of the Copyright Act providing consumers with the right to sell or otherwise transfer a copy of an audio recording to another person, following the same logic that allows you to sell a copy of a book or compact disc to a third party. However, note that file-based media raises an interesting problem: When you sell a book you've purchased to someone else, you no longer have a copy of that book. When you sell an MP3 file you've purchased, what's to prevent you from keeping a copy of that file around on your hard drive?

---

* How is the value of illegally available tracks calculated? That's for the courts to decide. Do not automatically assume that a CD with 13 songs and costing $13 retail has a value of $1 per track. Because every download of that track is potential lost revenue, the courts may conclude that even a single illegal copy on your site is valued at over $1,000.

Theoretically, a system could be established that would let you "check in" your copy of the file with some central database, or to log in and register the transfer of ownership. Such a system would be dependent on software that would only allow you to play files bearing a valid registration number. Needless to say, such a system would be fraught with complications, but this is at least possible in theory. In any case, it's important to distinguish between selling a copy of *a* copyrighted work from selling *your* copy of that same work.

This right meshes with traditional notions of property ownership, but potentially conflicts with some copyright protection mechanisms, which explicitly prevent such transfers through the identification of digital watermarks or other means. In fact, some believe that the First Sale Doctrine even specifically legitimizes the use of some copyright circumvention devices and applications, since it is possible that someone might procure a product like TotalRecorder or AudioJacker to save encrypted music to a non-encrypted format in order to transfer that piece of music to another person. Thus, tools like these may actually become necessary in order to preserve consumers' established rights. Otherwise, you'll never be able to sell a song you purchase from emusic.com or other online music vendors because SDMI (discussed later) will prevent its transfer.

International Issues

Some issues in the MP3 universe are complicated by the fact that the Internet is international in scope, but people live in individual countries and are subject to the laws of those countries. As you may have noticed, almost everything in this chapter is U.S.-centric, and refers to American organizations and laws. This raises some important questions for MP3 users in other countries. For example, once licensing fees and terms are established by the RIAA and DiMA, they're likely to feed royalties back into American organizations like ASCAP and BMI. What will that mean for Canadian webcasters? The Canadian equivalent of ASCAP is SOCAN, but SOCAN has, as of this writing, not yet weighed in on the webcasting issue. Repeat this confusing scenario for every wired country in the world and things get very messy very fast.

Another good example of the kind of confusion that can be caused by this disjunction is the case of the BladeEnc encoder (Chapter 5, *Ripping and Encoding: Creating MP3 Files*). BladeEnc's author lives in Sweden, and Swedish law prevents the patenting of algorithms. But MP3 *is* patented by its inventors, in both Germany and the U.S. BladeEnc's author distributes the BladeEnc source code under the terms of the LGPL (Lesser General Public License), under the advice of his ombudsman,* who has suggested that it's perfectly legal to distribute BladeEnc in Sweden without paying Fraunhofer their royalties. No attempt is made to prevent

---

* An ombudsman is a counselor or mediator, often involved in helping to resolve legal issues.

users in other countries from downloading and compiling the BladeEnc source code from the Swedish server, and it's not difficult to find binaries on servers in other countries, created from that source code. At this writing, the BladeEnc issue is officially unresolved. Keep on eye on *BladeEnc.cjb.net* for updates.

It is likely that similar international copyright questions will arise in the future, involving other codecs, technologies, and products. Unfortunately, this book can suggest no easy answers. It's a wild time for legal professionals these days.

The MP3 Patent

http://www.iis.fbg.de/amm/legal/ A great deal of confusion and misinformation surrounds the question of the MP3 patent itself, as it's involved in some way in every MP3 encoder and player available. Because many of these utilities are free for the download, many people automatically assume that MP3 must be a free specification. In fact, developers *can* freely download encoder source code offered by the International Standards Organization. Encoders based on this source are known as ISO-based encoders, and are referred to throughout this book.

It's worth noting that the ISO source is only a set of guidelines or suggestions. The ultimate goal of the source code is to help developers create applications that are capable of producing an MP3-compliant bitstream. The ISO code will get you there, but it won't necessarily offer the most efficient route. In any case, just because the source is available doesn't mean that developers are free to release utilities based on that source. If you compile and distribute binaries from the ISO source code, you may owe a fee to Fraunhofer IIS. The Fraunhofer IIS Institute, who spent nearly a decade developing MP3, demands that developers who have released ISO-based encoders pay licensing fees back to Fraunhofer IIS.

MP3 is an ISO-approved standard, but the intellectual property behind it is still owned and patented by the Fraunhofer IIS Institute (patents were registered in Germany in 1989 and again in the U.S. in 1996, while Thomson Multimedia owns a different set of patents on MP3). MP3 is not, at this writing, patented in other countries. In exchange for use of their intellectual property, Fraunhofer IIS (and THOMSON, a company with which Fraunhofer IIS partners) ask for something back from those who use the MP3 spec in their applications.

However, there's a difference between what they ask for and what they demand. If you merely distribute a free decoder, Fraunhofer IIS asks for nothing in return. If you sell your decoder, Fraunhofer IIS asks that you pay them $1.00 per copy.* However, Fraunhofer IIS's patent does not cover decoding, so they can't demand

---

* Although Fraunhofer IIS does not assert their patent against decoders of which less than 10,000 units have been sold.

this payment; it's voluntary on behalf of the developer. If you create a hardware-based decoder, the price doubles to $2.00 per unit, but again, this is a request for a voluntary payment. If users are required to pay for songs or tracks, Fraunhofer IIS demands that the agency offering the song for download pay $.01 per track.

The situation gets a little different with encoders, as this is where Fraunhofer IIS's patent kicks into gear. All distributors of MP3 encoders are required to pay patent licensing fees according to the schedule in Table 7-1. Developers of MP3 encoders must be prepared to pay Fraunhofer IIS substantial fees in exchange for the use of their intellectual property. Free encoders are not exempted from the responsibility to pay licensing fees.

Table 7-1. Fraunhofer IIS Licensing Fees

Number of encoders shipped	Fee per encoder
1–1,000	$25.00 per unit
1,001–2,000	$20.00 per unit
2,001–3,000	$15.00 per unit
3,001–10,000	$10.00 per unit
10,001–100,000	$5.00 per unit
More than 100,000	$2.50 per unit
PLUS a flat yearly fee of $15,000	

Some people think that it would be possible to create an encoder that doesn't use the scheme laid out in the ISO sources and thus circumvent the requirement to pay licensing fees. However, the patent is on tools that create an MP3-compliant bitstream. It doesn't matter how you get there; if your encoder can create MP3 files, you still owe money to Fraunhofer and THOMSON.

You know that "freeware" encoder you've been using for the last six months? Unless the developer has really deep pockets and has been paying Fraunhofer IIS out of their personal bank account, the vendor is probably in violation of the law. Typically, only encoders released by established companies such as MusicMatch, Real, Microsoft, or Be are fully paid up and licensed. Pretty much any freeware encoder you download and use is technically cheating Fraunhofer IIS out of the money they ask for the intellectual property they've contributed to the standard.

If a content provider charges for the download of songs, and if the encoder used to create those songs is covered by the Fraunhofer IIS patent (and it most surely is), Fraunhofer IIS is within their rights to demand (not just request) a payment. The required payment is currently $.01 per song.

The Serial Copy Management System (SCMS)

SCMS is described in the discussion of the AHRA earlier in this chapter. In essence, SCMS is a means by which manufacturers of digital audio recording devices can earn immunity from copyright infringement lawsuits if users of those devices distribute illegally copied music. An SCMS-compliant device must:

- Be registered with the Copyright Office

- Pay a royalty fee to the RIAA

- Disallow the creation of second-generation copies

SCMS has deeply ranging implications for MP3 recording devices (and, claims the Electronic Frontier Foundation, may have repercussions for Internet distribution as well). Many people have philosophical problems with the fact that SCMS presumes guilt on the part of the person using the device. An SCMS-compliant device places what many feel are unfair burdens on legitimate artists by disallowing them from copying their work around as they see fit. In this regard, SCMS rewards artists who are already signed to labels and penalizes unsigned artists who will not benefit from the royalty payment flowback; the government thus becomes a virtual agent for large artists and an adversary of small artists. SCMS also makes some hardware vendors jump through hoops to guarantee compliance and keep themselves out of hot water, and inconveniences users of those devices in several ways.

Nevertheless, the alternative is untenable to both large artists and labels, who do indeed stand to lose revenue if perfect and unlimited digital copying were to be allowed. Despite the best efforts of SCMS, however, the Internet has all but dwarfed concerns attached to external devices. The Internet is not a recording device, but it allows for nearly unfettered copying of copyrighted works, and cannot be as easily tamed as can hardware vendors.

The Secure Digital Music Initiative (SDMI)

www.sdmi.org In 1999, the recording industry decided to fight back against the MP3 phenomenon in a big way. More than 50 companies from all aspects of the recording industry, including the Recording Industry Association of Japan, tech industry leaders, the International Federation of the Phonographic Industry, and the five major record labels (BMG, EMI, Sony, Universal, and Warner) banded together to form what has become known as the Secure Digital Music Initiative, or SDMI. The group, realizing that MP3 was not a passing fad, that digital music distribution was not going to go away, and that competition among the many "secure" formats offered by various companies was likely to lead to chaos sooner than it was going to lead to solutions, decided to approach the problem from another angle and get copy protection mechanisms built into a much wider array of devices than those covered by SCMS. Because the Internet phenomenon is bigger than any one organization, and clearly can't be cut off at the knees, SDMI goes after what it can control: All of the mechanical means by which digital audio data enters and leaves devices, including portable devices, home stereo components, CDs, and yes, personal computers.

It's important to understand that SDMI does not represent any single technology or implementation. Rather, it's a framework in which many (possibly competing) technologies can interoperate within a single system. The goal, as stated by the industry, is to create technologies that will:

> ...respect the usage rules embedded in music by its creators... The Secure Digital Music Initiative brings together the worldwide recording industry and technology companies to develop an open, interoperable architecture and specification for digital music security. The specification will answer consumer demand for convenient accessibility to quality digital music, enable copyright protection for artists' work, and will enable technology and music companies to build successful businesses.

That's the rhetoric, but what's the reality? What exactly does SDMI mean for MP3 users? At this writing, it's a little difficult to say exactly, as full details of the SDMI implementation have not yet been fully worked out. What we do know, however, is that your portable MP3 player, your PC, your sound card, and your CD player will all conspire to control what you can and cannot copy into other audio formats.

SDMI faces an immense uphill battle. They must not only convince hardware manufacturers to implement SDMI capabilities in the equipment they produce, but they must convince consumers to adopt this equipment. The first part is easier than the second, because the forces behind SDMI have all the money and all the clout. They will be able to force legislation and wield threats. Convincing consumers that SDMI is a good thing will be a far more difficult task, as consumers aren't stupid, they know what they want, and they have already voted on unfettered MP3, even though a variety of security-minded formats already exist (see Chapter 9, *Competing Codecs and Other File Formats*). Consumers have a tendency to sensibly adopt the simpler, more open solution when provided with a choice. The battle between DVD and DIVX, which was formally won by DVD when DIVX withdrew from the battle in mid-1999, provides ample evidence of this tendency.

Phases I and II

However, the SDMI team has a pretty powerful ace up its sleeve. Because of the way SDMI is slated for roll-out, consumers will eventually find themselves unable to listen to the latest content without an SDMI-capable device. As much as we might like to fight the power, it may not be as simple as saying "I won't buy any SDMI-compliant hardware." The SDMI roll-out is scheduled to occur in two stages.

During Phase I, SDMI-compliant devices will be able to play either unprotected or SDMI-compliant music. This phase mostly represents the seeding of the market with SDMI-compliant devices, and consumers won't notice that anything has changed. However, all Phase I hardware and software will include a "time bomb." When a certain date arrives, Phase II will kick in and users will be prompted by their devices and applications to download new "screening" software. Without this screening update, users will not be able to play pirated versions of music created on Phase II SDMI hardware. Users will, however, still be able to play older unprotected music, just as they do now.

That scenario sounds fairly painless on the surface. After all, even Phase II SDMI devices will be able to play plain vanilla, unprotected MP3 files. However, consider the fact that computer hardware goes out of date rather quickly. Eventually, people will discard their old hardware and replace it (perhaps unwittingly) with newer, SDMI-compliant hardware. Copies of digital music made on that hardware will not be playable by other users of SDMI playback devices. And because record labels will be including digital watermarks on every track of every new CD they create, devices and applications will be able to easily distinguish between "marked" and "unmarked" content.

Over time, the pace of technological change will result in fewer and fewer people having access to non-SDMI hardware. Zillions of existing MP3 files will still be playable, but new music played on new hardware will soon be pirate-proof.

Holes in the facade

Or so the industry would have us believe. Of course there's always a way around, over, or under any barrier, and it probably won't be long before myriad hacks and workarounds are created to circumvent SDMI, both through hardware and through software. Present the computing world with a cracking challenge, and you've virtually thrown down the gauntlet. Hackers will see SDMI as just another challenge, and will no doubt discover myriad ways to circumvent SDMI's protection mechanisms. Illegal? Perhaps, but the fact remains that circumventions will exist. With the rising popularity of Linux, computer jocks find themselves in an environment that's not accountable to any corporation, and lacking Microsoft-style supervision and/or cooperation with the SDMI group. Linux machines may in fact become a sort of haven for users wanting to circumvent SDMI. And since Linux is also a server platform, SDMI-protected music will quickly find its way back out of Linux boxes and onto the Internet, in unprotected format.*

Of course, there are philosophical and political problems with SDMI as well. While SDMI claims to represent the interests of artists, membership in the SDMI working group has been both exclusive and expensive. No small-time artist, and few independent labels could afford the membership fee required to have their voice heard in SDMI decision-making sessions. One must keep in mind, however, that use of watermarks on audio CDs is not going to be forced on labels. If they choose to release compact discs without watermarks, they're free to do so.

In fact, some believe that SDMI is unfeasible at a technical level. For example, in order for SDMI to work on computers, each machine must be uniquely identifiable. But recall the public outcry that went up last year over the unique identifying string built into some Pentium chips. There are clearly some significant privacy issues at stake here. If files are tied to unique machine IDs, you run into another hurdle every time you upgrade your processor or motherboard (depending on where the identifying string is stored). Will you lose and have to replace all of your music? Will you have to re-register your machine with some central authority? There's a potential Pandora's box here.

Of course, any barrier that can be erected by the industry can be transcended by the clever user, and the organizations behind SDMI realize this. Their only hope is to erect a barrier high enough that the majority of consumers won't be bothered to try and jump over it. If they can block the majority of the population from easily pirating music, they will be better off than they are now (or, at least, that's their presumption).

Will SDMI fly, or will it die an ugly death at the hands of consumers? After all, it was consumers who killed DIVX in its crib by mobilizing the Internet to mass protest and educating millions of potential adopters. Whether you believe SDMI is good or bad, there's no question it faces a long and winding road to mass acceptance. However, remember too that DIVX was offered as an *option* to consumers. SDMI is not being put forth as an option; it may be forced upon the public, who will have no choice but to adopt it when their hardware goes out of date. If the forces behind SDMI are able to convince enough manufacturers to stand behind them, that is.

---

* I'm not suggesting that SDMI circumvention will only occur in the Linux world; only that many hackers gravitate toward Linux and that Linux does not live under corporate control like other operating systems do. SDMI circumvention techniques will undoubtedly exist on all platforms.

Technical difficulties and possible solutions

Thanks to technical editor Bruno Prior for his contributions to this section.

One of the proposed linchpins of SDMI is that it will allow users to create only so many copies of a given track, even for personal use. For example, you may be allowed to make four copies of a track: One for your computer, one for your home stereo, one for your car stereo, and one for your portable device. So what happens if you have two cars? What happens if the hard drive on your home stereo crashes? What if you want to store multiple copies of your music at different bitrates, or encoded with different encoders, for use in different situations? Theoretically, it should be possible to submit the original back to some governing organization and "check out" a replacement copy. But if you have more than four devices, you're going to have to do this over and over again, potentially each time you leave the house. Clearly, nobody is going to have the patience for that. At a certain threshold, such a plan becomes too inconvenient to be taken seriously.

Faced with barriers like these, customers are likely to seek out illegal circumvention techniques, potentially forcing law-abiding citizens to become scofflaws. Barriers this high will stifle the digital music distribution industry, rather than promote it.

More palatable—if it can be made easy enough to use—would be some form of public/private key system, similar to systems used in privacy protection mechanisms such as Pretty Good Privacy. A purchaser of music would submit their identity to an organization like Verisign, who would issue a public key to that person. The vendor would watermark and encrypt the audio tracks with the purchaser's public key before forwarding the encrypted file to the purchaser. The purchaser would then be able to decrypt the file with their private key and save the decrypted (but still watermarked) file to disk. Compliant software/hardware would require the availability of the private key to match the public key in the watermark in order to play the track.

Under such a scheme, users could create as many copies, permanent or temporary, as they liked, but would only be able to play them in the presence of the private key. Distributing one's private key to other users is not something most people would do, and any attempt to allow wholesale piracy by issuing protected files on the Internet would be easily traceable through the public key in the watermark. Any public keys so discovered could have their certification instantly revoked by the certification authority.

Such a schema could be taken even further by taking the 16-bit original and stripping every other bit to yield a lower-quality 8-bit version, which could be offered for free to the public as a sample download. Consumers who liked the track and wanted to purchase a high-quality version could submit their personal ID and receive the stripped bits, watermarked and encrypted, to rebuild the track at its original quality level. This would increase the attractiveness to the consumer and reduce the encrypting overhead for the server.

As with the officially proposed scheme, there are inconveniences to the user inherent in a key system as well, and it would be essential that all of the software and related tools required for such transactions be utterly simple and painless to use. However, such a scheme would not impose arbitrary limitations on the consumer's ability to create an unlimited number of digital copies of the music they already own.

More information

For more information on intellectual property, copyright, SDMI, and the political ramifications of MP3 issues in general, please visit the following sites, keeping in mind that most of these sites have their own agendas to protect. The News and Opinion sections of MP3.com are often good sources for counter-opinions:

10 Big Myths About Copyright Explained
www.templetons.com/brad/copymyths.html

The Digital Media Association (DiMA)
www.digmedia.org

The Electronic Frontier Foundation (EFF)
www.eff.org

Fraunhofer's take on Intellectual Copyright issues
www.iis.fhg.de/amm/techinf/ipmp/

The Recording Industry Association of America (RIAA)
www.riaa.com

SDMI: Boom or Bust for the Music Industry?
www.musicdish.com/downloads/sdmireport.pdf

Secure Digital Music Initiative (SDMI)
www.sdmi.org

SoundByting (RIAA subsidiary site)
www.soundbyting.com

World Intellectual Property Organization
www.wipo.org

8

In this chapter:
- *The Fundamentals of Internet Distribution*
- *Offering Files for Download*
- *Webcasting: Real-Time MP3 Broadcasting*
- *An Interview with MP3.com's "High Geek"*

Webcasting and Servers: Internet Distribution

It goes without saying that the Internet made the MP3 revolution possible, and by now you've probably spent a good bit of time hoovering tunes out of the ether and onto your own machine. But what if you want to make your own MP3 files available to others over the Web? What if you want to become a webcaster—set up your own Internet radio station and broadcast tracks in real time out to the music-hungry masses? This chapter covers distribution of MP3 files from web and FTP servers, shows you how to set up an MP3 broadcast system, and covers the bandwidth issues that invariably come into play. Note that this chapter does not cover playing back streamed MP3 audio. That's covered in the section "Listening to MP3 Streams" in Chapter 4, *Playlists, Tags, and Skins: MP3 Options*.

The Fundamentals of Internet Distribution

If you're confident that you have the right to distribute a particular collection of MP3 files, you've got some decisions to make. Do you plan to serve them from an account with an Internet Service Provider, or will you be running your own server? Are you setting up an FTP site for power users, or would you like to build a web site so users can simply click on links to begin their downloads? If you're working with an ISP, are you confident that you're not going to generate too much traffic? Most providers place upper limits on the amount of throughput they'll allow to move through your account without incurring additional fees. We'll look at these issues in the first part of this chapter.

If you're running your own server from home or the office, you have to consider bandwidth issues from two points in the chain: the speed of your personal Internet connection, as well any limits being placed on throughput by your upstream provider. There are simple formulas you can use to estimate the amount of bandwidth you're going to need, but keep in mind that your estimates are only that. Without knowing how fast your user's connections are going to be, there's no way to accurately determine up front how fat of a pipe you'll require.

If you plan on offering MP3 files on a permanent basis or want to be able to establish a presence quickly, you may want to look into some of the commercial options available. Many high-bandwidth sites exist solely for the purpose of helping artists to host their MP3 material easily, to make your content searchable, and to be listed in important indexes. Going with a commercial option can help make sure your content isn't being overlooked by the public. More on that in the "Commercial Options" section of this chapter.

Finally, you may decide that you want to offer more than simple file downloads to the public. If you'd like to run your own Internet radio station, there are plenty of tools available to help you do that. The simplest method of MP3 streaming is "MP3-on-demand," or "pseudo-streaming," which can be set up from any web server. More sophisticated Internet disc jockeys will want to set up a true broadcast server, in order to be listed in the indexes at *www.icecast.org* or *www. shoutcast.com* and to offer bandwidth-optimized audio streams to their listeners. The biggest difference between these two types of MP3 streaming is that true broadcasting is real-time. Like a radio station, users hear whatever is being broadcast at that moment, while pseudo-streaming is really more of a cross between a download and a broadcast. MP3-on-demand is covered in the "Offering Files for Download" section, while true broadcasting occupies the entire second half of this chapter.

Offering Files for Download

When deciding whether to offer your files for download or via real-time streams, remember that if you stream your files, most users won't be able to save the files to their own systems for later enjoyment. Remember also that unless you own the copyright to the files in question, streaming is your only legal option.* Assuming that you do own the copyright to your files, there are a number of ways to make your files available for download to other users.

Serving from an Internet Service Provider

Virtually every dial-up account with an ISP includes access to server space on the ISP's machines. Since ISPs are typically connected to very high-speed Internet backbones, speed is not usually an issue. However, just because the speed is

---

* And even then, you may have licensing issues to work out.

potentially there doesn't mean you automatically have access to it. Many ISPs place upper limits on outgoing transfer speeds from their servers in order to distribute loads fairly among their many users. In addition, many ISPs place an upper limit on the cumulative amount of data that can be transferred during a given period (usually one month). Exceed this amount, and you're liable to receive a hefty surcharge on next month's bill. You may not even receive notification when the limit has been exceeded, so be careful.

Legal Issues

Of course, there are legal issues to contend with as well. While copyright law is the same whether you're serving from the home, the office, or from an ISP, service providers may function as watchdogs, and revoke your account if they discover that you're distributing MP3 files illegally. While telecommunications laws dating back to the turn of the century have established that providers are not responsible for the content of transmissions flowing through their equipment, lawyers still wave big sticks. Precise interpretation of the law is sometimes made on a state-by-state basis, as well—in at least one case in the mid-90s, a service provider was arrested for allowing smut to travel through their system and onto the computers of juveniles residing in another state.

Rather than face court battles and their associated costs, service providers usually just comply with cease-and-desist letters sent to them by record industry lawyers, and will revoke accounts belonging to users who are in violation of the law. This is why searching the Internet for specific songs results in so many broken links and dead sites.

There's only one law that applies to offering MP3 files for direct download, either over the Web or through an FTP server: If you're the artist of the music being offered and you don't have a contractual obligation with a label or other agency, go for it. If you don't have rights to the music in question, don't do it. You have no legal right to redistribute the works of another artist, period.

Of course, not all MP3 files are music files, so the above might be more accurately and succinctly stated: If you're the copyright holder of the work in question, you can do whatever you like with it. If you're not the copyright holder, you're not legally allowed to do anything with the work without prior permission of the copyright holder.

Standard web downloads

If you choose to serve legitimate MP3 files from an ISP, you can simply transfer them into place on the server with any FTP client and link to them from your web pages like so:

```
<a href="../audio/mp3/neds_garage.mp3">Ned's Garage</a>
```

No special configuration of the server should be necessary. If the browser window starts to fill with ASCII garbage when users click such a link, you'll know that the server does not have a MIME type established for the MP3 file type. In this case, send a polite message to the server administrator asking them to set up MIME types as described in the following section, "Running Your Own Web Server." It may also be the case that your browser is not configured correctly to handle MP3 MIME headers sent by the server. See the sidebar "Configuring Your Browser" in Chapter 4.

Internet Storage Locker

Realizing that many people would like to be able to access their music as easily from work as from home, a company called myplay (*www.myplay.com*) has created an "Internet storage locker," which lets users store up to 250 MB of MP3 audio in a private location on the Internet. By using streaming players, users can listen to their own music collections regardless where they are at the moment—if you've got connectivity, you've got access to your music. myplay licenses tunes from major labels, which users can store in their lockers for free. In addition, users can upload music from their own computers, search for MP3 files in the wild and have them transferred to their lockers automatically, or drag MP3 URLs into a special Windows utility called the mplay DropBox, which will automatically upload those tracks to your locker.

Of course, myplay is potentially treading through a number of legal gray areas here, but their legal statement "House Rules" is very clear about the fact that users caught using the system for illegal purposes will be terminated immediately. Nevertheless, it's a system with a lot of potential, especially as broadband access becomes more ubiquitous.

Offering FTP access

Most ISPs do not offer anonymous FTP access to the world at large. Instead, they provide their subscribers only with username/password FTP accounts. While it's technically possible to give the world access to your files via FTP through an ISP by handing out the username and password, doing so would be foolish, as the FTP directory location probably points to the same directory where your HTML files are stored, and anybody would have unfettered access to your site.

If your ISP does allow for anonymous FTP access to a directory location separate from your HTML files, you're in business. Your ISP will provide instructions for using this service. Note that you will probably have to request this service specifically; your ISP may offer the service without advertising its availability. Users will be able to log into the FTP site with the username "anonymous" or "ftp" and a password consisting of their own email address.

If you find that anonymous users are not able to download files from the FTP server, you may have to tweak "permissions" settings for the parent directory containing the files (although in most cases the service provider will have established reasonable default permissions). Many graphical FTP clients include a graphical permissions control panel. Navigate to the directory containing the files and grant permission to the world to read (but not to write or execute) the directory. Alternatively (assuming you're dealing with a Unix/Linux server), you may be able to telnet in to the server and type:

```
chmod 744 directory_name
```

When uploading files to the FTP server, make sure the FTP client is set in binary mode (you should find this control somewhere in the FTP client's interface or perhaps buried in the preferences). In most cases, this will be default setting for the client and you won't need to touch a thing. If you're using command-line FTP, just type bin at the prompt to set binary mode. If you fail to transfer files in binary mode, they'll be corrupted and unplayable by your users (unless they run the files through a utility like uncook, covered in Chapter 4). Make sure your users know they have to download files in binary mode as well!

MP3-on-Demand

As described in the "Listening to MP3 Streams" section of Chapter 4, users are always free to play MP3 files directly from your server, rather than downloading them first. As a webmaster, you can make sure this happens (rather than it just being an option) by setting up an "MP3-on-demand" system. While you're at it, you can also let users listen to entire playlists from your server by clicking a single link.

Unlike true MP3 broadcasting, as described later in this chapter, MP3-on-demand (or "pseudo-streaming") doesn't require much setup on the part of the webmaster. Just create a plain text document containing full URLs to MP3 files on your server, one to a line, and save the file with an *.M3U* extension (again, ".m3u" stands for "MPEG URL"). For example, if your server is located at *www.mpegjam.com* and you store your files in a subdirectory called "tracks," an M3U file might look like this:

```
http://www.mpegjam.com/tracks/J/johnhardy.mp3
http://www.mpegjam.com/tracks/W/wild_ride.mp3
http://www.mpegjam.com/tracks/B/biloxi_blues.mp3
```

and saved as *Blues_Mix.m3u*. Next, you must make sure your web server's MIME database includes an appropriate association between the *.M3U* extension and the appropriate MIME type. Setting this association is dependent on the exact server you use, but it should be pretty clear. The association you want to set is:

```
audio/x-mpegurl     .m3u
```

Once the MIME type has been set and the M3U file placed on the server, a user accessing a link to an M3U file will find that his or her preferred MP3 player is launched and the first track in the list begins playing. Better players will show the entire M3U list in the playlist editor, allowing users to skip around between tracks at will.

Bandwidth considerations for MP3-on-demand

It is unlikely that many of your users will have fast enough connections to work comfortably with pseudo-streamed MP3 files at the standard bitrate of 128 kbps. In addition, your server probably won't be able to handle too many simultaneous users without maxing out its own available bandwidth. Therefore, you'll probably want to do one or more of the following:

- Encode the MP3 files you serve this way at a lower bitrate, or in mono, or at a lower sampling frequency.

- Tell users that your site is for high-bandwidth connections only.

- Limit use of your site to a high-speed LAN in your home, school, or organization.

- Use an option in your web server software to accept only a few simultaneous connections.

Because of these limitations, serious webcasters go with real (not pseudo-) streaming solutions, which are able to downsample or re-encode files at a lower bitrate on the fly, and offer much more control over the structure of the broadcast. However, just because MP3-on-demand configurations don't automatically downsample on the fly, as true broadcast servers can be configured to do, doesn't mean you can't set things up to do so manually. For instance, you might want to write a Perl script which, when invoked, pushes an MP3 file through a command-line downsampling routine and then pipes the output of that routine back to the user. Keep in mind, however, that such a solution is going to be very CPU-intensive. If you have plenty of storage space, you can get around this problem by running a script that will downsample all of your files to various bitrates or frequencies ahead of time. Your web interface can then offer users a choice among multiple connection speeds/quality levels.

If you'd like to go with a ready-made solution, check out Bitcasting's "MP3 Radio Station In A Box," which does just that (and works with RealAudio files as well). See *www.bitcasting.com.*

Commercial Options

If you don't want to be burdened with some of the more arcane technical responsibilities of running your own server, there are plenty of sites out there more than willing to provide you with free disk space and web pages. All they get in return (typically) are the advertising revenues generated by placing banner ads on your pages. Here are a few of the most popular, but there are dozens (if not hundreds) of similar sites out there, all with slightly different approaches and atmospheres.

MP3.com

www.mp3.com If you're an artist, you'll probably want to both set up your own web or FTP site and make sure your content is listed in one or more of the popular MP3 directory sites. The most popular, of course, is the ubiquitous MP3.com. If you're an unsigned artist or just a musical hobbyist, MP3.com offers the potential to get your music into thousands or millions of new ears, at no cost to you. The site also offers discussion boards where artists can gather and discuss all aspects of the Internet music distribution business. Artists can also keep an eye on MP3.com's dynamically generated download statistics to see how popular your music is in comparison to other MP3.com artists.

In addition, MP3.com will optionally create "DAM" (Digital Audio Music System) CDs of your music (in both MP3 and standard CD audio formats), let you determine the price, and keep a full 50% of the revenues—far, far more than artists can get through even the most generous record contracts. MP3.com users will be able to buy DAM CDs of your music as they surf your site.

As this book was going to press, MP3.com was beginning to position itself as a *Music Service Provider*, or MSP, with the intent to let users get at their music from anywhere on the planet. This potentially means that users will be able to keep a personal music collection on MP3.com servers, and then listen to it from home, work, a friend's house, or wherever they may happen to be. Rather than requiring users to download their files to each location, the system will probably allow users to create online playlists, and stream custom collections of music to themselves from any location. Playback may not be limited to MP3 software, either. Internet-savvy hardware may be capable of interfacing with MSPs such as MP3.com's as well. Of course, users with fast Internet connections will probably stand to gain the most from MSPs.

MP3.com isn't the only site on the Internet offering 100% legitimate, free songs. For another approach to the same basic model, take a look at *www.unsigned-music.com*. With the great success MP3.com has enjoyed, don't be surprised to find similar sites cropping up all over the place.

EMusic.com (formerly GoodNoise)

www.emusic.com EMusic works similarly to MP3.com, but charges $.99 (at this writing) per track for music downloads. The site has gained a reputation as being at the forefront of digital commerce for music. Why would users pay for tracks at EMusic when they can download them for free at MP3.com? Because EMusic works only with existing labels and signed artists, they offer music that may already be popularly heard on the radio. Whereas MP3.com is aimed more toward the joys of discovering new music you've never heard of, EMusic caters to fans looking to legitimately download music by their favorite artists. However, the unsigned artist isn't entirely left out of the loop; the site partners with the Internet Underground Music Archive (IUMA) to provide access to lesser-known artists.[*]

Some of the principal minds behind EMusic.com are, perhaps not coincidentally, also some of the founders of Pretty Good Privacy, the Internet's most popular encryption technology. In an atmosphere where labels would do anything to build excellent copy protection into digital music, don't be surprised if EMusic turns out to be a leader in this field at some point in the future.

Internet Underground Music Archive (IUMA)

www.iuma.com If your experience with the Web stretches back to the beginning, you'll probably have a fond place in your heart for IUMA, which became a home for artists to offer music to their customers digitally long before the MP3 revolution. The site has offered downloadable music in many different formats over the years, and currently focuses on MP3 and RealAudio. IUMA goes one step beyond MP3.com by offering not just server space for audio files, but the ability for artists to create their own complete web sites on IUMA servers, so artists can completely customize the viewing and learning experience for their audiences. IUMA's Artist Uplink feature makes it easy to create online calendars for shows and tour dates, a clean URL (e.g., *http://bandname.iuma.com/),* the addition of images and

---

[*] Emusic acquired IUMA in 1999.

Case Study: Bruce Lash Recounts His Experience with MP3 Distribution

Bruce Lash is an independent musician from Chicago, Illinois who has been experimenting with digital music distribution for quite some time. To get a sense for the ways in which the MP3 "revolution" affects artists, I asked Lash to recount some of his experiences promoting his music via MP3. As you'll read below, the MP3 dream doesn't always live up to the hype—while digital music distribution can definitely open new avenues to artists, it's not without its pitfalls, and much of its potential has yet to be realized.

I chose to interview Lash for several reasons: 1) Bruce is (for the most part) a one-man band, he does not perform live—his music is only viable in a recorded context and is therefore well-suited for digital distribution and promotion; 2) Bruce typifies the "do-it-yourself" approach to music making; 3) After listening to the music of hundreds of artists downloaded from MP3.com, I found that it was Bruce's tunes I kept coming back to again and again; his music resonated for me (I'm a big fan of Robert Wyatt, Syd Barrett, Nick Drake, Beck, and the like), and inspired me to buy CDs of every musical project he's been involved with to date. Lash typifies the case of the truly great singer/songwriter struggling independently for greater recognition. Of course, there are thousands of other musicians who walk in similar shoes; we're just using Bruce as an example. See Bruce's site at home.att.net/~bblash, or search MP3.com for "Bruce Lash."

Digital music distribution has been a double-edged sword for me. On the one hand, it's very exciting to be able to be heard around the world (this is especially true for someone {me} who doesn't perform before a live audience). On the other hand, it's easy for one's expectations to be unreasonably high. Wasn't that the way the Internet was sold to independent musicians?

People from all over the world have visited my site—I've sold CDs to people in places as unlikely as Pakistan. I once received a nice note from somebody in rural Costa Rica who liked what he heard on my pages, but didn't have the money to buy the CDs. Would I send him some anyway? You bet I would. I think it was one of the best things I did that year. His address read like bad directions through the Southern part of the country, literally saying: "Go 350 miles south of the main city to the pink house next to the big church and ask for Celeste." And it got there. That, to me, is a good Internet experience. There are people in Russia and Bosnia who wrote to the Virgineers [another of Lash's projects] asking for free CDs because they couldn't get currency out of their countries.Did we send them CDs? Yes. If our free little CD makes someone's life a little better in the Balkans, who are we to ask for money? So in this sense, yes, the Internet has greatly expanded the reach of my music. But I haven't really sold much of my music through MP3.com. In truth, I've had better luck selling through an on-line store (*www.cdbaby.com*).

—Continued—

I've never really liked MP3s. They take too long to download, and take up too much space on my hard drive. At the defacto bitrate of 128 kbps, they sound squirrelly. But if one wants to have a business as an independent artist on the Internet, one had better have MP3s available. I got into MP3.com pretty early. At the time, it seemed like a place that really wanted to "level the playing field," and I liked their attitude. I've had a good number of downloads over the months, and my songs were featured on the site at one point, which led to lots of downloads. I noticed, however, that the song itself was getting more hits than my artist page. People were apparently there more for the free music than to learn about the artist. As much as I wish more people were interested in really learning about artists, I can't fault them for that—everybody loves free stuff. I also became somewhat disillusioned when MP3.com came out with a program wherein artists pay to be a featured artist; it became clear to me that they had moved on from the "level playing field" phase of their operation.

But when it came time for me to manufacture "Prozak for Lovers," I was in email contact with a guy from Oklahoma City who had a friend who worked for a CD manufacturing company, and he was able to get me a good deal on the manufacturing cost. I wouldn't have known anything about the company, let alone get this deal, had I not been active on the Internet.

I've spent nearly two years promoting myself on the Internet. I posted on message boards (I still get hits from many of those posts). I sent CDs to on-line reviewers to get my name out there. I became a part of the independent music community as it exists on the Internet. I've also learned that non-Internet exposure is valuable. In fact, I've become more interested in non-Internet promotion as of late. Getting my music on the radio, or getting a review in a newspaper or magazine is very exciting. When you do the math, you find that people with access to the Internet are still a small lot compared to the number of people who have access to radios and newspapers and books. Despite the hype, much of the potential of digital music distribution has yet to be realized for artists like me.

As much as I've benefited from all of this experience and exposure, I've also noticed that my priorities have become skewed. I'm checking my stats too often rather than making music. I'm spending too much time thinking that something big might happen. Rock stardom is a very, very tall mountain to climb, and I haven't even gotten to the foothills yet. But I have no need for the journey—I'm able to produce quality recordings that I really like. If I didn't sell any CDs, I would still be able to make those records and it wouldn't matter whether anyone buys them.

—Continued—

> So, I've made a pact with myself to spend more time making music than pro-
> moting it. I'll keep my web pages up and respond to people who listen to my
> work and want to comment on it, but I will not take my eyes off of the prize:
> the chance to realize the sounds I hear in my head and massage them to the
> point where they sound good to my ears. My prize is my own musical freedom
> and happiness. I'd be foolish to want anything more.

biographical text, and more, all manageable through a web-based interface.
Despite the massive popularity of MP3.com, IUMA is the original, folks. The real
deal. Don't let anyone tell you different.

GarageBand.com

www.garageband.com Occupying a position somewhere between promotion of
unsigned artists (like MP3.com) and offering major label music for sale (like EMusic), GarageBand.com aims to work with the "bubbling" method alluded to in
Chapter 1, *The Nuts and Bolts of MP3*. By allowing users to vote for and review the
music of struggling musicians, GarageBand.com hopes to determine which of their
artists shows commercial potential statistically, and then to offer those artists actual
recording contracts. According to the site's founder, only about 600 of the 30,000
CDs published each year are actually profitable;* basically, just the discs that make
it into the Top 40. By gauging audience reactions before contracts are signed and
CDs pressed, GarageBand.com hopes to publish a higher proportion of profitable
music. The Talking Heads' Jerry Harrison is one of the site's co-founders.

Bandwidth: How Much Do You Need?

MP3 files may be small compared to uncompressed audio sources, but when you
start tossing a bunch of them over the wires, their cumulative impact on available
throughput can be huge. There are many factors that come into play when deciding how much throughput you need to keep your users happy. How many users
will you be serving simultaneously? If you're broadcasting, you'll almost certainly
be *downsampling*—lowering the quality of the audio to make it more Internet-
friendly. But by how much? If you're offering files for download, the equation is
purely a function of how many users you allow to connect simultaneously. If you
limit the number of connections, you may end up turning some users away, but
the ones who do get to connect will be guaranteed good throughput. If you don't,
you can offer more simultaneous downloads, but all downloads will be slow. In

---

* Ironically, this is just the kind of statistic labels use to justify their existence: That with such a low success
rate, we need someone to pour tons of money into distribution and promotion on lots of new music so
that a few artists can at least hope to succeed.

essence, it's your decision whether to place the bottleneck at their end of the line, or at yours. No one likes an unresponsive server.

So, exactly how much bandwidth do you need to serve up MP3 files from a web or FTP server you run yourself? You'll need to do some ballpark calculations, then do some real-world testing to make sure your calculations hold up okay. Trouble is, you don't have advance knowledge of the speed at which your users will be connecting, so the best you can do is to estimate. Having ten simultaneous modem users is very different from having ten simultaneous DSL or cable users:

```
U = Number of simultaneous users
S = Max connect speed of users (estimated)
O = Overhead. General Internet congestion. Estimated constant of .9
B = Bandwidth required
U x S x O = B
```

So let's assume you're going to allow 10 users to connect to your site simultaneously and you figure they're probably all using 33.6 K modems:

```
10 x 33.6 x .9 = 302.4
```

So your upstream connection must be capable of serving 302.4 K per second. In other words, your upstream path should be able to bear nearly ten times what a standard modem can download. If any of your users are on faster connections, your line will be saturated, and some of the users will get slower transfer speeds than their equipment is capable of.

It's important to remember that transfer speeds are often measured in bits per second, not bytes per second. There are eight bits in a byte, so 302.4 kbps is roughly equal to 38 kilobytes per second (38 K). If you've got a symmetric 384 kbps DSL connection, you're probably used to seeing your downloads speeds top out at around 42K (most browsers report download speeds in kilobytes/sec), so a 38K threshold would serve 10 simultaneous modem downloads pretty nicely.

Because MP3 fans are often download hogs, they're more prone to have fast connections than normal Internet users, so let's assume that half of your users are on 768 kbps DSL connections:

```
5 x 768k x .9 = 3456
5 x 33.6 x .9 = 151.2
---------------------------
Total: 3607.2, or 450K/sec.
```

As you can see, a few fast users can change the picture pretty dramatically—like grocery bills, these things can add up very quickly. Most web and FTP server software worth its salt includes a setting that will let you specify the maximum number of simultaneous users. More advanced software even offers the ability to let the administrator "throttle," or limit the maximum bandwidth available to any single user. If you plan to promote your site heavily, either be ready for the onslaught with a big fat pipe, or be prepared to face the wrath of disgruntled users.

Colocation

If you want to run your own server but can't get a fast enough connection to your home for an affordable rate, surf the sites of the ISPs in your area, looking for colocation options. With "colo," you supply the machine, install and set up the web server software, and maintain the site. But you store the machine on the premises of the service provider, taking advantage of their proximity to the high-speed Internet backbone. Most colo plans will also guarantee that someone will be around to reboot your machine if it hangs or crashes, or provide other QOS (Quality of Service) guarantees.

Free bandwidth

If you don't need a lot of server space, you may want to look into one of the generic "free web space" options such as GeoCities, Tripod, or XOOM. All run on a similar business model: Free web space in exchange for advertising banner eyeballs. The disadvantage to sites such as these is that they have a very low "cool" factor, and you don't get grouped together with other artists, have the opportunity to be featured as an "Artist of the Day" or similar, don't show up in the alphabetized artist indexes or searches, and may be subject to restrictions or limitations that don't fit your style. If free is what you're after, you're better off uploading to MP3.com or a similar site.

Running Your Own Web Server

It's easier than you may think to set up web server software on your own machine and grant access to the entire world. One of the nice things about working directly at the helm of your own server is that you don't have to build your site locally and then FTP it into place; all changes you make to your site are live immediately. Of course, there are issues that make this an unrealistic option for many users. The most prominent obstacle is, of course, bandwidth; this is really only an option for those with DSL or cable connections to the Internet (ISDN will do in a pinch, if you don't expect much traffic). Even then, some providers only offer their subscribers fast *downstream* bandwidth, assuming that most of their users will only want to download large files, not offer them for upload. Upstream bandwidth is sometimes constrained to a fraction of the download speed. This type of connection is known as *asymmetric.* Symmetric connections offer the same speed upstream and downstream, and are better suited for web server deployment. If you're not sure of your upstream bandwidth, check your provider's web site, contact them directly, or run some upload tests of your own. The other big issue is the ever-changing, dynamically assigned IP address (we'll address that in a minute).

Running your own web server doesn't mean you have to have a domain name associated with your machine; a server can run just fine from an IP address alone, though it won't be easy for your users to remember. If you want a domain name associated with your machine, you'll need to work with your ISP to obtain a static, unchanging IP address, then register a domain and ask your ISP to map that domain to your static IP address. Of course you'll want to make sure your machine is always running and always connected.

Setting up a web server is far easier than setting up a *secure* web server, and the importance of server security should not be understated. Once you've opened your machine's door to the rest of the world, there's no end to ways in which nefarious crackers can exploit vulnerabilities in a setup to alter or delete your data. While you're probably going to be safe with quick experiments, be sure to do additional research if you want to do this full time. A good place to start is Simson Garfinkel's book *Web Security and Commerce*, *www.oreilly.com/catalog/websec/*.

Server setup

Some operating systems come with built-in web servers. Windows NT comes with Internet Information Services (IIS), BeOS comes bundled with PoorMan, and Linux distributions almost always come with Apache. Even if your operating system doesn't include a web server, there are dozens of them to choose from, regardless of platform.

In all cases, setup involves the same simple steps: Choose a "root" directory on your machine representing the base directory for your server, a default filename to be served for directory accesses (e.g., if a file called *index.html* exists in the "images" subdirectory of your server's root and somebody access *www.mysite.com/ images/* they'll get served with *index.html* automatically), and enable the server. You'll probably also want to configure the server to be launched automatically when you start your machine.

Testing the server

Test your server by placing an HTML document under the server root, then enter your "loopback" address into a browser window, followed by the filename.

Assuming you created a file called *mp3.html*, you would enter one of the following:

```
http://localhost/mp3.html
http://127.0.0.1/mp3.html
```

These two are simply references to your own machine, hence the term "loop-back" Once that's working, find out your real IP address and use that instead.

Discovering this address may depend on whether you're connecting through a network card or over a dial-up connection. An easy way to learn your IP address In Windows is to click Start → Run and type *winipcfg.exe*. Select the PPP or Network Interface Card from the picklist in the resulting panel to learn your current IP address. In BeOS, right-click the Dial-Up Networking icon in the Deskbar and chose "Statistics," or use the Network preferences panel if you're not using a modem. In Linux, launch a terminal window and type `netstat`—your available network interfaces will be reported on the first few lines. In MacOS, you'll need a utility like IP Net Monitor or "Lucky Numbers"; check your favorite Mac software library. If the site works with that address, hand it out to your friends and go to town.

Establishing MIME types

MIME, or Multipurpose Internet Mail Extension, is a specification for formatting non-ASCII messages so they can be sent over the Internet. Originally developed to enable email attachments, MIME now forms the basis for file-transfer communications between browsers and web servers.

Before releasing your site to the public, make sure that when you click a link to an MP3 file, the browser either initiates a download of that file or launches an MP3 player. If the browser window fills up with ASCII garbage (older browsers only) or asks the user what he wants to do with the file, then you'll know that either the MP3 MIME type has not been established in the web server software or the user hasn't configured his browser's MIME types properly. It's crucial that the MIME type sent by the server matches one of the types registered in the user's browser so that the proper action can be taken (i.e., start a download or launch an associated application, rather than trying to display the file's data in the browser window), and as a webmaster, it's your responsibility to make sure you're carrying out your end of this deal.

On most platforms and most web servers, MIME types are registered in a table and consist of a simple association between the MIME type and filename extensions. In this case, you want to tell the server what MIME header to send when a file ending in MP3 is accessed:

```
audio/x-mpeg    .mp3
audio/mpeg      .mp3
```

Two MIME types are listed here because, unfortunately, the industry has yet to agree on a standard MIME type for MP3 files. Technically speaking, `audio/x-mpeg` is the correct MIME type, although `audio/mpeg` is in wide use as well. Essentially, MIME types preceded with `x-` refer to file types that have not yet been codified by international committee. Once a file type is deemed common enough to become a part of "the canon," the `x-` is removed and the type becomes official. Both of the above MIME types are in common use at this writing, even though the type has not yet been made official. You *may* want to additionally establish:

```
audio/x-mpegurl    .m3u
```

particularly if you plan to do any MP3 streaming from your server. Associate these with the extension *.M3U.*

Every web server has a different method of establishing MIME associations. Consult your server's documentation for details (in most cases, the MIME database can be easily found in the Options or Preferences).

 BeOS web servers do not utilize MIME tables, because all filetyping in BeOS is MIME-based to begin with. If the MP3 files on your system have correct filetypes, they'll be served up correctly regardless their filename extensions, or even without extensions (though it's a good idea to keep the *.mp3* extensions in place to make users of other platforms happy).

Dealing with dynamic IP addresses

If you connect to the Internet through a dial-up connection, chances are your IP address is drawn from a pool of available addresses and assigned to you at connect time. This is great for conserving on addresses, but terrible for people who want to run servers of any kind. The address you hand out for your server today will probably be different tomorrow, or even a couple of hours from now.

Fortunately, there are a number of ways to address this situation. None of them are as painless as securing a static address, but they do a fine job of working around a thorny problem. One way to get around it is to keep a page at a permanent location, on your ISP's server, for instance. This page will, in turn, simply provide a link or a redirect back to your machine. Every time you connect, a script or program will be run automatically that will regenerate this page and FTP it into place at the permanent location. Such a page can even tell users when your machine is off-line. Search your favorite software library for "dynamic IP" and you'll find many such solutions (try *hotfiles.com* for Windows, *macdownload.com* for MacOS, *freshmeat.net* for Linux, or *bebits.com* for BeOS).

In addition, there are web-based services that will do this job for you. In fact, these services go one better by allowing you to have an elegant URL and dynamic IP addressing at the same time. A good example of such a service is *www.dynip. com*. DynIP will make your machine appear as *mymachine.dynip.com* any time you're logged in, regardless of your IP address at the moment. The client software runs on all versions of Windows, plus some versions of MacOS and several Unix variants, including Linux.

Running Your Own FTP Server

There are three major advantages to running an FTP server rather than (or in addition to) a web server:

- Most FTP clients these days are capable of batch transfers. If you want your users to be able to download lots of files at once, FTP is the way to go, since users will be able to drag multiple files or even entire directory structures down from your machine and walk away while the transfer proceeds.

- FTP servers can exist somewhat more secretively than web servers. Web crawlers ("spiders") will eventually discover and index the contents of most web sites, which means they'll turn up in most search engines. Public knowledge of FTP sites, on the other hand, will generally only get around by word of mouth, or if you want it to. If you only want to give access to a small handful of select people, the rest of the world may never learn you're running an FTP server.

- FTP servers make it easy to establish users and groups with specific levels of permission, so you can offer one set of files to the general public and another set to your close friends, for example. This can also be done by using password protection on web sites, but it's generally easier to configure and manage the permissions lists on FTP servers; this is what they're designed to do.

On the downside, the Web is of course easier for users to navigate. Everybody knows how to use a web browser, while far fewer are comfortable with FTP. And of course you may *want* your content indexed by the search engines.

An FTP server is part of Windows NT's IIS package, is included in every Linux distribution, and is built into BeOS Networking. Third-party FTP servers are available for MacOS, Windows 95/98, and for virtually every platform in existence. Popular choices for Windows 95/98 include War FTPD and WS_FTP Server. Popular servers for MacOS include FTPd and Rumpus. Again, check your favorite software library for details.

Regardless of your platform, be extremely careful when setting up an FTP server for public access. Make sure users only have access to a limited corner of your hard drive, and if you set up access outside of that directory structure for select, trusted users, test very carefully to make sure you don't accidentally grant that access to the general public. Pay attention to read-only versus read/write permissions. Give a malicious person read/write permissions to the wrong location and they can wipe out entire directory structures right under your nose.

If you've set up an FTP site with a username/password pair but still want to be able to grant easy access to the general public (who may not be familiar with FTP client usage), you can use the following shortcut to let them log in to a protected FTP site through their web browser:

```
ftp://username:password@ftp.mysite.com/directory/path/
```

You can even use this construct in an HTML link:

```
<a href="ftp://username:password@ftp.mysite.com/directory/
path/">Click here!</a>
```

Most browsers developed since the mid-90s will properly parse out the username and password and pass it to the FTP server, which will then return the contents of **/directory/path/** to the browser. But remember: The username and password will be in plain view in the URL pane—you've just thrown all security out the window!

Webcasting: Real-Time MP3 Broadcasting

Just a few years ago, Internet pundits (like me) were waxing poetic about how one day we'd all be able to run TV and radio stations out of our homes as the new era of convergent media and speedy connections dawned. Well, guess what? It came true, and today you can broadcast audio signal out over the Internet in real time, ready to be heard by anyone who cares to listen. Thousands of users are queuing up their favorite tracks and personal creations, doing live call-in shows, variety shows, live interviews, even depressingly juvenile 24-hour live prank call shows.

In fact, just last week, riots again erupted in downtown Berkeley in protest of a real radio station having its freedom of speech curtailed by its parent company. Within hours, an Internet-based replacement show sprung to life and I was able to hear the voices of the "gagged" station employees, liberated by the openness of the Internet and the magic of streaming MP3.

Head over to *www.shoutcast.com, www.icecast.org, www.radiospy.com, www. mycaster.com, www.greenwitch.com, www.live365.com,* or any other directory of live MP3 radio, and you'll be amazed at the sheer number and variety of broadcast types being offered. And unlike your local radio environment, these broadcasts aren't constrained by the distance a signal can travel. All of them are available worldwide.

On the other hand, you don't necessarily get the same guarantee of quality you get with commercial or professional radio. Stations come up and down in the blink of an eye, they all broadcast at varying levels of quality, and the vast majority of them broadcast stuff you aren't really interested in hearing (just like real radio!). But at the same time, there are real gems out there: impromptu DJs broadcasting at decent quality levels, playing stuff you've never heard of but fall instantly in love with. It's a brave new world of "pirate" radio, as yet unfettered by the mandates of the FCC, anarchic, wonderful, and buzzing with a level of excitement the Internet hasn't seen since Mosaic hit the scene. Just as the world went nuts a few years ago when we realized that anyone could become a publisher, we now exhilarate in the fact that anyone can become a DJ and be heard around the world, instantly, and nearly for free.

While the notion of not being able to easily save the files you download may seem unappealing to some, the fact remains that not everybody wants to spend hours managing a huge MP3 collection, and sometimes we just want to let someone else control the horizontal and the vertical in the background while we work on other things. There are zillions of CDs and videocassettes out there, but we don't necessarily want to own all of them. The transience of radio and TV have an appealing place in our cultural landscape, and streaming MP3 fills the same kind of position in many people's lives. Many people are very happy to just listen in as the bits float by in the stream, enjoying them as they pass without feeling they have to "own" them.

 Note the legal situation changes somewhat in the case of Internet broadcasting. The legal distinction between offering MP3 downloads and streaming MP3 files is simple: If the ultimate destination of your files is the user's hard drive, you need legal rights to the music in question. If the music will be heard by the user but not stored for later playback, you should be able to obtain a "statutory license" for re-broadcast of the music in question. However, exact details on obtaining a statutory license were still being worked out by the relevant organizations at this writing, and negotiations appeared to have stalled. See the "Webcasting" section of Chapter 7, *The Not-So-Fine-Print: Legal Bits and Pieces* for additional information. You'll also find an excellent summary of the ongoing legal wranglings over webcasting in the Beginner's Guide at *www.radiospy.com.*

Commercial Internet Radio

SHOUTcast and icecast may be providing the most popular MP3 server software, but they're by no means the only sites offering directory listings. Other popular sites taking advantage of the popularity of MP3 streaming include Spinner.com, Tunes.com, SonicNet, and NetRadio. And how do they intend to make money? Without users clicking through dozens of pages to generate ad revenue, these sites look to other means, such as relationships with e-commerce sites like Amazon.com, and affinities with sites who pay a fee for purchases made via links. More importantly, the sites sell CDs and merchandise, and some of them experiment with ads embedded into streamed broadcasts as well. Small potatoes? Hardly. Both ImagineRadio and SonicNet were purchased by MTV in 1999. Meanwhile, a site called MP3Radio.com is partnering with hundreds of traditional radio stations around the world to help them get their standard transmissions and related MP3 downloads onto the Internet. The Web isn't just enabling a new flavor of radio, it's changing the way traditional radio operates as well.

How MP3 Broadcast Works

Streaming MP3 systems (which basically boil down to SHOUTcast and icecast, discussed later), are constructed modularly. A "source stream" module is used to organize and play the MP3 files themselves, and possibly to allow for live mixing of multiple sources, or to offer microphone input capabilities. The source stream may also interact with an MPEG codec to "downsample" the quality of the source stream to make it less bandwidth-intensive and more broadcast-friendly. The source stream sends the signal it generates on to a server module, which takes responsibility for distributing the source stream out to any currently listening clients. The source stream may or may not be running on the same machine as the server software, or even under the same operating system. The server software, in turn, may be redistributing streams from multiple source streams.

In a nutshell, the source streamer may be responsible for:

- "Down-sampling" audio signal to a reasonable distribution level

- Sending the currently playing track to the server

- Identifying the Internet and port addresses of the server

- Establishing appropriate data to be registered in public databases

- Connecting and disconnecting from the server

The server is responsible for:

- Replicating audio data from the source stream and sending it to listeners
- Logging all transactions
- Limiting or controlling the maximum number of concurrent users
- Disconnecting users whose connections have died
- Specifying the format of "metadata": titles, URLs, etc.

There are several advantages to keeping the broadcast system modular. First of all, it keeps a lot of complexity out of the source stream software itself (which will be WinAmp or Sonique for most users) that isn't needed by people who use that same software for normal (nonserving) playback. Second, it allows multiple users to send their data to a single server, which may remain under the control of a single administrator on some networks. But perhaps most importantly, it accommodates situations where you don't have much bandwidth on the source machine, but can partake of the services of another machine on a high-bandwidth pipe (possibly a friend's, or a machine at work or school). All you have to do is get a single stream of data out to the server, and the server can parse that data out to many listeners simultaneously. The modular system may provide security benefits in some cases. The source stream can be run on a user-friendly but insecure system like Windows 98, while the intensive network needs are take by a security-conscious system such as Linux.

To get a handle on the possible ways in which MP3 broadcast systems can be set up, study Figure 8-1. In scenario A, the source streamer (WinAmp) is being run on one machine (possibly Windows 98). Music being pumped out of the source streamer is sent to another machine (possibly Linux), which is running the server software. In scenario B, a single machine (possibly Windows 95) is running *both* the source streaming software and the server software. In either scenario, it is the server software that sends the audio stream out to multiple listeners. In both scenarios, the server software broadcasts the fact of its existence (but not the audio stream itself) to a directory listing server, such as the ones run by *shoutcast.com* and *icecast.org*. To learn about the existence of currently running servers, end users access a directory listing site. When they click on a link in the directory, they're connected directly with a streaming server.

Directory listing servers *do not* send audio data to users—they just keep track of currently running servers and help users make the connection. When a streaming server goes offline, it automatically disappears from the directory listing site.

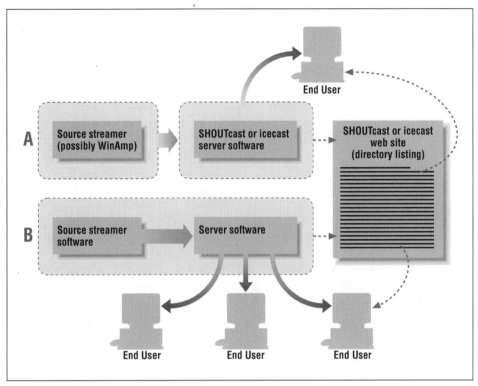

Figure 8-1. MP3 broadcast systems are constructed modularly to allow for maximum flexibility in implementation

The server is, in essence, an "intelligent repeater"; it knows how to listen to audio data coming from a source stream (e.g., the WinAmp DSP plug-in) and efficiently broadcast it to listening clients "out there." If the person controlling the source stream tells the server that the stream is to be publicly accessible, the server will send updates to the public web directory at *shoutcast.com* or *icecast.org* listing the name and description of the station along with a linked IP address so that listeners can check in with a single click.

If you don't tell the source streamer that the stream is meant for the public, your broadcasts will only be known to people who are specifically given the URL. Many people use this option to run a server at home that they listen to personally at work—a radio station for them and them alone.

Types of source streamers

There are two types of source streamers: The server may receive audio data from a *static file* source, or from a *re-encoding* source. Static sources simply broadcast MP3 files out over the network at the bitrate at which they've been encoded. Static streamers require a lot of bandwidth, but consume very little CPU or memory, as their task is very simple—just pass it on, brother. Re-encoding source streamers, on the other hand, must decode existing files to raw data and then re-encode them to downsampled, modem-friendly quality levels on the fly. As a result, they consume much less bandwidth, but are much more taxing on the machine's available resources. They also require access to an MPEG codec to do their job, while static streamers do not.

There are two popularly used MP3 broadcast solutions available: SHOUTcast and icecast. SHOUTcast is developed by NullSoft,* the makers of WinAmp, and some its functions are tightly integrated into WinAmp's. icecast is an open source alternative to SHOUTcast, and emerges from the Unix/Linux world. Fortunately, the two are nearly 100% compatible. You can send streams to an icecast server from WinAmp, or to the SHOUTcast server from shout or liveice, both of which are source streamers that come with icecast.

This willing compatibility between the two products is a refreshing change from the standards wars that usually boil around the introduction of new technologies. At this writing, icecast offers more security options than SHOUTcast, and uses less memory and CPU cycles than SHOUTcast (though this may change in the future). Both products are free (as in free beer), while only icecast is truly free (as in free speech and Open Source software). Both products' server modules run under most Unix-like operating systems and under Windows 95/98/NT. At this writing, only SHOUTcast offers a graphical user interface (though the SHOUTcast server is only quasi-GUI). icecast is completely command-line based, though this may change in the future. SHOUTcast is much more popular than icecast, and will receive the bulk of attention in the remainder of this chapter.

Working with SHOUTcast

In the SHOUTcast system, WinAmp itself is used as the source stream. WinAmp is used to organize and play music, while a WinAmp, Sonique, or other streaming output plug-in is used to send the stream off to an MPEG codec on the same machine for downsampling, and then on to the SHOUTcast server.

 Do not confuse the term "SHOUTcast server" or "server" in this section with the web site at *www.shoutcast.com*. The former refers to the server module running on your own machine or a machine to which you've been granted explicit permission to broadcast from. The SHOUTcast web site merely serves as a public directory of currently broadcasting servers. shoutcast.com does not replicate your stream or offer bandwidth or storage space to users—it just points to stations which are currently "on the air."

---

* NullSoft was purchased by AOL in mid-1999.

The server receives downsampled information from the WinAmp plug-in and passes audio data out to the Internet. Optionally, the system will also cause your "station" to be displayed in SHOUTcast's public directory of available radio stations.

Configure the plug-in

To get started, head over to *shoutcast.com* and download the DSP plug-in for WinAmp.[*] Install the included .DLL into WinAmp's plug-ins directory, restart WinAmp, launch the Preferences panel, and you'll find a new entry in the DSP category labeled "SHOUTcast source for WinAmp." Click Configure, and you'll see a panel similar to the one in Figure 8-2.

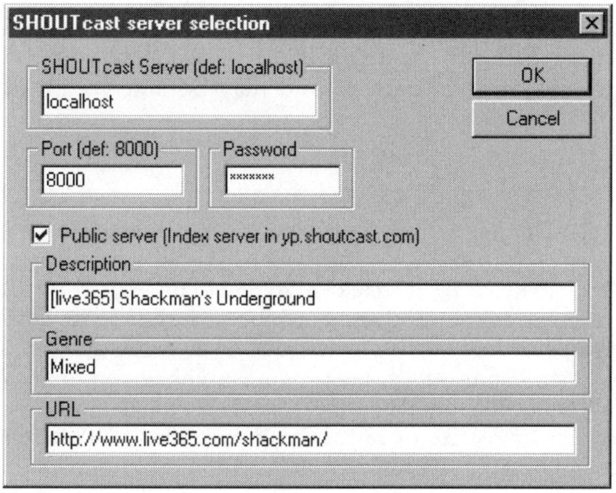

Figure 8-2. The SHOUTcast DSP plug-in for WinAmp

In the vast majority of cases, you'll want to leave the port address set to the default of 8000. You'll only need to change this if you're on a machine that's already using this port for another service (if unsure, ask your network administrator for advice).

The "Format" field represents the most critical choice you'll have to make as a station operator, as this is where you'll determine the balance between audio quality and the number of listeners your station can support. Because very few people have a fast enough connection to the Internet to listen to MP3 audio exactly as it's stored on your system, the SHOUTcast DSP *downsamples*: decreases the sample-rate and bitrate of the audio so it can be distributed effectively over POTS (plain old telephone service).

---

[*] WinAmp's DSP plug-in isn't the only source streamer available for use with SHOUTcast, but it's by far the most popular. Sonique and other players are also capable of sending audio streams to broadcast servers. However, we'll use WinAmp as an example in this section due to its broad popularity.

The configuration dialog for the DSP plug-in allows you to specify downsampling parameters, and here you'll have to do some calculations to take into account the speed of your Internet connection, and more importantly, the speed of your user's Internet connections. If you're broadcasting to a few known friends with high-speed connections, you'll probably want to set the ratio high, to give them maximum possible fidelity. If you're broadcasting to the general public, however, you'll probably want to assume that most of your users have a 33.6 kbps connection. Of course, as you probably know from experience, the maximum rated throughput of any given modem rarely represents the actual throughput after Internet overhead is taken into account. The safest bet for general streaming implementations is to select one of the 24 KB options in this dialog. That, however, means you're going to be broadcasting some very low fidelity music out into the world, which isn't a very happy prospect either. You'll need to choose your samplerate based on your perception of your target audience's available bandwidth. If you're reading this a couple of years from the time it was written (early 2000), you may have a very large audience of cable and DSL users, and may be able to afford a much higher samplerate.

It's important to distinguish between your own connection speed and that of your users, and to remember that your upstream bandwidth is going to be affected by Internet congestion. In addition, if you're using a 56 K modem, remember that the "56 K" label applies only to your downstream bandwidth. 56 K modem users rarely see better than 33.6 upstream bandwidth, so unless you've got a DSL or cable connection on the server machine, you'll probably want to limit your samplerate to 24 K even if you think your audience has a faster connection. If you're running the source streamer and the server software on separate machines, you'll need to take into account both the speed of your connection to the server machine and the speed of the server machine's outgoing connection. If you try to dish up more than can fit through the pipe from one end to the other, your users will experience drop-outs and lost signal. Be sure to do plenty of testing before marking your server as "public."

Install an appropriate codec

The DSP plug-in depends on the presence of an MP3 codec on you're system running the source streamer. Because NullSoft can't provide this codec without paying huge amounts of money to Fraunhofer, they assume that the user already has an appropriate MPEG codec installed. Fortunately, users can freely download the codec from Microsoft, or purchase a higher quality codec from a third party. To see if you have the codec installed on your system, launch the Windows Control Panel and navigate to Multimedia → Devices. Look under the Audio Compression

Codecs section for an entry labeled "'Fraunhofer IIS MPEG Layer-3 Codec." If you're using a recent version of Windows, or if you've installed the latest version of the Windows Media Player, you probably have this already. If you don't, you can install the codec that comes with the Microsoft NetShow tools package. You'll find a direct link to the latest version of this package at shoutcast.com's Downloads page.

Note, however, that the Microsoft-provided Fraunhofer codec is limited to streams of 56 kbps. While this should be plenty of resolution for almost all MP3 broadcast implementations, those with special high-bandwidth needs may install a high-end codec available from *www.opticom.de.*

 If you want to dish up files exactly as they're currently encoded, you won't need to do any downsampling during the serving process. However, this either means that A) your files are encoded at normal bitrates and you don't mind limiting your audience to owners of very fast connections only, or B) you've already encoded the files you intend to broadcast at relatively low bitrates and/or frequencies.

Configure the server

Once you've selected the SHOUTcast DSP plug-in in WinAmp's plug-in preferences panel, everything played in WinAmp will be sent on to the SHOUTcast server as well as to your own speakers. The server, however, will not redistribute music to the masses until it's been launched and enabled. Launch the SHOUTcast server (probably at *c:\program files\shoutcast\sc_serv.exe*) and you'll see a panel with a simple reporting window, which will show you what the server is up to at any given moment, as shown in Figure 8-3. The main window simply reports the server's transactions. All configuration is accomplished by editing a text file.

The default configuration of the server should be fine for starters, and you can now test the system. Make sure something is playing in WinAmp, then go to another machine, launch a broadcast-capable MP3 player, and enter the IP address of the host machine along with the port number. On a common "Class C" network, you might enter something like:

```
http://192.168.0.3:8000
```

If you have a real IP address, you might enter something like:

```
http://202.14.123.33:8000
```

After a brief delay, downsampled music being played through WinAmp on the remote machine should start to play on the client.

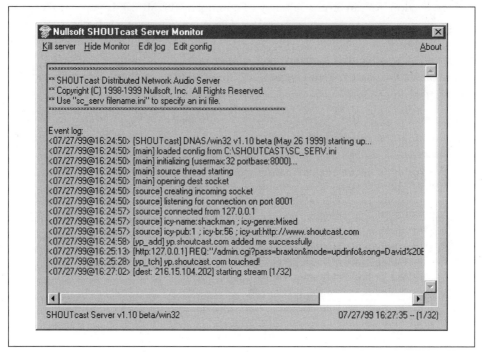

Figure 8-3. The SHOUTcast server offers little in the way of an interface

 Most of these instructions assume you're working in Windows, but the SHOUTcast server is available for Linux and other Unix-like platforms as well. Configuration instructions are virtually identical for both operating systems. Linux users will need to change permissions on the server binary with chmod u+x, and to make sure the config file is readable by the user who will by running the server. Note that if the user is not root, he will not be able to use port addresses lower than 1024. Note also that only the server component is available to Linux users, not the WinAmp source stream plug-in. Under *nix, substitute *sc_serv.conf* wherever it says *sc_serv.ini* in the text below.

Additional server options

Beyond the defaults, the server software offers a ton of additional options. All configuration of the SHOUTcast server is (at this writing) accomplished by editing the text file *sc_serv.ini*, which you'll find in the SHOUTcast installation directory. The file can also be accessed via the server's Edit Config pull-down menu. The config file is very heavily commented (commented lines begin with a semicolon) and should be relatively self-explanatory. Since *sc_serv.ini* is read into the server's memory when it's launched, you must kill and restart the SHOUTcast server after making any configuration changes. Note that many of the options in the config file are simple on/off switches, where "1" represents "on" and "0" represents "off." Here are brief descriptions of some of the most useful options:

Logging

The four logging options are quite intuitive, and let you specify the location and name of the file to which a traffic log is written, specify whether traffic is written to the screen in addition to the log file, and control the behavior of the "history" log, which can be parsed by other programs to create HTML graphs of ongoing traffic patterns. This can be set to */dev/null* on Linux machines if you want it disabled entirely, or *none* for Windows machines. The number of seconds between writes to the history log file can be specified on the *HistoryLogTime=* line.

Network configuration

Options set here determine the way your station interacts with the network. For example, you can change the port address your server is running on with the *PortBase=* line. The *SrcIP=ANY* line gives you control over who is allowed to broadcast MP3 streams through your server. By default, this is set to *ANY*, so that anybody running the DSP plug-in will be able to broadcast via your server. If you set this to your "loopback" IP of 127.0.0.1, only you will be allowed to use the server. If you want to limit use to people on your own network, you might use something like 192.168.*.*. Remember, however, that source streamers must still connect with the appropriate password, so you aren't completely exposed to the world.

If your server machine is bound to multiple IP addresses, you can specify which address the SHOUTcast server is on by editing the *DestIP=ANY* line. If your machine is running a DNS server, you can see the actual domain and machine names of the clients connecting to your server by editing the *NameLookups=0* line, though this may impact performance if your nameserver is slow.

Relays

You can cause your server to function as a "relay" server by uncommenting and editing the *RelayPort* and *RelayServer* lines (Figure 8-4). This allows you to re-broadcast incoming streams to another server for final distribution to "official" servers. Relay servers are particularly important for situations where you want to serve more listeners than the bandwidth available to a single server can accommodate.

Server configuration

Perhaps most important, this section lets you control specific parameters of your server's behavior. The *MaxUser=32* line lets you raise or lower the

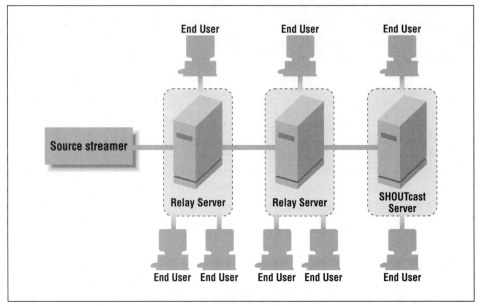

Figure 8-4. SHOUTcast/icecast "Relay" functions let administrators perform load-balancing across multiple machines

maximum number of clients that can be served by your station simultaneously. You'll need to tailor this line carefully to match the actual bandwidth available to your machine. To do this, multiply your available bandwidth by .9 in order to account for Internet congestion and overhead, then divide by the bitrate at which you intend to serve. For example, if you have a 384 kpbs upstream DSL connection and you want to serve MP3 audio at 24 kbps: $384 \times .9 / 24 = 14.4$. Thus, you should probably set the *MaxUsers* line to 14, or decrease the quality of the audio you're serving. Since the default is set to 32, it's important to edit this line if you're on anything less than a very fast connection. The version of the server available at this writing was capable of serving a maximum of 1,024 simultaneous users—pretty amazing, considering that 60 simultaneous users can saturate a typical T1 line!

If you're serving up a streaming MP3 server on a shared corporate or organizational network, it's very important that you consult with your sysadmin before beginning. Set a high number of *MaxUsers* without permission and it won't be long before you're hogging all the bandwidth your organization has at its disposal. Since the sysadmin's very existence is predicated on keeping all of his users happy, such a stunt is likely to land you in a Siberian cell block with nothing to eat but gruel and water. Be courteous, think ahead, and get permission before you begin.

The default password built into both the DSP plug-in and the SHOUTcast server is "changeme," and it's probably a very good idea to change this so that rogue users can't piggyback on your server's connection without your permission. Remember that the password in both the server config file and the DSP plug-in must match, so don't forget to change this in both places.

AutoDumpUsers and *AutoDumpSourceTime* can be used to specify whether your users will be disconnected automatically if the source stream becomes disconnected for some reason, and how long the server should wait before disconnecting those users.

If you'd like your users to hear an "intro" file as soon as they connect, before being transferred to the audio stream in progress, encode it at the same sample-rate and number of channels as the rest of your stream, then specify the file's name on the *IntroFile=* line. You can set a bitrate for the file in the filename itself, and then reference it on this line with the %d flag. For example, rename your intro file to *intro64.mp3*, then specify *IntroFile=c:\intro%d.mp3* to cause the file to be broadcast at 64 kbps. Similarly, if you haven't enabled *AutoDumpUsers*, you can provide an MP3 file that will be played automatically, over and over again, should the source stream disconnect. The same options for the intro file apply to the backup file.

You can also control the title that appears to users as they listen to your station. By default, this will simply be provided by the DSP plug-in, and will be read out of the currently playing track's ID3 tags. If you'd rather your users see a string like "Shackman's Underground," uncomment the `TitleFormat=` and append your preferred string. For extra credit, you can combine your station name with the title being sent by the source stream by using the %s flag; for example, if you use:

```
TitleFormat=Shackman's Underground: %s
```

and you're currently playing Billy Bang's "Valve #10," your users will see:

```
Shackman's Underground: Valve #10
```

Users can also be sent a URL, which makes it easy for them to visit your site if they decide they dig the tracks you're laying down and want to learn more. Because the *URLFormat* line can also accept the *%s* flag as an argument, you can allow users to arrive at a specific page on your web site via a custom CGI script. For example, if you use:

```
URLFormat=http://www.server.com/redirect.cgi?url=%s
```

then the name of the currently playing track will be passed to a CGI script running on the web server, and you can dish up additional information on that track. This presents a fantastic opportunity for artists and bands to encourage users to learn more about them as they listen, though you'll need some pre-existing CGI (probably perl) experience to pull this off.

All of this title, URL, and station ID information is known as "meta-data," and is constantly being sent to listening clients. Because meta-data will change as the source streamer moves from one track to the next, you can control how often the meta-data is sent as well. This interval is established not in seconds, but in bytes, and you can control how often meta-data is refreshed by tweaking the *MetaInterval=* line, though SHOUTcast recommends sticking with this default. If you're running a special broadcast consisting of zillions of very short tracks, you might want to make this shorter, but there's probably no good reason to make it longer, as the amount of bandwidth it consumes is so small as to be almost unmeasurable.

Extended logging

In addition to the standard logging capabilities described earlier, the SHOUTcast server is also capable of generating some pretty cool HTML-based logs and up-to-date reports, which you can access from anywhere thanks to the fact that SHOUTcast actually includes a built-in miniature HTTP server. So if you're running a SHOUTcast server from your home machine and want to see how popular it's been today from your desk at work, you can type in (substituting the actual IP address of the server, of course):

```
http://217.77.123.3:8000/current.html
```

In order to generate HTML reports, you'll need to create an HTML template file defining the look and feel of the report, then stuff it full of the allowable SHOUTcast logging keywords, in uppercase letters and embedded in HTML comments, as shown in Table 8-1. The server will treat each commented keyword like a variable, substituting in actual data from the history log.

Table 8-1. Special Remote Variables

Keyword	Keyword Function
<!-- LISTENERS -->	Number of active listeners
<!-- MAXLISTENERS -->	Number of maximum listeners configured in the server
<!-- LISTENERTABLE -->	Listeners listed in table format
<!-- GENRE -->	Genre string of currently playing track (from ID3 tag)
<!-- DESCRIPTION -->	The current description string
<!-- URL -->	The current URL string
<!-- HITS -->	Total number of hits since server was started
<!-- CURRENTSONG -->	Name of the current song

Once you've configured your template, you'll need to tell the server where to find it and how to treat it. The template is considered an input file, so edit the *CurrentLogIn=* to point to the template file. The generated HTML document is your output, to edit the *CurrentLogOut=* line to specify a path to the generated report, e.g., *CurrentLogOut=C:\current.html*. Finally, you can specify how often the report should be updated with the *CurrentLogTime=* line.

If you find that you need to run the server under one configuration one day and another configuration the next, you may want to make multiple copies of *sc_serv.ini*. You can then launch the server with a particular configuration from the DOS shell by typing something like:

```
sc_serv.exe sc_serv2.ini
```

Remote administration

Because the SHOUTcast server has (limited) built-in HTTP services, it's also capable of being administered remotely, i.e., from another machine anywhere on the Internet (Figure 8-5). Open any web browser and enter *http://ip_address:port* (substituting the real IP and port addresses) and a web page will be sent back to the browser listing the name of the station, the musical genre being played (as identified in the DSP plug-in), the bitrate being dished up, and the name of the currently playing track. Enter the correct password, click the Admin button, and you'll be passed to an administration page reporting full details on the current server configuration. While you can't change all server options remotely (or at least this was not possible at this writing), you can disconnect from the stream source with a single click, thereby disconnecting all currently connected users. Unfortunately, it is not possible to reconnect the source remotely, since this requires access to the DSP plug-in interface, not just to the server, so be careful!

In addition, you can view the entire log file that has been generated since the server was started, or just view information on the last few connections, by clicking the "tail logfile" link. Click the Usage Graph link to see an ASCII representation of the number of connections that have been established on a scale of time. You can also change the number of *MaxUsers* if necessary, but remember that doing so does not actually change the *sc_serv.ini* file, so you won't be making a permanent change here.

You can jump directly to the administration page without going through the "front door" by including your password in the URL. For example:

```
http://127.0.0.1:8000/admin.cgi?pass=zoomer23
```

might get you into administrative mode on your own machine. If you're not worried too much about people hijacking your machine, you can bookmark this URL for easy access in the future.

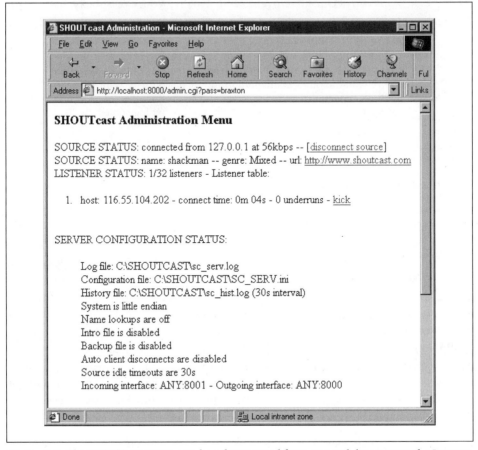

Figure 8-5. The SHOUTcast server can be administered from any web browser on the Internet in a limited fashion, as long as you can supply the correct password

Serving live streams, microphone input, and other formats

The SHOUTcast server is not limited to the distribution of existing MP3 files, but can handle any format that can be processed internally by WinAmp. Thus, streams from other sources that register in WinAmp's Input plug-ins can be encoded to low-samplerate MP3 on the fly, and served up just as you would serve up files. If your band is playing at a local club that has a decent Internet connection, you can take a line feed from the mixing board, run it into the input jack of your sound card, and hand your URL to the world so they can listen in from the comfort of their living rooms. However, there's a catch: The CD audio, line input, and MIDI input plug-ins do not use WinAmp's internal processor; WinAmp simply acts as a pass-through for these formats. To get around this limitation, you can install a third-party plug-in to replace the default plug-in. These alternatives will force WinAmp to handle the audio stream internally; it can pass the signal on to the SHOUTcast server. Look for the cd-da plug-in if you want to stream CD audio.

If you want to add a little vocal commentary to the mix as your station is broadcasting, tap Ctrl+L in WinAmp's playlist window and type *linerec://*. When you select the *linerec://* entry in the playlist, your station will be broadcasting anything coming through the sound card's input jack, including live input from your microphone. When you're done waxing poetic about your favorite artist, click on another song title in the playlist. Be careful though—if you leave the *linerec://* entry in place and the playlist cycles around to its entry again, it's all too easy to inadvertently broadcast what you might rather the world didn't hear.

Resource consumption

Since the SHOUTcast server doesn't have to hit the disk to retrieve MP3 data, or to run the MP3 decoding process, you'll actually find that running the SHOUTcast server consumes fewer machine resources than running an MP3 player locally. However, that's not the whole story—serving MP3 files *is* very taxing on network resources. Not only will you gobble up large amounts of outgoing bandwidth, but you'll be chugging through a ton of packets on the server machine as well. Linux users can run `tcdump` while the server is in use, and take a look at the output when you quit the utility. At 56 kbps, you'll probably find that you're processing around 20 packets per second, which can cause bottlenecks at around 10 users, depending on your machine and its particular configuration. This is where "repeaters" (see the "Relays" section of the server config file) come in handy—rather than trying to handle everything on one machine, run the server on different machines on the same LAN to distribute the load. This should only be necessary if your station is becoming very popular and you don't want to dedicate a machine expressly to the task of running your station.

Using publicly available servers

So SHOUTcast is all well and good for people with fast connections to the Internet, but what if you just have a dinky modem and no access to a machine on a fat pipe running the SHOUTcast server component? Does that mean you're stuck serving very low quality audio to just one or two people at a time? Fortunately, no. The advent of the WinAmp DSP plug-in signaled the appearance of sites such as *www.live365.com*, which provide server space and beefy bandwidth to those in need, absolutely free. In fact, live365 is so generous with their bandwidth that they'll actually let you stream your content to more people than you can probably reach with a typical DSL connection, without chewing up the bandwidth you might like to use for other purposes, such as running a standard web server. At this writing, live365 let anyone and their sister dish up 100 simultaneous streams of 56K audio, absolutely free, bringing the possibility of running your own station much closer to home for the average Joe. By the time you read this, it's a good bet live365 will have plenty of competitors with similarly generous offers.

Saving MP3 Streams

Since MP3 streams are typically broadcast in low-bitrate, heavily downsampled formats, it's not too likely that users will want to save them to disk for posterity. However, there are there those odd times when it can be desirable and/or convenient to trap a broadcast to disk—if you want to save a news broadcast in the middle of the night and listen to it in the morning, for example. That's really no different from videotaping a TV show to watch later, and doesn't necessarily run afoul of legal issues. Since the capacity to do so is conducive to piracy, however, most commercial MP3 players that support streaming make this impossible by design, or at least make the process difficult (if you try to use WinAmp's built-in DiskWriter plug-in for this purpose, you'll get nothing but a copyright violation alert box from WinAmp. Older version of WinAmp, however, do support saving MP3 streams to disk). There are a few select utilities dedicated to the task of pulling down streamed broadcasts to disk; check out X-FileGet, available at *www.2bsys.com* or search the Internet for tools like TotalRecorder or AudioJacker.

As tantalizing as the prospect of serving up 100 simultaneous streams may sound, keep in mind that very few stations actually attract this many listeners. Take a quick surf around the SHOUTcast or icecast directory pages and you'll see that only the very rare station attracts more than 10 simultaneous users, and these are stations that have risen to the top of the popularity heap with constant dedication to excellence, not just casual users broadcasting whenever the mood strikes. Trouble is, there are just so many hundreds of thousands of stations to choose from that the competition for listeners is immense.

Working with public servers is virtually the same as working with the SHOUTcast server, as described earlier in this chapter. You'll still need to install the WinAmp DSP plug-in, still need to make sure you've got a codec installed, and still need to create and manage a WinAmp playlist. Instead of connecting the source stream to the SHOUTcast server, you'll send your stream on to a unique set of IP and port addresses supplied to you by the public server. Detailed documentation is available at live365, should you run into any configuration issues.

While the MP3 broadcast tools covered in this chapter are by far the most common, they're not the only ones available. Check out Xing's StreamWorks and MP3Live! server and encoder combination (*www.xingtech.com/mp3/streamworks/*) for an interesting alternative.

Working with icecast

Those who prefer to stay on the open source side of the fence will be happy to learn that a functional equivalent to SHOUTcast exists, in the form of a server solution called icecast. In fact, there are very few functional differences between SHOUTcast and icecast, and icecast is designed to be completely compatible with SHOUTcast. You can broadcast source streams from WinAmp under Windows to another machine running the icecast server, and vice versa. You can broadcast from an icecast server to the public SHOUTcast directory, and vice versa. And since icecast is truly Open Source, it runs on more platforms than SHOUTcast (at least it did at this writing), including Linux, Windows 95/98/NT, BeOS, Solaris, and likely more by the time you read this. The icecast server offers more configuration options than SHOUTcast, and its development cycle is more rapid than that of its NullSoft cousin.

Unless your operating system comes bundled with a fully licensed MP3 codec, you'll need to locate and install one of your own if you want to stay legal (details can be found in the sections below). Both Microsoft and Be have paid a king's ransom to Fraunhofer and THOMSON for the right to include the MP3 codec in the OS (though Microsoft's is limited to 56 kbps).

By default, icecast will serve files only at the bitrate in which they're encoded (i.e., it's a static streamer). That means that if you want to accommodate listeners who log in via modem, you'll need to encode your files at very low bitrates to begin with. icecast ships with two source streamers: shout, for streaming static files, and liveice, for interacting with third-party codecs and for mixing multiple source streams, including microphone input.

Whether you decide to source your station from shout or liveice, start by firing up the icecast server. You should find it in the **bin** subdirectory of the icecast installation. From that directory, type:

```
./icecast
```

Don't follow the icecast command with an & for now, as you'll want to monitor its output while you get everything up and running. Later on you can run it in the background, and have the output dumped to a log file. By default, the log file will be created as *icecast.log* in the *icecast* directory.

Like SHOUTcast, icecast also has a text-based configuration file that you can tweak to establish additional parameters or to set up your station for unique situations. While the defaults will get you up and running quickly, do look through *icecast. conf*, which you'll find in the *etc* subdirectory of the icecast installation (you can optionally toss this into */etc* along with all of your other *.conf* files). At the very least, you should establish a password for connecting source streams after you verify that everything is running properly with the defaults.

Running shout

With icecast running, you can now send a source stream to it with WinAmp from another machine on the network, or use the *shout* command included with icecast. shout takes a ton of optional parameters, and can also be made to run with a configuration file encapsulating your most-used options. For starters, try:

```
shout localhost -P letmein -a -p ~/my_playlist.m3u -l -g funk -n "Mr. Toad's Wild
Ride"
```

In this case, shout would send its stream to the server "localhost" (i.e., your own machine; you can use any IP address here), would use the password "letmein," would play the playlist stored at */home/my_playlist.m3u*, would loop forever (return to the beginning of the playlist when it reached the end), would list its genre as "funk," and would broadcast its name as "Mr. Toad's Wild Ride." The −a flag is used to enable shout's automatic transfer bitrate correction feature. As it plays, it monitors its own transfer speed. If it finds itself going too fast or too slow, it will automatically correct for these variances.

To save yourself some typing, you can embed all of these options into a configuration file and simply launch shout with the −C flag followed by the path to the file. Take a look at *README.shout* for additional shout options and parameters.

 You'll notice that shout offers a −b flag to specify the bitrate. Since shout is a static streamer, it cannot actually change the bitrate of the files it sends. This option merely lets you broadcast the bitrate of your files for the benefit of users. This bitrate will appear in the readout window of most MP3 players, but it's up to you to make sure it accurately reflects the actual bitrate of your files!

Running liveice

If you need to downsample your files before sending them out into the ether, you'll want to source your stream through liveice rather than shout. Since liveice is a re-encoding streamer, it requires access to a codec. liveice can either use a "raw" codec stored in a central location in the OS as one does with Windows and BeOS, or simply utilize the decoding and encoding capabilities built into one of your existing MP3 players. No encoder is distributed with icecast or liveice; you'll need to obtain one elsewhere on the Internet. Use a search engine to track down encoders listed in *liveice.cfg*. By default, liveice looks for the existence of mpg123 (see Chapter 4) somewhere in your path for its decoding needs. Supported encoders include l3enc, Xing, LAME, etc. See icecast's documentation for details: the options are likely to grow in the future. Utilizing the Xing or LAME encoders may be well worth your while; both are more efficient than mpg123 (Xing in particular). For now, we'll stick with the defaults and assume you're using mpg123.

As you may recall, mpg123 can take certain command-line flags that force it to downsample the stream to a specific frequency (this capability should also be present in LAME by the time you read this). liveice simply calls mpg123 with these parameters and returns the resulting downsampled stream to the icecast server.

Running liveice in its default configuration is just as easy as running shout. Copy your playlist file and *liveice.cfg* (from the icecast distribution) to the liveice installation directory, make sure icecast is running, and type *./rveice*. You should now be able to open a streaming MP3 client such as Xmms on your own machine and open the URL *http://localhost:8000*. Naturally, an actual IP address can be substituted for "localhost" for network usage. Bitrate, samplerate, broadcast name, associated URL, and many other configuration options can be set by editing *liveice.cfg*.

liveice is capable of broadcasting multiple simultaneous streams, so you can, for instance, send high, medium, and low-bandwidth streams to various servers on fatter or thinner pipes all at once. Up to eight streams can be dished up simultaneously (bandwidth on the source streamer machine permitting, of course). After establishing the main settings in the top of the config file, look for:

```
ENCODER_STREAM_SET 0
```

section of the file and use *SAMPLERATE, BITRATE*, and other options to tweak the parameters for the first stream being sent. Move on to *SET 1* and do the same, and so on.

At the time of this writing, liveice's mixing capabilities were somewhat primitive (to say the least). The command line really isn't the ideal way to control live audio mixing, and a GUI interface was rumored to be in development. The command-line version of the mixer comes into play when you launch liveice with the –M flag. The playlist begins to play as normal, and two additional channels are opened. Audio can then be streamed into these channels from pipes set up elsewhere in the operating system, or from microphone. The keyboard controls in Table 8-2 are then in effect.

Table 8-2. liveice Keyboard Shortcuts

Action	Channel 1 key	Channel 2 key
Select next track on channel	1	A
Select prev track on channel	Q	Z
Start/Stop channel	2	S

Table 8-2. liveice Keyboard Shortcuts (continued)

Action	Channel 1 key	Channel 2 key
Reset channel	W	X
Increase volume on channel	3	D
Decrease volume on channel	E	C
Increase speed on channel	4	F
Decrease speed on channel	R	V
Sticky mode On/Random/Off	5	G
Preview channel	T	B
Random Track	U	M

If you're handy with bash or Perl scripting, you can automate an Internet broadcast almost entirely, setting up tracks to be mixed in advance. For an excellent Perl script built to handle much of this automation, check out IceDJ at *www.remixradio.com/icedj/*.

An Interview with MP3.com's "High Geek"

Sander van Zoest is the "High Geek" and Senior Web Engineer at MP3.com, one of the Web's most-trafficked sites. He also happens to have been among MP3.com's first employees. The author interviewed van Zoest via email.

Scot Hacker: How long have you been a part of MP3.com? When did it all start, and what was the original objective? Where is MP3.com based?

Sander van Zoest: MP3.com is based in San Diego, California. It was launched out of The Z Company, which was founded by our CEO, Michael Robertson. The Z Company was a small web shop that ran many web sites, such as Filez, the Net's largest and fastest file search engine, and Websitez, a domain name search engine. Greg Flores, our current Vice Present of Sales, told Michael about MP3, and in November 1997 they opened MP3.com.

The objective was to provide a one-stop site for the MP3 movement. It provided ground-breaking news and editorials by Michael Robertson, which can now be found on our site under the heading "Michael's Minute," and hardware and software sections to get new users started. In the summer of 1998 we started accepting MP3 music from musicians and artists around the world, to provide them with a revolutionary way of distributing their music.

What About Multicasting?

Internet veterans may have heard of a remarkable technology known as "IP Multicasting," which provides for more efficient distribution of high-bandwidth media than do traditional serving mechanisms. With traditional servers, a copy of the requested media is sent over the Internet to each client who requests it, even if they're sitting in side-by-side cubicles. The result is that for most of the journey from server to client, twice as much data is sent than is really necessary. The idea of multicasting is that the network and broadcast applications are given a new layer of intelligence, so they can determine whether data being sent to geographically proximate locations would be redundant. If a server is in France and 14 Americans are requesting an MP3 stream from it, the server only needs to send 1 stream to the U.S. Once the paths to the clients become divergent, they're split off to the individual users.

Clearly, IP multicasting is far more respectful of the Internet's bandwidth than standard serving techniques. In addition, multicasting can take a huge bandwidth burden off the server itself. Potentially, multicasting technology could make it feasible to run an MP3 broadcast server over a standard modem, which would clearly be a huge breakthrough for users who lack access to a high-bandwidth server.

The catch? Multicasting requires that all points in the chain be upgraded to handle the technology. All of the routers between the two points must be multicast aware, as does the TCP/IP stack in use and the broadcast application software. Fortunately, IP multicasting technology is slowly but surely shaping up at many points in the chain, and is becoming a more realistic possibility for broad deployment every day (it can already be used in some scenarios). Take a look at *www.live.com* and *www.ipmulticast.com* for more information. To learn more about the region of the Internet currently "roped off" for use in multicasting scenarios (commonly referred to as "the MBone"), see *www.live.com/mbone/*.

LIVE.COM offers a program called liveCaster, which is geared specifically toward serving up MP3 broadcasts over IP multicast. The site offers detailed instructions both on installed the liveCaster server software and on tuning into existing liveCaster streams with popular MP3 players.

I started working part time with Z Company in June of 1998, around the time of our first annual MP3 Summit, which was an attempt to gather all the influential people of the MP3 movement together under one roof. The event was held at the University of California, San Diego campus, and was when I realized how huge the MP3 movement was going to be. My good friend Josh Beck introduced me to Michael, and I knew I had to find a way to join their quest to revolutionize the music industry. In November of 1998, I joined Z Company as a full time employee.

SH: I can hardly imagine a site with more intense bandwidth requirements than MP3.com; you must be pumping out absolutely massive amounts of data. Tell me a bit about the server and connectivity infrastructure at MP3.com. How do you scale the system as you grow?

SVZ: We are really dedicated to providing every visitor with the best experience and we work some insane hours to accomplish this. Our servers are modified versions of the Apache Web Server and run on a variety of Unix machines ranging from Sun's Solaris, to Linux, to FreeBSD. Most of the systems are Linux machines, since most of our staff is familiar with the operating system and it performs quite well in our environment.

To provide constant uptime, we use some of our own load-balancing techniques and third-party network products.

SH: What kind of bandwidth are we talking about here? Do you have a hole in the back wall with a dozen T3s running out to the world or something?

SVZ: Our bandwidth requirements change by the day. Just to give you an idea, we host our site out of several different data centers to provide 24-hour access. We're working on bringing the content closer to you by sending you to the closest machines, network-wise, that we have. It's a big operation, especially since we do not control the content directly—the artists do, and we have to make sure they have the tools and infrastructure to keep their own sites up to date.

SH: What about the CD recording back-end for creating the DAM CDs? Do you have a whole CD factory on site?

SVZ: Yes, we have a just-in-time production facility that creates the DAM CDs and CD covers on the fly for each order. Each CD comes with the MP3s, Red Book audio tracks (for playing in your stereo system), and a multimedia interface with information about the artist and links to their web site.

SH: As astute users have observed, pointing a browser at mp4.com currently redirects back to mp3.com. Michael has stated several times that there's nothing sacred about MP3 itself, and that when/if the next big format comes along, the company will be ready for it. Do you do much internal testing of other file formats? Do you personally have a favorite digital music codec or file format, or is MP3 "it" for you?

SVZ: We are aware of the advantages and disadvantages of the MP3 format, but we plan to follow whatever standard the consumers want. Ultimately, it is the consumers who decide what format they would like to use. Without consumers there is no market, and without a market the artists will not be heard.

I, personally, do not really have a preferred format, though I do enjoy the freedom that MP3 provides. The fact that the MP3 specification is available and is a public standard, unlike formats such as MS Audio, Liquid Audio, or Real Audio, really opens the doors to allow anyone to use the format in the way they see fit. The patents held by the Fraunhofer Institute and THOMSON Multimedia do impose some limitations of use, but not nearly as much as the closed, proprietary formats. MP3 allows for a wide range of bitrates, so you can specify the amount of disk space relative to the quality you desire. You can store high-quality audio for use in home theater surround sound systems, or take it all the way down to AM radio quality for listening to music over your cell phone. It's all possible with the MP3 format; it just depends on how much disk space and bandwidth you have available.

SH: We're just now beginning to see the very first "stars" being born out of this new format, rising through the democratic model of MP3.com and hitting it big without necessarily ever having gone through the traditional rigamarole of touring, promoting, signing, and pressing. Do you see this new phenomenon as an exception to the rule, or do we have a new star-making process on our hands?

SVZ: It really depends on what your goals are as an artist and what you would consider "a star." The beauty of the Internet and the MP3 movement is that it provides the artist a way to market to their fans that really are into the music. It provides fans a way to really get in touch with the artists. It provides much more loyal fans and better communication between the artists and fans.

How many times have you bought a CD that you had heard so many times on the radio that you decided that you really liked the artist, only to find after a few listens that they really had just that one good song? It can be really hard to find the find the music you're really into via the traditional music industry. Via the MP3 movement, you'll be able to really get to know the artist, and have a much wider variety of music to choose from. If you're into African death metal bagpipes, chances are there are artists that can fill your need.

So, getting back to "stars." I personally think there will be a lot more and a much larger variety of stars coming out of this movement. You now have the ability to become "a local hero"—a star for a more specific community. I think this will be much more rewarding for the artist as well. Sure you're going to find artists such as "Red Delicious" that will appeal to the mainstream audience, but this new movement also provides others with the ability to be noticed within their own communities.

SH: What are some of the biggest obstacles you've faced from a technical perspective?

SVZ: Wow, this is a tough question. Probably the biggest challenge we face continually is in making sure that when artists change their sites on the back end, their changes appear live on the site as quickly as possible. While this might seem like a trivial task, the moment you add millions of visitors the balance between dynamic content and performance becomes an interesting but difficult task. And when you start dealing with more MP3 uploads than you can listen to in a day, you need to move the data around efficiently and as fast as possible.

Different interpretations of the MPEG Layer III Standard (ISO/IEC 11172-3:1993) also have been an obstacle. Because the MP3 spec is vague on precise implementation details, and because few developers actually read the full specification anyway, different encoders and decoders do things in slightly different ways. Since we've got artists uploading tracks created with the full range of available tools, we need to do things like determining whether or not a file is a valid MP3 file, how to handle free-form (no bitrate specified) files, and evaluate how players deal with bit reservoir variable bit rate (VBR) files—different encoders handle VBR MP3s differently. The objective was to have all MP3 files on our site usable by the majority of players, which was quite a task.

Another thing that's haunted us are the different ways various browsers, platforms, and players handled MIME types. We've also done quite a bit of troubleshooting with MP3 files to uncover bugs in encoders/players, and reported our findings to the appropriate authors.

SH: Are these things becoming a bigger problem as time goes on and the tools proliferate, or less of a problem as developers standardize and start to convene around a few standardized implementations?

SVZ: If all we did was fix bugs this would definitely become less of a problem, but with the demand for additional features such as embedding meta-data technologies such as ID3 and integration into every day appliances, I can see how this problem can get out of hand quickly. Open standards organizations and communication between developers and manufacturers will be the key.

SH: I've noticed that MP3.com has done a bit of work behind the scenes to prevent users from downloading files in big batches, with wget scripts for instance. What's the rational behind that? Do you think you'll ever open up straight FTP access, or are you purposely making sure users stay glued to the site?

SVZ: Our business is about data and content. It is what we do best! We prevent people from doing mass downloads for the protection of both the artists and ourselves. If we allow people straight access to our content without hitting up our web site, someone with enough bandwidth and disk space could possibly bring up a competing site with illegal content (they most likely would not have permission from the artist and/or copyright owners to do so). Of course, we also need the ability to display banner advertising to cover our costs. And we use HTTP cookies to track downloads and user customized content. Not all download utilities fully support HTTP/1.1 or cookies, which can be the cause of the problems.

So there are a lot of reasons why we limit batch downloads and do not open straight access to our content.

SH: What are your impressions of the many home/car/portable MP3 playback devices beginning to appear on the market and in the DIY scene? Do you think store shelves will start to fill up with these in the first decade of the millenium? Do you own any dedicated MP3 hardware yourself?

SVZ: I really think this is a great start towards better ways of managing your music and your access to it. Just imagine being able to carry your entire music collection with you wherever you go, and having it available to you any time of the day no matter where you are. I think there's a lot of potential for digital music devices, and I have heard rumors of gaming systems using MP3 and next-generation phones having built-in MP3 players. It is exciting and has the potential to be very popular with consumers. I myself have a Diamond Rio player and hope to get an MP3 car player in the future.

SH: Do you expect any of the copyright protection mechanisms built into MP3 hardware to adversely affect MP3.com's business, which is built on the premise that a lot of MP3 music is willfully and openly distributed by the artist?

SVZ: I do not think it will affect MP3.com's business. The artists should be able to determine the faith of their works and decide how they want to distribute their music. If there is no content then the hardware becomes useless. At the same time consumers are used to being able to use their music anywhere they see fit. They can play the songs in the car, in their stereo and even make a mixed tape and share it with their friends. It exposes music to others, who may become the artist's next fans. If the copyright protection mechanisms restrict this behavior, I am sure this will upset them as well.

SH: Would you say there's currently a "typical" MP3.com visitor, or does the site appeal to a broad cross-section of people? Do you see your demographic changing in near future?

SVZ: There doesn't seem to be a "typical" MP3 visitor, other then the fact that they most likely have an Internet connection, a computer, and are interested in music. :) Our most popular genre of music is electronic, but other genres such as rock, alternative, and hip-hop are catching up fast. In the early days we had a lot of early adopters visiting our site, but this has changed.

SH: Do you get many "Aunt Margaret" visitors? That is, do you see many visitors who are just beginning to learn about computers, or are most of your customers relatively computer-savvy?

SVZ: Yes, we get a decent amount. We have been working hard on making it easier for the computer novice by making our help section easy to help people get started. People had a lot of trouble setting up their browsers and installing MP3 players with control over the appropriate MIME types and extensions. So we have been working actively with player developers and internally on making this as simple as possible.

SH: You must get some very wild submissions from time to time. Are there any artists that have just been too "out there" for you to host? Do you ever reject submissions based on adult or violent content? Does MP3.com ever make aesthetic judgements? (e.g., if something was just *so* bad it was unlistenable by any sane human, would you still run it?). Any funny stories relating to MP3.com submissions?

SVZ: We have had just about everything on our site, from the latest Tom Petty tracks to comedian Tom Green, from hardcore noise to stuff that's just plain bizarre. In the early days, we had Beethoven's Fifth Symphony done entirely in farts. We have designated genres for adult content, and request that artists put "parental advisory" text around their songs where appropriate. I am not aware of any music we have denied unless it was in violation of copyright. Cover songs are also not allowed on our site for legal reasons. We expect the world to decide what they think is good music; something that one person cannot stand is someone else's favorite song.

SH: Who are some of your favorite musicians/bands?

SVZ: I personally really enjoy listening to music. I must have a collection of about a thousand CDs, and I seem to buy more every week or so. I mostly listen to a lot of dark electronic music ranging from X marks the pedwalk, Haujobb and Die Form, to Forma Tadre, Dementia Simplex, Violet Arcana, Internal, and Consequence. Some of these artists have music available on MP3.com, check them out if you're interested.

9

Competing Codecs and Other File Formats

MP3 isn't the only game in town. There are many other audio file formats out there trying to compete with MP3, with varying degrees of success. Some of the alternative formats are meant to establish security and guard against piracy, some aim to provide better audio quality at smaller file sizes, and most try to accomplish both goals at once. Despite the fact that some of the formats you'll read about in this chapter are technically superior to MP3, don't expect MP3 to go the way of the pterodactyl anytime soon. MP3 is deeply entrenched, and seems to have struck a near-optimal balance between simplicity, openness, and quality for most users. MP3 software and hardware is everywhere, not to mention the zillions of legal and illegal MP3 files themselves. Any contending format faces a massive uphill battle to popular acceptance, and the only way the world is liable to change horses in mid-stream is if the industry forces a new format upon us; a dubious proposition at best. Nevertheless, many of the competing formats represent excellent technology, and deserve consideration.

Because many of the competing formats are actually much more than simple audio codecs, we've broken this chapter up into two major categories: First we'll look at a few of the "architectures"—complete audio/video/multimedia authoring and playback platforms that encompass audio compression as a subset. Then we'll take a closer look at a few specific codecs in use out there, some of which are actually components of the larger architectures.

You'll also find a "What this technology means for MP3" follow-up at the end of each section. A codec comparison chart can be found at the end of the chapter, as well.

The Architectures

It's impossible to discuss the future of the MP3 scene without also touching on video issues. As available bandwidth and storage space increases, it's likely that users will increasingly begin to collect and swap movie clips and interactive presentations as readily as they do audio files today. RealPlayer G2, Windows Media, QuickTime 4.0, and MPEG-4 all represent complex, multifaceted presentation formats of which audio is but one component.

In the near future, users will be able to create and actually "participate" in interactive presentations that combine audio and video in ways we can only dream about today. For example, users might be able to download music videos that feature themselves as lead singer, pick up and carry objects through three-dimensional space, and enjoy it all through multi-channel home theatre systems.

 In contrast to MP3, many of the file formats, architectures, and codecs described in this chapter are proprietary technologies. The significance of this fact should not be underestimated. Even if alternative formats can be proven to provide distinct advantages over MP3, one should carefully consider the importance of keeping formats and specifications open. It is precisely MP3's openness and wide availability that has allowed it to flourish on all operating systems, and to give rise to an extensive industry of related software. In general, open standards promote the interests of consumers and most likely artists, while closed standards benefit labels, patent holders, artists, and other intermediaries in the traditional business model. Note that artists are caught in the middle here. While artists can benefit from greater exposure via file-based music distribution, they also stand to lose through piracy. A seemingly ideal compromise for most parties involved would be an open format such as MP3, but which still provided some sort of security or copy protection mechanism. Keep an eye open for news of the ability to protect MP3 files through advanced use of ID3v2 tags; this will afford us the benefits of MP3's nonproprietary nature while still satisfying the most important requirements of artists.

ASF/MS Audio/Windows Media Technologies

www.microsoft.com/windowsmedia/ Advanced Streaming Format, or ASF, is a subset of the Windows Media codec, which is designed to compress both audio and video into Internet-friendly sizes that can be streamed to users over 28.8 and faster modem connections. Windows Media includes a number of pieces that all work together, including compression tools, a playback component (Media Player) and a streaming server. Microsoft positions the codec as a replacement for two of its largest threats in Internet audio: RealAudio's G2 streaming codec, and MP3 itself.

Notes on Windows Media Nomenclature

Confused about the ASF/MS Audio/Windows Media nomenclature? Microsoft and others have used these terms nearly interchangeably, so you're not alone. Technically, "Windows Media Audio (WMA) files are ASF files that contain audio content compressed with the Windows Media Audio codec." According to Microsoft, "These files are named with the file extension 'WMA' so they can be easily identified as audio and distinguished from other ASF files that may have video." But a single codec encompasses both audio and video, and you can name your files with either *.WMA* or *.ASF* extensions—it's your choice, and most users stick to the *.ASF* extension, as do the examples shown in this section.

At its introduction, Microsoft claimed that MS Audio was capable of compressing audio nearly two times smaller than MP3 with comparable sound quality. Tests conducted by a number of organizations and individuals after the release yielded mixed results. However, most agreed that Microsoft's claims were close to true, with caveats. For example, some listeners found that stereo imaging was noticeably degraded in WMA, due to weak stereo compression algorithms used in the codec. Others noticed a persistent "echo" effect and general "thinness" in WMA files, along with a "blurring" or "rushing" at the high end (particularly with percussive or aggressive sounds) which MP3 does not have, even when both the WMA and MP3 files are encoded at 128 kbps. Finally, many listeners note that WMA performs very well with music, but terribly with the spoken word. Nevertheless, many listeners agreed that, with most types of audio signal, Microsoft had done a pretty good job with the format.

However, some critics noted that in its test, Microsoft had compared 64 kpbs mono WMA samples to 128 kbps stereo MP3s. As you may recall, 128 kbps stereo MP3s are basically two 64 kbps mono files working in conjunction (though some factors, such as joint stereo, make this a somewhat fuzzy definition). If listening conditions were sub-optimal and stereo effects were not easily perceptible, an unfair advantage could be shown in favor of WMA. And, in fact, many felt that the test's listening conditions were indeed sub-optimal. A fairer test would be to compare 64 kbps mono MP3 to 64 kbps mono WMA in such an environment.

But even though Microsoft makes available a streaming server component with no cost-per-stream fee, Microsoft is (so far) having trouble getting any significant buy-in on the Windows Media concept in general. Part of this is due to the fact that Real has been in this business for years, and had the market sewn up tight long ago. Microsoft is making some headway, but not what you'd expect given the overall quality of their product. Additionally, Real offers some server functions that are not present in Windows Media, such as better handling of artifacts introduced by lost packets in Internet transmission and their "SureStream" technology, which offers the ability to shift delivery rates to accommodate available bandwidth at any given moment. However, the better quality offered by Windows Media at lower bitrates will probably compensate for these omissions in most cases and for most users.

The best way to determine whether you should deliver your content via Windows Media, MP3, or RealAudio is to do some real-world tests. If you don't want to do all the encoding yourself, both Microsoft and Real have set up their own comparative listening tests, both of course aiming to prove that their own format is optimal. See *www.real.com/msaudio/* and/or *www.microsoft.com/windows/windowsmedia/en/compare/*.

Playing ASF files

The default player for all Windows Media, including ASF files, is the Windows Media Player. If your version of Media Player isn't yet configured to handle ASF files, the codec will be downloaded and installed automatically the first time you attempt to play one. This is a nice feature, but note that the codec isn't download-able except via MediaPlayer.

However, playback isn't limited to Media Player. Later versions of WinAmp, Sonique, and MusicMatch JukeBox also include ASF support, as does Diamond's RioPort. In addition, increasing numbers of portable and home stereo-based players are gaining ASF support. The portable market is an ideal candidate, because the limited amount of memory available on portable devices often limits total playback time to less than an hour with MP3. With Windows Media's tight compression, users are able to stuff more files of an acceptable quality into the limited amount of available memory. Because Microsoft is, well, Microsoft, expect to see ASF support starting to appear in virtually all major audio software and hardware products.

Does this mean that ASF could eventually topple MP3? That's certainly Microsoft's intention, but don't count on it happening anytime soon. The fact that ASF includes digital copyright protection mechanisms means many users will shun it, opting instead for the protection-free MP3 format already in such heavy use. In addition, people who encode to ASF now will be creating files that are not playable for users of alternative operating systems, or for users of MP3 players that don't support ASF. Since people naturally want their files to be playable by everyone, they'll likely opt for MP3. However, remember that Microsoft has applied to the International Standards Organization to have ASF declared a standard, which should theoretically open the doors to ASF support on all platforms and all players. In all likelihood, many large labels will side with Microsoft on ASF (Sony already has), which will mean that much legitimate content will become available only in ASF format. Many users will thus be forced to adopt the format, at least in part.

 It may become possible to convert ASF files to MP3. If an audio application supports both, and if its security features are not overly paranoid, the conversion may be as simple as pulling down File → Export. However, if an ASF file has security features enabled and the application respects these, export to other formats will likely not be possible. Your only recourse in that case may be to play back the ASF file normally and record the sound stream moving through the system with an audio recording application. Theoretically, in a system full of SDMI-enabled hardware, even this would be difficult, though clever users and hackers will always find a way. To convert MP3 files to ASF, see the next section.

Creating ASF files

To create ASF files, you'll need to download the Windows Media Tools from *www.microsoft.com/windowsmedia/.* The tools are very clearly documented, and you shouldn't have much difficulty figuring out how to use the Windows Media Encoder, as shown in Figure 9-1. Here we're creating an ASF file from an existing 128 kbps, 5.03 MB MP3 file. The output file was 64 kbps and 2.57 MB. Audio quality differences were negligible through an average-quality sound card and computer speakers, though a quality sound card and speakers uncovered notable weaknesses in the ASF file. Note, however, that you'll want to choose Custom Options when you launch the encoder if you want to re-encode an existing file. The resulting wizard will let you choose an existing WAV or .MP3 file (oddly, the option to choose MP3 as an input format is not available if you don't choose the right Wizard on startup). Because the encoder is capable of re-encoding existing MP3 files to the Windows Media format, you have the opportunity to re-do your entire collection and save space on your hard drive. If you're planning to distribute files, however, remember that the encoded files will not be playable by other users on other machines, due to the copy protection mechanisms built into the Windows Media system.

The Windows Media codec is also included in an increasing number of tools from third-party vendors. At this writing, ASF audio/video files could be created in Adobe Premiere, SonicFoundry SoundForge, and others.

Linking to and streaming ASF files

While you can always link to an ASF file in the standard manner:

```
<a href="windows_blues.asf">Click here to listen</a>
```

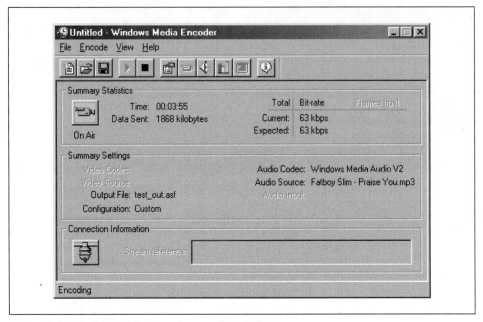

Figure 9-1. Windows Media Encoder gets the job done

doing so will simply initiate a download of *windows_blues.asf*, just as it would with an MP3 file. This may or may not be what you want. In many cases, you may want to let your listeners hear the file, but not save it to their hard drives easily. Because Media Player and most other audio players do not have a simple File → Save As... option, you can make it tougher for users to save your files by enveloping the file's URL in an ASX "locator" file. Doing so will not only give you a degree of protection against unwanted file saving, but it will also cause the file to be pseudo-streamed. In other words, the file will start playing for the user as soon as enough bits have been transferred, rather than forcing the user to wait through the entire download. Pseudo-streaming is managed by the client (in this case, Media Player) and can be done via any web server. We'll get to real streaming in a moment.

The role of the ASX file is to pass control of the download from the browser to the player. ASX is nothing more than a simple text document (in XML format, if you must know) that includes the reference to the actual ASF file (Figure 9-2). If you've worked with RealAudio before, you're already familiar with this process.

Create a new text file that looks like this:

```
<ASX version="3">
<Entry>
    <ref href="path\windows_blues.asf"/>
</Entry>
</ASX>
```

The href portion can be any form of URL: local, relative, or absolute. Save this file as *windows_blues.asx*. Then, in your page code, link to the *windows_blues.asx* rather than to *windows_blues.asf.* Upload the ASX and ASF files to your web server along with your HTML, and you're all set.

The ASX file can optionally include a number of additional options, including references to banners, images, copyright statements, and even playlists. See *msdn. microsoft.com/workshop/imedia/windowsmedia/crcontent/asx.asp/* for details.

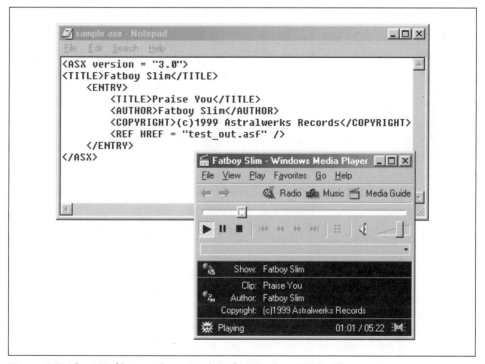

Figure 9-2. The ASX file provides meta-data for Windows Media Player

 Devious users can choose to save the ASX file to their hard drives by right-clicking the link in the browser. Once they have the ASX file, they can open it in a text editor, find the actual URL to the ASF file, and download it directly, thus circumventing your intention to prevent users from saving files to disk.

If you expect a lot of traffic on your site, or if you want to dish up live feeds with Windows Media at multiple simultaneous bitrates, you can set up the optional server components to manage and load-balance traffic, parse your available bandwidth, and deliver your audio in true streaming fashion, rather than pseudo-streaming. See *www.microsoft.com/windows/windowsmedia/serve/* for details.

Unfuck

The same day Microsoft officially rolled out MS Audio 4.0, including in their press release the phrase "proven digital rights management," a hack called "unfuck" surfaced in the MP3 community, capable of disabling the copyright protection in MS Audio files. Essentially, unfuck takes protected *.WMA* files, outputs them to WAV format, then re-encodes the WAVs in unprotected *.WMA* format. Testers at MP3.com tried the hack on one of their own Windows Media files and were successful in unlocking the file's protection mechanism. Microsoft vowed to tackle the situation with a software fix, but a permanent fix is theoretically impossible, since the crack works "outside" of the format itself. Like the Audiojacker and Totalrecorder programs that came before it, unfuck works by siphoning off the audio stream as it leaves the player, on its way to the sound card. Playback interception techniques will remain a staple of the audio hacking world, because there will always be a way to do so outside the control of any security mechanism currently in place (although hardware-based security mechanisms could theoretically make this much more difficult, if not impossible).

But the swiftness of the hack provided further evidence of the uphill battle faced by any vendor attempting to introduce security or digital rights management mechanisms into software and/or hardware: The hacking community is incredibly adroit, and apparently committed to overcoming any obstacles that lay in the path of free music distribution, with or without the approval of the artists and labels in question. The hack/counterhack tug-of-war inevitably follows on the heels of any product calling itself "secure."

Larger problems potentially loom. If utilities such as unfuck take off and end up representing a substantive threat to the music industry, they retain the right to revoke the device or software's SDMI-compliance rating (though MS Audio 4.0 is not SDMI-compliant since SDMI had not yet been finalized when it was released). If enough companies depart or are forced to depart from SDMI, the whole plan potentially unravels. Remember, though, that the Digital Millenium Copyright Act (see Chapter 7, *The Not-So-Fine-Print: Legal Bits and Pieces*) makes it illegal to circumvent copyright security mechanisms, so hackers caught behind the wheel of tools such as unfuck could face serious penalties. On the flip side, such hacks may be *necessary* to retain the user's right to make copies of music they already own. Anyone got an aspirin? The new Cold War is confusing.

What Windows Media means for the future of MP3

If for no other reason than the fact that Microsoft is able to include Windows Media playback tools with every copy of Windows (and, potentially, authoring tools as well), Windows Media stands a better chance of usurping MP3's domination than any other competing format, which is why I give the format such detailed coverage here. In addition, major labels and the SDMI group will of course work closely with Microsoft to work on and continue to improve file-based security models.

Marketing isn't the only thing Windows Media has going for it. The company has produced a format with excellent compression and fairly high quality, meaning that, in addition to the wide distribution of ASF/WMA files we're liable to see coming from major labels, millions of users will likely adopt the format for their personal use as well.

The biggest battle Windows Media faces is the fact that it arrived late to the game, when other architectures and formats had already formed an established user base. But Microsoft has demonstrated their ability to chart a new course on a dime (e.g., with Internet Explorer), and one should not underestimate their ability to achieve major consumer buy-in in a relatively short period of time.

Without releasing source code to their internal codecs, however, Microsoft will have trouble gaining any kind of favor with the alternative systems crowd, who form a large cross-section of the MP3 enthusiasts universe.

QuickTime

quicktime.apple.com It's a floor wax! It's a dessert topping! Ask a hundred people to define QuickTime, and you'll get a hundred different responses. That's because QuickTime isn't a single codec, but an umbrella format—an entire architecture encompassing dozens of different audio and video compression and multimedia playback techniques. QuickTime is a long-established industry leader used for creating multimedia presentations, delivering Internet video, embedding hypertext references in movies, creating interactive panoramic scenes, delivering streamed media to users over modems, synchronizing audio/video content through time-code sequences, and more. This flexibility has made QuickTime a multimedia leader not just on the Mac platform, but on virtually all platforms. Major browsers for Windows, for example, come bundled with the ability to play back QuickTime movies, even though the product is one of Apple's crown jewels. In fact, QuickTime may represent one of Apple's greatest successes in reaching users of non-Apple platforms.[*]

---

[*] Apple does, however, retain a few bits and pieces just for Mac users. For example, the excellent Sorenson codec can be used to generate very high quality movies with small file sizes. Many users of Windows and other platforms were frustrated when prerelease trailers for *Star Wars: The Phantom Menace* appeared at first only in Sorenson-encoded QuickTime format, playable only on MaM on the Macintosh.

It was QuickTime's extreme flexibility and wide adoption that led to the MPEG working group recommending to ISO that the QuickTime file format be adopted as a basis for the creation of MPEG-4 presentations (see the next section).

While QuickTime itself can be used for creating audio-only bitstreams, its primary role in practice is as a video and multimedia authoring/playback environment, with a reach extending far beyond that which concerns the audio-centric nature of this book. Audio-only QuickTime downloads are comparatively rare on the Internet, so we don't cover them here. QuickTime authors using Version 4.0 or later of the system, along with the QuickTime Streaming Server, can avoid the step of having to convert audio/video presentations to RealAudio or Windows Media formats before placing them online. Inclusion of the QDesign codec (covered later in this chapter) means that people using QuickTime for audio can take advantage of the extreme compression ratios that format provides.

Note that the QuickTime 4.0 player and above is capable of handling existing MP3 files, and QuickTime authors can embed MP3 files into their movies as soundtracks.

What QuickTime means for the future of MP3

Because QuickTime has been around for so long, and because its capabilities are so extensive, it's almost surprising that QuickTime hasn't become more popular as an audio-only distribution format. But search the Internet for downloadable music, or look through Apple's QuickTime Showcase, and you'll be hard-pressed to find much in the way of downloadable music unaccompanied by video. However, its inclusion of the QDesign codec, which threatens to give QuickTime a real edge in audio compression, is relatively new. It may take a while for users to catch on to the compression advantages they can achieve with QDesign. And, of course, the QuickTime Streaming Server means users will have an easy time of setting up Internet broadcasts of their own.

Considered as a complete audio/video compression solution, QuickTime will continue to be a major player and may even achieve greater buy-in as users wait patiently for MPEG-4 to reach maturity. As an audio-only solution, few people are turning to QuickTime over MP3, though there's not much stopping them. Again, only the openness of MP3 can really account for its popularity in the face of potentially superior solutions.

MPEG-4

Not just an audio coding standard, MPEG-4 is a complete, object-oriented scheme devised by the MPEG working group and completed in October 1998. The specification allows for the creation of low-bitrate audio/video presentations, aiming to cover every media possibility in the digital environment.

Much to the confusion of the general public, the terms AAC, VQF, MPEG-4, and MP4 are often used interchangeably. To clarify: MPEG-4 is the next-generation standard for specifying the compression and manipulation of audio and video objects, where an object is defined as "a component of a presentation" (even if it's the only component.) MP4 will most likely be the name of the file format that will encompass MPEG-4, while AAC and VQF are subsections of the MPEG-4 spec. The audio component of MPEG-4 is technically known as "MPEG-4, subpart 4, General Audio coder," or GA for short. In fact, GA is an umbrella term encompassing MPEG's AAC codec and Yamaha/Sony's VQF codec (both described independently in this chapter);* an MPEG-4 encoder should give you the option of creating either AAC or VQF files. Both AAC and VQF are capable of delivering better audio quality at 96 kbps than MP3 does at 160 kbps; i.e, they deliver the same level of quality as MP3 at lower bitrates.

Nomenclature is further confused by the release of a file format cheekily called "MP4" by Global Music Online, which is essentially a proprietary implementation of AAC (someone needs to explain all of this to Chuck D, who releases his own material in the proprietary "MP4" format).

It would be a mistake to think MPEG-4 is nothing but a more advanced compression format. In fact, the specification allows for some very futuristic features. If you have trouble visualizing the need for some of these features, picture the videophone in your house running over plain old telephone service, and checking out virtual items in a virtual store prior to buying. You might be able to "log in" to an interactive work of fiction, and manipulate objects in the characters' world. Virtually anything you can imagine that involves media and requires compression (i.e., to be transmitted or stored efficiently) will be able to benefit from the MPEG-4 spec. It's pretty amazing.

---

* Just because GA encompasses both AAC and VQF, don't be fooled into thinking that AAC and VQF are in fact MPEG-4 files in and of themselves—they're not. Converting between them should be possible given appropriate tools, but we're talking about three separate file formats here.

The important thing to remember is that MPEG-4 projects will not represent a single file format, but rather a variety of compressed formats delivered as independent objects, along with a scheme for "gluing" them together and defining their relationships and interactions through the BIFS description language (see later). This object-oriented model will allow for much more advanced control and customization options; audio and video can be compressed independently so that everything is optimized for both speed and functionality.

Some of the benefits that MPEG-4 will enable include:

Complete interactivity

Thanks to the Binary Format for Scenes (BIFS) description language, users will be able to "manipulate" objects in space—set objects into motion, "pick up and carry" objects in an audio/video environment, and do complete walkthroughs of three-dimensional scenes. These objects can be either synthesized (generated with 3D A/V modeling tools or CAD programs) or originate from "natural sources." For example, a source video might include footage of a wine glass sitting on a table. In its MPEG-4 implementation, you might be able to pick up the wine glass and "drink" from it.

BIFS will allow for full streaming support

Users will be able to begin partaking in a scene before the whole thing has been downloaded.

Support for "structured audio"

Provides a mechanism for the generation of sounds, rather than simply playing them back. In some ways, structured audio is similar to MIDI, with the critical distinction that structured audio describes *methods* of synthesis. As you may have experienced in the past, General MIDI often sounds "cheesy," because its palette is limited to the sounds built into your sound card. You have no guarantee that the sound of the MIDI file you're listening to is the same as the sound the creator heard on her own sound card. With structured audio, the actual sounds of the instruments being used are accurately described, which guarantees that the sound the artist hears is the sound you hear, while still retaining tiny file sizes (since the audio signal is described, rather than stored bit-by-bit).

Support for multiple tracks

From mono to multichannel surround sound.

Audio is represented in the form of objects

In fact, object support in MPEG-4 is actually more sophisticated for audio than for video. What will this get us? Authors will be able to create interactive scenes where audio sources appear to originate from different points in space, depending on the relation of the moving listener object (you) to the moving audio source. Authors can specify different sound scenes for different listening situations, so they can simultaneously optimize for playback of in-car audio and for home theater situations, for example. In fact, the object-oriented architecture of MPEG-4 borrows heavily from VRML (virtual reality modeling language), so three-dimensional soundscapes are built into the whole concept of MPEG-4. In another possible scenario, users may be able to take an existing recording and manipulate its tracks independently, as long as the musician packages the project in such a way as to make this possible.

The standard holds as a key objective decent audio quality at low bitrates

A number of ground-breaking techniques have been brought to bear on the problem (no single solution is the "official" one, since the objective is only to achieve compliant bitstreams, not to completely define the means of creating these bitstreams). Futuristic techniques such as morphology and fractal-based compression are being worked on. Whereas MP3 is pretty much able to duplicate CD quality at 160 kbps, AAC can achieve CD quality at 96 kbps, and good quality at 64 kbps. Remember: CD audio data is stored at 1411.2 kbps.

The possibility of including multiple "sound fonts" in a single audio file

The user could theoretically choose filters from a list and apply them to the audio in order to simulate the sound of different environments (from clubs to concert halls, for instance).

If some of these features sound familiar, perhaps it's because many of them are also found in Apple's QuickTime format and in the Windows Media system. In fact, ISO officially adopted QuickTime as the basis for MPEG-4 in February, 1998. Microsoft, as you can imagine, was not pleased; the company had been trying to get the organization to use what later became Windows Media in this role. Apple was backed by IBM, Netscape, Oracle, Silicon Graphics, and Sun Microsystems. The recommendation of the format by these companies to the ISO standards body was based on a consensus that the QuickTime format already provided many of the features ISO wanted to see in MPEG-4, such as real-time audio and video streaming, the ability to be streamed across different network protocols, and support for a huge array of pre-existing digital media types. The fact that QuickTime already enjoys broad adoption by media professionals couldn't have hurt either.

Playing and creating MPEG-4

At this writing, there is no *complete* implementation of the MPEG-4 standard. However, bits and pieces of it have been implemented in various products. Most notably, you'll find some AAC and, to a lesser extent, VQF support in many popular players. See those sections of this chapter for details. One of the early companies working on a complete MPEG-4 authoring suite is PsyTEL Telecom. Keep an eye on *www.psytel.com/mpeg4.htm*. Once the specification is finalized, expect to see many companies competing to create complete authoring solutions. As MP4 tools do become available, don't expect them to be free or inexpensive, like MP3 tools are. At least in the initial stages, MP4 authoring tools and encoders are likely to be highly complex and therefore expensive. Whether any freeware MP4 tools become available remains to be seen, although one can bet that if sample implementations are released, the Open Source community will be eager to develop Open Source MP4 authoring environments.

MPEG-4 copy protection

The MPEG-4 specification does not include its own means of implementing copyright protection. Instead, it provides a collection of "hooks" which other organizations can use to implement their own security mechanisms. The idea here is to keep MPEG-4 object-oriented and to help the format steer clear of becoming obsoleted by future advances in security technology. It's a safe bet that much thought will go into making sure security mechanisms are indeed secure, and possibly SDMI-compliant. Of course, virtually any security mechanism will be circumvented eventually,* but don't expect to find the same wealth of unprotected MP4 files floating around out there that one finds in the MP3 world. Of course, it may also be possible for people to create MP4 encoders that do not take advantage of security hooks. Coupled with non-SDMI hardware, such tools may make unprotected MP4 files possible. Everything remains to be seen on this front.

What MP4 means for the future of MP3

As you can see from the description above, MPEG-4 really is a completely different animal from MP3, since it encompasses so much more than just audio. As a result, asking what MP4 means for the future of MP3 is sort of the wrong question to ask. At this point in time (early 2000), MP4 is basically a non-issue for MP3 users. Much of it is still up in the air, there are very few tools available for creating MP4 files, and the ones that are available aren't quite mature yet. Licensing issues are still unresolved, and the industry isn't likely to launch another format that will be prone to the same problems MP3 has gotten itself into, with the patent holder scrambling around trying to collect fees *post facto* from developers who have implemented the technology without permission. It's not even clear yet who will be responsible for collecting MP4 licensing fees (although we do know that Dolby is handling licensing fees for AAC, one of the audio components of MP4).

---

* At this writing, security mechanisms built into DVD had just been cracked by Linux users trying to reverse engineer the format to create Linux DVD playback facilities. While they only stumbled across the security key because an application vendor had left it unencrypted, it is precisely this kind of human oversight that ultimately leads to the downfall of "uncrackable" security mechanisms.

When MP4 does reach maturity and is put into wider circulation, its extensive feature set will enable all kinds of futuristic audio applications, some of them fanciful and some genuinely useful. Tight compression, high quality, and multi-channel audio streams are likely to be the features of most interest to current MP3 users. It's more realistic to expect wider implementations of MP4 sub-components AAC and VQF before we see a complete MP4 implementation.

RealAudio

www.real.com Easily the most well-established corporate player in the Internet audio compression business, RealNetworks specializes in streaming audio and video, where it holds around 75% of the streaming market at this writing. However, Real is now facing competition from Microsoft's Windows Media services, which provide excellent codecs and publishing systems without the costs associated with Real's higher-end programs. Real holds the technological edge in certain key departments, however, and enjoys the mindshare they've earned by making their product a de facto standard half a decade before Microsoft emerged with anything that could be considered a serious challenge. Perhaps not coincidentally, Real's CEO is a highly competitive ex-Microsoftian who parted on bitter terms with the behemoth long ago.

While Real's algorithms were originally designed for very low bandwidth voice/ radio transmission (remember, these were the days of the 9600 baud modem), they've long since been optimized for music as well. The Real codec is now capable of generating comparatively high quality at virtually all bitrates, and can deliver quality close to that of FM radio at 20 to 34 kbps (though a bit of high-frequency distortion is a common criticism at higher bitrates under careful listening tests). Interestingly, some audiophiles have even been led to wonder aloud why MP3 gets all the action when virtually everyone out there has a Real player installed on their system, and the quality of G2 encodings is so good (G2 being the name of Real's latest encoding/playback system at this writing), as shown in Figure 9-3. Users can create RealAudio files either in Real Jukebox (Chapter 3) or with specialized tools available at extra cost from Real. Of course, such an argument ignores the openness of MP3 and the wide availability of tools. Real's encoder is also very fast.

Of course, the presence of Windows Media could have a significant impact on the matter, and Real has some interesting observations about Real products vis-a-vis Windows Media. Microsoft, of course, has published test results aiming to show that Windows Media can provide a superior alternative to Real. And Real, of course, has published a rebuttal proving just the opposite. The two make for interesting back-to-back reading are *www.microsoft.com/windows/windowsmedia/en/ compare/* and *www.real.com/msaudio/.*

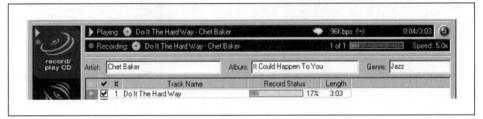

Figure 9-3. G2 files at 96 kbps often sound as good as MP3 files at 128 kbps

Perhaps one of the biggest reasons Real products haven't seen the widespread adoption of MP3 is because MP3 is primarily seen as a storage format, for building music collections, while Real has for so long positioned themselves as a streaming audio/video company. Few people even consider the possibility of saving Real files to their hard drives because for years they've clicked on a .ram link and had the file streamed to their Real players, without any option to save the file. There's nothing preventing anyone from downloading the G2 encoder and building a collection of music on their own hard drives, but it's just not what people think of doing first with Real technology. Nevertheless, you can easily use G2 encoder or the Real Jukebox covered in Chapter 3 to build your own collection of high-quality RealAudio files. If you want to use Real Jukebox to create Real Audio files rather than MP3, enter the Preferences menu, choose Encoding Options, and select "RealAudio."

What Real Player means for the future of MP3

Technically speaking, there's no real reason why users shouldn't be storing their collections in Real format rather than in MP3. But even Real has capitulated to the popularity of MP3 by promoting Real Jukebox so heavily, which creates MP3 and Real files with equal ease. While RealAudio files are ready to stream, Real's streaming server solution is still prohibitively expensive for casual users (though Real-Audio can easily be pseudo-streamed from any standard web server). And music can be compressed with audio quality equivalent to that of MP3 at smaller file sizes. Real Jukebox even gives you the option of enabling or disabling security features, so users who choose to use the product illegally can do so.

Real Jukebox (Figure 9-4) is being installed by millions of users, and some computer manufacturers are even pre-installing the tool on new machines. But despite its technical advantages, users are going to continue focusing their music encoding efforts where the rest of the world is: on MP3. Because Real Jukebox "swings both ways," it's apparent that Real knows this and is doing what it can to not be left out of the scene entirely. Expect Real to remain a major player in Internet streaming, but don't look for it to take over MP3s slot in file-based storage and distribution.

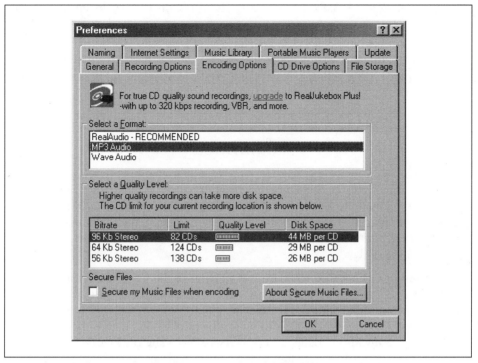

Figure 9-4. The free version of Real Jukebox is limited to 96 kbps encodings

The Codecs

In almost all cases, the alternatives to MP3 also use some form of perceptual codec, as described in Chapter 2, *How MP3 Works: Inside the Codec*. That means that all of these formats achieve their compression by discarding or reducing the amount of data representing inaudible sound (though the question of whether any sound is truly inaudible is still up for grabs; some diehard audiophiles maintain that even inaudible sounds contribute to music's overall atmosphere).

 This section only covers alternative audio *compression* schemes and file formats; there are many noncompressed formats that aren't really of interest to us here.

Throughout this discussion, keep in mind that if you decide to test some of these alternative codecs or formats, most of which claim smaller file sizes and higher quality, you're not going to get smaller files at the same bitrate. In other words, regardless of what format you use, 128 kbps means what it says: For every second of music, you store ~128,000 bits of data. The question is, how much quality can you get out of that much data? What you really want to discover is how low of a bitrate can you use and still get "CD quality" or "near CD quality" sound. Where there's money and improvements to be made, there's fierce competition. Don't expect it to let up anytime soon; anything could happen between now and next year.

AlbumDirect

At the time of this writing, it was too early to tell exactly what IBM has in store for us on the digital music distribution front. What we do know is that they've set up a broadband test system for the secure, paid delivery of digital music in selected geographical regions. The test, code-named "The Madison Project" and marketed as "AlbumDirect," will probably take on another name if it ever sees the light of day.

The intent of the test is to measure the reaction of the mainstream consumer, rather than focusing on people who use computers heavily and are already sold on MP3 or other formats; in other words, IBM wants to know how to sell John Q. Public on the idea of paid music downloads. The idea is that Warner Music, EMI, Sony Music, BMG, and Universal Music (The Big Five) are all looking for ways to cash in on digital distribution without losing control of the delivery chain, and IBM wants to provide them with the technology and mechanisms to do so.

We can expect whatever comes of AlbumDirect to be tied to a secure e-commerce system, flexible enough to interface with back-end databases at retail web sites. Users will be able to transfer downloaded music to hard drive or burn music directly to CD-ROM. One can also imagine cable-connected Internet kiosks in music stores that let users swipe their credit cards, enter the names of their 12 favorite songs, and have a custom CD burned on the spot. Similarly, online music retailers would be able to interact with Madison's back-end database to sell music directly to customers, undoubtedly skimming a commission for themselves in the process.

IBM has not revealed anything about the technology they intend to use; the codec, the security mechanism, and the distribution system are all "black boxes" at this point.

MPEG-1 Layer II

www.mpeg.org So whatever happened to this stalwart standard? Believe it or not, MPEG-1 Layer II (a.k.a. MP2) is still alive and kicking, and even in heavy use in some places. Defined as a standard for use in digital video, storage, and broadcasting in 1994, MP2 should not be considered obsolete just because it's old. Many television and video production studios still use MP2 heavily, and the format remains popular among owners of older computers, due to the fact that decoding MP2 is less computationally intensive than MP3. And don't be fooled for a second into thinking that MP2 sounds bad. In fact, many people feel that MP2 is still the quality king, and is able to create output more faithful to the original source signal than MP3. But what does that statement really mean when you're dealing with MP3 bitrates high enough to make the encoding nearly indistinguishable from the source file anyway? For most people, the answer is "not much."

The MP2 codec is much less complex than MP3's, so MP2 players are more efficient (consume fewer resources) and MP2 encoders are very fast. Of course, there is a downside—MP2 files are roughly 50% larger than corresponding MP3 files, and it was, after all, MP3's small file sizes that made it a good Internet citizen and contributed heavily to its widespread adoption.

Some encoding professionals also appreciate the fact that there is a wide array of DSP-based MP2 hardware out there for use in creating live broadcasts and encoding large collections of audio material. And because MP2 is used for the audio channel in MPEG video, the codec integrates neatly into existing video production systems.

Most quality MP3 encoders include an MP2 encoding option (check your preferences), and most major MP3 players also include the ability to decode MP2 files. Do some listening tests of your own, and you'll probably find that at higher bitrates, there just isn't all that much difference in output quality, and the larger file sizes created by MP2 encoding just aren't worth the storage space. Unless you have a very slow machine, you're better off just using a higher bitrate and sticking with MP3. And if you need to distribute your work over the Internet, forget about MP2 altogether.

What MP2 means for the future of MP3

MP2 does not figure heavily into the future of audio compression because, well, it doesn't compress very well. MP2 encoders are fast and the quality is very high, but while MP2 is not dead, it's not exactly moving forward, either. It offers nothing in the way of security or commerce, lacks an ID3 tagging system, and is favored only by users of older, slower machines. It will remain a stalwart component of some video production facilities (especially those in the third world, interestingly enough), but does threaten the dominance of MP3 in any way.

QDesign

www.qdesign.com One of the lesser-known, but perhaps most remarkable audio compression technologies vying for mind-share is QDesign's Music Codec, or QDMC. Like everyone else, QDesign is going for high quality at low bitrates. However, the company really does appear to be accomplishing some pretty amazing compression ratios with very small files. In some tests, files have been compressed at a ratio of 60:1 while maintaining relatively good quality. Not stellar quality, mind you, but good considering that level of extreme compression.

The secret lies in the approach QDesign has taken in designing their codec. While it's still based on perceptual models, like MPEG, they don't use the static filter-banks (or "transforms") that MPEG utilizes, because these start to break down at very low bitrates. Instead, the QDMC builds a source model from the original signal and breaks it down into "audio building blocks" and develops a custom set of filters for that particular audio signal. Thus, the QDMC is automatically optimized for every piece of music or voice it encodes. The result is that audible distortion is minimized at thresholds well below those where audible distortion enters the picture with traditional codecs. QDesign claims to be able to retain decent quality at bitrates of one bit per sample second.

As you might expect, encoding music with this technique takes longer than it takes to encode MP3, but this is true of nearly all the alternative coders covered in this section. QDesign licenses their coder for use in specialized applications and hardware. For example, they've partnered with Texas Instruments to create new chips for portable players (Figure 9-5), which will reportedly be capable of storing five times more music than portable MP3 devices, in the same amount of memory.

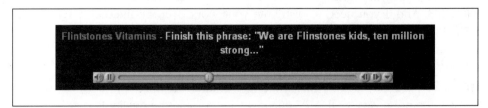

Figure 9-5. The QDesign player can be embedded directly into web pages

Perhaps even more significantly, Apple has adopted the QDesign codec as the basis of the audio component in QuickTime 4. If you've been playing QuickTime 4 files on MacOS or Windows lately, you may have heard the results of the QDesign codec without even knowing it. And since it's built into QuickTime, it automatically supports the Real Time Streaming Protocol (RTSP), rather than pseudo-streaming, as you might be forced to use with other formats. Finally, it means you can encode QDMC through any application that supports QuickTime 4 export, such as Apple QuickTime Pro or Terran Media Cleaner. You'll also find the codec built into popular tools such as Iomega's Record-It. QDesign also provides their own encoder.

If you do use QDesign's encoder, note that it's available in two versions: Basic and Professional. The Basic edition is limited to a few select bitrates, while the Pro edition gets you advanced coding parameters for further quality optimizations, pre-processing controls, faster compression options, and batch-encoding capabilities.

QDesign products plan to be fully compliant with the requirements of the SDMI, including watermarking and encryption mechanisms.

What QDesign means for the future of MP3

QDesign's codec achieves phenomenal compression ratios, but is, at this writing, gaining very few users. However, its inclusion in the QuickTime 4 architecture is liable to give it a much wider range of ears. As a proprietary codec, it lacks the kind of attention currently being shone on MP3 and other general codecs. But as a part of QuickTime, it may achieve a much broader user base. Nevertheless, expect much more attention to be directed toward the audio components of MPEG-4, Real Player G2, WindowsMedia, and QuickTime itself than on QDesign per se.

AAC

The Advanced Audio Codec, or AAC delivers better sound quality than MP3 at equivalent file sizes (or achieves similar quality at smaller file sizes),[*] and many people believe AAC may be the best candidate we've got for eventually replacing MP3. AAC was co-developed by engineers at the Fraunhofer Institute, AT&T, Lucent, Sony, Dolby, and others, and has been designated by the International Standards Organization (ISO) as a "next-generation MPEG audio standard." In addition, AAC is a component of the MPEG-4 audio coding specification, having been standardized in April, 1997 as ISO 13818-7. But while AAC may be the logical next step in the evolution of MPEG audio, AAC is just a small subset of the whole MPEG Layer IV specification—don't confuse AAC with MPEG Layer IV as a whole.

Unfortunately, AAC is not backwards-compatible with MPEG Audio Layers I, II, or III and was in fact called AAC-NBC (for Non-Backwards-Compatible) in its early stages. The advantage of breaking backwards compatibility was that AAC's developers were free to work with emerging technology breakthroughs without having

---

[*] According both to the author's own listening tests and to tests conducted by audio institutes including BBC research, NHK Science and Technical Research Labs, and the Communications Research Center of Canada. Double-blind listening tests demonstrate that AAC consistently provides superior audio quality when measured against popular codecs such as MP2 and MP3.

to saddle them with compatibility restrictions. The downside, of course, is that AAC files can't be played back by existing MP3 players without developers adding new modules or redistributing their applications.

Even though AAC was developed within the MPEG working group, many organizations and companies contributed to its development, including Fraunhofer, AT&T, Dolby Labs, Sony, the University of Hanover, and NEC. Unsurprisingly, Fraunhofer is responsible for the encoder's primary components and integrated the contributions of the other organizations and took responsibility for quality optimizations. Dolby Laboratories is responsible for managing all AAC licensing concerns.

But what makes AAC really interesting is not just the fact that it's better optimized than MP3, but the fact that it's built to work with up to 48 channels, rather than being constrained to mono or stereo. What could you possibly want with 48 channels? Granted, that's probably a little overkill for most applications, but think in terms of surround sound, multiple language options, and control and synchronization tracks, and you start to get the picture.

So, where can you get your hands on an AAC encoder and/or player? Unfortunately, that's the difficult part. At this writing, the pickings are mighty slim. Even though the spec has been in discussion since 1994, AAC has made almost no headway in the marketplace, due to two primary factors: Dolby's iron-grip holding of licensing rights and the complexity of the implementation itself. While you can find AAC plug-ins for some MP3 players and a smattering of AAC encoders at sites such as *www.mp3daily.com*, complete, full-blown implementations of the AAC codec are simply not out there except as proprietary implementations in players such as Liquid Audio's. As with MP3, the patent on AAC applies to the creation of a "compliant bitstream," rather than to any specific coder implementation. Theoretically, anybody could write their own software in a "clean room" environment capable of working with AAC files, but they would still owe the same licensing fees. And with the enormous complexity of the codec, it's not likely that this will happen anytime soon (if ever).

Meanwhile, the AAC source code available for download only allows developers to build a very low quality coder, certainly nothing that would impress an existing MP3 user. That pretty much leaves deep-pocketed investors to fork over big cash for the whole package. And right now, the biggest company who has decided to go for it is AT&T with their a2b player. And even the a2b player won't play AAC-compliant bitstreams, since AT&T has only implemented the portion of the spec they needed to satisfy their own criteria.

At this writing, there aren't many AAC encoders or players to choose from, and most of what is out there can't create bitstreams that are compliant enough to play properly in all decoders. Search the Internet for Astrid or Quartex AAC encoders, or check out MBSoft's AAC Encoder (*fly.to/mbsoft/*). K-Jöfol (*www.kjofol.org*) was one of the first audio players to handle AAC files for playback, but others are likely to support the format as well by the time you read this.

What AAC means for the future of MP3

While there are encoders and players for both AAC and VQF files out there right now, support is generally pretty sketchy, and you won't find a ton of files available for download encoded in these formats. The formats are not "vapor," but neither have they reached anything approaching widespread adoption.

The AAC format holds great promise, but until the industry loosens up around the format, it's going nowhere fast. Because MP3 got out of the industry's hands so quickly, one can surmise that they're going to try and hold onto AAC more tightly. Creating a second defacto standard may not be as easy this time. When and if the format does reach wide adoption, it will likely be on the industry's terms, not those of the public. Once again, ladies and germs, the best technology is not necessarily the winning technology.

Finally, encoding AAC is far more computationally intensive than encoding MP3. When and if AAC encoders do end up in public hands, users better be prepared to either be patient or get a faster machine.

a2b

www.a2bmusic.com One of the early corporate adopters of the AAC codec (covered earlier in this chapter) was AT&T's a2b, a proprietary player including security and digital rights management technologies for artists and labels. Because a2b is based on AAC, it's quality-to-compression ratio is very good. The player implements an Internet encryption scheme called CryptoLib and an electronic licensing system called PolicyMaker, for controlling terms of access and sharing of data (a2b files cannot be played on computers other than the ones to which they were downloaded). More information on CryptoLib and PolicyMaker can be found in the Technology section of a2b's site.

After early positive press, rumors have been floating around that a2b, as shown in Figure 9-6, may be stalling in the marketplace. For one thing, Liquid Audio established itself earlier with more backing and more technology (a2b does not, for example, support direct burning to CD or real-time streaming). In addition, the company was late to the table in taking a stand vis-a-vis SDMI and other initiatives on the industry's table. Meanwhile, AT&T executives appeared to be waffling over where to take the company next in the light of MP3's popularity. After a large group of key a2b engineers left the company en masse, some pundits saw failure in the cards for a2b.

However, a good number of big-name artists have lined up behind the company (including Aerosmith, Alanis Morissette,* and Bonnie Raitt), and of course AT&T has all the funding they need to stay in the game. If only they can find a strategy to set them apart from their competitors.

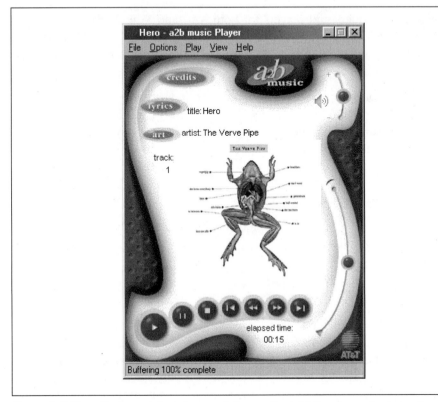

Figure 9-6. The a2b player is based around the excellent AAC codec and a pair of security technologies from AT&T

What a2b means for the future of MP3

a2b has been at this game for quite a while, but have yet to make a major dent in the market. The biggest reason, one can only surmise, is the fact that they've packaged up an excellent codec in a proprietary wrapper, which keeps interoperability at a minimum. Users are able to play back a2b files only on the same machine they downloaded to, and only through the a2b player. Without opening up their range of compatibility, a2b isn't going to increase their marketshare. Confusion within the company about MP3 isn't helping the situation any. It's the codec within the a2b player—AAC—that users should be excited about and waiting for.

---

* Morissette has also released tracks in MP3 format, so one shouldn't interpret her use of a2b as an exclusive endorsement.

Liquid Audio

www.liquidaudio.com Liquid Audio is one of the pioneers of the online music distribution business. Not that the product predated other methods of digital distribution, but they were one of the first to have a go at making money at it while simultaneously striving to satisfy the needs of the recording industry with integrated sales and security features.

The idea is that artists and labels are able to provide secure tracks or samples, along with built-in ordering capabilities. While you're listening, you can view album cover art, read the lyrics and liner notes, and take part in promotional deals. If you like a sample track, you can enter your credit card information and download the entire album digitally. Because Liquid Tracks are encrypted and watermarked, they must be played on the computer of the person who downloaded them. You can't just purchase Liquid Tracks and share them with your friends.

But while that part of the chain is no longer unusual among digital distribution systems, Liquid goes one step farther by integrating its capabilities with your CD-R device, so you can burn your purchases straight to CD, thus ending up with a product very similar to what you'd get at the record store (except that you never have to leave your chair and don't get the high-quality cover art). And before you get any big ideas, clever boy, no—you can't burn more than one CD copy of a purchased album (although you would still be able to create unprotected MP3 files from your newly burned CD...).

Liquid provides a three-part system, consisting of the Liquifier (their encoder), the Liquid MusicServer (which can be optionally used for streaming content), and Liquid Player itself, as shown in Figure 9-7. The encoder and player run on Windows and MacOS, while the server runs on Windows NT or Unix. The encoder includes digital watermarking options, as well as an "organizer" component that can be used to sift and sort through music collections, or prepare custom compilations for burning to CD. The organizer will let you mix and match Liquid Audio and MP3 files side by side. The Liquid Player offers access to complete lyrics, promotional deals, and built-in e-commerce technology so you can purchase tracks or entire albums online, then burn them to CD through the software's organizer component.

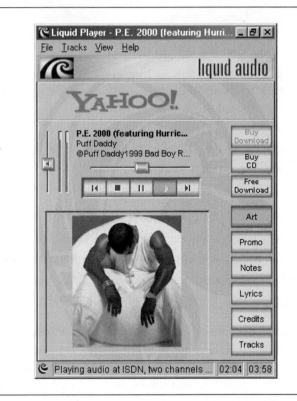

Figure 9-7. The Liquid Player offers complete access to e-commerce technology

 Even though you can download the Liquid Player for free, you're still asked to enter your credit card information in order to receive a "Liquid Passport," a digital ID that gets you into their database so they can verify your future purchases and, of course, track the music you're listening to and purchasing. Whether this scheme of forced tracking has Orwellian implications for personal privacy is a judgment each user has to make for herself.

Partially because Liquid Audio got a huge head start in theis part of the biz, they've got the de facto standard thing going for them, and fairly wide adoption by artists and labels looking for secure distribution (Figure 9-8). The company claims that more than 100,000 legally encoded songs are floating around out there, with quite a few big names on the roster (Dave Matthews Band and Marilyn Manson among them). Liquid Tracks also appear on a number of high-profile web sites, such as *Amazon.com* and *digital.yahoo.com*.

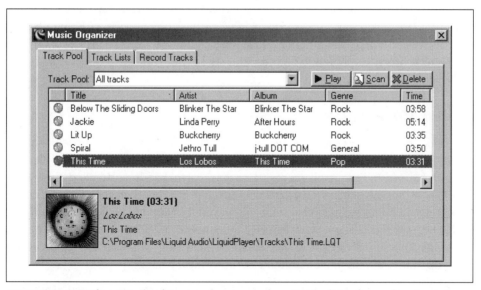

Figure 9-8. Liquid's organizer lets you organize and create playlists of your downloaded Liquid Tracks, then optionally burn them straight to audio CDs

Like QDesign (see later), Liquid is working with Texas Instruments to develop specialized chips with the Liquid Audio coder and security mechanisms built in, for use in the huge array of upcoming portable and home-based digital music playback devices. Many such devices could be in the channel on the market by the time you read this. While the Liquid Player is based originally on the AAC codec, it's important to note that the Liquid Player is not limited to playing files created with its own codec. Files created in Dolby Digital AC-3 (a format aimed chiefly at home theater and surround-sound implementations, not covered here) and AAC, Windows Media, and MP3 with the Genuine Music mark will also work in the Liquid Player. In addition, RealAudio fans can download a G2 plug-in that will let them listen to Liquid Tracks through the Real player. A variety of popular MP3 players also include Liquid support, including MusicMatch Jukebox, WinAmp, and the Diamond Rio and the Creative Labs' NOMAD (Chapter 6, *Hardware, Portables, Home Stereos, and Kits*).

The architecture of the Liquid System is constructed to support leading formats, not just to provide an added layer of convenience for users, but so that Liquid can easily be integrated with whatever mechanisms the SDMI churns out.

What Liquid Audio means for the future of MP3

Liquid is in basically the same boat as AT&T with their a2b player: excellent choice of codecs (AAC), shame about the proprietary implementation. One can't fault a company for wanting to add value to a spec and create a saleable package—it's a sound idea that used to work. But in today's climate, users want access, openness, and interoperability, which Liquid does not provide on the same scale that MP3 does. Still, some users will appreciate the convenience of being able to burn legitimate CDs full of commercial music, and to partake in other online "value-add" functions. Again, watch for the success of the AAC codec, not Liquid Audio itself.

Global Music's MP4

www.globalmusic.com Lest there be any confusion, this one is the poseur—a file format *based* on technology in MPEG-4, but proprietary. After creating the file format, Global Music One took matters into their own hands and called their files MP4 files. A smart business move, to be sure, but not one that gained them much respect among the technoscenti, since it introduces an unnecessary element of confusion into the picture. What happens when and if MPEG-4 becomes a popular implementation? If MP4 files are at all popular, they'll probably be forced to come up with a non-intuitive name for MPEG-4 files. Urgh.

That's not to say that Global Music One's files don't have their appeal. They are based on AAC, which as you read earlier in this chapter, is a high-quality format with great compression. And every MP4 file comes with its own built-in player, essentially "wrapped" around the audio data so users don't need to have an audio player configured to work with the file format—it all just works (assuming you're using Windows or MacOS, that is).

MP4 files encapsulated in a Digital Audio Postcard (DAP), as shown in Figure 9-9, are designed to be freely distributed by the copyright owner, and forwarded from one listener to another. The files can contain links to web sites where listeners can get more information, or purchase the album. The format received its first big boost in January 1999 when Public Enemy posted the song "Swindlers Lust" to its site for free download. Fittingly, the song is one long jab at the exploitative aspects of the recording industry.

While the format may be cool, its adoption has not exactly been rapid. Global Music posts new songs in MP4 format to its site regularly, and a few labels have jumped on board with it. But there's very little buzz out there, and the number of songs released in MP4 format is a barely perceptible trickle compared to the number of songs appearing out there in MP3 and other formats, both legitimately and not. And because many perceive Global Music as having made a bald-faced market grab in the face of an open standard, they've generated a good deal of ill will in the fiercely open Internet community. Open standards guarantee a certain level of interoperability, and hence success. Closed protocols aim to corner a segment of the market for the benefit of a single company. Most of the time, closed protocols unleashed on the Internet don't attract the biggest crowds.

Figure 9-9. Global Music's Digital Audio Postcard

What "MP4" means for the future of MP3

Global Music is onto something—until the time when we count on virtually everyone we know having MP3 playback software on their machines, Global's DAP system provides the ability to send music files to anyone without worrying in advance whether they have the right playback software installed or not. And the DAP package makes sure that artists can stay in touch with their latest creations and sales opportunities by allowing for embedded hyperlinks. But because Global Music (at this writing) does not offer an encoder that can be used by fans (Global Music works directly with labels), this version of "MP4" presents no threat to MP3.

VQF

www.yamaha-xg.com/english/xg/SoundVQ/ For a while there, the Internet went wild over the prospect of VQF. "MP3 is dead! Long live VQF!" said the fan sites. But at this writing, VQF seems to be going nowhere. Short for Transform-domain Weighted Interleave Vector Quantization, or TwinVQ for short, the format is very similar to AAC in terms of compression ratios and quality. In fact, this is no accident. Both technologies will ultimately appear in the MPEG-4 specification.

Originally developed by NTT (Nippon Telephone and Telegraph), the spec is now licensed and marketed by Yamaha, who make available one of the few VQF encoders available. VQF files typically retain near-CD-quality audio at an 18:1 compression ratio, similar to that of AAC. Because of the specification's complexity, decoders require 10–20% more CPU utilization than MP3 players, and the encoding process is much slower (though the ever-increasing speed of modern CPUs makes this kind of measurement less meaningful all the time). VQF files are known to stand up very well under conditions that stress MP3 encoding techniques. Some independent listening tests even showed that a 96 kbps VQF file had the same audio quality as a 192 kbps MP3 file, although detractors note that VQF sounds a bit thin when compared side-by-side with AAC.

It's difficult to explain the failure of VQF to catch on in a big way, except to note that it's a proprietary technology without cross-platform support. Perhaps it's not too late for VQF, but things aren't looking promising at this point.

You won't find nearly the proliferation of VQF files out there and available for download as you will MP3 files, but there are several thousand floating around. Popular MP3 players are capable of playing VQF, and curious users will find Yamaha's encoder and player kit at *www.yamaha-xg.com/english/xg/SoundVQ/* .

VQF files can be embedded into web pages or streamed, by means of a "locator" file similar to that used with ASF and RealAudio. A locator file consists of nothing but the URL of the *.VQF* file. Save the URL into a text document named with a *.VQL* extension and link to that instead of the .VQF itself. If you're serving *.VQF* files from your own server, you'll need to establish the appropriate MIME types (see Chapter 8, *Webcasting and Servers: Internet Distribution*, for more on that):

```
MIME type: audio
Subtype: x-twinvq
Extensions: .vqf, .vql

MIME type: audio
Subtype: x-twinvq-plugin
Extensions: .vqe
```

What VQF means for the future of MP3

Like AAC, VQF has a lot going for it... and is similarly hamstrung while music lovers wait for a variety of usable encoders and players to hit the scene. These, of course, are held up in politicking as the industry works out how to deal with licensing issues to keep VQF from becoming another runaway MP3. It's unfortunate that the needs of the industry and the desires of consumers are so consistently at odds. However, unlike AAC, VQF isn't even seeing the adoption into commercial products, as is true with the AAC coded in a2b and LiquidAudio. While users salivate at the opportunity to enjoy very high quality encoding at only 96 kbps, they'll continue to enjoy their MP3 files as they have been. And while VQF players and plug-in modules for WinAmp and other players were slowly beginning to increase in number, the single VQF encoder available—from Yamaha—had not been updated from its trial version of mid-1999.

It's not too late for VQF to take off, but the companies who hold its strings will need to act decisively before the format is written off in user's minds for good. At this writing, VQF does not present a viable threat to MP3.

While many of the file formats and codecs competing with MP3 for attention offer specific advantages, none have come close to usurping MP3's broad adoption, as shown in Table 9-1. MPEG-4 and QuickTime are not included here; their status as umbrella architectures makes comparison to straight codecs problematic.

Table 9-1. MP3 Compared To Other File Formats

File Format	Codec Used	Source Code Available	Strengths	Weaknesses	Security	OS Support
MP3	MPEG-1, Layer III	Yes (but licensing fees apply)	Widest interoperability between apps and operating systems. ID3 tags[a]	Not the smallest, not the best sounding	Virtually none, though ID3v2 allows for possible implementations	Windows, MacOS, Linux, BeOS, others
MP2	MPEG-1, Layer II	Yes (but licensing fees apply)	Fast encoding, consumes few CPU cycles	Larger file sizes	Virtually none (watermarks possible)	Windows, MacOS, Linux, BeOS, others
RealAudio (G2)	Proprietary (Multiple internal codecs)	No	Multiple OS support, small files, leader in streaming	Few apps support playback, proprietary	AT&T	Windows, MacOS, Linux, BeOS, others
a2b	Modified AAC	No	Small files, great quality, secure	Requires a2b player, few users	CryptoLib	Windows, MacOS
LiquidAudio	Modified AAC	No	Small files, great quality, secure, integrated sales features	Comparatively few users	Proprietary (Liquid Platinum)	Windows, MacOS
Global Music Online's "MP4"	Modified AAC	No	Small files, great quality, player is built in	Comparatively few users, snubbed industry with "MP4" name grab	Proprietary	Windows, MacOS
Windows Media	Proprietary (Windows Media Technologies 4.0)	No	Small files, good quality, security optional	Windows only unless adopted as ISO standard	Proprietary (Digital Rights Management)	Windows

Table 9-1. MP3 Compared To Other File Formats (continued)

File Format	Codec Used	Source Code Available	Strengths	Weaknesses	Security	OS Support
VQF	VQF	No	Small files, great quality, security possible	Few encoders or players. Industry still working out details	Can be added by vendor	Windows, others likely
AAC	AAC	No (likely in the future)	Small files, great quality, security possible	Mostly built into proprietary products, few "pure" encoders or players	Can be added by vendor	Windows, others likely
QDesign	Proprietary	No	Extremely small files, included in QuickTime 4.0	Proprietary, slow to take off (though signs are good)	Can use Quick-Time security features	Any format with full QuickTime support

[a] Although ID3 tags can theoretically be supported by other formats; it's a question of implementation rather than limitations in other formats.

Conducting Codec Comparison Tests

If you're sincerely interested in finding out for yourself which of the available codecs actually produces the highest quality output, there are a number of factors and considerations you'll want to bear in mind. First of all, it can be very difficult not to compare apples and oranges. Some codecs are optimized for quality, others for file size. Most of them attempt to strike a balance between the two, but only you can say what's most important for your collection. If you're looking for compatibility with a wide range of hardware devices, you may be willing to make some sacrifices in order to have access to the widest range of files "out there." If you've got gobs of disk space to spare and don't plan on doing much Internet distribution, you may want to go with a format like MP2 rather than the more popular MP3. If you want to run an Internet radio station, you may decide that RealAudio has more built-in technology than MP3 or Microsoft's competing ASF.

All of that said, when it's time to actually start encoding samples, take care to choose a variety of types of music. In particular, seek out music which is difficult for some encoders to get right. If you've got a favorite song and you've noticed repeatable glitches when listening to MP3 encodings of it, don't *avoid* that track—*use* it! The idea is to stress-test encoders under conditions that will really show their flaws. If you use music that's very dense or very constant, the differences between encoders will be less noticeable. Seek out music that features isolated instruments, so you can hear their subtleties rather than having them masked by the other instruments in the band or orchestra. Solo vocal passages can be especially revealing, as can acoustic guitars, harpsichords, and snare drums. Orchestral music and loud or bright pop music may not be your best choices.

You'll also want to set aside sufficient time for thorough tests. If you look around on the Internet, you're liable to find a number of tests of downloadable samples encoded with various techniques. Unfortunately, some of these tests provide samples of only a few seconds length. Short clips may cover only the most dramatic pieces of music, ignoring more subtle passages where the real testing action is. Downloadable tests are interesting for informing yourself, but cannot substitute for a test run by you, with your own music, on your own system, with lots of time to sit down and listen carefully.

As described in Chapter 4, one of the best ways to listen to multiple encodings up close and personal is to decode them back to WAV format and burn them to an audio CD you can listen to on your home stereo. Unfortunately, it can be difficult to transform many of the alternative formats back to WAV without the assistance of either illegal tools or tools that pass signal through your sound card, thus introducing artifacts with an extra digital-analog conversion step.

—Continued—

Regardless, in all cases you'll be looking for the "transparency" of the given format. In other words, you want to discover the degree to which the encoder in question intrudes on the quality of the original source file. In a perfect world, the encoded file is tiny and its audio quality is indistinguishable from that of the source file. Such an encoder would be said to have total transparency.

Appendix: ID3v1 Genres

Genre identifiers in the ID3v1 specification can be referenced either by name or by identifying number (as is common with tools such as id3ren, covered in Chapter 4). Table A-1 lists the genre names and IDs commonly accepted as "standard;" officially, any other value will be considered as "Unknown." Table A-2 lists WinAmp's extensions to the standard, which are also filtering into wide usage.

Table A-1. ID Numbers Assigned to Common Music Categories in the ID3 Tag Specification

0 Blues	20 Alternative	40 AlternRock	60 Top 40
1 Classic Rock	21 Ska	41 Bass	61 Christian Rap
2 Country	22 Death Metal	42 Soul	62 Pop/Funk
3 Dance	23 Pranks	43 Punk	63 Jungle
4 Disco	24 Soundtrack	44 Space	64 Native American
5 Funk	25 Euro-Techno	45 Meditative	65 Cabaret
6 Grunge	26 Ambient	46 Instrumental Pop	66 New Wave
7 Hip-Hop	27 Trip-Hop	47 Instrumental Rock	67 Psychedelic
8 Jazz	28 Vocal	48 Ethnic	68 Rave
9 Metal	29 Jazz+Funk	49 Gothic	69 Showtunes
10 New Age	30 Fusion	50 Darkwave	70 Trailer
11 Oldies	31 Trance	51 Techno-Industrial	71 Lo-Fi
12 Other	32 Classical	52 Electronic	72 Tribal
13 Pop	33 Instrumental	53 Pop-Folk	73 Acid Punk
14 R&B	34 Acid	54 Eurodance	74 Acid Jazz
15 Rap	35 House	55 Dream	75 Polka
16 Reggae	36 Game	56 Southern Rock	76 Retro
17 Rock	37 Sound Clip	57 Comedy	77 Musical
18 Techno	38 Gospel	58 Cult	78 Rock & Roll
19 Industrial	39 Noise	59 Gangsta	79 Hard Rock

Table A-2. Audio Categories Specified in WinAmp's Extensions to the ID3 Standard,
Commonly Supported in Other ID3-compliant MP3 Players

80 Folk	97 Chorus	114 Samba	131 Indie
81 Folk-Rock	98 Easy Listening	115 Folklore	132 BritPop
82 National Folk	99 Acoustic	116 Ballad	133 Negerpunk
83 Swing	100 Humour	117 Power Ballad	134 PolskPunk
84 Fast Fusion	101 Speech	118 Rhythmic Soul	135 Beat
85 Bebob	102 Chanson	119 Freestyle	136 Christian-GangstaRap
86 Latin	103 Opera	120 Duet	137 HeavyMetal
87 Revival	104 Chamber Music	121 Punk Rock	138 BlackMetal
88 Celtic	105 Sonata	122 Drum Solo	139 Crossover
89 Bluegrass	106 Symphony	123 A capella	140 ContemporaryChristian
90 Avantgarde	107 Booty Bass	124 Euro-House	141 ChristianRock
91 Gothic Rock	108 Primus	125 Dance Hall	142 Merengue
92 Progressive Rock	109 Porn Groove	126 Goa	143 Salsa
93 Psychedelic Rock	110 Satire	127 Drum&Bass	144 TrashMetal
94 Symphonic Rock	111 Slow Jam	128 Club-House	
95 Slow Rock	112 Club	129 Hardcore	
96 Big Band	113 Tango	130 Terror	

Glossary

AES/EBU

A high-end digital audio connection interface found almost exclusively on expensive and/or dedicated equipment. Use of AES/EBU in MP3-related situations is rare and probably overkill, though it does occur in some studio implementations.

AIFF

One of several standard uncompressed audio formats, popular primarily on Macintosh computers. AIFF is essentially uncompressed PCM audio wearing a slightly different file header.

Algorithm

A rule or series of rules and processes described in programmatic terms to achieve a conversion between formats. The MP3 codec is an algorithm utilizing mathematical descriptions and forumulae to remove "unnecessary" data from uncompressed audio.

Big Five

Standard nomenclature for the five largest recording labels in the world, which together control a huge portion of the world's music distribution industry. The labels in "The Big Five" are Warner Music, EMI, Sony Music, BMG, and Universal Music.

Bitrate

A measure of the number of bits allocated to each second in a given data stream. MP3 encoders allow users to specify a bitrate before encoding begins; higher bitrates mean larger files and higher MP3 quality.

Bitstream

A series of bits running through a device or conduit (such as an MP3 player or Internet broadcast). An MP3-compliant bitstream can be reassembled into an intelligible audio signal.

Broadcast

The practice of "pushing" MP3 over the Internet directly to an MP3 player, either via genuine streaming (i.e., from a SHOUTcast or icecast server) or via pseudo-streaming, wherein the player "pulls" a bitstream down from a standard web server. Broadcast differs from download in that the user does not explicitly save an MP3 file to her file system.

Buffer

A chunk of MP3 data stored in memory prior to the moment of playback, for the purpose of alleviating skips caused by network latency or slow/flaky storage devices (such as some CD-ROM drives.) Buffers can also be helpful for slow machines or systems that have to do a lot of processor-intensive tasks simultaneously. Buffer size can typically be adjusted by the user.

CBR

Constant Bitrate. The standard method of MP3 encoding, wherein each second of audio is allocated the same number of bits. For example, a 128 kbps MP3 file is a CBR file. Contrast with VBR.

CDDB

The Compact Disk Database. A public database accessible on the Internet at *www.cddb.com*, which matches unique identifying strings for hundreds of thousands of compact discs with the album name, artist name, and track listings. The CDDB enables many MP3 ripper/encoder tools to assign meaningful names and ID3 tags to tracks as they're being encoded.

CD-R, CD-RW

CD-Recordable and CD-Recordable/Writeable. These are abbreviations referring to recordable compact disc technology. CD-R drives and discs allow data to be written to a given area of the disk only once, while CD-RW devices can be recorded to multiple times. However, there are distinct drawbacks to CD-RW technology; see Chapter 5, *Ripping and Encoding: Creating MP3 Files* for details.

Codec

Short for compressor/decompressor, this term refers to any algorithm capable of compressing or decompressing a bitstream, such as MP3. The complex but efficient MP3 codec is built into both encoders and players.

DAC

Digital-to-Analog Converter. Any unit that performs the function of transforming digitally stored audio signal into traditional analog signal, which must happen at some point in the playback chain in order for the signal to be audible. Most modern sound cards include an on-board DAC, while many audiophiles prefer to use external DACs for their (typically) superior fidelity.

DAE

Digital Audio Extraction. The capability of most modern CD-ROM drives to extract digital data from an audio CD, which virtually all modern ripping/encoding tools require. Without a DAE-capable CD-ROM drive, users must trap the analog audio signal moving through the system to an uncompressed audio format, and then encode that.

DAO

Disc-At-Once. The capability of some CD-ROM burning software to let you burn discs without a two-second delay between tracks. Not generally an issue for mixed collections, but useful for live shows and for music containing audible inter-song segues.

Decoder

Any software or hardware capable of transforming an MP3 bitstream back into uncompressed signal, which may be either audible output or an uncompressed audio file on disk. Any MP3 player can be called a decoder, as can any tool that turns MP3 files into WAV or AIFF files.

DSP

Digital Signal Processor. A programmable chip dedicated to a specific task, such as decoding video or MP3 on-the-fly. Most portable MP3 units, for example, contain custom DSPs programmed solely for the task of turning MP3 bitstreams into audible signal.

Dynamic range

An audio term referring to range of volume changes in a given audio stream. A musical piece that has both quiet and loud passages would be said to have a lot of dynamic range.

Encoder

For our purposes, any tool capable of transforming uncompressed audio signal into an MP3-compliant bitstream, which may be either a live broadcast or an MP3 file.

Equalization

The process of adjusting the audible character of an audio signal by raising or lowering frequency bands. The purpose of equalization is to compensate for deficiencies in the source material, the playback hardware, or the listening environment, although equalizers are often used simply to pump up the bass or other frequencies some listeners find attractive. Equalization can be easily over-used, resulting in poor fidelity.

Filterbanks

During the encoding process, the signal is broken down into multiple "sub-bands," or cross-sections of the signal that can be treated separately by the encoder for optimal results. These cross-sections are known as "filterbanks," or "transforms."

Flash memory

Any silicon chip that can have data written to it in blocks, rather than one byte at a time, and that retains the data it stores even when a power supply is removed. Flash memory is commonly used with portable MP3 players to provide reprogrammable storage space in a compact form factor. Users load up flash memory cards (such as a SanDisk MMCs or Sony MemorySticks) with MP3s and take them along when they leave the house or office, so they have access to a potentially unlimited supply of music throughout the day.

Fletcher-Munson curve

A specific configuration of an equalizer that takes advantage of the fact that the ear is not as sensitive to low and high frequencies when music is being played at low volumes. Boosting these frequencies somewhat above normal can help music to sound more natural at lower volumes (see Chapter 4, *Playlists, Tags, and Skins: MP3 Options*).

Frame

MP3 files consist of thousands of very short sections, much as a movie consists of thousands of tiny still shots. Each frame is stuffed with as many bits as are allocated in the encoder's bitrate preferences, and is preceded by header data describing additional information about the data to come (encoding method, ownership, etc.) See Chapter 2, *How MP3 Works: Inside the Codec*, for details.

Frequency (Hz)

The technical description of audio pitch, measured in cycles per second, or Hertz (Hz). In general, humans cannot hear frequencies below 20Hz (20 cycles per second), nor above 20KHz (20,000 cycles per second).

FTP

File Transfer Protocol. One of the simplest (and oldest) methods of distributing data on the Internet. Many MP3 files are distributed through FTP servers rather than via the Web. While most web browsers are capable of accessing FTP servers, you'll probably want to use a dedicated FTP client if you end up downloading many files this way.

Huffman coding

A method of reducing the size of any given data set by seeking out redundancies and describing them mathematically. Huffman coding is used in virtually every computer compression technique, including ZIP and JPEG. MP3 encoders make a Huffman pass for added compression after running through the psychoacoustic techniques outlined in Chapter 2.

ID3

MP3 files allow users to store "meta-data" in the file itself in the form of "ID3 tags." There are two versions of ID3. ID3v1 stores only artist, album, song, genre, year, and a brief comment, and appears at the end of the file. ID3v2 allows for the storage of up to 256 MB of arbitrary data, and appears (more usefully) at the beginning of the file. See Chapter 4 for more information.

ISO

International Standards Organization. This group exists to codify and create formal standards out of defacto standards created by independent organizations working either solo or in concert. ISO has formally codified the MP3 work done by Fraunhofer, AT&T, and others.

Jacking

A colloquial term referring to the process or extracting an audio signal from the computer before it heads out for the sound card and toward the speakers. "Jacking" is commonly used to circumvent piracy protection schemes.

Kbps

Kilobits-per-second. A measure of the bitrate of an MP3 stream in terms of thousands of bits per second. 128 kbps is the defacto standard bitrate for MP3 audio downloaded from the Internet, but is considered sub-par from a fidelity standpoint. Most serious MP3 users encode at 160 or 192 kbps.

Lossiness

Compression techniques are either lossless or lossy. In lossless compression, the act of decompression restores every bit of the original source material. In lossy compression, some data is irretrievably discarded in the compression process. MP3 is a lossy compression format.

M3U

In on-demand streaming situations, URLs to MP3 files are listed in a simple text file. The M3U file is downloaded and passed to the MP3 player, which takes responsibility for downloading the MP3 files at the specified URLs. M3U stands for MPEG URL.

Masking

The portion of the MP3 encoding process that analyzes signal for subtle differences in pitch or notes close together in time. Because the human auditory perception system is only sensitive to such changes if they're sufficiently separated in time, some of the data describing them can be discarded. Auditory and temporal masking processes are explained in Chapter 2.

MIME

Multipurpose Internet Mail Extension. The Internet-standard technique used for mapping filename extensions to filetypes, so that browsers can launch downloaded files into appropriate helper applications. For example, the MIME type of an MP3 files is *audio/x-mpeg*, which is associated with the extension *MP3*. It is up to the operating system or browser on the receiving end to determine what to do with any given MIME type.

Moore's Law

Gordon Moore, who helped to invent microprocessors and was once the chairman of Intel Corporation, noted that the number of transistors that could be squeezed into a given space effectively doubled every 18 months to two years, in a pattern dating back to the very invention of computing devices. As a result, processors made two years from now will be either half the size of today's at the same speed, or the same size and twice as fast. Additionally, the next cycle always lets you buy twice the horsepower at the same cost, or the same horsepower at half the cost, in comparison to the current batch of processors. Moore's Law has successfully predicted the evolution of computing horsepower since around 1900, with no end in sight (until we run up against the lower size limit imposed by the width of atoms themselves, but that's another story). See *The Age of Spiritual Machines*, Ray Kurzweil, Viking Penguin 1999.

MPEG

While this technically stands for "Motion Picture Experts Group," the term is almost always used to refer to a family of audio and video compression technologies. The family is broken down into major classes and, within those classes, "layers" defining specific strengths, bandwidths, and samplerates. See Chapter 1, *The Nuts and Bolts of MP3* for more information.

MP3

An abbreviation for MPEG-1, Layer III, a subclass of the MPEG family of audio and video compression technologies. Also the filename extension typically used with audio files of this class, e.g., *Grateful_Dead-Black_Star.mp3*.

PCM

Pulse Code Modulation. The standard format for raw, uncompressed signal, audio in particular. Each PCM sample is represented by eight bits, for a total of 64 kbps. Data on an audio CD is stored in PCM format, for example.

Perl

Practical Extraction and Report Language. A popular, cross-platform scripting language which excels at text handling and processing. Available for every operating system under the sun, Perl is the most common language used in CGI (Common Gateway Interface) back-ends for web servers, and is often used for building custom MP3 solutions for home networks, broadcast interfaces, and for building indexes of MP3 files on a given system.

Playlist

A text file referencing one or more paths to MP3 files on a system. Playlists allow users to create custom playback sequences on their hard drives without physically rearranging files. Playlists can typically be created by dragging MP3 files or directories into a player's playlist editor window, by running system queries, or by using a specialized playlist creation tool such as Helium for Windows.

Plug-in

A software module designed to extend the functionality of some other software. Many popular MP3 players accept plug-ins, and have spawned entire cottage industries of plug-in development. Plug-ins generally fall into four categories: Visualizers, DSP/Effects, Input/Output, and General Purpose/Miscellaneous. See Chapter 4 for details on specific plug-ins.

Pseudo-streaming

A streaming technique wherein the client (user's) MP3 player downloads a file directly to itself, rather than being handed a file that's already been downloaded. The process differs slightly from true MP3 broadcast. Also called "MP3-on-demand." More information on streaming techniques can be found in Chapters 4 and 8.

Psychoacoustics

The study of the relationship between the human hearing mechanism and the brain. MP3's tremendous compression capabilities are a direct result of findings originating in the field of psychoacoustics.

Relay server

An intermediary server in a broadcast system that intercepts an MP3 broadcast and redistributes it to multiple users, thereby making more bandwidth available to the source streamer so multiple users can tune in simultaneously.

RIAA

The Recording Industry of America. A trade group representing the interests of artists and labels, and involved in an ongoing battle to stamp out music piracy. The RIAA is also actively investigating methods to accommodate the new era of file-based digital music distribution.

Ripping

The process of extracting audio files from audio CDs, using a computer. Because audio CDs don't contain a filesystem similar to that of consumer operating systems, audio data must be accessed via other means. Most modern MP3 encoders do their ripping transparently in the background, although one can also use separate ripping tools. See Chapter 5 for details.

Samplerate

A measure of how many times per second a given audio signal is digitally represented (whether it be "live" or stored on disk). Typically described in Kilohertz, "samplerate" should not be confused with "bitrate," which refers to the amount of storage dedicated to each second of signal, rather than the frequency with which samples are taken from the source material.

SDMI

The Strategic Digital Music Initiative. An initiative proposed by many corners of the recording industry to fight music piracy at both the hardware and software levels, by creating a security specification for audio CDs, sound cards, and music playback software. By getting all links in the chain to speak the same language, the hope of the industry is that piracy will become more difficult. The proposal, however, has many detractors, and its ultimate acceptance faces many obstacles. More on SDMI can be found in Chapter 7, *The Not-So-Fine-Print: Legal Bits and Pieces.*

Signal

A somewhat abstract term. Technically, signal could be described as "a fluctuating AC voltage, current, or electrical field strength representing the part of the music, tone, audio, etc., that you want, distinct from the part that you don't want, which is noise." Noise, however, is an equally abstract term, and can refer to line hum, audio byproducts from recording/playback equipment, or even portions of a recording the artist feels detracts from the musical experience. Variations in signal represent coded information, such as music. The terms "signal" and "noise" are interdependent, defining one another, and are also context-dependent: they may mean different things in different situations.

Skin

A collection of bitmap images that can be assembled together and used as a "dressing" for the user interface of software, such as an MP3 player. Many popular MP3 players for multiple operating systems accept WinAmp skins, while other players define their own skin requirements. Skins have no effect on playback performance; their purpose is merely aesthetic.

Sound stage

The aural illusion of a sense of "space" in music, even when heard through two speakers. The "perfect" sound stage is of course perceived at a live, unamplified concert, although quality recordings and playback equipment are able to recreate much of the "presence" of an actual sound stage. Low bitrate MP3 encodings have difficulty projecting a quality sound stage.

S/PDIF

Sony/Phillips Digital Interface. A digital interconnection schema yielding higher quality than the plastic "Toslink" optical connectors found on some equipment. S/PDIF connectors are found on many modern sound cards, and can be used with a digital amplifier or outboard DAC to obtain maximum fidelity from computer sound equipment.

SSFDC

Solid State Floppy Disk Card. An industry specification providing flash memory cards with a set of common mechanisms and interfaces to ensure interoperability across devices. For example, an SSFDC memory card will work as easily in your portable MP3 player as it does in your digital camera or your cell phone.

Streaming

Any technique wherein MP3 (or other audio/video formats) is played back on the client machine as it's being downloaded, rather than after download is complete. The two main types of streaming are "broadcast," where the server is preprocessing the stream to meet bandwidth restrictions, and "MP3-on-demand" or "pseudo-streaming," which takes place on a standard web server.

Toe-in

The technique of pointing a pair of speakers slightly in toward the center of the listening space to achieve the best possible sound stage.

Toslink

Plastic optical cable used for interconnecting some digital output devices (such as sound cards or DVD players) with some digital amplifiers and DACs. While of fairly good quality, S/PDIF is generally considered to yield superior audio quality to Toslink.

USB

Universal Serial Bus. A connection specification for low-bandwidth computer peripherals, including everything from mice and keyboards to MP3 players. USB circumvents the "IRQ dilemma" resulting from limitations in the x86 architecture. USBv2 will offer the same flexibility, but will be capable of faster throughputs, making it suitable for use with video devices as well. When shopping for MP3 hardware, you'll probably want to make sure it offers a USB connectivity option.

UUencoding

A technique for encoding binary data as ASCII data, useful for posting binaries (such as MP3 files) to Usenet groups. Most modern newsreaders are capable of decoding UUencoded data on the fly, though independent UUdecoders are available for virtually all platforms. See Chapter 3, *Getting and Playing MP3 Files* for details.

VBR

Variable Bitrate. A technique for encoding MP3 audio wherein each frame is allotted an amount of data optimized for the moment of music it represents. Passages with little musical variation can occupy very little space, while more complex passages are allotted more. Users can specify a VBR "threshold," so they can still control whether they end up with large, high-quality files, or the opposite. Contrast with CBR.

Watermark

A digital "imprint" embedded in a music file, with the intention of preventing piracy. A watermarked file is intended to be played back only on the machine on which it was created. While it is possible to watermark MP3 files via ID3v2, no existing implementations were known at this writing. Watermarking will likely become more prevalent in nonMP3 file formats.

WAV

The defacto standard in uncompressed audio data, used extensively under Microsoft Windows. WAV files are usually straight PCM audio files with a WAV header. There is no difference in quality between PCM, AIFF, and WAV.

Wavelength

The distance between the peak of one wave and the peak of the next, measured in Hz, or cycles per second. Wavelength corresponds to pitch: The closer the peaks of the waves, the higher the pitch.

Webcasting

The process of running an "Internet radio station" by broadcasting MP3 or other audio formats over the Internet in real time. Users tune in to webcasts and hear what's being broadcast at that moment in time (as with traditional radio), rather than having random access to a playlist, as they do with MP3-on-demand.

WMA/ASF

Windows Media Audio/Active Streaming Format. A set of Microsoft technologies for compressing audio and video signal, designed to be competitive with MP3 and RealAudio alike. These formats are described in detail in Chapter 9, *Competing Codecs and Other File Formats*.

Index

About the Author

Scot Hacker has been obsessed with music since his early teens, and has been a digital audiophile for half a decade. After earning a B.A. in Philosophy at UC Santa Cruz, he made a living writing reviews of jazz and improvised music for *The Utne Reader* and *The Cadence Journal of Jazz and Blues* before graduating to the role of Content Manager and Production Editor at ZDNet. Hacker's interest in digital audio and fine computer systems has evolved into a series of regular articles for *PC Magazine*, Byte.com, *Windows Sources*, ZiffNet, Japan's *ASCII* magazine, and the CompuServe network, as well as television appearances and trade show gigs. Hacker is the author of the definitive *The BeOS Bible*, a best-selling guide to the high-performance operating system optimized for digital media, including audio compression, encoding, and playback.

Colophon

Our look is the result of reader comments, our own experimentation, and feedback from distribution channels. Distinctive covers complement our distinctive approach to technical topics, breathing personality and life into potentially dry subjects.

The animal on the cover of *MP3: The Definitive Guide* is a hermit crab (*Coenobita perlatus*). The hermit crab is commonly found in the Indian and Pacific Oceans, and inhabits the areas surrounding the Islands of Aldabra, Mauritius, and Samoa. Despite the name of the hermit crab, which alludes to a solitary lifestyle, *Coenobita perlatus* are very social creatures. They characteristically travel in groups of 25 or more, and have been found living in colonies of over 100 in the wild.

Hermit crabs make their homes by occupying the discarded shells of gastropds in order to protect their soft, coiled abdomens and inner organs. They prefer shells that fit snuggly in order to prevent evaporation of moisture. Most hermit crabs carry water in their shells, which they use for breathing and a water source when they are far away from the sea.

Maureen Dempsey was the production editor and copyeditor for *MP3: The Definitve Guide*. Colleen Gorman and Clairemarie Fisher O'Leary were the proofreaders. Melanie Wang, Nicole Arigo, and Madeleine Newell provided quality control. Brenda Miller wrote the index.

Hanna Dyer designed the cover of this book, based on a series design by Edie Freedman. The cover image is a 19th-century engraving from the Dover Pictorial Archive. Kathleen Wilson produced the cover layout with QuarkXPress 3.32 using Adobe's ITC Garamond font.

Alicia Cech designed the interior layout based on a series design by Nancy Priest. Mike Sierra implemented the design in FrameMaker 5.5.6. The text and heading fonts are ITC Garamond Light and Garamond Book. The illustrations that appear in the book were produced by Robert Romano and Rhon Porter using Macromedia FreeHand 8 and Adobe Photoshop 5. This colophon was written by Maureen Dempsey.

Whenever possible, our books use RepKover™, a durable and flexible lay-flat binding. If the page count exceeds RepKover's limit, perfect binding is used.